Structured
ANS COBOL

Mike Murach & Associates, Inc.

4697 West Jacquelyn Avenue
Fresno, California 93722
(209) 275-3335

Structured
ANS COBOL

Part 2: An advanced course
using 1974 or 1985 ANS COBOL

Second edition

Mike Murach
Paul Noll

Editorial team

Mike Murach
Paul Noll
Judy Taylor
Anne Prince
Pat Bridgemon

Production team

Steve Ehlers
Carl Kisling

Other products in our COBOL series

Instructor's Guide for *Structured ANS COBOL, Part 2*
Minireel for *Structured ANS COBOL, Part 2*

Structured ANS COBOL, Part 1 by Mike Murach and Paul Noll
Instructor's Guide for *Structured ANS COBOL, Part 1*
Minireel for *Structured ANS COBOL, Part 1*

How to Design and Develop COBOL Programs
      by Paul Noll and Mike Murach
The COBOL Programmer's Handbook by Paul Noll and Mike Murach
Case Studies, Instructor's Guide and *Minireel* for *How to Design and Develop COBOL Programs*

Report Writer by Steve Eckols
VS COBOL II: A Guide for Programmers and Managers (Second Edition)
      by Anne Prince
VSAM for the COBOL Programmer (Second Edition)
      by Doug Lowe

CICS for the COBOL Programmer, Part 1 by Doug Lowe
CICS for the COBOL Programmer, Part 2 by Doug Lowe
Instructor's Guide and *Minireel* for *CICS for the COBOL Programmer*

IMS for the COBOL Programmer, Part 1: DL/I Data Base Processing by Steve Eckols
IMS for the COBOL Programmer, Part 2: Data Communications and MFS by Steve Eckols

20 19 18 17 16 15 14 13 12 11 10 9 8 7 6 5 4 3

Library of Congress Catalog Card Number: 86-61654

ISBN: 0-911625-38-0

Contents

Preface

This book is a long overdue revision of our 1979 book: *Structured ANS COBOL, Part 2*. The first edition was used in dozens of colleges and junior colleges for classroom instruction, and in thousands of businesses for inhouse training. Nevertheless, it needed revision badly, due to changes in COBOL, changes in data processing procedures, and changes in training requirements.

What this book does

This book is the second in a two-part series for COBOL training. It is designed to teach a programmer or a programmer trainee to use the advanced capabilities of the COBOL language. Because file handling is a critical skill in COBOL, section 2 shows you how to handle sequential, indexed, and relative files in COBOL. It also shows you how to sort or merge files within a COBOL program. Then, section 3 shows you how to use other functions and features of COBOL. Specifically, this section shows you how to use the COPY library, how to call and write subprograms, how to define and process tables, how to manipulate characters, and how to use the features of 1985 COBOL.

Because we feel that an effective programmer must use effective programming techniques, this book gives extensive coverage to modern program-development techniques. Specifically, chapter 1 shows you how to design a program from the top down using a structure chart; how to plan the modules of a program using pseudocode; and how to test a program from the top down. This chapter is designed for students who haven't read *Structured ANS COBOL, Part 1*. Then, chapter 11 presents the structure and logic of edit, update, and file maintenance programs. As a result, students who complete this course should not only be able to code COBOL, they should be able to develop programs using effective procedures for design, planning, and testing.

Who this book is for

This book is intended for COBOL trainees who have completed an

1

introductory course in COBOL. Although it is the second book in a two-part series that starts with *Structured ANS COBOL, Part 1*, it can be used for an advanced course no matter what book was used for the introductory course. Figure P-1 summarizes the COBOL skills that a student should have before starting this book, so you can see that any introductory book should satisfy these prerequisites. For those students who haven't read *Part 1*, chapter 1 of this book quickly introduces the structured programming techniques that the students must be familiar with in this course.

We also recommend this book for programmers who want to increase their knowledge so they can make full use of the COBOL language. In our experience, many professional programmers make little effort to learn how to use the functions and features of COBOL that they don't already know. As a result, they often don't handle files as efficiently as they should. Also, they either don't use or they misuse verbs like SET, SEARCH, PERFORM VARYING, INSPECT, STRING, and UNSTRING. That's why this book can significantly improve the effectiveness of the average COBOL programmer.

Since this book presents standard COBOL as defined in the 1974 and 1985 standards, it teaches COBOL that can be used on any computer system that supports COBOL. Although standard COBOL has minor variations as you move from one computer system to another, examples are given throughout the book that apply to microcomputers, minicomputers, and IBM mainframes. In fact, each COBOL chapter ends with a topic on compiler dependencies that highlights any of the code that may vary from one compiler to another. In general, any program in this text will run on any system that supports COBOL with only a couple minor changes, and these changes are clearly specified.

Since IBM mainframes are the most widely-used systems today, all of the program examples in this text have been run on an IBM mainframe. As a result, this book is particularly easy to use if you're going to develop your programs on an IBM mainframe. As I said, though, the variations required by other systems are also presented, and they are trivial.

How to use this book

If you're reading this book as part of a course, your instructor should guide you through it. On the other hand, if you're reading this book on your own, you should realize that the chapters don't have to be read in sequence from chapter 1 through chapter 12. Instead, the chapters are grouped into four sections as shown by the table in figure P-2. As you can see, you can read section 2, 3, or 4 any time after you complete chapter 1. However, you don't need to read chapter 1 if you've read *Structured ANS COBOL, Part 1*.

What the student should be able to do before starting this book

1. Design, code, and test report preparation programs in COBOL using sequential input files and printer output files.

2. Define data items in the Data Division using the following language elements:

    01 through 49 levels
    PICTURE clause
    VALUE clause
    USAGE clause
    REDEFINES clause
    88 levels

3. Code procedures in the Procedure Division using the following language elements:

    OPEN, CLOSE, and READ statements for disk input files
    OPEN, CLOSE, and WRITE statements for printer output files
    MOVE statement
    ADD, SUBTRACT, MULTIPLY, DIVIDE, and COMPUTE statements
    PERFORM and PERFORM UNTIL statements
    IF and nested IF statements
    Relation, sign, class, and condition tests
    ACCEPT DATE/DAY/TIME statement
    DISPLAY statement
    STOP RUN statement

Figure P-1   The prerequisites for this course

Beyond this, you don't have to read the chapters within a section in sequence. As you can see in figure P-2, sections 3 and 4 are organized on a "random" basis. This means that you can read the chapters in these sections in any sequence you choose. Similarly, section 2 is organized on a random basis once you finish chapter 2. This means that you can read chapters 3, 4, and 5 in any sequence you want once you finish chapter 2.

This type of organization, which we call *modular organization*, gives you a number of options as you use this book. If, for example, you want to learn all of the COBOL elements in section 3 before you learn how to handle files as described in section 2, that's one option. Beyond this, you can go back and forth between the chapters of sections 2, 3, and 4 within the limits summarized in figure P-2. In fact, once you read chapters 1 and 2, you can read the remaining chapters in any sequence you want. As a result, in contrast to most courses, your learning can be teacher-directed or student-directed, but it won't be textbook-directed.

If you would like a recommended sequence of study, I suggest that you simply go from chapter 1 through chapter 12 in sequence, skipping over any topics or chapters that don't apply to your system or compiler. But don't feel that you should rigidly adhere to any sequence. Feel free to change the sequence whenever a subject arouses your interest. There is no better atmosphere for learning than the one created when you study something in search of an answer.

To help you learn from this book, each topic or chapter is followed by terminology lists and behavioral objectives. If you feel you understand the terms in each terminology list, it's a good indication that you've understood the content of the topic or chapter you've just read. In other words, we don't expect you to be able to define the terms in a list, but you should recognize and understand them. Similarly, if you feel that you can do what each objective requires, it's a good indication that you've learned what we wanted you to learn in each topic or chapter.

To give you a chance to apply your learning, appendix C presents problems on a chapter-by-chapter basis. These problems are related since they all operate upon the same master file. If you can code and test all of the problems in this appendix, we feel that this book has accomplished its primary objective.

So you get the maximum benefit from your programming time, the problems in appendix C don't ask you to develop programs from scratch. Instead, they ask you to modify one of the three programs provided in that appendix. This lets you concentrate on the new COBOL elements, rather than on the ones you already know.

Although the problems in appendix C test your ability to use COBOL, they don't test your ability to design and develop programs from scratch. And they don't test your ability to develop programs that have complex structural and logical requirements. As a result, appendix D presents four more case studies. These case studies not only test your command of COBOL, but also your ability to design, plan, code, and test programs with varying structural and logical requirements.

Like the case study problems in appendix C, the case studies in appendix D are designed to get the maximum benefit from your programming time. As a result, case study 2 asks you to enhance the edit program you developed for case study 1. Similarly, case study 4 asks you to modify the sequential update program you developed for case study 3 so it updates an indexed master file on a random basis. As we see it, if you can develop the programs required by these case studies, you are programming at a level that is representative of an experienced programmer in industry.

Section	Chapters	Section title	Prerequisites	Organization
1	1	Required background	Skills listed in figure P-1	
2	2-5	File handling in COBOL	Chapter 1	Random after chapter 2
3	6-10	COBOL by function or feature	Chapter 1	Random
4	11-12	Related subjects	Chapter 1	Random

Figure P-2   The basic organization of this book

Related books

This book is only one book in our COBOL training series. *Structured ANS COBOL, Part 1* is a course for novices. It teaches a beginner how to use a subset of COBOL for developing report preparation programs. Then, *Report Writer* teaches you how to use the Report Writer feature of COBOL. If you use Report Writer in your shop, you can read our book on it any time after you complete either *Part 1* or *Part 2* in our COBOL series.

Perhaps the most important book we've ever done for COBOL programmers is called *How to Design and Develop COBOL Programs*. It shows experienced COBOL programmers how to design, code, and test programs that are easy to debug and maintain. And it shows them how to increase their productivity, often by 200 percent or more. As an accompanying reference, we offer the *The COBOL Programmer's Handbook*, which summarizes the procedures and techniques presented in the text. It also presents seven model programs that you can use as guides for developing your own programs. Because this text and handbook present techniques and examples that will help you at any stage of your COBOL training, we recommend that you get them and use them throughout your training and career.

Beyond this, we offer books that teach the COBOL programmer how to use CICS and IMS or DL/I on IBM mainframes. We have books on other subjects that the IBM COBOL programmer must know, like VSAM, TSO, ICCF, and JCL. And we are publishing new books each year. So please check our current catalog for titles that may be of interest to you.

Instructor's materials

If you're an instructor in a school or business, you will probably be interested in the *Instructor's Guide* that is available with this book. It presents complete solutions for the case studies in appendixes C and D. It gives you ideas and summary information for administering an advanced COBOL course. And it gives you masters for most of the figures in the text so you can make overhead transparencies from them.

A *minireel* is also available with this course. It is a 1600-bpi tape that contains files of test data, COPY members, and source programs. In brief, it provides all of the solutions to the case studies in appendixes C and D, as well as the COPY members and files you'll need for running the case study solutions on your system.

Incidentally, we also offer instructor's guides and minireels for other courses in our COBOL series. These courses include *Structured ANS COBOL, Part 1* and *How to Design and Develop COBOL Programs*.

Reference manuals

Although this book represents a complete course in COBOL, we recommend that students have access to the basic COBOL reference manuals for their system. On an IBM mainframe, for example, two manuals are usually enough for the version of COBOL that is being used: the COBOL reference manual and the programmer's guide for using COBOL. On other systems, one manual is usually enough.

In general, you shouldn't have to refer to these manuals as you do the case studies. Occasionally, though, a problem may come up that is specific to your system, not to standard COBOL. Then, you can research the problem yourself in your system's manuals. Also, as we point out in chapter 12, it's good to page through your system's COBOL manuals at some time during your training to find out what features your version of COBOL provides.

About Paul Noll

Paul Noll originated the program development techniques we recommend in this book when he was working as a training manager for Pacific Telephone back in the mid-1970's. In 1978, he became an independent COBOL consultant. Since then, he has conducted seminars in hundreds of companies throughout the United States and Canada. His books have been used by thousands of programmers around the world, and, based on a COBOL survey we did in 1984, we believe that more than 3000 COBOL shops now use Paul's methods for program development. As far as we can tell, that means that Paul's methods are the most widely-used methods for structured program development. We've used Paul's methods in our own company since 1979, and we're convinced that they're the most effective methods currently available.

Paul is listed as a co-author of this book in the sense that he developed the basic methods that are taught in this book. He also reviewed the manuscript for this book as a double check on its technical accuracy. As a result, we feel that he has made an important contribution to the educational and technical quality of this book.

Conclusion

Paul and I believe that this book will help you learn COBOL better than any competing book or course will. We're confident that this book will teach you how to use COBOL as the best professional programmers use it. We're also confident that you'll learn more efficiently when you use this book than you would if you were using any competing book or course.

If you have comments about this book, we welcome them. If you check the last few pages of this book, you'll find a postage-page comment form. You'll also find a postage-paid order form in case you want to order any of our products. We hope you find this book useful, and thanks for being our customer.

Mike Murach
Fresno, California
October 20, 1986

Required background

Structured ANS COBOL, Part 1 not only teaches you a subset of COBOL, it also teaches you how to develop COBOL programs using structured programming techniques. If you haven't read *Part 1*, we assume that you at least know how to use the subset of COBOL that it teaches. On the other hand, we don't assume that you know how to use the structured programming techniques that it presents. As a result, this section introduces you to those techniques.

If you've read *Structured ANS COBOL, Part 1*, you can skip this section. Similarly, if you're already familiar with the techniques of structured programming, you can probably go through this section quickly, concentrating only on the techniques you aren't familiar with. As you will see, the techniques that we recommend are quite straightforward, so they are relatively easy to apply to the development of COBOL programs.

Chapter 1

An introduction to structured COBOL

If you've read *Structured ANS COBOL, Part 1*, you don't have to read this chapter. Instead, you can continue with the COBOL instruction in sections 2 and 3 of this book. If you haven't read *Part 1*, this chapter will prepare you for the COBOL instruction that follows.

Topic 1 of this chapter presents a structured COBOL program so you can see what we mean when we refer to a "structured" program. This topic also shows you what you ought to know before you start this book. Next, topic 2 introduces you to the techniques of structured programming so you can use them when you do the case studies for this course. Then, topic 3 presents a procedure for developing structured programs that you can use when you do the case studies.

Topic 1 Presenting a structured COBOL program

Today, most programmers will tell you that they develop "structured" COBOL programs. This implies that they are using modern techniques for program development, which in turn implies that they are developing high-quality programs at a high rate of productivity. Unfortunately, the facts don't bear this out.

The truth is that most COBOL programmers today work at pathetically low levels of productivity. That's why the backlog of programs waiting to be developed has reached an all-time high. Similarly, the programs developed by the average programmer today are anything but high-quality. They are difficult to understand and maintain, and they don't even work correctly all of the time. That's why most computer departments spend more money on the maintenance of old programs than they spend on the development of new programs.

Fortunately, it doesn't have to be that way. Structured programming techniques do make it is possible to develop high-quality COBOL programs at a high rate of productivity. You just have to know which "structured" techniques to use and how to use them.

In this book, we'll show you how to use COBOL, but we'll also show you how to use effective structured techniques for developing COBOL programs. In this topic, then, I'm going to show you what we mean by a "structured" COBOL program. I'll start by presenting one. Then, I'll point out its essential characteristics.

A structured report preparation program

Appendix A of this book gives the complete documentation for a structured COBOL program. It's the program we used as an example in chapter 5 of *Structured ANS COBOL, Part 1*. If you take a moment now to look at the program specifications, the structure chart, and the COBOL listing for this program, I think you'll find that they're quite easy to read and understand.

The program specifications   The program specifications consist of a program overview, a COBOL record description for the inventory master file used as input to the program, and a print chart used for the investment listing prepared by the program. Naturally, we've simplified this program so it's more useful for illustration than a complete production program would be. But I think this program illustrates most of the essential design and code that any report preparation program requires.

The structure chart   The *structure chart*, which we developed using top-down design, is an index to the paragraphs of the COBOL program. As you can see in the COBOL listing, the coding for the top-level module (box) of the structure chart can be found in the first paragraph of the Procedure Division. It is named 000-PREPARE-INVESTMENT-LISTING so it corresponds to the number and name of the module on the structure chart. Similarly, every other paragraph in the COBOL listing corresponds to one module shown on the structure chart. In contrast, the striped boxes on the structure chart represent subprograms named SYSDATE and SYSTIME that are called by the program.

The COBOL listing   The COBOL listing shows how COBOL can be used to create a program that is easy to read and understand. Because of its readability, a program like this is more likely to be reliable than a less readable program, and it's going to be easy to maintain. Are the programs you've been writing as easy to read as this one? If not, I hope you'll soon realize how much there is to gain by making only a few changes to your development methods.

Three characteristics of a structured program

As we see it, a structured program is an effective program. The problem is that some people say their programs are structured when they aren't. That's why we'd like to identify the three characteristics that we feel are essential to a structured program.

Characteristic 1: A structured program is designed from the top down so each module represents one independent function that can be coded in a single COBOL paragraph   I think most professional programmers agree with the first part of this statement. You have to design a program from the top down, and each module on the structure chart (or other design document) should represent an independent function. Then, these functions can be divided into their subordinate functions. And so on.

The problem is that programmers disagree about what independence is, what a function is, and when you should stop designing a program. As we see it, most programmers allow more than one function to be combined in a single module of a program. They don't create modules that are independent. And they don't design each program down to a low enough level.

To illustrate, compare the structure chart in appendix A with the chart in figure 1-1. Both are for the same program. Both programmers think they have created modules that represent single, independent functions. And both programmers think they have designed down to a low enough level. But each module in the structure chart in the appendix can be coded in a single COBOL paragraph using 1974 COBOL, while two of the modules in the chart in figure 1-1 can't be.

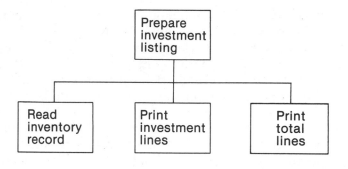

Figure 1-1   An unacceptable design for the report preparation program of appendix A

That in turn means that the program represented by the chart in figure 1-1 will be more difficult to code, test, and maintain than the one in appendix A.

Because it is impossible to develop an effective COBOL program based on the design in figure 1-1, Paul Noll tries to give a specific guideline for knowing how far down to design a program. He says that a program should be designed from the top down until each module can be coded *in a single COBOL paragraph.* That way, you'll usually be able to code each module of the program in 50 statements or less. In addition, your structure chart will be an index to each paragraph of the COBOL program. In contrast, you can't tell how many paragraphs the design in figure 1-1 will require.

As you will see in chapter 10 of this book, the inline PERFORM statement of 1985 COBOL lets you code functions in one paragraph that would take two or more paragraphs using 1974 COBOL. As a result, if you're using 1985 COBOL, Paul's principle should be modified so it says that a program should be designed from the top down until each module can be coded in a single COBOL paragraph *without using inline PERFORMs.* When you actually code the program, you may decide to combine paragraphs by using an inline PERFORM, but you should first design the program so it can be coded without using them. If you do combine two or more paragraphs into one, you must modify the structure chart so it corresponds to the COBOL code.

Incidentally, although we use structure charts as the design documents for the programs in this book, other design documents can be used for structured programs. The essential characteristic we're talking about is the design, not the design document. As a result, you can use other styles of structure charts or diagrams to design your program. As far as we're concerned, no matter what design document you use, a program is structured if it consists of modules that are designed from the top down, represent independent functions, and can be coded in single COBOL paragraphs without inline PERFORMs.

Characteristic 2: Each module on the design document of a structured program is coded as a single COBOL paragraph   As long as you've taken the trouble to design a program so each module can be coded in a single COBOL paragraph, you should code the modules that way. Then, the structure chart for a program is an index to the COBOL code: one module on the chart corresponds to one paragraph in the program.

Although this principle seems obvious enough to us, some people who say they write structured programs don't agree with this. Some people say each module should be coded as a section, which can consist of more than one paragraph. Some say each module should be coded as a series of paragraphs. And some say each module should be coded as a subprogram. But as soon as you code the modules of a program in one of these three ways, you start to defeat the purposes of structured programming. Your design document is no longer a guide to the paragraphs of the program, and it becomes more difficult to enforce coding standards.

As you will see, though, it's not always possible to code each module of a program as a single COBOL paragraph. In chapter 5, for example, you'll learn that the SORT statement in 1974 COBOL forces you to use sections that consist of more than one paragraph. But this is an exceptional case. In most cases, you'll be able to code each module of a program as a single COBOL paragraph, and the quality of your programs will be improved if you do.

Characteristic 3: A structured program is coded so it's easy to read and understand   I don't think anyone is going to disagree with this characteristic of structured programs. The more readable a program is, the easier it is to test and maintain. Nevertheless, not enough has been said about how COBOL programs should be coded so they are as readable as possible within some practical limits. As a result, many programmers develop "structured" programs that are difficult to read and understand. They just don't know how to improve the readability of their programs.

To illustrate this point, look at the coding samples in figure 1-2. The first is taken from a production program that the programmer calls "structured." The second is taken from a program that is part of a "structured" software package for payroll. By our standards, both can be improved considerably. The first isn't structured; it is unmaintainable foolishness. The second isn't that bad, but it violates some of the standards that we feel are important for readability. If you compare either of these samples with the code in appendix A, I think you'll see that our coding standards can lead to significant improvements in readability.

In this book and in *Part 1*, all of the programming examples are written in a readable style. They were developed using the standards

A coding sample from a "structured" production program

```
AA43.  PERFORM KK.
       IF ITMSTS20 = ' ' GO TO AAA43.
       IF ITMSTS20 = 'N' AND ITMSTS70 (A, SS) = 'N'
       PERFORM A54G THRU X54G GO TO B43
       IF ITMSTS20 = 'N' PERFORM CC43 PERFORM A54J
       MOVE '25' TO ACT40 MOVE ITMSTS20 TO ITMSTS40 GO TO B43.
       IF ITMSTS70 (A, SS) = 'N' GO TO CC43.
AAA43. PERFORM EQCHEC.
       IF EQWORK1 = EQWORK2 GO TO QQ43.
       IF EQWORK2 = SPACES GO TO QQ43.
       GO TO CC43.
QQ43.  PERFORM EE THRU KK.
B43.   PERFORM A54D THRU X54D GO TO D42.
CC43.  MOVE '40' TO ACT40.
   .
   .
```

A coding sample from one program of a "structured" software package

```
LEVEL-1 SECTION.
MAIN-LOGIC.
    PERFORM OPENING-PROCEDURE.
    IF OPENING-PROCEDURE-SUCCESSFUL
        IF PR-CTL-USE-JOB-NUMBER-FLAG IS = 'N'
            PERFORM JOB-NOS-NOT-SELECTED-MESSAGE,
            MOVE UNSUCCESSFUL TO OPENING-PROCEDURE-STATUS,
        ELSE
            PERFORM ENTER-MENU-SELECTION,
            IF NOT END-KEY-PRESSED
                PERFORM JOB-FILE-MAINTENANCE UNTIL
                END-KEY-PRESSED.
    PERFORM CLOSING-PROCEDURE.
MAIN-LOGIC-EXIT.
    PERFORM WAIT-MESSAGE-ROUTINE.
    EXIT PROGRAM.
    STOP RUN.
LEVEL-2 SECTION.
OPENING-PROCEDURE.
    PERFORM OPEN-CRT-FILE.
    PERFORM OPEN-PR-CONTROL-FILE.
    IF PR-CONTROL-FILE-STATUS IS = I-O-OK
        MOVE FILE-IS-OPEN TO PR-CONTROL-FILE-OPEN-STATUS,
        PERFORM READ-PR-CONTROL-FILE,
    ELSE
        MOVE UNSUCCESSFUL TO OPENING-PROCEDURE-STATUS.
   .
   .
```

Figure 1-2　　Two samples of "structured" COBOL code that are difficult to read

presented in *The COBOL Programmer's Handbook*, which we published in 1985. If you copy the style used in these programs, you're going to write readable programs too.

Other characteristics of structured programs

We believe that the three characteristics we've just presented are the essential characteristics of a structured program. However, there are others. For instance, a structured program should make effective use of COPY members and subprograms. Also, the documentation for a structured program should be a by-product of the development process. We're not going to present these characteristics, though, because they are relatively trivial when compared with the three we've just mentioned.

Beyond this, we could describe and discuss the relationships between the modules of a structured program: what proper subordination is and topics like that. But that's beyond the scope of this chapter and this book. If you pattern your programs after the examples in this book, you're going to write programs that we consider to be structured.

Curiously, many people say that one of the characteristics of a structured program is that it doesn't use GOTO statements. In fact, structured programming started as an attempt to develop programs without GOTO statements. We haven't mentioned this as an essential characteristic of a structured program, though, because we believe it has led many people to believe that a structured program is simply one without GOTO statements. And we certainly don't agree with that. None of the programs in this book use GOTO statements unless they are required, because we feel that a program is easier to code, test, debug, and modify when it doesn't use GOTO statements. However, we've seen programs with no GOTOs at all that are illogical messes. As a result, we feel that the avoidance of GOTO statements is a secondary characteristic of a structured program, not a primary characteristic.

What you should know before you start this course

Structured ANS COBOL, Part 1 teaches three aspects of COBOL programming: (1) the COBOL language for report preparation programs; (2) structured programming techniques; and (3) procedures for compiling and testing a program. If you've taken a different introductory COBOL course, however, chances are good that you have satisfied the prerequisities for this course.

In terms of COBOL, the program in appendix A is a good indication of what you should know before you start this course. If you can read and understand this program, you have met the COBOL prerequisites for this course. In fact, if you understand all of its COBOL code except for the use of the COPY and CALL statements, you still have met the COBOL prerequisities for this course because the use of the COPY and CALL statements is also presented in this book. Perhaps the most difficult aspects of the COBOL code in appendix A are the nested IF statements, compound conditions, and condition names, so be sure you understand how they are used.

In terms of structured programming, we're going to assume that you don't have the background given in *Structured ANS COBOL, Part 1*, because most introductory courses are weak when it comes to structured programming techniques. As a result, the next topic in this chapter introduces you to the structured programming techniques presented in *Part 1*. Then, when you develop the case studies for this course, you should be able to use these techniques, even if you haven't used similar techniques before.

In terms of procedures for compiling and testing programs, we assume that you already know how to enter programs into your system, how to compile the programs and correct the diagnostics, and how to test the programs. Obviously, if you've written programs before, you've had to learn how to do these tasks. As a result, topic 3 of this chapter presents a general procedure that you can use when you develop the case studies for this course, but it doesn't present specific information about entering, compiling, or testing programs.

In summary, the prerequisites for this course are minimal. *Part 1* presented relatively little COBOL for an introductory course so it could emphasize the structure and logic of report preparation programs. As a result, if you've taken another introductory COBOL course, you most likely will have met the prerequisities for this course. Then, this book will teach you all of the significant features of COBOL that weren't presented in your introductory course, and it will emphasize the structure and logic of edit, update, and maintenance programs.

Terminology

structure chart

Objective

List and describe the three characteristics of a structured COBOL program.

Topic 2   An introduction to structured programming

The term *structured programming* refers to a collection of techniques that are designed to help you improve both your productivity and the quality of your programs. The techniques include structured program design, structured module planning using pseudocode, structured coding, and top-down testing. In this book, all of the programs have been developed using structured design and structured coding.

I'll start this topic by presenting the theory of structured programming. Next, I'll show you how to design a program using a structure chart and how to plan the modules of a program using pseudocode. Then, I'll show you how to code the structures of structured programming in COBOL and how to code and test a program from the top down.

The theory of structured programming

The basic theory of structured programming is that any program, in any language, can be written using three logical structures: sequence, selection, and iteration. These structures, illustrated in figure 1-3, have only one entry point and one exit point. In contrast, unstructured programs allow for multiple entry and exit points.

The first structure, the *sequence structure*, is simply a set of imperative statements executed in sequence, one after another. The entry point is at the start of the sequence; the exit point is after the last statement in the sequence. A sequence structure may consist of a single function or of many functions.

The second structure, the *selection structure*, is a choice between two, and only two, functions based on a condition. You should realize, though, that one of the functions may be null. In other words, if the condition is not met, the flow of control may pass directly to the structure's exit point with no intervening statements or structures. This structure is often referred to as the IF-THEN-ELSE structure, and most programming languages have code that approximates it.

The third structure, the *iteration structure*, is often called the DO-WHILE structure. It provides for doing a function as long as a condition is true. As you can see in variation 1 of the iteration structure, the condition is tested before the function is performed. When the condition is no longer true, the program continues with the next structure.

Related to the DO-WHILE structure are the DO-UNTIL and the COBOL PERFORM-UNTIL structures. As you can see in the DO-UNTIL structure in figure 1-3, the condition is tested *after* the function is performed and the function is performed until a condition is

The sequence structure

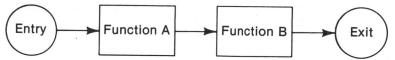

The selection structure (IF-THEN-ELSE)

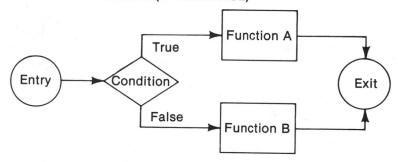

Variation 1 of the iteration structure (DO-WHILE)

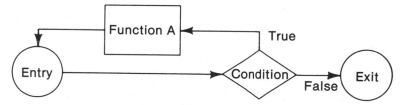

Variation 2 of the iteration structure (DO-UNTIL)

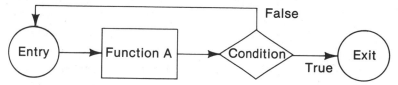

Variation 3 of the iteration structure (COBOL PERFORM-UNTIL)

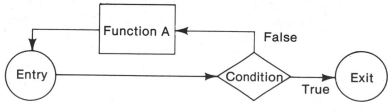

Figure 1-3   The basic structures of structured programming

true. In the PERFORM-UNTIL structure, the function is also performed until the condition is true, but the condition is tested *before* the function is performed.

Again, let me stress that all of the structures in figure 1-3 have only one entry point and one exit point. As a result, a program made up of these structures will have only one entry point and one exit point. This means the program will be executed in a controlled manner from the first statement to the last. These characteristics make up a *proper program*.

To create a proper program, any of the three structures can be substituted for a function box in any of the other structures. The result will still be a proper program. Conversely, two or more of the basic structures in sequence can be treated as a single function box. This means that structures of great complexity can be created with the assurance that they will have only one entry point and one exit point.

If you've never written an unstructured program, you may have a hard time understanding the significance of structured programming. But take my word for it: Allowing for multiple entry and exit points makes a program hard to read, understand, and change. It also makes it hard to code and debug in the first place. And the difficulty increases dramatically as the programs get longer. So the theory of structured programming is an important contribution to the art of programming because it places necessary restrictions on program structure.

How to design a program from the top down using a structure chart

In this book, each program is presented with the structure chart for its design. To create a structure chart, we recommend a five-step procedure. This procedure should help you design any of the programs required by the case studies for this course. When you design a program from the top down, you are using a technique called *structured program design*, or *top-down program design*.

Step 1: Design the function boxes for the first two levels   To design a structure chart, you start with a top-level module that represents the entire program. Next, you decide on the one functional module that will be performed repeatedly during the execution of the program, and you draw this module at the second level of the chart. Then, you decide whether your program requires any functional modules that need to be performed before or after this primary module at the second level. If so, you draw boxes for these functions to the left or the right of the primary module.

To illustrate, figure 1-4 represents the first two levels of the chart for the investment-listing program shown in appendix A. The top-level box is named "prepare investment listing," and the primary module at the second level is named "prepare investment line." The

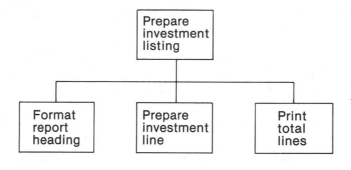

Figure 1-4   The first two levels of the structure chart for the investment-listing program of appendix A

prepare-investment-line module is the primary module because it will be executed repeatedly during the program, once for each master record until all records in the master file have been read and processed. In other words, a primary module represents the processing for one input record or one set of input records.

Because the investment-listing program must get the date and time into the first heading line of the investment listing, the module to the left of the prepare-investment-line module is named "format report heading." This module will get the date and time and edit them into the appropriate fields in the heading lines. If other functions must be performed before the primary module is executed, they can also be drawn to the left of the primary module. For instance, a program that uses a table might require a module to load the table from a file into storage at the start of the program (table handling is covered in chapter 8 of this text).

Because the investment-listing program must print two total lines after all investment lines have been printed, the module to the right of the prepare-investment-line module is named "print total lines." If other functions must be performed after the function of the primary module has been completed, they can also be drawn to the right of the primary module.

To name the functions and subfunctions represented by the boxes of a chart, you use a verb, one or two adjectives, and a noun. Thus, the name of the top-level box in the chart in figure 1-4 is "prepare investment listing." And the names of the modules in the second level of the chart are "format report heading," "prepare investment line," and "print total lines."

As you get more experience with top-down design, you'll realize that all programs can be charted at the first two levels with a structure similar to the one in figure 1-4. Every program has at least one primary function, although it may not be related to a set of input records. And most programs require functions that must be performed before or after the primary function.

Step 2: Design the subordinate function boxes until each module of the program can be coded in single COBOL paragraph   Step 2 is to divide the modules at the second level into their subordinate functions and subfunctions until each module of the program can be coded in a single COBOL paragraph. To illustrate, figure 1-5 shows the functions and subfunctions that I designed for the modules in figure 1-4.

To start, I asked what subordinate modules (if any) the format-report-heading module required. Without any subordinates, I knew that I could code the format-report-heading box in a single COBOL paragraph. However, I also knew that two subprograms were available for getting the system date and system time. As a result, I drew boxes for these subprograms on the structure chart.

If you're not familiar with subprograms, they are presented in chapter 7 of this book. When you use a subprogram, it should be shown as a separate box on the structure chart for the program. Also, a stripe should be drawn at the top of each subprogram box, and the name of the subprogram should be written in this striped area. Thus, the names of the two subprograms in the chart in figure 1-5 are SYSDATE and SYSTIME.

After I designed the subordinates for the format-report-heading module, I designed the subordinate functions for the prepare-investment-line module. As you can see in figure 1-5, I designed three functions subordinate to this module. Each time the prepare-investment-line module is executed, it must (1) read an inventory master record, (2) compute the required inventory fields, and (3) print an investment line if the investment amount is greater than $10,000.

I then asked if any of these modules required subordinates, and I decided that only the print-investment-line module needed one. Whenever page overflow occurs, the report headings must be printed on the new page. As a result, the print-heading-lines module is subordinate to the print-investment-line module.

If the read or compute modules required subordinates, of course, I would have drawn them at the next level of the chart. And I would have continued this process until I had designed down to the lowest level. For this simple program, though, figure 1-5 presents all of the functional modules that are required by the prepare-investment-line module.

Last, I asked whether the print-total-lines module required any subordinates. I decided that it didn't. As a result, figure 1-5 represents all the functional modules required by the investment-listing program. In addition, I'm confident that I can code any one of them in a single COBOL paragraph.

When you draw modules on a structure chart, keep in mind that a left-to-right sequence of execution is expected at each level of subordination. At the third level in figure 1-5, for example, you would expect the subordinates for the prepare-investment-line module to be executed in the sequence of read, compute, and print. However, when you actually code the program, that may not be the case. So the

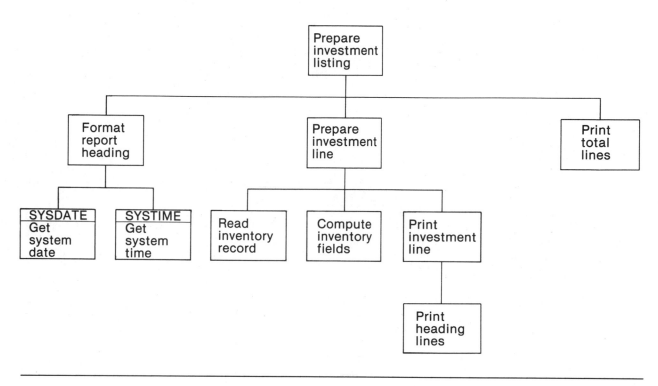

Figure 1-5   The expanded structure chart for the investment-listing program of appendix A

expected sequence can be varied as required by the program specifications. In other words, you can't always tell what the sequence will be at the time that you design a program's modules.

Step 3: Add one function box for each I/O statement   In step 3, you add one function box for each I/O operation required by a program. If you look at the chart in figure 1-6, for example, you can see that I added four write modules for the printer file, though three of them are the same. I didn't add a read module for the inventory master file, because the chart already had one.

In general, when you add I/O modules to a program, the objective is for you to code only one READ or WRITE statement for each file used by the program. But this isn't always possible. For instance, a print file usually requires one WRITE statement that skips to the top of a page as well as one WRITE statement that spaces one or more lines based on the value in a space-control field. As a result, each print file will usually require two WRITE statements (and two different types of write modules on the structure chart).

When you isolate the I/O statements in their own modules like this, you end up with a more efficient program and one that is easier to modify. This also makes it easier to provide for functions like counting the number of records read or written by a program, because you

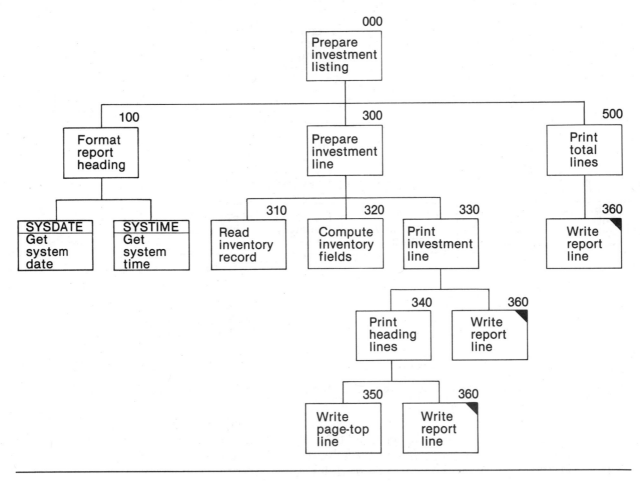

Figure 1-6   The complete structure chart for the investment-listing program of appendix A

can code functions like this in the related I/O module. The alternative in a large program is to have several READ or WRITE statements for each file dispersed throughout the program, a practice that can make the logic of the program difficult to follow.

Step 4: Shade the common modules   In step 4, you shade the upper righthand corners of the modules that are used in more than one place in the program. These modules are called *common modules*. In figure 1-6, for example, the write-report-line modules are common modules, so their corners are shaded. Although this program doesn't illustrate it, modules that aren't I/O modules can also be common modules, in which case they should be shaded too.

Step 5: Number the modules   In step 5, you number all of the modules except the subprogram modules. For most programs, a simple numbering system like the one used in figure 1-6 is adequate. That means you give the top-level module a number of 000. Next, you number the modules in the second level by hundreds, but you leave enough space between the hundreds to provide for the modules at the lower levels of the chart. That's why the modules in the second level of figure 1-6 are numbered 100, 300, and 500. Finally, you number the modules at the next levels by tens.

Note that the numbers do *not* indicate at what level a module can be found. This means that you can add modules to the chart at any level without changing the numbers of any of the other modules. For instance, you could add a module 200 as a subordinate to module 000. You could add a module 325 as a subordinate to module 300. Or, you could add a module 335 as a subordinate to module 330. As a result, a structure chart like this is easy to enhance or modify.

How to plan the modules of a program using pseudocode

Once you have completed the structure chart for a program, you can use *pseudocode* to plan the code for the program modules before you actually code them. For instance, figure 1-7 gives the pseudocode for all of the modules charted in figure 1-6. Pseudocode lets you plan the operations and logic of a module using only the legal structures of structured programming. And it lets you plan the modules quickly and easily.

When you use pseudocode, you should realize that it is a personal language. As a result, you don't have to follow rigid coding rules. In general, you should capitalize all of the structure words like DO, UNTIL, IF, and ELSE. Beyond this, you simply try to state what each module must do in a style that you feel comfortable with.

To illustrate typical variations in the ways that people use pseudocode, figure 1-8 shows three different forms of pseudocode for module 000 of the structure chart in figure 1-6. In the first style, only the structure words DO and UNTIL are capitalized. In the second style, PERFORM is used instead of DO and all COBOL words are capitalized. In the third style, all of the words are capitalized. If you compare the differences, you can see they're trivial. But books on pseudocode often stress these kinds of differences, and you may work in a shop someday that stresses them too. So I want you to be aware that differences do exist.

When you use pseudocode, you should use indentation to make the code as readable as possible. This is illustrated by the code in figure 1-7. In the DO-UNTIL statement in module 000, for example, the UNTIL portion is indented four spaces. Similarly, in the nested IF statements in module 300, indentation is used to show the levels of nesting.

When you use pseudocode, you should realize that you don't have to plan every aspect of a module. You'll note in figure 1-7, for example, that I didn't bother to plan the logic of modules 100, 320, 340, and 500 in detail because I know the logic is trivial. Similarly, you

```
000-prepare-investment-listing.

    Open files.
    DO 100-format-report-heading.
    DO 300-prepare-investment-line
        UNTIL all master records have been read.
    DO 500-print-total-lines.
    Close files.
    Stop run.

100-format-report-heading.

    Format report heading.

300-prepare-investment-line.

    DO 310-read-inventory-record.
    IF NOT invmast-eof
        DO 320-compute-inventory-fields
        IF investment-amount > 10000
            DO 330-print-investment-line.

310-read-inventory-record.

    Read record
        AT END
            move 'Y' to invmast-eof-switch.
    IF NOT invmast-eof
        add 1 to record-count.

320-compute-inventory-fields.

    Compute inventory fields.

330-print-investment-line.

    IF page-overflow
        DO 340-print-heading-lines.
    Format investment-line.
    DO 360-write-report-line.
    Move 1 to space-control.
```

Figure 1-7   Pseudocode for the investment-listing program charted in figure 1-6 (part 1 of 2)

may decide that a "format" statement like the one in module 330 is obvious so you don't have to show it in your pseudocode.

Similarly, you don't necessarily have to plan every module in a program when you use pseudocode. For instance, modules 100, 320, 330, 340, 350, 360, and 500 in figure 1-7 are relatively trivial. As a result, you may only want to plan modules 000, 300, and 310 for this program. When you design a structured program, you'll usually find that just a few modules are complicated enough to require planning. On the other hand, if you're not sure how a module should be coded, it's worth taking the time to plan it with pseudocode.

```
340-print-heading-lines.

    Print the heading lines using modules 350 and 360
    to actually write the lines.

350-write-page-top-line.

    Write a page-top line.
    Move 1 to line-count.
    Move 2 to space-control.

360-write-report-line.

    Write a line after advancing space-control lines.
    Add space-control to line-count.

500-print-total-lines.

    Format total lines and print them using module 360 to
    write them.
```

Figure 1-7   Pseudocode for the investment-listing program charted in figure 1-6 (part 2 of 2)

How to code a structured program in COBOL

Structured coding implies three things. First, it implies that you have a structured design for the program. Second, it implies that the program will be coded using only the accepted structures of structured programming. And third, it implies a style of coding that is designed to increase the readability of a program. Since I've just shown you how to design a program using a structure chart, I will now discuss briefly the coding for the accepted structures and give you some guidelines for increasing the readability of your programs.

How to code the accepted structures in COBOL   To review, the accepted structures of structured programming are the sequence, selection, and iteration structures. In COBOL, any statement without conditions is a sequence structure. Similarly, a succession of two or more of these statements is a sequence structure. Thus, a simple PERFORM statement is a sequence structure, a series of MOVE statements is a sequence structure, and a series of arithmetic statements without ON SIZE ERROR clauses is a sequence structure.

To code a selection structure, you code an IF statement. Within the IF statement, you use indentation to show how the IF and ELSE parts of a statement are related. You also use indentation to show how the parts of nested IF statements are related.

To code an iteration structure, you code a PERFORM UNTIL statement. This has the logic shown in variation 3 of the iteration structure in figure 1-3. Using 1985 COBOL, you can also code varia-

Simple pseudocode

```
Open files.
DO 100-format-report-heading.
DO 300-prepare-investment-line
    UNTIL all master records have been read.
DO 500-print-total-lines.
Close files.
Stop run.
```

Pseudocode plus COBOL

```
OPEN files.
PERFORM 100-FORMAT-REPORT-HEADING.
PERFORM 300-PREPARE-INVESTMENT-LINE
    UNTIL INVMAST-EOF.
PERFORM 500-PRINT-TOTAL-LINES.
CLOSE files.
STOP RUN.
```

Pseudocode plus COBOL using all capital letters

```
OPEN FILES.
PERFORM 100-FORMAT-REPORT-HEADING.
PERFORM 300-PREPARE-INVESTMENT-LINE
    UNTIL INVMAST-EOF.
PERFORM 500-PRINT-TOTAL-LINES.
CLOSE FILES.
STOP RUN.
```

Figure 1-8   Different forms of pseudocode for module 000 of the investment-listing program

tion 2 of the iteration structure. You do this by coding the WITH TEST AFTER clause in the PERFORM UNTIL statement as described in chapter 10 of this book.

Guidelines for readability   A primary goal of structured programming is to create code that is easy to read because a program that is readable is easier to develop, test, debug, and maintain than one that isn't. As a result, the program in appendix A and all of the other programs in this book have been coded using guidelines that help produce more readable code.

In general, the code in all of the programs is presented in the same sequence. The SELECT statements and FD statements for the files are in sequence with input files first, I-O files second, and output files third. The groups in the Working-Storage Section are in sequence by (1) work fields such as switches and counters, and (2) record descriptions in the same order as the related files listed in the SELECT statements. Within the record descriptions, the print line descriptions are in sequence by heading lines, body lines, and total lines. In the

Procedure Division, all paragraphs are in sequence by module number. When you use standard sequences like this, it makes it easier for you to locate code as you test and maintain your programs.

Although there are many ways to achieve vertical spacing in a source listing, we recommend that blank comment lines be used for this purpose. A *blank comment line* is a line with an asterisk in column 7 and spaces in columns 8 through 72. In general, we use these lines to set off division and section headers and to highlight groups of data names in the Data Division and paragraphs in the Procedure Division.

In the Data Division, we group related data items to make it easier to find them. We also try to create data names that are meaningful so it's easy to tell what they represent. We use condition names whenever we think they can improve clarity. And we indent and align clauses to improve readability.

In the Procedure Division, we code each box on the structure chart with a single COBOL paragraph. We also use indentation and alignment to make all statements as easy to read as possible.

These, then, are the main guidelines for readability that are illustrated by the programs in this book. If you use them in your programs, we're confident that you will develop programs that are relatively easy to read, test, debug, and maintain.

How to test a program using top-down testing

When you design a program on a top-down basis using structured design, you can develop it using *top-down coding and testing*. In fact, we recommend that you use top-down coding and testing on any program that takes more than a day to develop. And you may want to use it when you develop the case studies for this course.

When you use top-down coding and testing, you don't code the entire program and then test it. Instead, you code and test in phases. You normally start by coding the top-level module and one or more of the modules in the second level. Then, after correcting any bugs, you add one or more modules to this coding and test again. When this much of the program runs correctly, you code a few more modules, add them to what you have, and test again. You continue in this way until all the modules have been coded and you are testing the entire program. Because top-down coding and testing always go together, the phrase *top-down testing* implies top-down coding.

The primary benefit of top-down testing is improved testing efficiency (or improved productivity). To illustrate, imagine a typical COBOL program of 2000 lines or more. If you test the entire program at once with all of its bugs, it's likely that your testing will proceed very inefficiently. For example, it may take several hours of testing just to debug a couple of minor clerical errors. But if you test on a top-down basis, testing proceeds in increments of a few modules at a time. Then, it is relatively easy to find any bugs that are discovered during a test phase because they almost have to be in the modules just added or in the interfaces between the old modules and the new.

How to create a top-down test plan   When you use top-down testing, you start by developing a top-down test plan like the one in figure 1-9. In this plan for the investment-listing program that is charted in figure 1-6, five modules are tested in phase 1, three more are added in phase 2, and the last two are added in phase 3. Then, phase 4 tests data complexities and phase 5 is a volume test. Since the read module (module 310) isn't tested until phase 3, no test data is needed for the first two phases.

When you create a test plan, you have considerable choice as to what modules you test in each phase. As long as you proceed from the top down and add one or more modules in each phase, you are adhering to the principles of top-down testing. Whether you add one, two, or more modules at a time depends on your experience and on the length and complexity of the modules. In a short program like the investment-listing program, it doesn't matter too much what sequence you use, but in a larger, more realistic program, you must carefully plan the development sequence.

In general, your goal should be to use the sequence of testing that will be most efficient in terms of coding and testing. As a result, when you develop your test plan, you should ask questions like: Where are the major module interfaces in the program? Where, if anywhere, in the structure chart do I have doubts about the design? In what modules do I have doubts about how the coding should be done? In most cases, you should try to code and resolve the major problems first.

After you test the first two or three levels of a program, it often becomes a case of mop up. Eventually, you have to code and test all of the modules, so you may as well take them one group at a time, introducing data that applies to each group as you go along.

Incidentally, you don't have to code the file or data definitions required by a module until you add the module to the program. For instance, since the read module in figure 1-6 isn't added to the program until phase 3, you don't have to code the FD statement for the inventory master file until phase 3. On the other hand, since module 330 requires the data descriptions for the fields in the inventory master file, you have to code its record description as part of your coding for phase 2.

How to code program stubs   To use top-down testing, you must code *program stubs*, or *dummy modules*, for the modules in a phase that are called, but not tested. Using the test plan in figure 1-9, for example, modules 310, 320, and 330 are dummy modules in phase 1, so you must code program stubs for them. Similarly, modules 310 and 320 are dummy modules in phase 2.

In phase 1 of figure 1-9, the program stubs for modules 320 and 330 don't have to do anything because the modules that are being tested don't require any data that is developed by them. As a result,

Program: INV3520 Prepare investment listing	Page: 1
Designer: Mike Murach	Date: 04/03/86

Test phase	Data	Data source
1. Modules 000, 100, 300, 500 and 360	None	Not applicable
2. Add modules 330, 340, and 350	None	Not applicable
3. Add modules 310 and 320	Three records: one with investment amount less than $10,000; one with investment amount equal to $10,000; one with investment amount greater than $10,000	Self
4. All modules	Phase 3 data plus records that test the ON SIZE ERROR conditions of the arithmetic statements	Self
5. Page overflow	Phase 4 data plus enough records to cause page overflow	Utility

Figure 1-9   A top-down test plan for the investment-listing program of appendix A

you can code just the paragraph name for each module. Module 310, however, should contain the following statement:

```
MOVE 'Y' TO INVMAST-EOF-SWITCH.
```

This simulates the end of the input file so the program can end properly.

If you want to make sure that the modules are called correctly, you can code program stubs to display messages to that effect. For instance, you can code this statement at the beginning of the stub for module 310:

```
DISPLAY '310-READ-INVENTORY-RECORD'.
```

When executed, this stub will display or print the paragraph name of the module to show that it has been executed. Then, if you code similar statements in the stubs for modules 320 and 330, the printed output will indicate whether or not the dummy modules were called.

In phase 2 of figure 1-9, the program stubs should develop some data in order to test module 330. To do this, the program stubs can be coded as in figure 1-10. Here, module 310 is expanded. It now simulates the reading of one input record the first time it is executed by moving data into the record area for the inventory master file. The second time it's executed, RECORD-COUNT isn't less than one, so Y is moved to INVMAST-EOF-SWITCH indicating that all records in the master file have been read. Similarly, module 320 simulates the calculation of the inventory fields by moving values into INVESTMENT-AMOUNT and NO-OF-MONTHS-STOCK. If the stubs are coded like this, module 330 can print the data for one investment line so all of the modules except the stubs will get tested.

When you code program stubs, you must try to be practical. At some point, it becomes more practical to code the actual module than it is to simulate the function of the module. If, for example, you look at the stub for the read module in figure 1-10, you can see that the code for the stub is longer than the code for the actual module will be. So is it worth coding this stub? That, of course, depends on the program, the module, and your experience. In the case of the read stub in figure 1-10, I think it's worth coding it that way, because you simulate a one-record file before you even have to create a test file.

Discussion

You should now be able to use top-down design, pseudocode, structured coding, and top-down testing as you develop the case studies for this course. If you use these techniques, I believe you'll be able to develop high-quality programs in a minimum of time.

The input stub

```
310-READ-INVENTORY-RECORD.
*
    DISPLAY '310-READ-INVENTORY-RECORD'.
    IF RECORD-COUNT < 1
        MOVE '11111AAAAAAAAAAAAAAAAAAAAA2222233333'
            TO IM-DESCRIPTIVE-DATA
        MOVE '444445555566666' TO IM-INVENTORY-DATA
        MOVE '7777778888888999999999' TO IM-SALES-DATA
        ADD 1 TO RECORD-COUNT
    ELSE
        MOVE 'Y' TO INVMAST-EOF-SWITCH.
```

The processing stub

```
320-COMPUTE-INVENTORY-FIELDS.
*
    DISPLAY '320-COMPUTE-INVENTORY-FIELDS'.
    MOVE 12000.00 TO INVESTMENT-AMOUNT.
    MOVE 12.0 TO NO-OF-MONTHS-STOCK.
```

Figure 1-10   The program stubs for phase 2 of the test plan in figure 1-9

To help you design the case studies for this course, chapter 11 presents structure charts and pseudocode for typical edit, update, and maintenance programs. You can use these designs as models for your case study programs. That's why we recommend that you read chapter 11 before you start the case studies.

Although the structured programming techniques presented in this topic should help you develop the case study programs for this course, you should realize that this has just been an introduction to these techniques. That's why we offer two other books on structured programming for the COBOL programmer. The first, called *How to Design and Develop COBOL Programs*, is a 528-page book that presents all aspects of structured programming, including other techniques for design, planning, and coding. The second, called *The COBOL Programmer's Handbook*, presents complete guidelines for developing structured programs as well as model programs that you can use as a basis for developing your own programs. These books are used in thousands of COBOL shops throughout the country, and we believe that at least one set belongs in every COBOL shop to answer the development questions that frequently occur.

Terminology

structured programming
sequence structure
selection structure
iteration structure
proper program
structured program design
top-down program design
common module
pseudocode
structured coding
blank comment line
top-down coding and testing
top-down testing
program stub
dummy module

Objectives

1. Explain the theory of structured programming.

2. Given case study specifications, design the program using a structure chart, plan the coding of its modules using pseudocode, code it in structured style using the guidelines for readability presented in this chapter, and test it using top-down testing.

Topic 3 A student's procedure for developing COBOL programs

Since you should have developed one or more programs before taking this course, we assume that you've already used some procedure for developing COBOL programs. As much as possible, though, you should follow a standard development procedure. To some extent, this procedure will vary from one company or school to another. As a starting point, though, figure 1-11 lists the seven tasks of the student's procedure for developing COBOL programs that we presented in *Structured ANS COBOL, Part 1*. In most training environments, you'll use a procedure like this when you develop the case study programs for this course.

Although this topic probably doesn't present much that you don't already know, we still recommend that you read it. It will give you a better idea of what the book does and what the book assumes.

Task 1: Get complete program specifications

As a programmer, it is your responsibility to make sure you know exactly what a program is supposed to do before you start to develop it. You must know not only what the inputs and outputs are, but also what processing is required to derive the desired output from the input. If you are assigned a programming problem that isn't adequately defined, be sure to question the person who assigned it until you're confident that you know what the program is supposed to do.

Most companies have standards for what a complete program specification must include. In general, it should include at least three items: (1) some sort of program overview; (2) record layouts for all files used by the program; and (3) print charts for all printed output prepared by the program. Other documents may be required for specific programs, but these are the most common ones.

The program overview   *Program overviews* can be prepared in many different forms. Most companies have their own standards. What's important is that a program overview presents a complete picture of what the program is supposed to do.

Appendix A shows the kind of program overview we use in our shop. You will work with program overviews like this when you do the case studies for this course. As you can see, the form is divided into three parts. The top section is for identification. It gives the name and number of the program as specified by the system documentation, along with the name of the program designer and the date. The middle part of the form lists and describes all of the files that the program requires. In addition, it tells what the program will do with each of those files: use them only for input, use them only for output, or use them for update.

The last section of the form is for processing specifications. It's this section, of course, that is the most critical. Here, you must make sure that all of the information you need to develop the program has been provided. If it isn't all there, you must develop it yourself.

Record layouts   In our shop, we use COBOL descriptions for the record layouts of the files used by a program. This is illustrated by the record description for the inventory master file in appendix A. Usually, these descriptions are available as COPY members so we can copy them into our programs. COBOL descriptions are easier to create and maintain than other forms of record layouts, and they're easier to understand. If you're not familiar with COPY libraries, they are presented in chapter 6 of this book. Whether or not you use COPY libraries, though, the record layouts for the case studies in this course will be presented as COBOL record descriptions.

Print charts   We assume you're already familiar with print charts like the one in appendix A. A chart like this simply indicates the print positions to be used for each item on the report. Since many programs require printed output, you will use print charts often.

Note in the upper lefthand corner of the print chart in appendix A that the date and time are printed as part of the heading. Similarly, the page number and program name are printed in the upper righthand corner of the report. This is a standard practice in many companies.

Task 2:   Design the program using a structure chart

To design a COBOL program, most programmers use top-down design as presented in topic 2 of this chapter. Design is a critical task in the process of program development because it affects the tasks that follow. If you create an effective design for a program, you can code and test the program efficiently. If you don't design a program effectively, coding is likely to be inefficient and testing is often a nightmare. In chapter 11, you'll be shown effective designs for typical edit, update, and maintenance programs.

Task 3:   If necessary, plan the critical modules of the program using pseudocode

In many cases, you'll be able to code and test your programs using only the program specifications and your structure charts. Sometimes, though, you'll want to plan the critical modules of a program before you code them. To do this, we recommend the use of pseudocode as presented in topic 2 of this chapter.

Analysis

1. Get complete program specifications.

Design

2. Design the program using a structure chart (chapter 11).
3. If necessary, plan the critical modules of the program using pseudocode (chapter 11).

Implementation

4. Code the program (chapters 2 through 10) and enter it into the system.
5. Compile the program and correct its diagnostics.
6. Test and debug the program.
7. Document the program.

Note: If you use top-down testing, you repeat tasks 4, 5, and 6 for each phase of your test plan.

Figure 1-11   A student's procedure for developing COBOL programs

Pseudocode is useful because it corresponds closely to COBOL code, yet you can write it much more quickly. As a result, you can plan several modules of a program in a fraction of the time it would take you to actually code them. On the other hand, there's no sense in coding a program twice: once in pseudocode and once in COBOL. That's why we recommend the use of pseudocode only when necessary.

Task 4:   Code the program and enter it into the system

We assume that you already know how to code a report preparation program and enter it into your system. The main purpose of this book is to teach you how to use the features and functions of the COBOL language that you don't already know. By using these features and functions, you should be able to develop edit, update, and maintenance programs as well as report preparation programs.

We also assume that you will use an interactive system for developing the case study programs for this course. Although you may be handcoding your programs on coding forms before you enter them into the system, this isn't really necessary. Instead, you can code a program as you enter it into the system using your structure chart and pseudocode as a guide for your entries. In fact, with a little practice, you'll find that you can enter a program directly into the system much faster than you can handcode it and then enter it. So find out if this is acceptable in your school or company.

If you're interested in what version of COBOL this book teaches, it teaches COBOL for use by any compiler that is based on the 1974 or 1985 COBOL standards. For the most part, in fact, this book teaches a subset of COBOL that will compile on either type of compiler. In addition, chapter 10 presents the main features of the 1985 COBOL standards. And chapters 2 through 9 present elements of the 1985 code that are closely related to the subjects of these chapters. So there's no confusion about what code is 1974 and what code is 1985, all of the 1985 code is shaded in the language summaries presented within chapters 2 through 9.

Because all systems require some compiler dependent code, the last topic in chapters 2 through 10 points out coding elements that may vary from one system to another. More specifically, these topics present the compiler dependent code for: (1) the Microsoft COBOL compiler as used on an IBM PC; (2) the Wang VS compiler as used on a Wang VS system; (3) the VS COBOL compiler as used on an IBM mainframe under the DOS/VSE operating system; (4) the VS COBOL compiler as used on an IBM mainframe under the OS/MVS operating system; and (5) the VS COBOL II compiler as used on an IBM mainframe under OS/MVS. As a result, if you're using one of these compilers, you shouldn't have to refer to any of the reference manuals for your system when you want to find out how to code the compiler dependencies.

If you're not using one of the five compilers I just listed, you will have to find out how to code the compiler dependencies for your system. However, these dependencies are usually trivial. With the exception of the program in chapter 10, all of the programs in this book will run on any system with a 1974 compiler as long as you change: (1) the system names in the SELECT statements so they are acceptable to your system; (2) the single quotation marks (') to double marks (") if double marks are required by your compiler; and (3) COMP-3 usage to COMP usage if COMP is appropriate for your system.

Task 5:   Compile the program and correct its diagnostics

We assume that you already know how to compile a program and correct its diagnostics. Since appendix B presents the proper formats for all of the language you will learn, it should be relatively easy for you to correct the diagnostics that relate to the COBOL you will learn in this book.

Task 6: Test and debug the program

We assume that you already know how to test and debug a program on your system whether it runs to a normal or abnormal termination. However, you probably haven't been using top-down testing as you developed your programs. Now that you know what it is, though, you may want to use it as you develop some of the longer case study programs. So find out if this is acceptable in your school or company. If you use top-down testing, you repeat tasks 4, 5, and 6 for each phase of your test plan.

Task 7: Document the program

Documentation in data processing terminology refers to the collection of records that specifies what is being done and what is going to be done within a data processing system. For each program in an installation, there should be a collection of documents referred to as *program documentation*. As a programmer, one of your jobs is to provide this documentation for each program you write.

Fortunately, some of the most important components of program documentation are by-products of the program development process: the program overview, the record layouts, the print chart, and the design document. In addition, you should include the final compiler listing since it is the only document that shows the actual programming details. And you may be asked to include your listings of test data and test run output. For production programs, your shop standards should specify what's required for program documentation.

For your case study programs, you should provide (1) your design document, (2) your final compiler listing, and (3) listings of your test run output, plus any additional items your instructor requests.

Discussion

This topic is designed to give you a better idea of what you must do to develop a COBOL program in a training environment. If you follow the procedure shown in figure 1-11, you should be able to do your case study assignments with relative efficiency. In addition, you may want to use top-down testing for your longer programs, in which case you will repeat tasks 4, 5, and 6 for each phase of your test plan.

In contrast to the procedure in figure 1-11, figure 1-12 presents a typical procedure for developing COBOL programs in a production environment. Here, you can see that the programmer should get related COPY members and subprograms as a task in the analysis

Analysis

1. Get complete program specifications.
2. Get related programs, COPY members, and subprograms.

Design

3. Design the program using a structure chart.
4. If necessary, plan the critical modules of the program using pseudocode.

Implementation

5. Plan the testing of the program by creating a test plan.
6. If necessary, code the job control procedures for the test runs.
7. If necessary, create the test data for the test runs.
8. Code and test the program using top-down testing.
9. Document the program.

Figure 1-12   A professional procedure for developing COBOL programs

phase. You'll learn more about this in chapters 6 and 7. Although COPY members and subprograms are used in only a few of the program examples in this book, you should realize that they're used in most professional programs.

In the implementation phase in figure 1-12, you can see that the procedure suggests that you plan the testing, code the procedures for the test runs, and create the test data for the test runs before any coding is done. Although these testing techniques aren't covered in this book, these tasks show how important it is to test a program in a carefully-controlled manner.

Terminology

program overview
documentation
program documentation

Objective

List and describe the seven tasks of the student's development procedure presented in this topic.

File handling in COBOL

This section consists of four chapters that show you how to handle files in COBOL. This is the most important section in this book because file handling is a critical skill in COBOL. Chapter 2 shows you how to handle sequential files; chapter 3 shows you how to handle indexed files; chapter 4 shows you how to handle relative files; and chapter 5 shows you how to sort or merge files within a COBOL program. Although relative files are used infrequently, every COBOL programmer should know how to handle sequential and indexed files; and in large shops, every COBOL programmer should know how to use the sort/merge feature of COBOL.

This section is designed so you have to read chapter 2 on sequential files before you read the other three chapters. However, once you read chapter 2, you can read the other chapters in whatever sequence you want. If you're reading this book on your own, I would recommend that you read chapters 2, 3, and 5 first. Then, you can read chapter 4 whenever you are assigned a program that uses a relative file.

Chapter 2

Sequential file handling

In your introductory COBOL course, you learned how to write programs that read simple sequential files. In this chapter, you'll learn how to write and update the records in sequential files. You'll learn how to handle variable-length records as well as fixed-length records. And you'll learn how to handle the I/O errors that may occur when a program processes sequential files.

In topic 1 of this chapter, you'll learn the concepts you need to know for handling sequential files. In topic 2, you'll learn how to write programs that process sequential files of fixed-length records. In topic 3, you'll learn how to write programs that process files of variable-length records. And, in topic 4, I'll present some compiler dependent code that is related to sequential file handling.

Topic 1   Sequential file handling concepts

A *sequential file* can reside on either a tape or a disk device. In either case, the records of the file are stored one after another in consecutive order. Usually, one field within each record contains a key value that's used to sequence the records in the file. When a sequential file is created, the records are written on the device one after another starting with the first record position and continuing until all of the records have been written on the file or there's no more room for the next record. When a sequential file is read, the records are read starting with the first record and continuing until an end-of-file record is read.

To illustrate a sequential file, figure 2-1 presents a simple, ten-record employee file in sequence by social security number. As you can see, the file occupies ten consecutive disk locations, but these ten locations don't have to be the first ten on the disk. They can be anywhere on the disk. If the file were stored on magnetic tape instead of disk, it would occupy ten consecutive tape locations.

In this example, the social security number field is the *key field*, or just *key*. The key field for a sequential file contains the data that the file is sequenced by. Of course, the key field doesn't have to be the first field in a record. It can be located anywhere within the record.

Because sequential files are relatively simple conceptually, there's no point in dwelling on them. In this topic, I'll simply review blocked records, introduce you to variable-length records, and present some volume and file concepts.

Blocked records

To improve the efficiency of a computer system, records within a sequential file are often *blocked*. This simply means that more than one record is stored between gaps on a disk or on a magnetic tape. In figure 2-2, for example, the records are blocked with five records to a block, so you can say that the *blocking factor* is 5.

Blocking can improve processing efficiency, because an entire block of records is read or written at one time. It can improve tape or disk usage, because less tape or disk space is used for the gaps between records. I mention blocking because you sometimes have to specify the blocking factors of the files that are processed by your COBOL programs. From a conceptual point of view, though, it doesn't matter whether the records within a file are blocked or unblocked. Although blocking improves I/O efficiency, your program still processes only one record at a time.

Disk location	Social security number	First name	Middle initial	Last name	Employee number
1	213-64-9290	Thomas	T	Bluestone	00008
2	279-00-1210	William	J	Collins	00002
3	334-96-8721	Constance	M	Harris	00007
4	498-27-6117	Ronald	W	Westbrook	00010
5	499-35-5079	Stanley	L	Abbott	00001
6	558-12-6168	Marie	A	Littlejohn	00005
7	559-35-2479	E	R	Siebart	00006
8	572-68-3100	Jean	B	Glenning	00009
9	703-47-5748	Paul	M	Collins	00004
10	899-16-9235	Alice		Crawford	00003

Figure 2-1   A sequential employee file on disk in sequence by social security number

Variable-length records

Thus far, all of the sequential files you have used have had *fixed-length records*. That is, all of the records in the file have had the same record length.

When the records in a file vary in length, they are referred to as *variable-length records*. Sometimes, for example, a file will consist of more than one type of record. Then, if these record types have different lengths, the file consists of variable-length records. For instance, a set of records representing one transaction may contain a header record that is 250 bytes long, detail records that are 50 bytes long, and a trailer record that is 150 bytes long. In this case, the maximum record length in the file is 250 bytes.

Another type of variable-length record consists of a *root segment* plus a variable number of other segments. For example, inventory records that give warehouse locations may be in variable-length format. In this case, the root segment of each record contains the basic inventory data like item number, item description, and so on. Then, the root segment is followed by a variable number of location segments that specify a warehouse location (typically, warehouse number and bin number), the quantity stored there, and maybe even the date it was stored. There is one of these segments for each warehouse location in which some of the item is stored. As a result, an item stored in only one location has only one of these location segments attached to its root segment; an item stored in ten locations has ten location segments.

Like fixed-length records, variable-length records are stored one after another in consecutive order. If the records are blocked, each block contains as many records as will fit in the maximum block size. So the system knows how long the blocks and the records are, each block and each record is preceded by a short field, as illustrated in

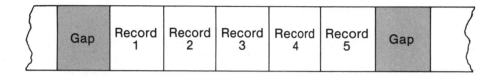

Figure 2-2   The concept of blocked records

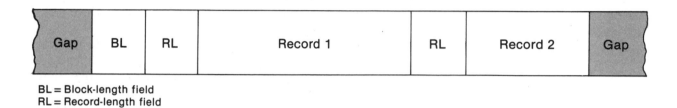

BL = Block-length field
RL = Record-length field

Figure 2-3   The format of blocked variable-length records

figure 2-3. For each record, the record length is given in the record-length field that precedes the record. The record length is the number of bytes in the record itself, plus the number of bytes in the record-length field (usually, four). For each block, the block length is given in the block-length field that precedes the block. The block length is the sum of the record lengths, plus the number of bytes in the block-length field (usually, four).

Variable-length records can be useful because they make efficient use of tape or disk storage. If, for example, an inventory record can have from zero through 20 location segments, all 20 have to be provided for in a fixed-length record whether or not they contain data. In a variable-length record, though, only the actual number of location segments used by an inventory item are stored in the inventory record. This can make a dramatic difference in the size of the file as it resides on a tape or a disk.

In practice, though, variable-length records aren't used much. One reason for this is that sorting a file of variable-length records usually takes considerably longer than sorting a comparable file of fixed-length records. As a result, if a file is going to need sorting, you must question whether the file wouldn't be more efficient with fixed-length records than with variable-length records.

Determining block size

When you write a program that reads a sequential file, you normally are given the block size as part of the program specifications. For fixed-length records, you are given the blocking factor for the file. For variable-length records, you are given the maximum block size.

However, when you write a program that creates a sequential file, you may not be given the block size. Then, it may be your job to determine the block size. If you know your operations group is going to change the block size for your program after you test it and before it is put into production, this presents no problem. In this case, you simply select a block size that is consistent with your test data. You understand that your program will be changed later so it uses a block size that maximizes program and storage efficiency.

On the other hand, if you are asked to select an efficient block size, you should know that block sizes of around 4000 bytes tend to maximize program and storage efficiency. This means that blocks of this size minimize the number of I/O operations required to read or write a file, while they maximize the amount of data that can be stored on a tape or disk. Although larger block sizes can improve these two factors even more, they continue to increase the size of your program, which can decrease its efficiency. As a result, block sizes of around 4000 bytes tend to be optimal.

Today, almost all tape files consist of blocked records, so you have to use the BLOCK CONTAINS clause in the FD statements for these files. If this clause is omitted, unblocked records are assumed. Although most sequential disk files are also blocked, it's becoming common for the operating system to determine an efficient block size for each disk file. As a result, the programmer doesn't know what the actual block size for each file is and doesn't have to use the BLOCK CONTAINS clause in the FD statement for the file.

Volume and file relationships

A *volume* is a unit of a storage medium that can be mounted on an I/O device like a disk or tape drive. For tape devices, a volume is a tape reel. For disk devices, a volume is a disk pack. For years, most disk volumes were removable, just like tape volumes, but today many disk volumes are non-removable.

The data stored on a volume is organized into one or more *files*. As you undoubtedly know by now, a file is a collection of related records that are treated as a unit. These files can have several different relationships with volumes.

The simplest case of a file-volume relationship is a single file on a single volume. For instance, it's common for tape volumes to contain just one file. Logically, this is called a *single-file volume*, as illustrated by file A in figure 2-4. Although it's less common for a disk volume to

Single-file volume

Tape volume

File-A	Unused

Multi-file volume

Tape volume

File-B	File-C	File-D	File-E	File-F	File-G

Multi-volume file

Tape volume

File-H (part 1 of 5)

Tape volume

File-H (part 2 of 5)

Tape volume

File-H (part 3 of 5)

Tape volume

File-H (part 4 of 5)

Tape volume

File-H (part 5 of 5)	Unused

Figure 2-4   Volume and file relationships

contain only one file, it isn't unheard of, particularly when a large file is stored on a disk drive with a removable disk pack.

For disk devices, it's more likely that a volume will hold several or many files. Then, it's called a *multi-file volume*. Files B, C, D, E, F, and G in figure 2-4 illustrate this file-volume relationship. Multi-file volumes are common on both disk and tape.

Some files are too large to fit on a single tape or disk volume. That doesn't mean that the file can't be stored, however, because it's possible for parts of one file to be stored on different volumes in a *multi-volume file*. This is illustrated by file H in figure 2-4. Large multi-volume files can be found on disk devices, but you're more likely to find them on tape because tape is an economical storage medium for large files.

In general, you don't have to know whether a file is a multi-volume file or whether it's on a multi-file volume when you code a COBOL program. These relationships are handled by the operating system. However, you do have to provide job control language that identifies the files or volumes that your program uses. If, for example, you write a program to create a multi-volume file, the operating system will automatically handle the switching from one volume to another as the file is created, but your job control language will probably have to identify the volumes to be used. Similarly, if your program reads one file from a multi-file volume, the operating system will find the file for your program, whether the file is on tape or disk, but your job control language must identify the file, and it may also have to identify the volume.

Terminology

sequential file	volume
key field	file
key	single-file volume
blocked records	multi-file volume
blocking factor	multi-volume file
fixed-length records	
variable-length records	
root segment	

Objectives

1. Describe the characteristics of a sequential file.

2. Describe the format of blocked, variable-length records.

3. Explain the difference between a multi-file volume and a multi-volume file.

Topic 2   COBOL for sequential files of fixed-length records

Figure 2-5 summarizes the COBOL code that you use when you write programs that process sequential files. After I tell you more about this code, I will present three programs that use it. You shouldn't have much trouble with sequential files of fixed-length records, because they're relatively simple from a conceptual point of view. Also, you should already know how to read this type of file.

The SELECT statement

If you review the format for the SELECT statement in figure 2-5, you can see three new clauses. As a result, you can code a SELECT statement for a sequential file like this:

```
SELECT INVMAST  ASSIGN TO AS-INVMAST
                ORGANIZATION IS SEQUENTIAL
                ACCESS IS SEQUENTIAL
                FILE STATUS IS INVMAST-FILE-STATUS.
```

Here, the system name is suitable for the VS COBOL or VS COBOL II compiler running under OS/MVS on an IBM mainframe. Note in figure 2-5, though, that sequential organization and access are assumed when the ORGANIZATION and ACCESS clauses are omitted. As a result, most programmers omit these clauses for sequential files.

The FILE STATUS clause gives the name of a field that is updated by the system as each I/O statement for the file is executed. The FILE STATUS field must be defined in working storage with a picture of XX. Then, after each I/O operation, the program can examine the value in this field to determine how the operation turned out and what error condition (if any) occurred.

Figure 2-6 summarizes the FILE STATUS codes for sequential files. The first code, 00, indicates that the last I/O operation was successful. The second code, 10, indicates that the last operation was successful, but the AT END condition occurred. Both of these are expected outcomes. In contrast, codes from 30 through 99 indicate that more serious errors have occurred. As you'll see in the program examples in this topic, a program normally should terminate itself when one of these conditions occurs.

The FD statement

As the summary in figure 2-5 indicates, you code the FD statement for

SELECT statement

```
SELECT file-name
    ASSIGN TO system-name
    [ORGANIZATION IS SEQUENTIAL]
    [ACCESS MODE IS SEQUENTIAL]
    [FILE STATUS IS data-name]
```

FD statement

```
FD  file-name
    [LABEL RECORDS ARE STANDARD]
    [RECORD CONTAINS integer-1 CHARACTERS]
    [BLOCK CONTAINS integer-2 RECORDS]
```

Procedure Division statements

```
     ⎧INPUT    file-name-1 [WITH NO REWIND] ...⎫
OPEN ⎪OUTPUT   file-name-2 [WITH NO REWIND] ...⎪ ...
     ⎨I-O      file-name-3 ...                  ⎬
     ⎩EXTEND   file-name-4 ...                  ⎭

READ file-name [NEXT] RECORD
    [INTO data-name]
    [AT END imperative-statement-1]

WRITE record-name
    [FROM record-name]

REWRITE record-name
    [FROM data-name]

CLOSE file-name-1 [WITH NO REWIND]  ...
```

Note: All 1985 COBOL elements are shaded.

Figure 2-5   COBOL statement formats for handling sequential files of fixed-length records

FILE STATUS codes	Meaning
00	Successful completion of I/O operation
10	End-of-file condition during read operation (AT END condition)
30-39	Permanent error condition with unsuccessful completion of I/O operation
40-49	Logical error condition with unsuccessful completion of I/O operation
90-99	Defined by implementor

Figure 2-6   FILE STATUS codes for I/O operations on sequential files

a sequential file using the LABEL RECORDS, RECORD CONTAINS, and BLOCK CONTAINS clauses. Because almost all sequential files have standard labels, the LABEL RECORDS clause is optional in the 1985 COBOL standards as indicated by the shading over the brackets for this clause. When it is omitted, it means that the label records are standard. As a result, you probably won't code this clause when you start using a 1985 compiler.

The RECORD CONTAINS clause specifies the number of characters (bytes) in each fixed-length record. When you code this clause, the compiler compares the number of bytes specified in it with the number of bytes derived from the record description that follows the FD statement. If they aren't equal, a diagnostic message is printed. As a result, you should code this clause, because it may help you identify a coding problem. It's also good documentation.

If your program is processing blocked tape records, you should code the BLOCK CONTAINS clause to show how many records are stored or are going to be stored in each block. Similarly, you have to code this clause for blocked disk records on some systems. On other systems, though, the system itself calculates and keeps track of the block size for sequential disk files, so you don't have to code it. In this book, we don't use the BLOCK CONTAINS clause in any of the programs because it isn't required on IBM mainframes when using VSAM files.

Procedure Division statements

The OPEN statement   If you check the format for the OPEN statement, you can see that you can open a file four ways: INPUT, OUTPUT, I-O, and EXTEND. INPUT means that a file will only be used for input by the program. OUTPUT means that the file will be created by the program. I-O means that a disk file will be read by the program, but it also means that the records in the file can be written back onto the file in the same disk locations that they were read from. EXTEND means that a disk file will be *extended* by the program. When a file is extended, records are added to the file after the last record in the file.

The WITH NO REWIND clause applies only to tape files. Normally, when an OPEN statement for a tape file is executed, the tape is rewound and positioned at the first record of the first file on the tape. When the NO REWIND clause is coded, though, the tape isn't rewound. As a result, it is sometimes useful when processing files on a multi-file reel of tape. If, for example, three transaction files are stored on one reel of tape, the NO REWIND clause can leave the tape positioned at the start of the second or third file after the first or second file has been processed. This clause is rarely used, though; I only mention it here so you'll be aware that it exists.

The READ statement   Since you've used READ statements for sequential files already, the format in figure 2-5 should be familiar to you. Note, however, that the 1985 standards provide for the word NEXT to be used after the file name. It is an optional word that simply means that each READ statement reads the next sequential record, so we don't recommend its use, and we won't use it in the programs in this book.

The WRITE statement   The WRITE statement can be used only for a file that has been opened as OUTPUT or EXTEND. When it's executed, it writes a record in the next available record location. In other words, the WRITE statement adds a record to a file.

The REWRITE statement   The REWRITE statement can be used only for a file that has been opened as I-O. Before it can be executed, a READ statement must be executed. This positions the file at a certain record location. Then, the REWRITE statement writes a record into this location. In other words, the REWRITE statement is used to change records that are already on a file.

The CLOSE statement   The CLOSE statement simply lists the files to be closed. For tape files, though, the NO REWIND clause can be coded after the file name. Then, the file isn't rewound as part of the CLOSE operation. If the NO REWIND clause isn't coded, the tape is rewound. Here again, you may find this clause useful when processing multi-file tapes, but you will probably use it rarely, if at all.

1985 code for I/O statements   As you will see in chapter 10, the 1985 standards provide for some new code in the I/O statements for sequential files. Specifically, a NOT AT END clause is allowed in a READ statement, and the READ, WRITE, and REWRITE statements can be ended by the END-READ, END-WRITE, and END-REWRITE delimiters. In general, you won't need to use the END delimiters, but the NOT AT END clause can help you to improve the readability of your code, as you'll see in chapter 10.

Three illustrative programs

Because sequential files of fixed-length records are relatively simple in concept, you shouldn't have much trouble with the COBOL for processing them. As a result, I'll only present three short programs in this topic.

An edit program that extends a sequential file   Figure 2-7 gives a program overview for a simple edit program. This program reads a sequential file of inventory transactions; it produces a sequential file of valid transactions and another sequential file of invalid transactions. Note, though, that the file of valid transactions is to be extended. This means the VALTRAN file already exists and the program should add the valid records to it after the last record in the file. In contrast, the error transaction file is an output file so it will be created by the program.

This program is unrealistic, of course, because it has been simplified for illustrative purposes. As a result, the transaction record is short and only a limited amount of validity checking is required. Also, the program just writes the invalid records on the file of error transactions. In practice, though, an edit program often prints a listing of invalid records so they can be corrected and processed later on.

Figure 2-8 presents the structure chart for this program. It consists of only six modules. The two we'll concentrate on are modules 330 and 340, which contain the WRITE statements for the files.

Figure 2-9 presents the source code for this program. If you check the SELECT statements for the valid transaction file and the error transaction file, you can see that they are defined with FILE STATUS fields named VALTRAN-FILE-STATUS and ERRTRAN-FILE-STATUS. These fields are defined in working storage with pictures of XX.

In module 330, you can see the WRITE statement for the valid transaction file. The IF statement that follows it checks the FILE STATUS field to see how the WRITE operation turned out. If the FILE STATUS field has a value of 00, it means the operation was successful, so the program continues. However, if the file status value is anything other than 00, a message like this is displayed:

```
INV1100   A   2   WRITE ERROR FOR VALTRAN
INV1100   A   2   ITEM NUMBER = 32014
INV1100   A   2   FILE STATUS = 30
```

```
┌─────────────────────────────────────────────────────────────────────────────┐
│                                                                               │
│  Program: INV1100    Edit inventory transactions      Page: 1                 │
│                                                                               │
├─────────────────────────────────────────────────────────────────────────────┤
│                                                                               │
│  Designer: Mike Murach                               Date: 09-03-86           │
│                                                                               │
└─────────────────────────────────────────────────────────────────────────────┘
```

Input/output specifications

```
┌─────────────────────────────────────────────────────────────────────────────┐
│                                                                               │
│   File           Description                             Use                  │
│                                                                               │
├─────────────────────────────────────────────────────────────────────────────┤
│                                                                               │
│   INVTRAN        Inventory transaction file             Input                 │
│   VALTRAN        Valid inventory transaction file       Extend                │
│   ERRTRAN        Invalid inventory transaction file     Output                │
│                                                                               │
│                                                                               │
│                                                                               │
│                                                                               │
│                                                                               │
│                                                                               │
└─────────────────────────────────────────────────────────────────────────────┘
```

Process specifications

```
┌─────────────────────────────────────────────────────────────────────────────┐
│                                                                               │
│  This program edits a file of inventory transactions (INVTRAN).  If all       │
│  of the fields in a transaction are valid using the editing rules             │
│  below, the record is valid.  Then, the record should be written in the       │
│  valid transaction file (VALTRAN).  But if one or more fields is              │
│  invalid, the record is invalid.  Then, the record should be written in       │
│  the invalid transaction file (ERRTRAN).  The format of the records in        │
│  all three transaction files is the same.                                     │
│                                                                               │
│  The basic processing requirements for each inventory transaction            │
│  follow:                                                                      │
│                                                                               │
│  1.  Read the transaction record.                                            │
│                                                                               │
│  2.  Edit the fields in the record.                                          │
│                                                                               │
│  3.  If the record is valid,                                                 │
│          write the record in the valid transaction file.                     │
│                                                                               │
│  4.  If the record is invalid,                                               │
│          write the record in the invalid transaction file.                   │
│                                                                               │
│  Editing rules:                                                               │
│                                                                               │
│  IT-ITEM-NO              Must be numeric                                       │
│  IT-VENDOR-NO            Must be numeric                                       │
│  IT-RECEIPT-QUANTITY     Must be numeric                                       │
│                                                                               │
└─────────────────────────────────────────────────────────────────────────────┘
```

Figure 2-7   The program overview for an edit program that extends a sequential file of valid transactions

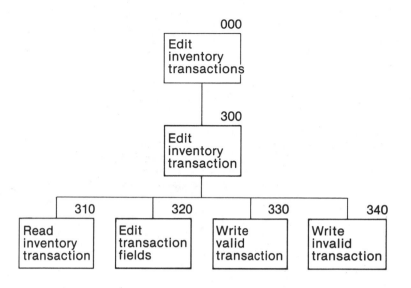

Figure 2-8   The structure chart for the edit program

Also, the end-of-file switch for the input file is turned on so the program will end.

Similarly, in module 340, you can see the WRITE statement for the error transaction file. After this statement, the FILE STATUS field is checked to make sure the operation was successful. If it wasn't, an error message is displayed and INVTRAN-EOF-SWITCH is turned on so the program will end before another transaction is read.

Otherwise, you should be able to understand this program without much trouble. Note that a FILE STATUS field isn't used for the input file because an input error normally doesn't cause any serious problems. In contrast, if the program doesn't catch an output error, it's possible that the program will end normally so no one will be aware that the file wasn't created or extended properly. Since this will cause errors later on, it's common to check for errors when writing records on a sequential file. More about this in topic 4.

```
 IDENTIFICATION DIVISION.
*
 PROGRAM-ID.  INV1100.
*
 ENVIRONMENT DIVISION.
*
 INPUT-OUTPUT SECTION.
*
 FILE-CONTROL.
     SELECT INVTRAN    ASSIGN TO SYS020-AS-INVTRAN.
     SELECT VALTRAN    ASSIGN TO SYS021-AS-VALTRAN
                       FILE STATUS IS VALTRAN-FILE-STATUS.
     SELECT ERRTRAN    ASSIGN TO SYS022-AS-ERRTRAN
                       FILE STATUS IS ERRTRAN-FILE-STATUS.
*
 DATA DIVISION.
*
 FILE SECTION.
*
 FD  INVTRAN
     LABEL RECORDS ARE STANDARD
     RECORD CONTAINS 21 CHARACTERS.
*
 01  INVENTORY-TRANSACTION.
*
     05   IT-ITEM-NO          PIC X(5).
     05   IT-VENDOR-NO        PIC X(5).
     05   IT-RECEIPT-DATE     PIC X(6).
     05   IT-RECEIPT-QUANTITY PIC X(5).
*
 FD  VALTRAN
     LABEL RECORDS ARE STANDARD
     RECORD CONTAINS 21 CHARACTERS.
*
 01  VALID-TRANSACTION       PIC X(21).
*
 FD  ERRTRAN
     LABEL RECORDS ARE STANDARD
     RECORD CONTAINS 21 CHARACTERS.
*
 01  ERROR-TRANSACTION       PIC X(21).
*
 WORKING-STORAGE SECTION.
*
 01  SWITCHES.
*
     05   INVTRAN-EOF-SWITCH  PIC X        VALUE 'N'.
          88   INVTRAN-EOF                 VALUE 'Y'.
     05   VALID-TRAN-SWITCH   PIC X.
          88   VALID-TRAN                  VALUE 'Y'.
*
 01  FILE-STATUS-FIELDS.
*
     05   VALTRAN-FILE-STATUS PIC XX.
     05   ERRTRAN-FILE-STATUS PIC XX.
*
 PROCEDURE DIVISION.
*
```

Figure 2-9   The edit program (part 1 of 2)

```
     000-EDIT-INVENTORY-TRANS.
*
         OPEN INPUT   INVTRAN
              EXTEND VALTRAN
              OUTPUT ERRTRAN.
         PERFORM 300-EDIT-INVENTORY-TRAN
             UNTIL INVTRAN-EOF.
         CLOSE INVTRAN
               VALTRAN
               ERRTRAN.
         DISPLAY 'INV1100   I   1   NORMAL EOJ'.
         STOP RUN.
*
     300-EDIT-INVENTORY-TRAN.
*
         PERFORM 310-READ-INVENTORY-TRAN.
         IF NOT INVTRAN-EOF
             PERFORM 320-EDIT-TRANSACTION-FIELDS
             IF VALID-TRAN
                 PERFORM 330-WRITE-VALID-TRAN
             ELSE
                 PERFORM 340-WRITE-INVALID-TRAN.
*
     310-READ-INVENTORY-TRAN.
*
         READ INVTRAN
             AT END
                 MOVE 'Y' TO INVTRAN-EOF-SWITCH.
*
     320-EDIT-TRANSACTION-FIELDS.
*
         MOVE 'Y' TO VALID-TRAN-SWITCH.
         IF         IT-ITEM-NO NOT NUMERIC
             OR  IT-VENDOR-NO NOT NUMERIC
             OR  IT-RECEIPT-QUANTITY NOT NUMERIC
             MOVE 'N' TO VALID-TRAN-SWITCH.
*
     330-WRITE-VALID-TRAN.
*
         WRITE VALID-TRANSACTION FROM INVENTORY-TRANSACTION.
         IF VALTRAN-FILE-STATUS NOT = '00'
             DISPLAY 'INV1100   A   2   WRITE ERROR FOR VALTRAN'
             DISPLAY 'INV1100   A   2   ITEM NUMBER = ' IT-ITEM-NO
             DISPLAY 'INV1100   A   2   FILE STATUS = '
                 VALTRAN-FILE-STATUS
             MOVE 'Y' TO INVTRAN-EOF-SWITCH.
*
     340-WRITE-INVALID-TRAN.
*
         WRITE ERROR-TRANSACTION FROM INVENTORY-TRANSACTION.
         IF ERRTRAN-FILE-STATUS NOT = '00'
             DISPLAY 'INV1100   A   3   WRITE ERROR FOR ERRTRAN'
             DISPLAY 'INV1100   A   3   ITEM NUMBER = ' IT-ITEM-NO
             DISPLAY 'INV1100   A   3   FILE STATUS = '
                 ERRTRAN-FILE-STATUS
             MOVE 'Y' TO INVTRAN-EOF-SWITCH.
```

Figure 2-9   The edit program (part 2 of 2)

A sequential update program   Figure 2-10 gives the program specifications for a sequential update program. This program updates the records in an inventory master file based on the data in a file of valid inventory transactions (the file created by the edit program in figure 2-9). The output is a new master file with the same record format as the original (old) master file. If a transaction can't be processed because no record in the old master file has the same item number, it should be written on a new file of error transactions.

Here again, this program has been simplified for illustrative purposes. As a result, only one field in a master record is updated by a transaction record. In practice, of course, many fields in a master record are likely to be updated by a single transaction. Also, a typical update program is likely to print a listing of all error transactions so they can be corrected and processed later on.

Figure 2-11 presents a structure chart for this program. Module 300 is called "process inventory transaction," which indicates that the logic of the program is based on the reading of the transaction file, not the master file. Module 320 is called "get inventory master," which implies more than just reading the next record. In this case, as you can deduce from modules 330 and 340, it means write the previously-read master record on the new master file and read a master record from the old master file. Finally, module 350 is called "update inventory master," which means update the record in main memory. Note, however, that this has nothing to do with reading or writing a master record. The reads and writes of the old and new master files are controlled by module 320.

Figure 2-12 gives the COBOL code for this program. It has two input files and two output files, and both output files are defined with FILE STATUS fields. If you check the read modules in the Procedure Division, you can see that both of them move HIGH-VALUE to the key field for the file when the AT END condition is reached. To do this, you must use the INTO option of the READ statement because fields defined in the File Section for a file aren't available to the program after the AT END clause has been executed for the file. Also, to use HIGH-VALUE, the key fields must be defined with pictures of X(5), not 9(5). In case you're not familiar with this figurative constant, HIGH-VALUE represents the highest value that can be defined for a computer system, so it will always be greater than any field it's compared to.

Beyond this, the only aspect of this program that you might have difficulty with is the logic in modules 000, 300, and 320. As background, you should know that the logic of a sequential update program is based on a comparison of the key fields in the master and transaction records that are read. These key fields are sometimes called *control fields* because this comparison controls the logic of the program. If the key field of a transaction record and the key field of a master record are equal, the records are *matched*. This means that the transaction record applies to the master record, so the master record

Program: INV1200 Update inventory file	Page: 1
Designer: **Mike Murach**	Date: 09-03-86

Input/output specifications

File	Description	Use
VALTRAN	Valid inventory transaction file	Input
INVMAST	Old inventory master file	Input
NEWMAST	New inventory master file	Output
ERRTRAN	Unmatched inventory transaction file	Output

Process specifications

This program updates an inventory master file (**INVMAST**) based on the data in a file of valid inventory transaction records (**VALTRAN**). The output is a new master file that contains the updated master records (**NEWMAST**).

If a transaction has the same item number as a master record, the transaction matches the master record. Then, the transaction data should be used to update the master record: The on hand quantity in the master record should be increased by the receipt quantity in the transaction record.

If a matching master record can't be found for a transaction, the transaction is unmatched. Then, the transaction record should be written on the file of error transactions (**ERRTRAN**).

Both **VALTRAN** and **INVMAST** are in sequence by item number. Also, the record formats for **VALTRAN** and **ERRTRAN** are the same, and the record formats for **INVMAST** and **NEWMAST** are the same.

The basic processing requirements follow:

1. Read a transaction record.

2. If necessary, get inventory master records until a record with a matching or greater item number is found. This includes writing the previous master record to the new master file.

3. If the transaction is matched,
        the matching master record should be updated.

4. If the transaction is unmatched,
        the record should be written on the file of error transactions.

Figure 2-10   The program specifications for a sequential update program (part 1 of 2)

The record layout for the transaction record

```
01   INVENTORY-TRANSACTION.
*
     05   IT-ITEM-NO                 PIC X(5).
     05   IT-VENDOR-NO               PIC X(5).
     05   IT-RECEIPT-DATE            PIC X(6).
     05   IT-RECEIPT-QUANTITY        PIC S9(5).
```

The record layout for the inventory master record

```
01   INVENTORY-MASTER-RECORD.
*
     05   IM-DESCRIPTIVE-DATA.
          10   IM-ITEM-NO            PIC X(5).
          10   IM-ITEM-DESC          PIC X(20).
          10   IM-UNIT-COST          PIC S999V99.
          10   IM-UNIT-PRICE         PIC S999V99.
     05   IM-INVENTORY-DATA.
          10   IM-REORDER-POINT      PIC S9(5).
          10   IM-ON-HAND            PIC S9(5).
          10   IM-ON-ORDER           PIC S9(5).
     05   FILLER                     PIC X(30).
```

Figure 2-10   The program specifications for a sequential update program (part 2 of 2)

should be updated based on the transaction data. Similarly, if the key of a transaction record isn't equal to the key of any master record, it means the transaction record is unmatched (an *unmatched transaction*). This means that the transaction can't be processed, so it is considered to be an error transaction. Finally, if the key of a master record isn't equal to the key of any transaction record, it means that the master record is unmatched (an *unmatched master*). This means that there are no transactions for the master record. In this case, the master record should be written on the new master file unchanged.

In module 000 in figure 2-12, LOW-VALUE is moved to the key field of the master file before any records are read. In contrast to HIGH-VALUE, LOW-VALUE represents the lowest value that can be defined for a computer system. Then, module 300 is performed until the all-records-processed switch is turned on. As you will see in module 300, this switch is turned on when the key fields in both the transaction and master files are equal to HIGH-VALUE.

Module 300 starts by performing module 310 to read one transaction record. Then, it performs module 320 until the key field in the master record isn't less than the key field in the transaction record. Since the key field in the master record was set to LOW-VALUE in module 000, this means module 320 will be performed at least once. When module 300 stops performing module 320, the master record

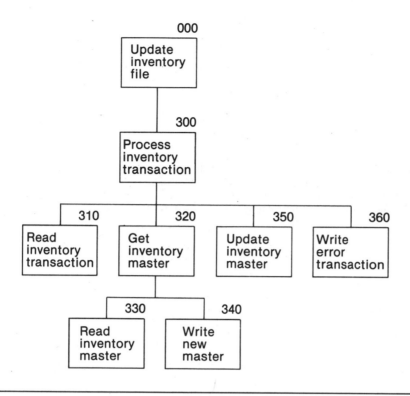

Figure 2-11   The structure chart for the sequential update program

will either match the transaction record or its key field will be greater than the key field in the transaction record. Then, the IF statement in module 300 determines whether the transaction is matched or unmatched and performs either module 350 or 360 based on this determination. It also turns the all-records-processed switch on if both key fields are equal to HIGH-VALUE.

The logic of module 320 is based on the notion that a record shouldn't be read from the old master file until the previous record has been written on the new master file. As a result, it uses a FIRST-EXECUTION switch to read an old master record without writing a new one the first time the module is executed. After that, though, the module writes a new master record before reading the next old master record. That way, you can be sure that all of the records from the old master file have been written on the new master file.

If you check modules 340 and 360, you can see that they are coded much like the write modules in the edit program. After a WRITE statement has been executed, the FILE STATUS field is checked to make sure the operation was successful. If it wasn't, an appropriate message is displayed and the all-records-processed switch is turned on so the program will end before any more records are read.

```
 IDENTIFICATION DIVISION.
*
 PROGRAM-ID.   INV1200.
*
 ENVIRONMENT DIVISION.
*
 INPUT-OUTPUT SECTION.
*
 FILE-CONTROL.
     SELECT VALTRAN    ASSIGN TO SYS020-AS-VALTRAN.
     SELECT INVMAST    ASSIGN TO SYS021-AS-INVMAST.
     SELECT NEWMAST    ASSIGN TO SYS022-AS-NEWMAST
                       FILE STATUS IS NEWMAST-FILE-STATUS.
     SELECT ERRTRAN    ASSIGN TO SYS023-AS-ERRTRAN
                       FILE STATUS IS ERRTRAN-FILE-STATUS.
*
 DATA DIVISION.
*
 FILE SECTION.
*
 FD  VALTRAN
     LABEL RECORDS ARE STANDARD
     RECORD CONTAINS 21 CHARACTERS.
*
 01  VALID-TRANSACTION-AREA     PIC X(21).
*
 FD  INVMAST
     LABEL RECORDS ARE STANDARD
     RECORD CONTAINS 80 CHARACTERS.
*
 01  MASTER-RECORD-AREA         PIC X(80).
*
 FD  NEWMAST
     LABEL RECORDS ARE STANDARD
     RECORD CONTAINS 80 CHARACTERS.
*
 01  NEW-MASTER-AREA            PIC X(80).
*
 FD  ERRTRAN
     LABEL RECORDS ARE STANDARD
     RECORD CONTAINS 21 CHARACTERS.
*
 01  ERROR-TRANSACTION          PIC X(21).
*
 WORKING-STORAGE SECTION.
*
 01  SWITCHES.
*
     05   ALL-RECORDS-PROCESSED-SWITCH  PIC X      VALUE 'N'.
          88   ALL-RECORDS-PROCESSED               VALUE 'Y'.
     05   FIRST-EXECUTION-SWITCH        PIC X      VALUE 'Y'.
          88   FIRST-EXECUTION                     VALUE 'Y'.
*
 01  FILE-STATUS-FIELDS.
*
```

Figure 2-12   The sequential update program (part 1 of 3)

```
        05    NEWMAST-FILE-STATUS       PIC XX.
              88   NEWMAST-SUCCESSFUL                    VALUE '00'.
        05    ERRTRAN-FILE-STATUS       PIC XX.
              88   ERRTRAN-SUCCESSFUL                    VALUE '00'.
*
   01   INVENTORY-TRANSACTION.
*
        05    IT-ITEM-NO                PIC X(5).
        05    IT-VENDOR-NO              PIC X(5).
        05    IT-RECEIPT-DATE           PIC X(6).
        05    IT-RECEIPT-QUANTITY       PIC S9(5).
*
   01   INVENTORY-MASTER-RECORD.
*
        05    IM-DESCRIPTIVE-DATA.
              10   IM-ITEM-NO                PIC X(5).
              10   IM-ITEM-DESC              PIC X(20).
              10   IM-UNIT-COST              PIC S999V99.
              10   IM-UNIT-PRICE             PIC S999V99.
        05    IM-INVENTORY-DATA.
              10   IM-REORDER-POINT          PIC S9(5).
              10   IM-ON-HAND                PIC S9(5).
              10   IM-ON-ORDER               PIC S9(5).
        05    FILLER                         PIC X(30).
*
   PROCEDURE DIVISION.
*
   000-UPDATE-INVENTORY-FILE.
*
        OPEN INPUT    VALTRAN
                      INVMAST
             OUTPUT   NEWMAST
                      ERRTRAN.
        MOVE LOW-VALUE TO IM-ITEM-NO.
        PERFORM 300-PROCESS-INVENTORY-TRAN
             UNTIL ALL-RECORDS-PROCESSED.
        CLOSE VALTRAN
              INVMAST
              NEWMAST
              ERRTRAN.
        DISPLAY 'INV1200  I  1  NORMAL EOJ'.
        STOP RUN.
*
   300-PROCESS-INVENTORY-TRAN.
*
        PERFORM 310-READ-INVENTORY-TRAN.
        PERFORM 320-GET-INVENTORY-MASTER
             UNTIL IM-ITEM-NO NOT < IT-ITEM-NO.
        IF        IM-ITEM-NO = HIGH-VALUE
              AND IT-ITEM-NO = HIGH-VALUE
              MOVE 'Y' TO ALL-RECORDS-PROCESSED-SWITCH
        ELSE
              IF IM-ITEM-NO = IT-ITEM-NO
                    PERFORM 350-UPDATE-INVENTORY-MASTER
              ELSE
                    PERFORM 360-WRITE-ERROR-TRAN.
```

Figure 2-12   The sequential update program (part 2 of 3)

```
*
 310-READ-INVENTORY-TRAN.
*
     READ VALTRAN INTO INVENTORY-TRANSACTION
         AT END
             MOVE HIGH-VALUE TO IT-ITEM-NO.
*
 320-GET-INVENTORY-MASTER.
*
     IF FIRST-EXECUTION
         PERFORM 330-READ-INVENTORY-MASTER
         MOVE 'N' TO FIRST-EXECUTION-SWITCH
     ELSE
         PERFORM 340-WRITE-NEW-MASTER
         PERFORM 330-READ-INVENTORY-MASTER.
*
 330-READ-INVENTORY-MASTER.
*
     READ INVMAST INTO INVENTORY-MASTER-RECORD
         AT END
             MOVE HIGH-VALUE TO IM-ITEM-NO.
*
 340-WRITE-NEW-MASTER.
*
     WRITE NEW-MASTER-AREA FROM INVENTORY-MASTER-RECORD.
     IF NOT NEWMAST-SUCCESSFUL
         DISPLAY 'INV1200  A  2   WRITE ERROR FOR NEWMAST'
         DISPLAY 'INV1200  A  2   ITEM NUMBER = ' IM-ITEM-NO
         DISPLAY 'INV1200  A  2   FILE STATUS = '
             NEWMAST-FILE-STATUS
         MOVE 'Y' TO ALL-RECORDS-PROCESSED-SWITCH.
*
 350-UPDATE-INVENTORY-MASTER.
*
     ADD IT-RECEIPT-QUANTITY TO IM-ON-HAND.
*
 360-WRITE-ERROR-TRAN.
*
     WRITE ERROR-TRANSACTION FROM INVENTORY-TRANSACTION.
     IF NOT ERRTRAN-SUCCESSFUL
         DISPLAY 'INV1200  A  3   WRITE ERROR FOR ERRTRAN'
         DISPLAY 'INV1200  A  3   ITEM NUMBER = ' IT-ITEM-NO
         DISPLAY 'INV1200  A  3   FILE STATUS = '
             ERRTRAN-FILE-STATUS
         MOVE 'Y' TO ALL-RECORDS-PROCESSED-SWITCH.
```

Figure 2-12   The sequential update program (part 3 of 3)

A sequential update-in-place program   Usually, a sequential update program reads an old master file, updates its records, and creates a new master file. Sometimes, though, it's efficient for a sequential file to be *updated in place*. This means that an updated record is written back on the file in the location that it was read from. Then, the program only uses one master file; it doesn't require an old master file and a new one.

To illustrate, figures 2-13 and 2-14 present the structure chart and COBOL code for the same program that is presented in figures 2-10 through 2-12. In contrast to the program in figure 2-12, though, the program in figure 2-14 updates the master file in place. If you compare the structure charts for these programs, you'll see that the only difference is that the chart in figure 2-11 calls module 340 "write new master," while the chart in figure 2-13 calls it "rewrite inventory master."

If you review the code in figure 2-14, you can see in module 000 that the master file is opened as I-O. This means that records can be written back onto the file using the REWRITE statement. Then, in module 340, you can see the use of the REWRITE statement. After it is executed, its FILE STATUS field is checked to make sure the operation was successful. If it wasn't, a message is displayed and a switch is turned on so the program will end.

When a file is updated in place, you don't need to rewrite a master record unless it has been changed. In fact, it is inefficient to do so. As a result, you should code a program like this so it doesn't rewrite the unchanged master records.

In figure 2-14, a MASTER-UPDATED switch is turned on and off throughout the execution of the program so the program can decide when a master record needs to be rewritten on the master file. As you can see, this switch is off when the program begins. Then, it is turned on in module 350 after a master record is updated, and it is turned off in module 340 after a master record has been rewritten on the master file. In module 320, you can see that the program only calls module 340 to rewrite a master record when this switch is on.

Incidentally, this program is designed and coded so it will process more than one transaction for a single master record. Otherwise, its structure and code could be simplified.

Also, please note that this program will read all of the records in the master file, even though none will be updated after the last transaction record has been read. We wrote the program this way for two reasons. First, we wanted to keep the program as much like the sequential update program in figure 2-12 as possible. Second, a production program is likely to be written like this so control data can be accumulated from each master record. If it weren't for these requirements, we would have written the program so processing ends after the last transaction record has been read.

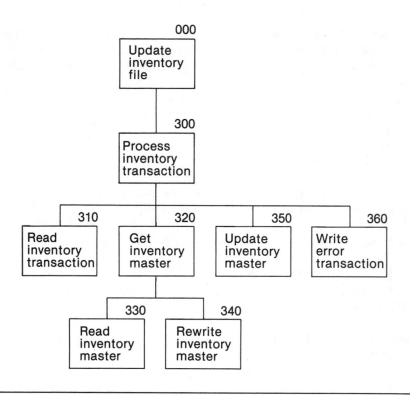

Figure 2-13   The structure chart for the sequential update-in-place program

Discussion

In this topic, I've emphasized the COBOL required for sequential files, not the logic of programs that use sequential files. However, if you study the programs in this topic, I think you'll understand them without too much difficulty. If you do have problems with them, keep in mind that chapter 11 presents more information about the structure and logic of edit, update, and maintenance programs.

Terminology

extending a file   unmatched transaction
control field   unmatched master
matched record   updating in place

Objective

Given program specifications that require the use of one or more sequential files, develop a COBOL program that satisfies the specifications.

```
  IDENTIFICATION DIVISION.
*
 PROGRAM-ID.  INV1200.
*
 ENVIRONMENT DIVISION.
*
 INPUT-OUTPUT SECTION.
*
 FILE-CONTROL.
      SELECT VALTRAN   ASSIGN TO SYS020-AS-VALTRAN.
      SELECT INVMAST   ASSIGN TO SYS021-AS-INVMAST
                       FILE STATUS IS INVMAST-FILE-STATUS.
      SELECT ERRTRAN   ASSIGN TO SYS022-AS-ERRTRAN
                       FILE STATUS IS ERRTRAN-FILE-STATUS.
*
 DATA DIVISION.
*
 FILE SECTION.
*
 FD  VALTRAN
     LABEL RECORDS ARE STANDARD
     RECORD CONTAINS 21 CHARACTERS.
*
 01  VALID-TRANSACTION-AREA    PIC X(21).
*
 FD  INVMAST
     LABEL RECORDS ARE STANDARD
     RECORD CONTAINS 80 CHARACTERS.
*
 01  MASTER-RECORD-AREA        PIC X(80).
*
 FD  ERRTRAN
     LABEL RECORDS ARE STANDARD
     RECORD CONTAINS 21 CHARACTERS.
*
 01  ERROR-TRANSACTION         PIC X(21).
*
 WORKING-STORAGE SECTION.
*
 01  SWITCHES.
*
     05  ALL-RECORDS-PROCESSED-SWITCH  PIC X     VALUE 'N'.
         88  ALL-RECORDS-PROCESSED               VALUE 'Y'.
     05  MASTER-UPDATED-SWITCH         PIC X     VALUE 'N'.
         88  MASTER-UPDATED                      VALUE 'Y'.
*
 01  FILE-STATUS-FIELDS.
*
     05  INVMAST-FILE-STATUS    PIC XX.
         88  INVMAST-SUCCESSFUL             VALUE '00'.
     05  ERRTRAN-FILE-STATUS    PIC XX.
         88  ERRTRAN-SUCCESSFUL             VALUE '00'.
*
 01  INVENTORY-TRANSACTION.
*
```

Figure 2-14   The sequential update-in-place program (part 1 of 3)

```
    05   IT-ITEM-NO              PIC X(5).
    05   IT-VENDOR-NO            PIC X(5).
    05   IT-RECEIPT-DATE         PIC X(6).
    05   IT-RECEIPT-QUANTITY     PIC S9(5).
*
 01  INVENTORY-MASTER-RECORD.
*
    05   IM-DESCRIPTIVE-DATA.
         10   IM-ITEM-NO              PIC X(5).
         10   IM-ITEM-DESC            PIC X(20).
         10   IM-UNIT-COST            PIC S999V99.
         10   IM-UNIT-PRICE           PIC S999V99.
    05   IM-INVENTORY-DATA.
         10   IM-REORDER-POINT        PIC S9(5).
         10   IM-ON-HAND              PIC S9(5).
         10   IM-ON-ORDER             PIC S9(5).
    05   FILLER                       PIC X(30).
*
 PROCEDURE DIVISION.
*
 000-UPDATE-INVENTORY-FILE.
*
    OPEN INPUT   VALTRAN
         I-O     INVMAST
         OUTPUT ERRTRAN.
    MOVE LOW-VALUE TO IM-ITEM-NO.
    PERFORM 300-PROCESS-INVENTORY-TRAN
        UNTIL ALL-RECORDS-PROCESSED.
    CLOSE VALTRAN
          INVMAST
          ERRTRAN.
    DISPLAY 'INV1200  I  1   NORMAL EOJ'.
    STOP RUN.
*
 300-PROCESS-INVENTORY-TRAN.
*
    PERFORM 310-READ-INVENTORY-TRAN.
    PERFORM 320-GET-INVENTORY-MASTER
        UNTIL IM-ITEM-NO NOT < IT-ITEM-NO.
    IF         IM-ITEM-NO = HIGH-VALUE
           AND IT-ITEM-NO = HIGH-VALUE
        MOVE 'Y' TO ALL-RECORDS-PROCESSED-SWITCH
    ELSE
        IF IM-ITEM-NO = IT-ITEM-NO
            PERFORM 350-UPDATE-INVENTORY-MASTER
        ELSE
            PERFORM 360-WRITE-ERROR-TRAN.
*
 310-READ-INVENTORY-TRAN.
*
    READ VALTRAN INTO INVENTORY-TRANSACTION
        AT END
            MOVE HIGH-VALUE TO IT-ITEM-NO.
*
 320-GET-INVENTORY-MASTER.
*
```

Figure 2-14   The sequential update-in-place program (part 2 of 3)

```
     IF MASTER-UPDATED
         PERFORM 340-REWRITE-INVENTORY-MASTER
         PERFORM 330-READ-INVENTORY-MASTER
     ELSE
         PERFORM 330-READ-INVENTORY-MASTER.
*
 330-READ-INVENTORY-MASTER.
*
     READ INVMAST INTO INVENTORY-MASTER-RECORD
         AT END
             MOVE HIGH-VALUE TO IM-ITEM-NO.
*
 340-REWRITE-INVENTORY-MASTER.
*
     REWRITE MASTER-RECORD-AREA FROM INVENTORY-MASTER-RECORD.
     IF NOT INVMAST-SUCCESSFUL
         DISPLAY 'INV1200  A  2  REWRITE ERROR FOR INVMAST'
         DISPLAY 'INV1200  A  2  ITEM NUMBER = ' IM-ITEM-NO
         DISPLAY 'INV1200  A  2  FILE STATUS = '
             INVMAST-FILE-STATUS
         MOVE 'Y' TO ALL-RECORDS-PROCESSED-SWITCH.
     MOVE 'N' TO MASTER-UPDATED-SWITCH.
*
 350-UPDATE-INVENTORY-MASTER.
*
     ADD IT-RECEIPT-QUANTITY TO IM-ON-HAND.
     MOVE 'Y' TO MASTER-UPDATED-SWITCH.
*
 360-WRITE-ERROR-TRAN.
*
     WRITE ERROR-TRANSACTION FROM INVENTORY-TRANSACTION.
     IF NOT ERRTRAN-SUCCESSFUL
         DISPLAY 'INV1200  A  3  WRITE ERROR FOR ERRTRAN'
         DISPLAY 'INV1200  A  3  ITEM NUMBER = ' IT-ITEM-NO
         DISPLAY 'INV1200  A  3  FILE STATUS = '
             ERRTRAN-FILE-STATUS
         MOVE 'Y' TO ALL-RECORDS-PROCESSED-SWITCH.
```

Figure 2-14   The sequential update-in-place program (part 3 of 3)

Topic 3   COBOL for sequential files of variable-length records

As I mentioned in topic 1, variable-length records are used infrequently. In fact, in many COBOL shops, they aren't used at all. As a result, you should find out whether or not you need to study this topic before you actually start it.

When you write programs that process sequential files of variable-length records, you use the same code that I presented in topic 2. However, you code the FD statement for a variable-length file somewhat differently than you do for a fixed-length file. After I present the considerations for the FD statement, I'll show you how to handle input and output files of variable-length records.

The FD statement

Figure 2-15 presents the format of an FD statement for a file of variable-length records. As you can see, the LABEL RECORDS clause is coded just as it is for a file of fixed-length records. However, the BLOCK CONTAINS and RECORD CONTAINS clauses are coded somewhat differently.

The BLOCK CONTAINS clause gives the maximum number of characters (bytes) that a block can contain. This includes any bytes that are used to specify record lengths and block length as described in topic 1. When the BLOCK CONTAINS clause is coded in this way, an output block of records isn't written until its size is greater than the maximum block size minus the maximum record size. If, for example, a file consists of 50-, 100-, and 200-byte records and the maximum block size is 4000, a new block won't be written on the file until the block size is greater than 3800 bytes (4000 minus 200).

Although COBOL lets you specify the maximum number of records rather than the maximum number of characters, you should avoid doing this because it leads to smaller block sizes than the CHARACTERS option leads to. If, for example, you code the BLOCK CONTAINS clause like this:

```
BLOCK CONTAINS 20 RECORDS
```

the blocks will always receive 20 records, whether they are short records or long records. As a result, if the file consists of 50-, 100-, and 200-byte records and twenty 50-byte records in succession are created, the block size will be only 1000 bytes (20 times 50), which is far short of the optimum 4000 bytes. Since this decreases processing efficiency and wastes tape or disk space, you shouldn't use this form of the BLOCK CONTAINS clause.

The RECORD CONTAINS clause for a file of variable-length

```
FD   file-name

     [LABEL RECORDS ARE STANDARD]

     BLOCK CONTAINS integer-1 CHARACTERS

   ⎧ RECORD CONTAINS integer-2 TO integer-3 CHARACTERS      ⎫
   ⎪ RECORD IS VARYING IN SIZE                              ⎪
   ⎨         [[FROM integer-4] [TO integer-5] CHARACTERS]   ⎬
   ⎪         [DEPENDING ON data-name]                       ⎪
   ⎩                                                        ⎭
```

Note: All 1985 COBOL elements are shaded.

Figure 2-15   The FD statement for a file of variable-length records

records gives the minimum and maximum number of characters (bytes) per record. This doesn't include any bytes used to specify the record length as described in topic 1. As a result, this clause

```
RECORD CONTAINS 26 TO 368 CHARACTERS
```

means that the record sizes will range from 26 through 368 bytes.

If you're using 1985 COBOL, you can also specify the record size using a clause like this:

```
RECORD IS VARYING IN SIZE
     FROM 26 TO 368 CHARACTERS
     DEPENDING ON RECORD-SIZE
```

Here, the FROM and TO phrases are optional, but it's good to include them so it's easy to tell what the minimum and maximum size of a record should be. Usually, a compiler treats the FROM phrase as documentation, but it compares the maximum record size given in the TO phrase with the maximum size of the record description that follows the FD statement. If these sizes aren't the same, the compiler will print a diagnostic message.

The DEPENDING ON phrase in the FD statement for a variable-length file in 1985 COBOL is also optional. If you use it, the data name you code must be defined in the Working-Storage Section of the program. Then, before a record is written on the file, the length of the record must be stored in that field.

Handling files that contain record types of more than one length

In topic 1, I explained that some files consist of more than one type of record, each type with a different record length. For instance, a file may contain records with lengths of 50, 100, 250, and 500 bytes. Then, the record size varies from 50 to 500 bytes. To show you how to process variable-length files that contain several types of records, let me present a few examples.

File creation   To create this type of file, you can describe each record type after the FD statement as shown in figure 2-16. The effect of describing multiple record types in this way is similar to that of the REDEFINES clause. Here, only one input area is used for all three record types, but different data names are used to refer to the fields within that area. In other words, the input area is redefined by each set of record descriptions.

To write the records in a file like this, you must use a different WRITE statement for each record type. This is one of the cases in which you must use more than one WRITE statement for a single output file. Since each WRITE statement gives the record name of a different record description, the system can determine what the length of each output record is.

Figure 2-17 illustrates another way to create a file like this using the RECORD IS VARYING clause of the 1985 standards. When you use this clause, the DEPENDING ON phrase gives the name of the field that will tell the system the size of each record that is written on the file. In the Procedure Division in this example, you can see that the record size is moved to VLTRANS-RECORD-SIZE before each record is written.

File reading   To read a variable-length file, you can use one of two basic techniques. The first one is suggested by the coding in figure 2-16. Here, all of the record types are completely defined in the File Section. Then, when a record is read, the program tests the record code to determine what type of record has been read, and it adjusts its processing accordingly. In this case, of course, the records are processed in the storage area defined by the File Section.

If your program needs to process the records of a variable-length file in working storage, you can use the technique illustrated in figure 2-18. Here, the record area for the transactions is defined in the File Section, but the record description for each transaction type is defined in the Working-Storage Section. Then, when a record is read, the program tests the record code to find out what type of record has been read and moves the record type to the corresponding area in working storage. These MOVE statements work properly when a larger area is moved to a smaller one because the number of characters moved is determined by the length of the receiving field, not the length of the sending field.

```
DATA DIVISION.
      .
      .
FD  VLTRANS
    LABEL RECORDS ARE STANDARD
    BLOCK CONTAINS 4000 CHARACTERS
    RECORD CONTAINS 18 TO 128 CHARACTERS.
*
 01  HEADER-RECORD.
*
     05   HDR-RECORD-CODE        PIC X.
     05   HDR-FIELD-1            PIC X(30).
     05   HDR-FIELD-2            PIC X(30).
     05   HDR-FIELD-3            PIC X(30).
     05   HDR-FIELD-4            PIC X(30).
     05   HDR-FIELD-5            PIC S9(7).
*
 01  DETAIL-RECORD.
*
     05   DET-RECORD-CODE        PIC X.
     05   DET-FIELD-1            PIC X(6).
     05   DET-FIELD-2            PIC X(6).
     05   DET-FIELD-3            PIC S9(5).
*
 01  TRAILER-RECORD.
*
     05   TLR-RECORD-CODE        PIC X.
     05   TLR-FIELD-1            PIC X(50).
     05   TLR-FIELD-2            PIC S9(6).
     05   TLR-FIELD-3            PIC S9(7).
*

      .
      .
PROCEDURE DIVISION.
      .
      .
    WRITE HEADER-RECORD.
      .
    WRITE DETAIL-RECORD.
      .
    WRITE TRAILER-RECORD.
      .
      .
```

Figure 2-16   Generalized code for creating a variable-length file that contains records of more than one length (1974 standards)

```
          FD  VLTRANS
              LABEL RECORDS ARE STANDARD
              BLOCK CONTAINS 4000 CHARACTERS
              RECORD IS VARYING IN SIZE
                  FROM 18 TO 128 CHARACTERS
                  DEPENDING ON VLTRANS-RECORD-SIZE.
          *
           01  VLTRANS-RECORD-AREA        PIC X(128).
          *
          WORKING-STORAGE SECTION.
          *
           01  WORK-FIELDS.
          *
              05  VLTRANS-RECORD-SIZE    PIC 9(3).
          *
           01  HEADER-RECORD.
          *
              05  HDR-RECORD-CODE        PIC X.
              05  HDR-FIELD-1            PIC X(30).
              05  HDR-FIELD-2            PIC X(30).
              05  HDR-FIELD-3            PIC X(30).
              05  HDR-FIELD-4            PIC X(30).
              05  HDR-FIELD-5            PIC S9(7).
          *
           01  DETAIL-RECORD.
          *
              05  DET-RECORD-CODE        PIC X.
              05  DET-FIELD-1            PIC X(6).
              05  DET-FIELD-2            PIC X(6).
              05  DET-FIELD-3            PIC S9(5).
          *
           01  TRAILER-RECORD.
          *
              05  TLR-RECORD-CODE        PIC X.
              05  TLR-FIELD-1            PIC X(50).
              05  TLR-FIELD-2            PIC S9(6).
              05  TLR-FIELD-3            PIC S9(7).
          *
                     .
                     .
          PROCEDURE DIVISION.
                     .
                     .
              MOVE 128 TO VLTRANS-RECORD-SIZE.
              WRITE VLTRANS-RECORD-AREA FROM HEADER-RECORD.
                     .
                     .
              MOVE 18 TO VLTRANS-RECORD-SIZE.
              WRITE VLTRANS-RECORD-AREA FROM DETAIL-RECORD.
                     .
                     .
              MOVE 64 TO VLTRANS-RECORD-SIZE.
              WRITE VLTRANS-RECORD-AREA FROM TRAILER-RECORD.
                     .
                     .
```

Figure 2-17   Generalized code for creating a variable-length file that contains records of more than one length (1985 standards)

```
 FD   VLTRANS
      LABEL RECORDS ARE STANDARD
      BLOCK CONTAINS 4000 CHARACTERS
      RECORD CONTAINS 18 TO 128 CHARACTERS.
*
 01   TRANSACTION-AREA.
*
      05   TR-RECORD-CODE          PIC X.
           88   TR-HEADER-RECORD                    VALUE 'H'.
           88   TR-DETAIL-RECORD                    VALUE 'D'.
           88   TR-TRAILER-RECORD                   VALUE 'T'.
      05   FILLER                  PIC X(127).
*
         .
         .
         .
 WORKING-STORAGE SECTION.
         .
         .
 01   HEADER-RECORD.
*
         .
         .
*
 01   DETAIL-RECORD.
*
         .
         .
*
 01   TRAILER-RECORD.
*
         .
         .
 PROCEDURE DIVISION.
         .
         .
      PERFORM 300-READ-TRANSACTION-RECORD.
      IF NOT VLTRANS-EOF
          IF TR-HEADER-RECORD
             MOVE TRANSACTION-AREA TO HEADER-RECORD
          ELSE
             IF TR-DETAIL-RECORD
                MOVE TRANSACTION-AREA TO DETAIL-RECORD
             ELSE
                IF TR-TRAILER-RECORD
                   MOVE TRANSACTION-AREA TO TRAILER-RECORD.
         .
         .
```

Figure 2-18   Generalized code for reading a variable-length file that contains records of more than one length

Handling files that contain records
with a varying number of segments

As I described in topic 1, the other type of variable-length record consists of a root segment plus a varying number of other segments. To illustrate the processing for this type of file, I'm going to present one program that creates a file like this and another one that prepares a report from it.

A file creation program   Figure 2-19 presents the program overview for a program that creates a file of variable-length customer records. The customer records consist of a root segment plus from one through 20 invoice segments. This file is created by reading a file of fixed-length invoice records that are sorted into sequence by customer number.

Figure 2-20 presents the structure chart for this program. Quite simply, to create one variable-length customer record, the program must read one or more invoice records (module 310), format the root segment of the customer record (module 320), format as many invoice segments as are needed (module 330), and write the customer record on the file when there are no more invoice records for the customer (module 340).

Figure 2-21 gives the COBOL listing for this program. If you check the FD and record description for the customer record in the File Section, you can see that a record will be from 26 to 368 bytes long. The root segment, which is 8 bytes long, contains the customer number and a field indicating the number of invoice segments in the record. If, for example, bytes 7 and 8 in the root segment contain a value of 11, the customer has 11 unpaid invoice segments within the record. The invoice segment is 18 bytes long. As a result, a record consisting of one root segment plus one invoice segment will be 26 bytes long (8 plus 18); a record consisting of the root segment plus 20 invoice segments will be 368 bytes long (20 times 18 plus 8).

If you took the *Part 1* course, you should be familiar with the OCCURS DEPENDING ON clause in the customer record description. Otherwise, this code is explained in topic 1 of chapter 8 in this book. Briefly stated, though, the OCCURS portion of the clause gives the range of occurrences for a group or elementary item in a record. Then, the DEPENDING ON phrase names a field that tells the actual number of times the field or fields will occur. Quite logically, the DEPENDING ON field must always be coded in the root segment of a record, and the root segment must be coded before the variable segments.

The DEPENDING ON phrase in the OCCURS clause is required in a program that creates this type of record when you use 1974 COBOL so the system can figure out how long each record will be. However, it isn't required in a program that reads records from a file like this. Also, when you use 1985 COBOL, you can code the

Program: CUST1100 Create VL customer file	Page: 1
Designer: **Mike Murach**	Date: 09-03-86

Input/output specifications

File	Description	Use
CUSTINV	**Fixed-length customer invoice file**	Input
VLCUST	**Variable-length customer file**	Output

Process specifications

**This program creates a variable-length customer file from a file of
fixed-length invoice records. The invoice records are in sequence by
customer number.**

**There can be from one through 20 invoices for a customer. If there
are more than 20 for one customer, the program should display an error
message. Then, the program should end.**

Figure 2-19   The program specifications for a file creation program that creates a file of
variable-length customer records (part 1 of 2)

The record layout for the invoice record

```
01  INVOICE-RECORD.
*
    05  IR-CUSTOMER-NO          PIC  X(6).
    05  IR-INVOICE-DATE         PIC  X(6).
    05  IR-INVOICE-NO           PIC  X(5).
    05  IR-INVOICE-AMOUNT       PIC  S9(5)V99.
    05  FILLER                  PIC  X(56).
```

The record layout for the customer record

```
01  CUSTOMER-RECORD.
*
    05  CR-ROOT-SEGMENT.
        10  CR-CUSTOMER-NO      PIC  X(6).
        10  CR-INVOICE-COUNT    PIC  S99.
    05  CR-INVOICE-SEGMENT      OCCURS 1 TO 20 TIMES
                                DEPENDING ON CR-INVOICE-COUNT
                                INDEXED BY SEGMENT-INDEX.
        10  CR-INVOICE-DATE     PIC  X(6).
        10  CR-INVOICE-NO       PIC  X(5).
        10  CR-INVOICE-AMOUNT   PIC  S9(5)V99.
```

Figure 2-19   The program specifications for a file creation program that creates a file of variable-length customer records (part 2 of 2)

DEPENDING ON clause in the FD statement for the file so it isn't necessary in the record description. Since the use of the DEPENDING ON phrase in the OCCURS clause leads to inefficient object code, we recommend that you avoid using it whenever you can.

The Procedure Division of the program in figure 2-21 should be fairly easy to follow. Module 000 performs module 300 until all invoice records have been read. In module 300 and its subordinates, SEGMENT-INDEX is used to keep track of the number of invoice segments stored in each customer record. If you're not familiar with indexes, they are explained in topic 1 in chapter 8 of this book.

The first time module 300 is executed it reads the first invoice record, sets the control field (OLD-CUSTOMER-NO) equal to the control field in the first record (IR-CUSTOMER-NO), and sets SEGMENT-INDEX to one. Then, module 300 calls module 330 to construct the variable segment for the first record. As long as the invoice records that follow are for the same customer number, module 330 is called to add more invoice segments to the record. However, if SEGMENT-INDEX isn't less than 21, an error has occurred because the program provides for a maximum of 20 segments per record. As a result, module 300 displays an error message and moves Y to CUSTINV-EOF-SWITCH so the program will end.

When module 300 determines that the customer number in the

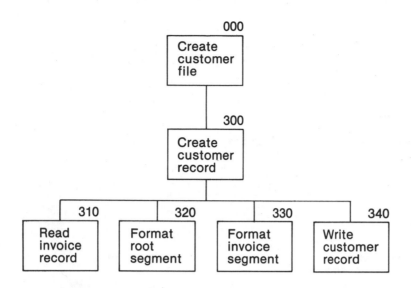

Figure 2-20   The structure chart for the file creation program (variable-length records)

next invoice record is greater than the one in the preceding record, it calls module 320 to format the root segment of the customer record. This includes storing the proper value in CR-INVOICE-COUNT, which is the DEPENDING ON field in the record description. Then, module 300 calls module 340 to write the complete record into the current block of records.

As I mentioned before, this program uses SEGMENT-INDEX to keep track of the number of invoice segments per record. It is set to one in module 300 in the processing for the first record. It is also set to one in module 320 after the root segment for the current record has been created. Then, after each variable segment has been created by module 330, SEGMENT-INDEX is increased by one. As a result, module 320 must set the index down by one before it sets CR-INVOICE-COUNT in the root segment to SEGMENT-INDEX.

If you check the code in module 340, you can see that the WRITE statement for the file is coded just as if the file contained fixed-length records. Also, the testing of the FILE STATUS field is handled in the same way whether the file contains fixed- or variable-length records.

One thing you should realize when creating variable-length files is that the number of characters given in the BLOCK CONTAINS clause of the FD statement represents only the maximum block size. The actual block sizes will vary. As the master records are written by the WRITE statement, the I/O routine checks the space remaining in the block it is currently building. In the program in figure 2-21, if a maximum size record doesn't fit in the remaining space without exceeding the 4000-byte maximum given in the BLOCK CONTAINS clause, the current block is written and another block is started.

```
 IDENTIFICATION DIVISION.
*
 PROGRAM-ID.     CUST1100.
*
 ENVIRONMENT DIVISION.
*
 INPUT-OUTPUT SECTION.
*
 FILE-CONTROL.
     SELECT CUSTINV   ASSIGN TO SYS021-AS-CUSTINV.
     SELECT VLCUST     ASSIGN TO SYS022-AS-VLCUST
                       FILE STATUS IS VLCUST-FILE-STATUS.
*
 DATA DIVISION.
*
 FILE SECTION.
*
 FD  CUSTINV
     LABEL RECORDS ARE STANDARD
     RECORD CONTAINS 80 CHARACTERS.
*
 01  CUSTOMER-INVOICE-AREA        PIC X(80).
*
 FD  VLCUST
     LABEL RECORDS ARE STANDARD
     BLOCK CONTAINS 4000 CHARACTERS
     RECORD CONTAINS 26 TO 368 CHARACTERS.
*
 01  CUSTOMER-RECORD.
*
     05   CR-ROOT-SEGMENT.
         10  CR-CUSTOMER-NO       PIC X(6).
         10  CR-INVOICE-COUNT     PIC S99.
     05   CR-INVOICE-SEGMENT      OCCURS 1 TO 20 TIMES
                                  DEPENDING ON CR-INVOICE-COUNT
                                  INDEXED BY SEGMENT-INDEX.
         10  CR-INVOICE-DATE      PIC X(6).
         10  CR-INVOICE-NO        PIC X(5).
         10  CR-INVOICE-AMOUNT    PIC S9(5)V99.
*
 WORKING-STORAGE SECTION.
*
 01  SWITCHES.
*
     05   CUSTINV-EOF-SWITCH      PIC X      VALUE 'N'.
         88   CUSTINV-EOF                    VALUE 'Y'.
     05   FIRST-RECORD-SWITCH     PIC X      VALUE 'Y'.
         88   FIRST-RECORD                   VALUE 'Y'.
*
 01  FILE-STATUS-FIELDS.
*
     05   VLCUST-FILE-STATUS      PIC XX.
         88   VLCUST-SUCCESSFUL              VALUE '00'.
*
 01  CONTROL-FIELDS.
```

Figure 2-21   The variable-length file creation program (part 1 of 3)

```
*
     05   OLD-CUSTOMER-NO           PIC X(6).
*
 01   INVOICE-RECORD.
*
     05   IR-CUSTOMER-NO            PIC X(6).
     05   IR-INVOICE-DATE           PIC X(6).
     05   IR-INVOICE-NO             PIC X(5).
     05   IR-INVOICE-AMOUNT         PIC S9(5)V99.
     05   FILLER                    PIC X(56).
*
 PROCEDURE DIVISION.
*
 000-CREATE-CUSTOMER-FILE.
*
     OPEN INPUT   CUSTINV
          OUTPUT  VLCUST.
     PERFORM 300-CREATE-CUSTOMER-RECORD
         UNTIL CUSTINV-EOF.
     CLOSE CUSTINV
           VLCUST.
     DISPLAY 'CUST1100  I   1   NORMAL EOJ'.
     STOP RUN.
*
 300-CREATE-CUSTOMER-RECORD.
*
     PERFORM 310-READ-INVOICE-RECORD.
     IF FIRST-RECORD
         MOVE IR-CUSTOMER-NO TO OLD-CUSTOMER-NO
         SET SEGMENT-INDEX TO 1
         MOVE 'N' TO FIRST-RECORD-SWITCH
     ELSE
         IF IR-CUSTOMER-NO > OLD-CUSTOMER-NO
             PERFORM 320-FORMAT-ROOT-SEGMENT
             PERFORM 340-WRITE-CUSTOMER-RECORD
             MOVE IR-CUSTOMER-NO TO OLD-CUSTOMER-NO.
     IF NOT CUSTINV-EOF
         IF SEGMENT-INDEX < 21
             PERFORM 330-FORMAT-INVOICE-SEGMENT
         ELSE
             DISPLAY 'CUST1100  A   2   OVER 20 OPEN ITEMS'
             DISPLAY 'CUST1100  A   2   INVOICE NO. = '
                 IR-INVOICE-NO
             DISPLAY 'CUST1100  A   2   CUSTOMER NO. = '
                 IR-CUSTOMER-NO
             MOVE 'Y' TO CUSTINV-EOF-SWITCH.
*
 310-READ-INVOICE-RECORD.
*
     READ CUSTINV INTO INVOICE-RECORD
         AT END
             MOVE HIGH-VALUE TO IR-CUSTOMER-NO
             MOVE 'Y' TO CUSTINV-EOF-SWITCH.
*
 320-FORMAT-ROOT-SEGMENT.
*
```

Figure 2-21   The variable-length file creation program (part 2 of 3)

```
        MOVE OLD-CUSTOMER-NO TO CR-CUSTOMER-NO.
        SET SEGMENT-INDEX DOWN BY 1.
        SET CR-INVOICE-COUNT TO SEGMENT-INDEX.
        SET SEGMENT-INDEX TO 1.
*
   330-FORMAT-INVOICE-SEGMENT.
*
        MOVE IR-INVOICE-DATE    TO CR-INVOICE-DATE (SEGMENT-INDEX).
        MOVE IR-INVOICE-NO      TO CR-INVOICE-NO (SEGMENT-INDEX).
        MOVE IR-INVOICE-AMOUNT TO CR-INVOICE-AMOUNT (SEGMENT-INDEX).
        SET SEGMENT-INDEX UP BY 1.
*
   340-WRITE-CUSTOMER-RECORD.
*
        WRITE CUSTOMER-RECORD.
        IF NOT VLCUST-SUCCESSFUL
            DISPLAY 'CUST1100  A  3   WRITE ERROR FOR VLCUST'
            DISPLAY 'CUST1100  A  3   CUSTOMER NO. = '
                CR-CUSTOMER-NO
            DISPLAY 'CUST1100  A  3   FILE STATUS = '
                VLCUST-FILE-STATUS
            MOVE 'Y' TO CUSTINV-EOF-SWITCH.
```

Figure 2-21   The variable-length file creation program (part 3 of 3)

A report preparation program   Figure 2-22 presents the program overview for a program that prepares a report by reading the file created by the program in figure 2-21. The report is just a listing with no headings or total lines, but it illustrates the requirements for reading a file of variable-length records.

Figure 2-23 presents the structure chart for this program. The basic logic is to read a record (module 310), add the invoice amounts in the invoice segments to derive the total amount owed (module 320), and write a line on the report (module 330).

The program is given in figure 2-24. To start, note that the DEPENDING ON clause isn't coded in the customer record description in the File Section. It isn't required because the block and record lengths are recorded in each block read by the system. By omitting the DEPENDING ON clause, the program will execute more efficiently. Nevertheless, the program uses the field named CR-INVOICE-COUNT to determine how many invoice segments it should process in each record.

If you don't use the DEPENDING ON clause, you shouldn't use the FROM phrase in the OCCURS clause either because it will lead to a diagnostic. That's why the OCCURS clause for the invoice segment specifies 20 occurrences, not from 1 to 20 occurrences.

In the Procedure Division, the invoice segments in each record are processed by module 300 using a PERFORM VARYING statement. If you're not familiar with this code, you can study it in topic 1 of chapter 8 in this book. Otherwise, you shouldn't have any trouble understanding this program.

Program: CUST3100 Prepare customer listing	Page: 1
Designer: **Mike Murach**	Date: **09-03-86**

Input/output specifications

File	Description	Use
VLCUST	**Variable-length customer file**	**Input**
CUSTLST	**Print file: Customer listing**	**Output**

Process specifications

This program summarizes the data in a variable-length customer file.
It prints one line on the customer listing for each record in the
customer file. This line consists of only customer number and the
total amount owed by the customer. To simplify the program for
illustrative purposes, no headings or total lines are required on the
listing.

The total amount owed is derived by adding the invoice amounts in all
of the invoice segments for the customer. There can be from one
through 20 invoices for a customer.

Figure 2-22   The program overview for a report preparation program that prints one line for each
variable-length customer record

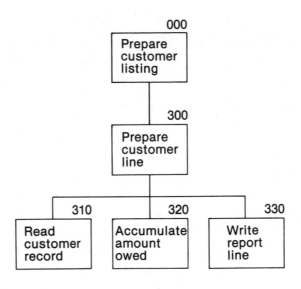

Figure 2-23   The structure chart for the report preparation program

Discussion

One reason why variable-length records aren't used much is that variable-length sorts are slower than fixed-length sorts. So if a file is going to need sorting, you must question whether the file wouldn't be more efficient with fixed-length records than with variable-length records. For instance, the records in the invoice file described in this topic could be treated as fixed-length records of 368 bytes each. Then, if a record contained the data for only one invoice, the last 19 invoice segments wouldn't be used. Although this means wasted storage space on tape or disk devices, it also means you don't need OCCURS DEPENDING ON to create the file and the file can be sorted more efficiently.

Which approach is better? It depends, of course, on other considerations. How much do the records vary in length...if most of the records are near maximum length, why not treat them as fixed-length records? How limited is storage space...is it a small system with limited disk space available to it? And how much sorting does the file require? While these considerations may rule out variable-length records in a large shop, they may reveal the need for variable-length records in a small shop.

```
 IDENTIFICATION DIVISION.
*
 PROGRAM-ID.     CUST3100.
*
 ENVIRONMENT DIVISION.
*
 INPUT-OUTPUT SECTION.
*
 FILE-CONTROL.
     SELECT VLCUST    ASSIGN TO SYS020-AS-VLCUST.
     SELECT CUSTLST   ASSIGN TO SYS006-UR-1403-S.
*
 DATA DIVISION.
*
 FILE SECTION.
*
 FD  VLCUST
     LABEL RECORDS ARE STANDARD
     BLOCK CONTAINS 4000 CHARACTERS
     RECORD CONTAINS 26 TO 368 CHARACTERS.
*
 01  CUSTOMER-RECORD.
*
     05  CR-ROOT-SEGMENT.
         10  CR-CUSTOMER-NO        PIC X(6).
         10  CR-INVOICE-COUNT      PIC S99.
     05  CR-INVOICE-SEGMENT        OCCURS 20 TIMES
                                   INDEXED BY SEGMENT-INDEX.
         10  CR-INVOICE-DATE       PIC X(6).
         10  CR-INVOICE-NO         PIC X(5).
         10  CR-INVOICE-AMOUNT     PIC S9(5)V99.
*
 FD  CUSTLST
     LABEL RECORDS ARE OMITTED
     RECORD CONTAINS 132 CHARACTERS.
*
 01  PRINT-AREA                    PIC X(132).
*
 WORKING-STORAGE SECTION.
*
 01  SWITCHES.
*
     05  VLCUST-EOF-SWITCH  PIC X      VALUE 'N'.
         88  VLCUST-EOF                VALUE 'Y'.
*
 01  TOTAL-FIELDS           COMP-3.
*
     05  AMOUNT-OWED         PIC S9(5)V99.
*
 01  CUSTOMER-LINE.
*
     05  CL-CUSTOMER-NO      PIC X(6).
     05  FILLER             PIC X(3)        VALUE SPACE.
     05  CL-AMOUNT-OWED      PIC ZZ,ZZZ.99.
     05  FILLER             PIC X(114).
```

Figure 2-24   The report preparation program with a variable-length input file (part 1 of 2)

```
*
 PROCEDURE DIVISION.
*
 000-PREPARE-CUSTOMER-LISTING.
*
     OPEN INPUT  VLCUST
          OUTPUT CUSTLST.
     PERFORM 300-PREPARE-CUSTOMER-LINE
         UNTIL VLCUST-EOF.
     CLOSE VLCUST
           CUSTLST.
     STOP RUN.
*
 300-PREPARE-CUSTOMER-LINE.
*
     PERFORM 310-READ-CUSTOMER-RECORD.
     IF NOT VLCUST-EOF
        MOVE ZERO TO AMOUNT-OWED
        PERFORM 320-ACCUMULATE-AMOUNT-OWED
           VARYING SEGMENT-INDEX FROM 1 BY 1
           UNTIL SEGMENT-INDEX > CR-INVOICE-COUNT
        MOVE CR-CUSTOMER-NO TO CL-CUSTOMER-NO
        MOVE AMOUNT-OWED     TO CL-AMOUNT-OWED
        MOVE CUSTOMER-LINE  TO PRINT-AREA
        PERFORM 330-WRITE-REPORT-LINE.
*
 310-READ-CUSTOMER-RECORD.
*
     READ VLCUST
        AT END
           MOVE 'Y' TO VLCUST-EOF-SWITCH.
*
 320-ACCUMULATE-AMOUNT-OWED.
*
     ADD CR-INVOICE-AMOUNT (SEGMENT-INDEX) TO AMOUNT-OWED.
*
 330-WRITE-REPORT-LINE.
*
     WRITE PRINT-AREA
        AFTER ADVANCING 1 LINE.
```

Figure 2-24   The report preparation program with a variable-length input file (part 2 of 2)

Terminology

None

Objective

Given program specifications that require the use of one or more sequential files of variable-length records, develop a COBOL program that satisfies the specifications.

Topic 4 Compiler dependent code

With only a couple of changes, the programs presented in topics 2 and 3 of this chapter will run on any system that uses 1974 or 1985 ANS COBOL. In general, you have to change the system names so they are acceptable on your compiler. You have to change the single quotation marks to double marks if they are required by your compiler. And you have to change COMP-3 usage to COMP usage if COMP is appropriate for your compiler.

On the other hand, I/O operations vary considerably from one system to another. Besides the differences in system names, you should be aware of differences related to the use of FD statements, variable-length records, FILE STATUS fields, and files opened in extend mode.

System names in SELECT statements

You should already know how to code system names for sequential files on your system. To review, though, figure 2-25 presents system names for disk files on some common systems when you're using the Microsoft, Wang VS, IBM VS, or IBM COBOL II compilers. In general, the names are relatively simple when you're using compilers on microcomputers and minicomputers, and they're more complicated when you're using a mainframe compiler.

On an IBM mainframe, there can be two kinds of sequential files: VSAM and non-VSAM. As you can see in figure 2-25, the format of a system name for a VSAM file is different than one for a non-VSAM file. In this book, all the programs are written for VSAM files.

FD statements

When you're using files of fixed-length records, some systems require the BLOCK CONTAINS clause to give the blocking factor for the file on disk. Then, if the clause is omitted, a blocking factor of one is assumed. On other systems, though, the BLOCK CONTAINS clause is treated as documentation because the system determines the most efficient blocking factor for each type of file.

On an IBM mainframe, the interpretation of the coding depends on whether the file is a VSAM or non-VSAM file. If it's a VSAM file, the BLOCK CONTAINS clause can be omitted because blocking has no meaning for VSAM file organizations. In contrast, for non-VSAM sequential files, the VS compiler assumes unblocked records when the clause is omitted. As a result, since disk records in a sequential file are normally blocked, you should usually code a BLOCK CONTAINS clause for a non-VSAM sequential file on an IBM mainframe. In this

Microsoft COBOL

    Format: `"DISK"`

    Example: `"DISK"`

Wang VS COBOL

    Format: `"parameter-reference-name" "DISK"`

    Example: `"INVMAST" "DISK"`

Note: The *parameter-reference-name* must be eight or fewer letters or digits, starting with a letter. For consistency, this can be the same name as the file name.

IBM VS COBOL on a DOS/VSE system

    Format: `SYSnnn-UT-device-S-name`
                 (for a non-VSAM file)

                 `SYSnnn-AS-name`
                 (for a VSAM file)

    Examples: `SYS020-UT-3350-S-INVMAST`
                 (for a non-VSAM file)

                 `SYS020-AS-INVMAST`
                 (for a VSAM file)

Notes: 1. The SYS number is a number between SYS000 and SYS240 that is used to identify a specific I/O device. Find out what numbers you should use on your system.

        2. The *device* is a number like 3350 for the 3350 disk drive. Find out what device numbers you should use on your system.

        3. The *name* consists of from three to seven letters or digits, starting with a letter. For consistency, this can be the same name as the file name. This name is used to relate the file description in the program with a file on a disk.

        4. UT stands for utility device, S stands for sequential organization, and AS stands for sequential organization in a VSAM file.

Figure 2-25   The formats of system names for sequential disk files on some common COBOL compilers (part 1 of 2)

IBM VS COBOL or COBOL II on an OS/MVS system

Format: [comments-][S-]ddname
               (for a non-VSAM file)

               [comments-]AS-ddname
               (for a VSAM file)

Examples: INVMAST
               (for a non-VSAM file)

               AS-INVMAST
               (for a VSAM file)

Note: The *ddname* is made up of eight or fewer letters or digits, starting
          with a letter. For consistency, this name can be the same as the file
          name. This name is used to relate the file description in the program
          with a file on an I/O device outside of the program.

Figure 2-25   The formats of system names for sequential disk files on some common COBOL
                    compilers (part 2 of 2)

book, though, all of the example programs process VSAM files, so you
won't see the BLOCK CONTAINS clause used in them from now on.

     When you process a non-VSAM sequential disk file on an IBM
mainframe using the OS/MVS operating system, the BLOCK
CONTAINS clause should specify zero records. This means that the
blocking factor will be given outside of the COBOL program (in the
job control statements for running the program). This is useful
because it means that the blocking factor can be changed without
changing the COBOL program.

     In any event, you should already know how to code FD
statements for sequential files on your system. If you don't, you should
find out right away.

Variable-length records

Not all compilers support the use of variable-length records, so you
can start by finding out if your compiler does provide for them.
Similarly, not all compilers support the OCCURS DEPENDING ON
clause, so you may be limited as to what type of variable-length
records your system can create.

     For instance, neither the Microsoft COBOL compiler nor the
Wang VS compiler supports variable-length files that contain
OCCURS DEPENDING ON clauses. However, they do provide for
files that contain more than one type of record as illustrated in figures
2-16 through 2-18. In contrast, the IBM mainframe compilers provide
for both types of variable-length records within both VSAM and non-
VSAM files.

FILE STATUS fields

Before the 1974 standards were published, an error condition was handled by the operating system when an I/O operation was unsuccessful. Then, the 1974 standards introduced FILE STATUS fields that could be used within an application program to determine what I/O errors had occurred. This raised a question: Which program should handle an I/O error condition—the application program or one of the programs of the operating system?

Today, the handling of I/O error conditions varies from one system to another. On some systems, the operating system still handles the I/O error conditions, so you don't have to use FILE STATUS fields within your programs. On our Wang VS system, for example, the operating system takes care of the error conditions, so we don't use FILE STATUS fields in any of our programs.

On other systems, though, the operating system assumes that the application program will handle the I/O error conditions. On an IBM mainframe operating under DOS/VSE, for example, the operating system will ignore unsuccessful I/O operations. As a result, an application program must check the FILE STATUS fields to detect any unsuccessful I/O operations, and it must handle these error conditions accordingly. If it doesn't handle them, the program may continue running to its normal termination, even though an output file hasn't been created properly.

Because of these variations, you must find out when and how to use FILE STATUS fields in your shop. Should you use them at all? Should you use them only after WRITE and REWRITE statements? Should you use them after all I/O statements including OPEN, CLOSE, and READ statements? When you use them, what actions should you take for each type of condition? And so on. If your shop uses FILE STATUS fields, it should have standards for using them in a consistent manner.

As you will see in the next two chapters, you can use FILE STATUS fields for indexed and relative files in much the same way that you use them for sequential files. The only thing that differs is what some of the error codes mean. For all three types of files, though, 00 indicates a successful I/O operation. Because of these similarities, we won't illustrate the use of FILE STATUS fields in the programs in the next two chapters, except when they are required no matter what system you're using. Keep in mind, though, that your shop standards may require you to use FILE STATUS fields in all of your file handling programs.

Files opened in extend mode

According to the ANS standards, a file opened in extend mode can't be created by the program; the file must already exist so records can be added to it. The exception to this is an optional file that is opened in extend mode, but optional files aren't covered in this book because they're not very useful.

When using some compilers, though, any file opened in extend mode can be either created or extended. In this case, the file has to be defined so the operating system can find it, but the file doesn't have to contain any records. When the file is empty, it can be referred to as a *null file*. Then, if the file that is opened in extend mode is a null file, the program creates the file. But if the file contains one or more records, the program extends the file. When using the IBM VS COBOL compiler under DOS/VSE, for example, a VSAM sequential file can be either created or extended when the file is opened in extend mode. Although you won't need this create-or-extend capability often, it sometimes comes in handy. As a result, you may want to find out whether your compiler provides for it.

Discussion

The use of sequential files is more standardized than the use of indexed or relative files. That's why sequential files on tape are often used to transfer data from one type of computer system to another. On the other hand, all I/O operations are to some extent dependent on the system and the compiler you're using. As a result, you must learn how to use the compiler dependent code for your system.

Terminology

null file

Objective

Find out how to use the compiler dependent code for sequential files on your system.

Chapter 3

Indexed file handling

In this chapter, you will learn how to process indexed files. Topic 1 presents the concepts you need to know for processing indexed files. Topic 2 shows you the COBOL you need for programs that process indexed files with one index. Topic 3 shows you the COBOL you need for programs that process indexed files with alternate indexes. And topic 4 presents some compiler dependent code related to the handling of indexed files.

Topic 1   Indexed file handling concepts

Sequential file organization has its advantages, but it also has its limitations. For instance, a blocked sequential file makes maximum use of the storage capacity of a disk device, but it has many of the limitations of a tape file. To update a sequential file, all of the records in the file must be read rather than just those affected by transactions, and the entire file has to be rewritten in order to add a record to the file. In contrast, the records in an indexed file can be read sequentially or randomly, and records can be added to the file without having to rewrite the entire file.

When the records in a file are stored with *indexed file organization*, the file is referred to as an *indexed file*. For this type of file, *indexes* are kept that allow the records in the file to be accessed on both a sequential and a random basis. Indexed files can have one or more indexes, and you need to understand how these indexes are used before you can write COBOL programs for indexed files.

Indexed files with one index

Figure 3-1 illustrates an indexed file with one index. The entries in the index are based on the value of a *key field* within each data record. In this example, the key field is employee number. This key field is the *primary key* of the file, and the index associated with this key is the *primary index* of the file.

In a primary index, there is one and only one key for each record in the file. That means there are no *duplicate keys* in the file. To say this another way, the keys in a primary index are *unique*.

When a file is organized in this way, a program can locate any record in the file on a random basis if it knows the key for that record. First, the program finds the key in the primary index. Then, it accesses the desired record by using the disk location provided in the index.

Notice in figure 3-1 that the employee numbers in the data records don't have to be in any particular sequence. However, the entries in the index are always maintained in key sequence. That's what makes it possible to access the records in the file sequentially. To do so, the entries in the index are read sequentially and the disk locations are used to retrieve the records in sequential order by key.

Indexed files with more than one index

All indexed files have one primary index. However, an indexed file can also have one or more *alternate indexes*. Alternate indexes make it possible to access records in an indexed file by a key field other than the primary key field. The keys used in an alternate index are called *alternate keys*. Unlike primary keys, alternate keys don't have to be unique. In other words, more than one record in a file can have the same alternate key.

An indexed file can have more than one alternate index. For instance, an employee file could have alternate indexes based on social security number and last name. When a file has more than one index, each alternate index is independent. In other words, alternate indexes never point to one another. As you will see, alternate indexes point to entries in the primary index.

Unique alternate keys   Figure 3-2 shows the same employee file as in figure 3-1, but this time the file has an alternate index with unique keys. The alternate key is social security number. Since social security numbers are unique, there will be only one record in the file for each record in the index.

To access records in the file randomly using an alternate index, a program first looks up the alternate key (social security number in figure 3-2) in the alternate index. This index entry gives the value of the primary key (employee number). The program then looks up this key in the primary index to find the location of the data record. Once the location is known, the record can be retrieved.

To access records from a file sequentially by alternate key, the entries in the alternate index are read in sequence. These entries are always maintained in alternate key sequence just as the entries in the primary index are maintained in primary key sequence. Each entry retrieved from the alternate index points to an entry in the primary index which gives the disk location of the next data record to be retrieved.

Non-unique alternate keys   Figure 3-3 illustrates the same employee file as in figures 3-1 and 3-2, but this time the file has an alternate index that contains last names. Since it's possible for more than one employee to have the same last name, the index may have duplicate keys. In other words, the index has *non-unique keys*.

When a program accesses records randomly by an alternate index with non-unique keys, only the first record with the specified key is retrieved. As a result, to access all of the records with that key, the subsequent records must be retrieved sequentially. In other words, the file must be accessed on both a random and sequential basis within a single program. Otherwise, processing files based on non-unique keys is quite similar to processing files based on unique keys.

Discussion

This topic has presented a conceptual view of how indexed files are organized. But how these concepts are actually implemented will vary

Primary index   **Data records**

Employee number	Disk location		Disk location	Social security number	First name	Middle initial	Last name	Employee number
00001	5		1	213-64-9290	Thomas	T	Bluestone	00008
00002	2		2	279-00-1210	William	J	Collins	00002
00003	10		3	334-96-8721	Constance	M	Harris	00007
00004	9		4	498-27-6117	Ronald	W	Westbrook	00010
00005	6		5	499-35-5079	Stanley	L	Abbott	00001
00006	7		6	558-12-6168	Marie	A	Littlejohn	00005
00007	3		7	559-35-2479	E	R	Siebart	00006
00008	1		8	572-68-3100	Jean	B	Glenning	00009
00009	8		9	703-47-5748	Paul	M	Collins	00004
00010	4		10	899-16-9235	Alice		Crawford	00003

Figure 3-1   An indexed employee file with one index

from one system to another. In fact, the process of accessing records in an indexed file is usually much more complicated than this topic has indicated. From the point of view of the COBOL programmer, though, you only need to understand that indexed files can be accessed either sequentially or randomly, by primary keys or alternate keys. You don't need to know exactly how your system implements this access method.

Terminology

indexed file organization	duplicate keys
indexed file	unique keys
index	alternate index
key field	alternate key
primary key	non-unique keys
primary index	

Objectives

1. Explain how the primary index is used to access records in an indexed file, both sequentially and randomly.

2. Explain how an alternate index with unique keys is used to access records in an indexed file, both sequentially and randomly.

3. Explain how an alternate index with non-unique keys is used to access records in an indexed file, both sequentially and randomly.

Alternate index

Social security number	Employee number
213-64-9290	00008
279-00-1210	00002
334-96-8721	00007
498-27-6117	00010
499-35-5079	00001
558-12-6168	00005
559-35-2479	00006
572-68-3100	00009
703-47-5748	00004
899-16-9235	00003

Primary index

Employee number	Disk location
00001	5
00002	2
00003	10
00004	9
00005	6
00006	7
00007	3
00008	1
00009	8
00010	4

Data records

Disk location	Social security number	First name	Middle initial	Last name	Employee number
1	213-64-9290	Thomas	T	Bluestone	00008
2	279-00-1210	William	J	Collins	00002
3	334-96-8721	Constance	M	Harris	00007
4	498-27-6117	Ronald	W	Westbrook	00010
5	499-35-5079	Stanley	L	Abbott	00001
6	558-12-6168	Marie	A	Littlejohn	00005
7	559-35-2479	E	R	Siebart	00006
8	572-68-3100	Jean	B	Glenning	00009
9	703-47-5748	Paul	M	Collins	00004
10	899-16-9235	Alice		Crawford	00003

Figure 3-2　An indexed employee file with unique alternate keys

Alternate index

Last name	Employee number
Abbott	00001
Bluestone	00008
Collins	00002
Collins	00004
Crawford	00003
Glenning	00009
Harris	00007
Littlejohn	00005
Siebart	00006
Westbrook	00010

Primary index

Employee number	Disk location
00001	5
00002	2
00003	10
00004	9
00005	6
00006	7
00007	3
00008	1
00009	8
00010	4

Data records

Disk location	Social security number	First name	Middle initial	Last name	Employee number
1	213-64-9290	Thomas	T	Bluestone	00008
2	279-00-1210	William	J	Collins	00002
3	334-96-8721	Constance	M	Harris	00007
4	498-27-6117	Ronald	W	Westbrook	00010
5	499-35-5079	Stanley	L	Abbott	00001
6	558-12-6168	Marie	A	Littlejohn	00005
7	559-35-2479	E	R	Siebart	00006
8	572-68-3100	Jean	B	Glenning	00009
9	703-47-5748	Paul	M	Collins	00004
10	899-16-9235	Allice		Crawford	00003

Figure 3-3　An indexed employee file with non-unique alternate keys

Topic 2   COBOL for indexed files with one index

In this topic, I'll present the COBOL you need to know to process indexed files that have one index. First, I'll show you the code for sequential processing. Then, I'll show you the code for random processing. Last, I'll show you a program that uses both sequential and random processing.

SEQUENTIAL PROCESSING

Figure 3-4 summarizes the COBOL code you use when you write programs that process indexed files sequentially. Most of the code should look familiar to you because it is similar to the code for handling sequential files. However, the SELECT statement must be coded somewhat differently for an indexed file than it is for a sequential file. The FILE STATUS codes are somewhat different for an indexed file. And two new statements are available for indexed files: the START and DELETE statements. In the explanations that follow, I'll emphasize the differences in the code for indexed and sequential files.

The SELECT statement

When you code the SELECT statement for an indexed file, you have to indicate that the file is indexed. You do this by coding the ORGANIZATION clause like this:

```
ORGANIZATION IS INDEXED
```

If you don't code this clause, the compiler will assume the file is sequential.

When you process an indexed file sequentially, you should code the ACCESS MODE clause like this:

```
ACCESS MODE IS SEQUENTIAL
```

Although sequential processing is assumed when this clause is omitted, it's a good idea to include it because it helps document the program.

If you refer to the summary in figure 3-4, you can see that the ACCESS MODE clause can be coded SEQUENTIAL or DYNAMIC. When you specify *dynamic access*, it means that the file can be accessed either sequentially or randomly. Unless you need to access a file both ways, though, it's usually best to code the specific access you'll be using. Later on in this topic, I'll introduce you to a program that uses dynamic access. Otherwise, I'll only mention dynamic access when it affects the way a statement is coded.

SELECT statement

```
SELECT file-name

    ASSIGN TO system-name

    ORGANIZATION IS INDEXED

    [ACCESS MODE IS {SEQUENTIAL}]
                    {DYNAMIC   }

    RECORD KEY IS data-name-1

    [FILE STATUS IS data-name-2]
```

FD statement

```
FD  file-name

    [LABEL RECORDS ARE STANDARD]

    [RECORD CONTAINS integer-1 CHARACTERS]

    [BLOCK CONTAINS integer-2 RECORDS]
```

Figure 3-4   COBOL formats for sequential processing of indexed files (part 1 of 2)

The RECORD KEY clause in the SELECT statement for an indexed file specifies the key that's used to index the file. This field must be defined within the record description for the file in the File Section of the program.

The last clause in the SELECT statement is the FILE STATUS clause. As you learned in chapter 2, the FILE STATUS clause specifies a field that is updated by the system as each I/O statement for a file is executed. This field is a two-digit field that is defined in the Working-Storage Section of the program. If necessary, you can use the FILE STATUS field to identify the specific status that results from an I/O operation for a file.

Procedure Division statements

```
       ⎧ INPUT    file-name-1 ... ⎫
       ⎪ OUTPUT   file-name-2 ... ⎪
OPEN  ⎨ I-O      file-name-3 ... ⎬
       ⎩ EXTEND   file-name-4 ... ⎭
```

```
                              ⎧ EQUAL TO                   ⎫
                              ⎪ =                          ⎪
                              ⎪ GREATER THAN               ⎪
START file-name [KEY IS  ⎨ >                          ⎬  data-name]
                              ⎪ NOT LESS THAN              ⎪
                              ⎪ NOT <                      ⎪
                              ⎪ GREATER THAN OR EQUAL TO  ⎪
                              ⎩ >=                         ⎭
```

   [INVALID KEY imperative-statement]

READ file-name [NEXT] RECORD

   [INTO identifier]

   [AT END imperative-statement]

WRITE record-name

   [FROM identifier]

   [INVALID KEY imperative-statement]

REWRITE record-name

   [FROM identifier]

   [INVALID KEY imperative-statement]

DELETE file-name RECORD

   [INVALID KEY imperative-statement]

CLOSE file-name-1 ...

Note: All 1985 COBOL elements are shaded.

Figure 3-4   COBOL formats for sequential processing of indexed files (part 2 of 2)

FILE STATUS codes

Figure 3-5 summarizes the FILE STATUS codes for indexed files, both for sequential and random processing. The first code, 00, indicates that the last I/O operation was successful. The second code, 02, has to do with alternate keys so I will discuss it in the next topic. The third code, 10, indicates that the AT END condition occurred during a sequential reading operation. The next four codes (21, 22, 23, and 24) all indicate invalid key conditions. The rest of the codes indicate more serious error conditions that usually lead to program termination.

If the INVALID KEY clause of an I/O statement is coded, it is executed when any of the four invalid key conditions in figure 3-5 occurs. These conditions are somewhat self-explanatory, but let me describe them briefly.

Code 21 indicates that an out-of-sequence record is being read or written on a sequential basis. This status can't result from a random I/O operation. It normally occurs when an indexed file is being created on a sequential basis.

Code 22 indicates that a duplicate key was found in an index that doesn't allow duplicates. This normally occurs when a file is being created or when records are being added to a file. Often, codes 21 and 22 indicate serious errors that force early termination of a program. But sometimes they indicate a problem with only a few records, so the program can continue.

Code 23 indicates that the desired record wasn't found during a random I/O operation. This status can't result from a sequential I/O operation. It occurs any time a program tries to access a record with a key that isn't in a file. As a result, it indicates a problem with only one record, and it occurs fairly often in programs that randomly process the records in a file.

Code 24 indicates that the program tried to perform an operation on an area of the disk that is beyond the space assigned to the file. This can happen when a sequential file creation program tries to write a record on the file. It can also happen when a random file maintenance program tries to add a record to a file. Normally, this type of error shouldn't occur during the execution of an indexed file handling program, but when it does, the program usually has to terminate itself.

Procedure Division statements

The OPEN statement   Note in figure 3-4 that the EXTEND option is shaded indicating that it is a part of the 1985 COBOL standards. In the 1974 standards, an indexed file couldn't be opened in extend mode. However, the EXTEND option can only be used if the file is opened for sequential access; it can't be specified for a file that is

FILE STATUS codes	Meaning
00	Successful completion of I/O operation
02	Successful completion of I/O operation but duplicate key detected
10	End-of-file condition during read operation (AT END condition)
21	Invalid key condition: Sequence error
22	Invalid key condition: Duplicate key
23	Invalid key condition: Record not found
24	Invalid key condition: Boundary violation
30-39	Permanent error condition with unsuccessful completion of I/O operation
40-49	Logical error condition with unsuccessful completion of I/O operation
90-99	Defined by implementor

Figure 3-5   FILE STATUS codes for I/O operations on indexed files

opened for dynamic access, even if the file is only accessed sequentially.

The INVALID KEY clause   Two of the statements you were introduced to in the last chapter (WRITE and REWRITE) and both of the new statements I'll present here (START and DELETE) use the INVALID KEY clause when processing indexed files. The INVALID KEY clause is executed whenever an invalid key condition occurs. As I explained earlier, there are four conditions that can cause the execution of the INVALID KEY clause. They are represented by codes 21 through 24 in the summary in figure 3-5.

The INVALID KEY clause is optional because you can control the four invalid key conditions by analyzing the FILE STATUS field after each I/O operation. However, you'll often find that it's more efficient to use the INVALID KEY clause. In general, we recommend that you code the INVALID KEY clause, at least as the first step in your error processing routines.

The START statement   The START statement can be used for a file that is opened as INPUT or I-O. It specifies the key at which sequential processing should begin. When you use this statement, the starting key must be placed in the RECORD KEY field before the START statement is executed. Then, the KEY clause of the START statement can be used to establish the first record to be processed in the file.

To start processing at the first record equal to or greater than the value in the RECORD KEY field, you can use the START statement like this:

```
MOVE '1000' TO INV-ITEM-NUMBER.
START INVMAST
    KEY IS NOT < INV-ITEM-NUMBER.
```

Then, the file is positioned to read the first record whose key value is greater than or equal to 1000. Note that the record isn't actually read; the file is simply positioned so the next READ statement will retrieve that record.

If you refer back to figure 3-4, you can see that the 1985 standards provide for a relational operator stated as GREATER THAN OR EQUAL TO. Although this means the same as NOT LESS THAN, I think it makes the relationship a little more apparent. More about the 1985 relational operators in chapter 10.

As you can see in figure 3-4, the KEY clause of the START statement is optional. If it's omitted, the file will be positioned at the first record whose key value is equal to the value placed in the key field. However, if that record doesn't exist, an invalid key condition will occur due to a record not found condition (code 23). Since that usually won't be what you intended, it's a good idea to code the KEY clause so you can specify the exact relationship you want.

The READ statement   Although the READ statement has the same format for accessing indexed files sequentially as it does for accessing sequential files, there is one point I would like to make. If you specify dynamic access, you must code the word NEXT on the READ statement to access the records sequentially. If you don't, random processing is assumed. You'll see an example of the READ NEXT statement when I present dynamic processing.

The REWRITE statement   REWRITE statements can only be used on files that are opened as I-O. When a REWRITE statement is executed for an indexed file in sequential access, the record to be rewritten is specified by the value in the key field of the file. That key should be the key of the last record read from the file. In other words, a READ statement must be executed before a REWRITE statement can be executed.

The DELETE statement   The DELETE statement is used to delete records from a file. It can only be used on a file that is opened as I-O. When it's used in sequential access mode, it deletes the record that was read by the last READ statement. In this case, the INVALID

KEY clause should never be executed because the record to be deleted is obviously on the file.

When the DELETE statement is used in dynamic access mode, however, it deletes the record indicated by the value in the key field for the file. In other words, it deletes a record on a random rather than a sequential basis. As a result, you should code the INVALID KEY clause in a statement like this in case the record to be deleted can't be found in the file.

Two illustrative programs

Sequential processing of indexed files is similar to the processing of sequential files, so you shouldn't have any problems with it. In fact, the sequential update program I'll present in a minute is almost identical to the update-in-place program I presented in the last chapter. Before I present that program, though, I want to show you a program that creates an indexed file. It starts on the next page.

Program:	INV1100 Create inventory file		Page: 1
Designer:	Anne Prince		Date: 09-03-86

Input/output specifications

File	Description	Use
INVMAST	Sequential inventory master file	Input
INVMSTI	Indexed inventory master file	Output

Process specifications

This program creates an indexed file of inventory master records from a sequential file of master records. The records in the sequential file are in sequence by item number, which is the key of the indexed file.

The basic processing requirements follow:

1. Read a sequential inventory record.

2. Write an indexed inventory record.

Figure 3-6   The program overview for an indexed file creation program

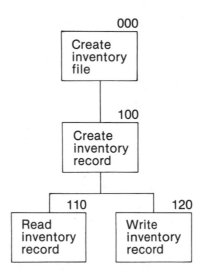

Figure 3-7   The structure chart for the file creation program

A file creation program   Figure 3-6 presents a program overview for a program that creates an indexed inventory master file from a file of sequential inventory records, and figure 3-7 presents the structure chart for this program. As you can see, the processing is quite simple. For each record in the sequential file, a record is written on the indexed file.

Notice that the program overview says that the records in the sequential file are in sequence by item number, which is the key field of the indexed file. If any records are out of sequence or if two or more records have the same key value, an invalid key condition will occur when the WRITE statement is issued for the indexed file.

Figure 3-8 presents the program listing for the file creation program. There are only four things I want to point out in this program. First, the SELECT statement for the indexed file indicates that the file has indexed organization and will be accessed sequentially. It also specifies that the key field for the file is IR-ITEM-NO. Remember that the key field must be specified even if the file is being accessed sequentially.

Second, look at the record description for the indexed file in the File Section of the program. Even though I didn't have to define each individual field in the record, I did have to define the key field. The name of the key field has to be the same as the name of the field specified in the RECORD KEY clause of the SELECT statement.

Third, notice that I coded a single record description for the master record in working storage that I used for both the sequential and indexed files. I was able to do this because the records have identical formats. Then, when a record is read from the sequential file, the INTO clause on the READ statement places the record in this working

```
 IDENTIFICATION DIVISION.
*
 PROGRAM-ID. INV1100.
*
 ENVIRONMENT DIVISION.
*
 INPUT-OUTPUT SECTION.
*
 FILE-CONTROL.
     SELECT INVMAST   ASSIGN TO SYS020-AS-INVMAST.
     SELECT INVMSTI   ASSIGN TO SYS021-INVMSTI
                      ORGANIZATION IS INDEXED
                      ACCESS IS SEQUENTIAL
                      RECORD KEY IS IR-ITEM-NO.
*
 DATA DIVISION.
*
 FILE SECTION.
*
 FD  INVMAST
     LABEL RECORDS ARE STANDARD
     RECORD CONTAINS 80 CHARACTERS.
*
 01  SEQUENTIAL-RECORD-AREA  PIC X(80).
*
 FD  INVMSTI
     LABEL RECORDS ARE STANDARD
     RECORD CONTAINS 80 CHARACTERS.
*
 01  INDEXED-RECORD-AREA.
*
     05  IR-ITEM-NO       PIC X(5).
     05  FILLER           PIC X(75).
*
 WORKING-STORAGE SECTION.
*
 01  SWITCHES.
*
     05  INVMAST-EOF-SWITCH     PIC X     VALUE 'N'.
         88  INVMAST-EOF                  VALUE 'Y'.
*
 01  INVENTORY-MASTER-RECORD.
*
     05  IM-DESCRIPTIVE-DATA.
         10  IM-ITEM-NUMBER      PIC X(5).
         10  IM-ITEM-DESC        PIC X(20).
         10  IM-UNIT-COST        PIC S999V99.
         10  IM-UNIT-PRICE       PIC S999V99.
     05  IM-INVENTORY-DATA.
         10  IM-REORDER-POINT    PIC S9(5).
         10  IM-ON-HAND          PIC S9(5).
         10  IM-ON-ORDER         PIC S9(5).
     05  FILLER                  PIC X(30).
*
```

Figure 3-8   The indexed file creation program (part 1 of 2)

```
 PROCEDURE DIVISION.
*
 000-CREATE-INVENTORY-FILE.
*
     OPEN INPUT   INVMAST
          OUTPUT INVMSTI.
     PERFORM 100-CREATE-INVENTORY-RECORD
         UNTIL INVMAST-EOF.
     CLOSE INVMAST
           INVMSTI.
     DISPLAY 'INV1100  I  1   NORMAL EOJ'.
     STOP RUN.
*
 100-CREATE-INVENTORY-RECORD.
*
     PERFORM 110-READ-INVENTORY-RECORD.
     IF NOT INVMAST-EOF
         PERFORM 120-WRITE-INVENTORY-RECORD.
*
 110-READ-INVENTORY-RECORD.
*
     READ INVMAST INTO INVENTORY-MASTER-RECORD
         AT END
             MOVE 'Y' TO INVMAST-EOF-SWITCH.
*
 120-WRITE-INVENTORY-RECORD.
*
     WRITE INDEXED-RECORD-AREA FROM INVENTORY-MASTER-RECORD
         INVALID KEY
             DISPLAY 'INV1100  A  2   WRITE ERROR FOR INVMSTI'
             DISPLAY 'INV1100  A  2   ITEM NUMBER = ' IR-ITEM-NO
             MOVE 'Y' TO INVMAST-EOF-SWITCH.
```

Figure 3-8   The indexed file creation program (part 2 of 2)

storage area. When a record is written to the indexed file, the FROM clause on the WRITE statement writes the record from this same area.

Finally, notice in module 120 that the WRITE statement is coded with the INVALID KEY clause. If any errors occur when this statement is executed (such as a sequence error or duplicate key error), the statements associated with the INVALID KEY clause will be executed. In this case, a message is displayed showing the key for the record that was being written when the error occurred and the end-of-file switch is turned on.

As I promised in the last chapter, I didn't use the FILE STATUS clause to check for I/O errors in this program. However, if you use FILE STATUS fields in your shop, you would probably want to use one for the indexed file to determine the exact cause of an invalid key condition on the WRITE statement.

Program:INV1200   Update inventory file (sequential)   Page: 1

Designer: Mike Murach   Date: 09-03-86

Input/output specifications

File	Description	Use
VALTRAN	Valid inventory transaction file	Input
INVMAST	Inventory master file	Update
ERRTRAN	Unmatched inventory transaction file	Output

Process specifications

This program updates an inventory master file (INVMAST) based on the data in a sequential file of valid inventory transaction records (VALTRAN). The master file should be read on a sequential basis, and the updated records should be rewritten on the master file. The master file is indexed by item number.

If a transaction has the same item number as a master record, the transaction matches the master record. Then, the transaction data should be used to update the master record: The on hand quantity in the master record should be increased by the receipt quantity in the transaction record.

If a matching master record can't be found for a transaction, the transaction is unmatched. Then, the transaction record should be written on the file of error transactions (ERRTRAN).

VALTRAN is in sequence by item number. Since INVMAST is being accessed sequentially, its records will also be retrieved in item-number sequence. Also, the record formats for VALTRAN and ERRTRAN are the same.

The basic processing requirements follow:

1. Read a transaction record.

2. If necessary, get inventory master records until a record with a matching or greater item number is found. This includes rewriting the last master record that was updated.

3. If the transaction is matched,
        the matching master record should be updated.

4. If the transaction is unmatched,
        the record should be written on the file of error transactions.

Figure 3-9   The program overview for a program that sequentially updates an indexed file

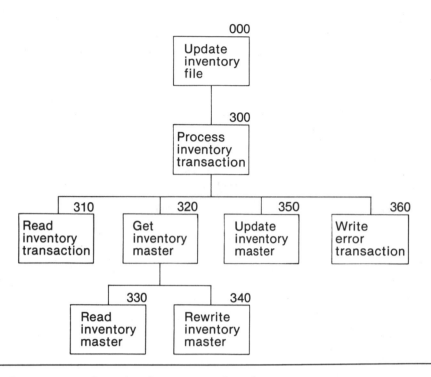

Figure 3-10   The structure chart for the sequential update program

A sequential update program   Figure 3-9 presents a program over-view for a sequential update program. The specifications for this pro-gram are identical to those for the update-in-place program in the last chapter, except that the master file has indexed organization. The records in the inventory master file are updated based on the data in a file of valid inventory transactions. After all transactions for an item have been processed, the record is rewritten to the file.

Figure 3-10 presents the structure chart for this program. It is iden-tical to the chart for the sequential update-in-place program in figure 2-13. Then, figure 3-11 gives the COBOL code for this program, which is almost the same as the code for the update-in-place program in figure 2-14. In fact, there are only three differences.

First, the SELECT statement for the indexed file specifies indexed organization and a record key named MR-ITEM-NO. Se-cond, the key field for the file is defined in the record description in the File Section. Third, I used the INVALID KEY clause on the REWRITE statement for the indexed file, and I didn't check FILE STATUS codes for this file.

Like the sequential update-in-place program, this program reads all the records in the master file, even though none are updated after the last transaction record is processed. Since this is inefficient, you should keep in mind that the program wouldn't actually be coded that way unless it had to accumulate control data from each master record.

```
 IDENTIFICATION DIVISION.
*
 PROGRAM-ID.  INV1200.
*
 ENVIRONMENT DIVISION.
*
 INPUT-OUTPUT SECTION.
*
 FILE-CONTROL.
     SELECT VALTRAN   ASSIGN TO SYS020-AS-VALTRAN.
     SELECT INVMAST   ASSIGN TO SYS021-INVMAST
                      ORGANIZATION IS INDEXED
                      ACCESS IS SEQUENTIAL
                      RECORD KEY IS MR-ITEM-NO.
     SELECT ERRTRAN   ASSIGN TO SYS022-AS-ERRTRAN.
*
 DATA DIVISION.
*
 FILE SECTION.
*
 FD   VALTRAN
      LABEL RECORDS ARE STANDARD
      RECORD CONTAINS 21 CHARACTERS.
*
 01   VALID-TRANSACTION-AREA    PIC X(21).
*
 FD   INVMAST
      LABEL RECORDS ARE STANDARD
      RECORD CONTAINS 80 CHARACTERS.
*
 01   MASTER-RECORD-AREA.
*
     05   MR-ITEM-NO           PIC X(5).
     05   FILLER               PIC X(75).
*
 FD   ERRTRAN
      LABEL RECORDS ARE STANDARD
      RECORD CONTAINS 21 CHARACTERS.
*
 01   ERROR-TRANSACTION        PIC X(21).
*
 WORKING-STORAGE SECTION.
*
 01   SWITCHES.
*
     05   ALL-RECORDS-PROCESSED-SWITCH  PIC X      VALUE 'N'.
          88   ALL-RECORDS-PROCESSED               VALUE 'Y'.
     05   MASTER-UPDATED-SWITCH         PIC X      VALUE 'N'.
          88   MASTER-UPDATED                      VALUE 'Y'.
*
 01   INVENTORY-TRANSACTION.
*
     05   IT-ITEM-NO           PIC X(5).
     05   IT-VENDOR-NO         PIC X(5).
     05   IT-RECEIPT-DATE      PIC X(6).
```

Figure 3-11   The sequential update program (part 1 of 3)

```
    05   IT-RECEIPT-QUANTITY     PIC S9(5).
*
 01  INVENTORY-MASTER-RECORD.
*
    05   IM-DESCRIPTIVE-DATA.
         10   IM-ITEM-NO              PIC X(5).
         10   IM-ITEM-DESC            PIC X(20).
         10   IM-UNIT-COST            PIC S999V99.
         10   IM-UNIT-PRICE           PIC S999V99.
    05   IM-INVENTORY-DATA.
         10   IM-REORDER-POINT        PIC S9(5).
         10   IM-ON-HAND              PIC S9(5).
         10   IM-ON-ORDER             PIC S9(5).
    05   FILLER                       PIC X(30).
*
 PROCEDURE DIVISION.
*
 000-UPDATE-INVENTORY-FILE.
*
    OPEN INPUT   VALTRAN
         I-O     INVMAST
         OUTPUT ERRTRAN.
    MOVE LOW-VALUE TO IM-ITEM-NO.
    PERFORM 300-PROCESS-INVENTORY-TRAN
         UNTIL ALL-RECORDS-PROCESSED.
    CLOSE VALTRAN
          INVMAST
          ERRTRAN.
    DISPLAY 'INV1200  I  1   NORMAL EOJ'.
    STOP RUN.
*
 300-PROCESS-INVENTORY-TRAN.
*
    PERFORM 310-READ-INVENTORY-TRAN.
    PERFORM 320-GET-INVENTORY-MASTER
         UNTIL IM-ITEM-NO NOT < IT-ITEM-NO.
    IF        IM-ITEM-NO = HIGH-VALUE
          AND IT-ITEM-NO = HIGH-VALUE
        MOVE 'Y' TO ALL-RECORDS-PROCESSED-SWITCH
    ELSE
        IF IM-ITEM-NO = IT-ITEM-NO
            PERFORM 350-UPDATE-INVENTORY-MASTER
        ELSE
            PERFORM 360-WRITE-ERROR-TRAN.
*
 310-READ-INVENTORY-TRAN.
*
    READ VALTRAN INTO INVENTORY-TRANSACTION
        AT END
            MOVE HIGH-VALUE TO IT-ITEM-NO.
*
 320-GET-INVENTORY-MASTER.
*
    IF MASTER-UPDATED
        PERFORM 340-REWRITE-INVENTORY-MASTER
        PERFORM 330-READ-INVENTORY-MASTER
```

Figure 3-11   The sequential update program (part 2 of 3)

```
      ELSE
          PERFORM 330-READ-INVENTORY-MASTER.
*
 330-READ-INVENTORY-MASTER.
*
      READ INVMAST INTO INVENTORY-MASTER-RECORD
          AT END
              MOVE HIGH-VALUE TO IM-ITEM-NO.
*
 340-REWRITE-INVENTORY-MASTER.
*
      REWRITE MASTER-RECORD-AREA FROM INVENTORY-MASTER-RECORD
          INVALID KEY
              DISPLAY 'INV1200  A  2  REWRITE ERROR FOR INVMAST'
              DISPLAY 'INV1200  A  2  ITEM NUMBER = ' IM-ITEM-NO
              MOVE 'Y' TO ALL-RECORDS-PROCESSED-SWITCH.
      MOVE 'N' TO MASTER-UPDATED-SWITCH.
*
 350-UPDATE-INVENTORY-MASTER.
*
      ADD IT-RECEIPT-QUANTITY TO IM-ON-HAND.
      MOVE 'Y' TO MASTER-UPDATED-SWITCH.
*
 360-WRITE-ERROR-TRAN.
*
      WRITE ERROR-TRANSACTION FROM INVENTORY-TRANSACTION.
```

Figure 3-11   The sequential update program (part 3 of 3)

RANDOM PROCESSING

Figure 3-12 summarizes the COBOL code you use when you write programs that process indexed files randomly. There are no new statements here, but there are a few variations you should be aware of. After I discuss these variations, I will present a random update program that uses some of these COBOL elements.

The SELECT statement

The only difference between the SELECT statement for an indexed file processed sequentially and one processed randomly is in the ACCESS MODE clause. For a randomly accessed file, you must specify either RANDOM or DYNAMIC access. Random access means that records will be accessed depending on their key values. Dynamic access means that records in the file can be accessed both sequentially and randomly. If a program is only going to process a file on a random basis, though, we recommend that you specify RANDOM in this clause, not DYNAMIC.

Procedure Division statements

The OPEN statement   If you look at the OPEN statement in figure 3-12, you'll notice that there isn't an EXTEND option. That makes sense because records don't have to be added at the end of a file when you use random access. Similarly, you can't use the EXTEND option on a dynamic access file, even if the records are going to be accessed sequentially.

The READ statement   The only difference in the READ statement is that the INVALID KEY clause can be coded for random access, and the AT END clause can't be coded because it has no meaning for a random read. Before a READ statement is executed, the key of the desired record must be placed in the field specified in the RECORD KEY clause. Then, if no record exists with that key, an invalid key condition occurs.

The WRITE, REWRITE, and DELETE statements   Although the formats of the WRITE, REWRITE, and DELETE statements are the same for random access as they are for sequential access, the way these statements are processed is different. For sequential access, the record processed depends on the location of the record pointer when the statement is issued. For random access, the record processed depends on the value in the key field for the file. As a result, you don't have to issue a READ statement for a record before you issue a REWRITE or DELETE statement for it.

SELECT statement

```
SELECT file-name

     ASSIGN TO system-name

     ORGANIZATION IS INDEXED

     ACCESS MODE IS {RANDOM }
                    {DYNAMIC}

     RECORD KEY IS data-name-1

     [FILE STATUS IS data-name-2]
```

FD statement

```
FD  file-name

    [LABEL RECORDS ARE STANDARD]

    [RECORD CONTAINS integer-1 CHARACTERS]

    [BLOCK CONTAINS integer-2 RECORDS]
```

Figure 3-12   COBOL formats for random processing of indexed files (part 1 of 2)

When the WRITE statement is executed, it adds a record to a file. As a result, the INVALID KEY clause should only be executed if a duplicate key is already stored in the file or if a boundary violation occurs (there's no room for the record in the disk space allocated to the file). When the REWRITE statement is executed, it writes a record on the file in the location assigned to a record with a specific key. As a result, its INVALID KEY clause should only be executed if a record with the specified key doesn't already exist on the file. Similarly, the DELETE statement tries to delete a record with a specific key from the file. As a result, its INVALID KEY clause should only be executed if a record with the specified key doesn't already exist on the file. In most programs, a record is read before a REWRITE or DELETE statement is executed for that key value so the program knows that the record already exists.

Procedure Division statements

```
      (INPUT     file-name-1 ...)
OPEN {OUTPUT    file-name-2 ...}
      (I-O       file-name-3 ...)


READ file-name RECORD

    [INTO identifier]

    [INVALID KEY imperative-statement]


WRITE record-name

    [FROM identifier]

    [INVALID KEY imperative-statement]


REWRITE record-name

    [FROM identifier]

    [INVALID KEY imperative-statement]


DELETE file-name RECORD

    [INVALID KEY imperative-statement]


CLOSE  file-name-1 ...
```

Note: All 1985 COBOL elements are shaded.

Figure 3-12   COBOL formats for random processing of indexed files (part 2 of 2)

Program: INV1200   Update inventory file (random)   Page: 1

Designer: Anne Prince   Date: 09-03-86

Input/output specifications

File	Description	Use
VALTRAN	Valid inventory transaction file	Input
INVMAST	Inventory master file	Update
ERRTRAN	Unmatched inventory transaction file	Output

Process specifications

This program updates an inventory master file (INVMAST) based on the
data in a file of valid inventory transaction records (VALTRAN). The
inventory master file is indexed by item number and should be updated
randomly.

If a master record is found with the same item number as a
transaction, the transaction data should be used to update the master
record: The on hand quantity in the master record should be increased
by the receipt quantity in the transaction record.

If a master record is not found for a transaction, the transaction
record should be written on the file of error transactions (ERRTRAN).
The record format for ERRTRAN is the same as for VALTRAN.

The basic processing requirements follow:

1. Read a transaction record.

2. Read the master record with the same item number as in the
      transaction record.

3. If a master record is found,
        the master record should be updated and rewritten.

4. If a master record is not found,
        the transaction record should be written on the file of error
        transactions.

Figure 3-13   The program overview for a program that randomly updates an indexed file

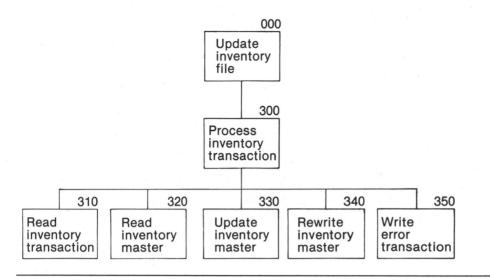

Figure 3-14 The structure chart for the random update program

A random update program

Figure 3-13 presents a program overview for a program that updates an indexed file of inventory records based on the data in a sequential file of valid inventory transactions. This program is just like the sequential update program I presented earlier in this topic, except that the records are processed on a random, rather than a sequential, basis.

As you can see in the program overview, I have assumed that the transaction file is in no particular sequence, so the program reads a transaction, reads the master record with the same key, changes the master record, and then rewrites it. If the transaction file were in sequence by record key, however, this would be inefficient. In that case, the program should check to make sure that all the transactions for a record have been processed before the master record is rewritten on the file.

Figure 3-14 presents the structure chart for this program. It has modules to read an inventory transaction, to read a master record on a random basis, to update the data in the master record, to rewrite the master record, and to write an error transaction. All of these modules are controlled by module 300.

Figure 3-15 presents the code for this program. It should be easy enough to understand. In the SELECT statement for the inventory master file, I specified RANDOM access. In module 300, if a master record is found with the same key as a transaction, modules 330 and 340 are called to update the master record and rewrite it on the file. Otherwise, module 350 is called to write the transaction record on the error file.

```
 IDENTIFICATION DIVISION.
*
 PROGRAM-ID.  INV1200.
*
 ENVIRONMENT DIVISION.
*
 INPUT-OUTPUT SECTION.
*
 FILE-CONTROL.
      SELECT VALTRAN   ASSIGN TO SYS020-AS-VALTRAN.
      SELECT INVMAST   ASSIGN TO SYS021-INVMAST
                       ORGANIZATION IS INDEXED
                       ACCESS IS RANDOM
                       RECORD KEY IS MR-ITEM-NO.
      SELECT ERRTRAN   ASSIGN TO SYS022-AS-ERRTRAN.
*
 DATA DIVISION.
*
 FILE SECTION.
*
 FD  VALTRAN
     LABEL RECORDS ARE STANDARD
     RECORD CONTAINS 21 CHARACTERS.
*
 01  VALID-TRANSACTION-AREA     PIC X(21).
*
 FD  INVMAST
     LABEL RECORDS ARE STANDARD
     RECORD CONTAINS 80 CHARACTERS.
*
 01  MASTER-RECORD-AREA.
*
     05   MR-ITEM-NO          PIC X(5).
     05   FILLER              PIC X(75).
*
 FD  ERRTRAN
     LABEL RECORDS ARE STANDARD
     RECORD CONTAINS 21 CHARACTERS.
*
 01  ERROR-TRANSACTION         PIC X(21).
*
 WORKING-STORAGE SECTION.
*
 01  SWITCHES.
*
     05   VALTRAN-EOF-SWITCH           PIC X     VALUE 'N'.
          88  VALTRAN-EOF                        VALUE 'Y'.
     05   MASTER-FOUND-SWITCH          PIC X.
          88  MASTER-FOUND                       VALUE 'Y'.
*
 01  INVENTORY-TRANSACTION.
*
     05   IT-ITEM-NO          PIC X(5).
     05   IT-VENDOR-NO        PIC X(5).
     05   IT-RECEIPT-DATE     PIC X(6).
```

Figure 3-15   The random update program (part 1 of 3)

```
     05   IT-RECEIPT-QUANTITY      PIC S9(5).
*
 01  INVENTORY-MASTER-RECORD.
*
     05   IM-DESCRIPTIVE-DATA.
          10   IM-ITEM-NO           PIC X(5).
          10   IM-ITEM-DESC         PIC X(20).
          10   IM-UNIT-COST         PIC S999V99.
          10   IM-UNIT-PRICE        PIC S999V99.
     05   IM-INVENTORY-DATA.
          10   IM-REORDER-POINT     PIC S9(5).
          10   IM-ON-HAND           PIC S9(5).
          10   IM-ON-ORDER          PIC S9(5).
     05   FILLER                    PIC X(30).
*
 PROCEDURE DIVISION.
*
 000-UPDATE-INVENTORY-FILE.
*
     OPEN INPUT   VALTRAN
          I-O     INVMAST
          OUTPUT  ERRTRAN.
     PERFORM 300-PROCESS-INVENTORY-TRAN
         UNTIL VALTRAN-EOF.
     CLOSE VALTRAN
           INVMAST
           ERRTRAN.
     DISPLAY 'INV1200  I  1  NORMAL EOJ'.
     STOP RUN.
*
 300-PROCESS-INVENTORY-TRAN.
*
     PERFORM 310-READ-INVENTORY-TRAN.
     IF NOT VALTRAN-EOF
         PERFORM 320-READ-INVENTORY-MASTER
         IF MASTER-FOUND
             PERFORM 330-UPDATE-INVENTORY-MASTER
             PERFORM 340-REWRITE-INVENTORY-MASTER
         ELSE
             PERFORM 350-WRITE-ERROR-TRAN.
*
 310-READ-INVENTORY-TRAN.
*
     READ VALTRAN INTO INVENTORY-TRANSACTION
         AT END
             MOVE 'Y' TO VALTRAN-EOF-SWITCH.
*
 320-READ-INVENTORY-MASTER.
*
     MOVE IT-ITEM-NO TO MR-ITEM-NO.
     MOVE 'Y' TO MASTER-FOUND-SWITCH.
     READ INVMAST INTO INVENTORY-MASTER-RECORD
         INVALID KEY
             MOVE 'N' TO MASTER-FOUND-SWITCH.
*
 330-UPDATE-INVENTORY-MASTER.
```

Figure 3-15   The random update program (part 2 of 3)

```
✿
     ADD IT-RECEIPT-QUANTITY TO IM-ON-HAND.
✿
 340-REWRITE-INVENTORY-MASTER.
✿
     REWRITE MASTER-RECORD-AREA FROM INVENTORY-MASTER-RECORD
         INVALID KEY
             DISPLAY 'INV1200  A  2   REWRITE ERROR FOR INVMAST'
             DISPLAY 'INV1200  A  2   ITEM NUMBER = ' IM-ITEM-NO
             MOVE 'Y' TO VALTRAN-EOF-SWITCH.
✿
 350-WRITE-ERROR-TRAN.
✿
     WRITE ERROR-TRANSACTION FROM INVENTORY-TRANSACTION.
```

Figure 3-15   The random update program (part 3 of 3)

In module 320, which is designed to read an inventory master record, the item number in the transaction record is first moved to the key field in the master record, MR-ITEM-NO. Next, MASTER-FOUND-SWITCH is turned on. Then, the READ statement tries to read the master record with the key value specified in MR-ITEM-NO. If it can't find this record, the INVALID KEY clause is executed so MASTER-FOUND-SWITCH is turned off. The result of this code is to turn the MASTER-FOUND condition on if the record is found and to turn it off if it isn't found. This condition is used in module 300 to control the processing of the program.

If you have a 1985 COBOL compiler, a module like 320 can be coded in a more straightforward manner by using the NOT INVALID KEY clause as in this example:

```
MOVE IT-ITEM-NO TO MR-ITEM-NO.
READ INVMAST INTO INVENTORY-MASTER-RECORD
    INVALID KEY
        MOVE 'N' TO MASTER-FOUND-SWITCH
    NOT INVALID KEY
        MOVE 'Y' TO MASTER-FOUND-SWITCH.
```

This, of course, has the same result as the code in figure 3-15. The 1985 COBOL code is presented in more detail in chapter 10.

DYNAMIC PROCESSING

As I've already mentioned, a program can process a file using both sequential and random access if you specify DYNAMIC access for the file. This type of processing can be referred to as *dynamic processing*. When you use dynamic access for a file, you can process it using the COBOL elements presented in the sequential processing summary in figure 3-4 as well as the elements in the random processing summary in figure 3-12.

In general, dynamic processing is more useful in interactive programs than it is in batch programs. During the execution of an interactive program, for example, the computer user may want to get the data from one record on a random basis, look over the data in the next few records in the file on a sequential basis, examine another record on a random basis, and so on. In contrast, a batch program (one that isn't interactive) can usually be coded quite effectively without using dynamic access.

Because this book doesn't show you how to code interactive programs, I don't want to use one to illustrate dynamic access. As a result, I'll use a batch report preparation program to illustrate dynamic processing, even though you wouldn't actually code the program in this way. After I show you how you can use dynamic access in this program, I'll show you how you can code it without using dynamic access.

A report preparation program that uses dynamic access

Figure 3-16 presents the program specifications for a report preparation program that processes an indexed file of inventory location records. For each inventory transaction, which represents a receipt to inventory, the program is supposed to list all of the inventory locations in which some stock for that item number is stored. As you can deduce from the print chart, one line is printed for each inventory location record that is read for an item. Needless to say, the location listing is unrealistically simple, but it isn't unrealistic to display data like this on a screen during the execution of an interactive program.

For each item number, there may be none, one, or more location records in the inventory location file. The key for this file consists of the item number followed by a two-digit sequence number. The first location record for each item number has a sequence number of 01; the second location record for an item has a sequence number of 02; and so on. Because of this, the program that prepares the report could read the location records using random access. However, to illustrate dynamic access, the program is going to read only the first location record for each inventory item on a random basis. The other records for each transaction will be read on a sequential basis.

Figure 3-17 presents the structure chart for this program. To support dynamic access, module 320 prepares only the first location line for each transaction record, and module 330 reads the first location record for each transaction on a random basis. Then, module 340 prepares the location lines for the other location records for each transaction, and module 350 reads the records in the location file on a sequential basis. Incidentally, I numbered the print modules in this chart starting with module 360 so all of the print modules will be at the end of the compiler listing.

Program: INV3100 Prepare location listing	Page: 1
Designer: Anne Prince	Date: 09-03-86

Input/output specifications

File	Description	Use
VALTRAN	Valid inventory transaction file	Input
INVLOC	Inventory location file	Input
LOCLIST	Print file: Inventory location listing	Output

Process specifications

This program reads a sequential file of valid transaction records
(VALTRAN) that represent receipts to inventory. These records are in
a random sequence. As the program reads this file, it prints a
listing of the possible inventory locations in which each inventory
item can be stored. It gets these locations from a file of location
records (INVLOC).

The inventory location file is an indexed file. The key for each
record is made up of item number and a sequence number. The sequence
number ranges from 01 through as many different location records as
there are for an item number. If, for example, item number 23354 has
five location records that apply to it, the location record keys are
2335401, 2335402, 2335403, 2335404, and 2335405.

The basic processing requirements follow:

1. Read a transaction record.

2. Read all the location records for the item number represented by
    the transaction. For each location record, print a line on the
    location listing. If there are no location records for a
    transaction, print a line on the location listing that indicates
    that no location records have been found.

Figure 3-16   The program specifications for a report preparation program that retrieves the records
                in an indexed file (part 1 of 2)

The record layout for the transaction record

```
01   INVENTORY-TRANSACTION.
*
     05   IT-ITEM-NO            PIC  X(5).
     05   IT-VENDOR-NO          PIC  X(5).
     05   IT-RECEIPT-DATE       PIC  X(6).
     05   IT-RECEIPT-QUANTITY   PIC  S9(5).
```

The record layout for the inventory location record

```
01   INVENTORY-LOCATION-RECORD.
*
     05   IL-RECORD-KEY.
          10   IL-ITEM-NO            PIC  X(5).
          10   IL-SEQUENCE-NO        PIC  XX.
     05   IL-LOCATION-DATA.
          10   IL-WAREHOUSE-NO       PIC  X(2).
          10   IL-LOCATION-NO        PIC  X(4).
          10   IL-BIN-NO             PIC  X(2).
          10   IL-CAPICITY           PIC  S9(5).
          10   IL-QUANITY-STORED     PIC  S9(5).
          10   IL-QUANITY-AVAILABLE  PIC  S9(5).
     05   FILLER                     PIC  X(50).
```

The print chart for the inventory location listing

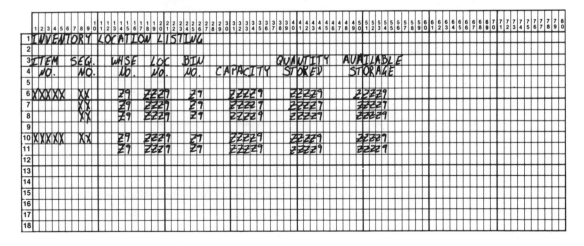

Figure 3-16   The program specifications for a report preparation program that retrieves the records in an indexed file (part 2 of 2)

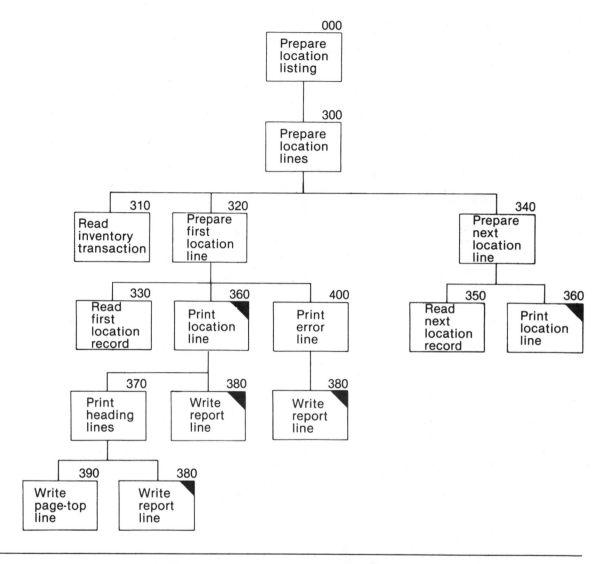

Figure 3-17   The structure chart for the report preparation program when dynamic access is used

Figure 3-18 presents the COBOL code for this program. Since it merely combines the sequential and random access code you've already learned into a single program, you should be able to understand it without much difficulty.

To read the first location record for each transaction, module 330 moves the key of the first location record into the location record area. It does this by moving the item number from the transaction along with sequence number 01 into the key area. Then, it turns LOCATION-FOUND-SWITCH on. Last, it reads the location record

```
 IDENTIFICATION DIVISION.
*
 PROGRAM-ID.  INV3100.
*
 ENVIRONMENT DIVISION.
*
 INPUT-OUTPUT SECTION.
*
 FILE-CONTROL.
     SELECT VALTRAN   ASSIGN TO SYS020-AS-VALTRAN.
     SELECT INVLOC    ASSIGN TO SYS021-INVLOC
                      ORGANIZATION IS INDEXED
                      ACCESS IS DYNAMIC
                      RECORD KEY IS LR-RECORD-KEY.
     SELECT LOCLIST   ASSIGN TO SYS006-UR-1403-S.
*
 DATA DIVISION.
*
 FILE SECTION.
*
 FD  VALTRAN
     LABEL RECORDS ARE STANDARD
     RECORD CONTAINS 21 CHARACTERS.
*
 01  VALID-TRANSACTION-AREA    PIC X(21).
*
 FD  INVLOC
     LABEL RECORDS ARE STANDARD
     RECORD CONTAINS 80 CHARACTERS.
*
 01  LOCATION-RECORD-AREA.
*
     05  LR-RECORD-KEY.
         10  LR-ITEM-NO        PIC X(5).
         10  LR-SEQUENCE-NO    PIC XX.
     05  FILLER               PIC X(73).
*
 FD  LOCLIST
     LABEL RECORDS ARE OMITTED
     RECORD CONTAINS 132 CHARACTERS.
*
 01  PRINT-AREA               PIC X(132).
*
 WORKING-STORAGE SECTION.
*
 01  SWITCHES.
*
     05  VALTRAN-EOF-SWITCH           PIC X      VALUE 'N'.
         88  VALTRAN-EOF                         VALUE 'Y'.
     05  LOCATION-FOUND-SWITCH        PIC X.
         88  LOCATION-FOUND                      VALUE 'Y'.
*
 01  PRINT-FIELDS             COMP-3.
*
     05  SPACE-CONTROL        PIC S9.
```

Figure 3-18   The report preparation program that uses dynamic access (part 1 of 5)

```
     05  LINES-ON-PAGE            PIC S999   VALUE +55.
     05  LINE-COUNT               PIC S999   VALUE +99.
*
 01  INVENTORY-TRANSACTION.
*
     05  IT-ITEM-NO               PIC X(5).
     05  IT-VENDOR-NO             PIC X(5).
     05  IT-RECEIPT-DATE          PIC X(6).
     05  IT-RECEIPT-QUANTITY      PIC S9(5).
*
 01  INVENTORY-LOCATION-RECORD.
*
     05  IL-RECORD-KEY.
         10  IL-ITEM-NO               PIC X(5).
         10  IL-SEQUENCE-NO           PIC XX.
     05  IL-LOCATION-DATA.
         10  IL-WAREHOUSE-NO          PIC X(2).
         10  IL-LOCATION-NO           PIC X(4).
         10  IL-BIN-NO                PIC X(2).
         10  IL-CAPACITY              PIC S9(5).
         10  IL-QUANTITY-STORED       PIC S9(5).
         10  IL-QUANTITY-AVAILABLE    PIC S9(5).
     05  FILLER                       PIC X(50).
*
 01  HEADING-LINE-1.
*
     05  FILLER  PIC X(30)  VALUE 'INVENTORY LOCATION LISTING'.
     05  FILLER  PIC X(102) VALUE SPACE.
*
 01  HEADING-LINE-2.
*
     05  FILLER  PIC X(20)  VALUE 'ITEM  SEQ.  WHSE   LO'.
     05  FILLER  PIC X(20)  VALUE 'C  BIN           QUA'.
     05  FILLER  PIC X(20)  VALUE 'NTITY   AVAILABLE    '.
     05  FILLER  PIC X(72)  VALUE SPACE.
*
 01  HEADING-LINE-3.
*
     05  FILLER  PIC X(20)  VALUE ' NO.    NO.    NO.  NO'.
     05  FILLER  PIC X(20)  VALUE '.  NO.  CAPACITY   ST'.
     05  FILLER  PIC X(20)  VALUE 'ORED      STORAGE    '.
     05  FILLER  PIC X(72)  VALUE SPACE.
*
 01  LOCATION-LINE.
*
     05  LL-ITEM-NO               PIC X(5).
     05  FILLER                   PIC X(2)     VALUE SPACE.
     05  LL-SEQUENCE-NO           PIC X(2).
     05  FILLER                   PIC X(4)     VALUE SPACE.
     05  LL-WAREHOUSE-NO          PIC Z9.
     05  FILLER                   PIC X(2)     VALUE SPACE.
     05  LL-LOCATION-NO           PIC ZZZ9.
     05  FILLER                   PIC X(3)     VALUE SPACE.
     05  LL-BIN-NO                PIC Z9.
     05  FILLER                   PIC X(4)     VALUE SPACE.
     05  LL-CAPACITY              PIC ZZZZ9.
```

Figure 3-18   The report preparation program that uses dynamic access (part 2 of 5)

```
    05    FILLER                   PIC X(4)       VALUE SPACE.
    05    LL-QUANTITY-STORED       PIC ZZZZ9.
    05    FILLER                   PIC X(5)       VALUE SPACE.
    05    LL-QUANTITY-AVAILABLE    PIC ZZZZ9.
    05    FILLER                   PIC X(78)      VALUE SPACE.
*
 01   LOCATION-ERROR-LINE.
*
    05    LEL-ITEM-NO              PIC X(5)        VALUE SPACE.
    05    FILLER                   PIC XX.
    05    FILLER                   PIC X(24)
                                   VALUE 'NO LOCATION RECORD FOUND'.
    05    FILLER                   PIC X(101)     VALUE SPACE.
*
 PROCEDURE DIVISION.
*
 000-PREPARE-LOCATION-LISTING.
*
     OPEN INPUT   VALTRAN
                  INVLOC
          OUTPUT LOCLIST.
     PERFORM 300-PREPARE-LOCATION-LINES
         UNTIL VALTRAN-EOF.
     CLOSE VALTRAN
           INVLOC
           LOCLIST.
     DISPLAY 'INV3100   I   1   NORMAL EOJ'.
     STOP RUN.
*
 300-PREPARE-LOCATION-LINES.
*
     PERFORM 310-READ-INVENTORY-TRAN.
     IF NOT VALTRAN-EOF
         PERFORM 320-PREPARE-FIRST-LOC-LINE
         IF LOCATION-FOUND
             PERFORM 340-PREPARE-NEXT-LOCATION-LINE
                 UNTIL NOT LOCATION-FOUND.
*
 310-READ-INVENTORY-TRAN.
*
     READ VALTRAN INTO INVENTORY-TRANSACTION
         AT END
             MOVE 'Y' TO VALTRAN-EOF-SWITCH.
*
```

Figure 3-18   The report preparation program that uses dynamic access (part 3 of 5)

```
 320-PREPARE-FIRST-LOC-LINE.
*
     PERFORM 330-READ-FIRST-LOCATION-RECORD.
     MOVE 2 TO SPACE-CONTROL.
     IF LOCATION-FOUND
         PERFORM 360-PRINT-LOCATION-LINE
     ELSE
         PERFORM 400-PRINT-ERROR-LINE.
*
 330-READ-FIRST-LOCATION-RECORD.
*
     MOVE IT-ITEM-NO TO LR-ITEM-NO.
     MOVE '01'        TO LR-SEQUENCE-NO.
     MOVE 'Y' TO LOCATION-FOUND-SWITCH.
     READ INVLOC INTO INVENTORY-LOCATION-RECORD
         INVALID KEY
             MOVE 'N' TO LOCATION-FOUND-SWITCH.
*
 340-PREPARE-NEXT-LOCATION-LINE.
*
     PERFORM 350-READ-NEXT-LOCATION-RECORD.
     IF LOCATION-FOUND
         PERFORM 360-PRINT-LOCATION-LINE.
*
 350-READ-NEXT-LOCATION-RECORD.
*
     READ INVLOC NEXT RECORD INTO INVENTORY-LOCATION-RECORD
         AT END
             MOVE 'N' TO LOCATION-FOUND-SWITCH.
     IF IT-ITEM-NO NOT = IL-ITEM-NO
         MOVE 'N' TO LOCATION-FOUND-SWITCH.
*
 360-PRINT-LOCATION-LINE.
*
     IF LINE-COUNT > LINES-ON-PAGE
         PERFORM 370-PRINT-HEADING-LINES.
     IF LR-SEQUENCE-NO = '01'
         MOVE IT-ITEM-NO              TO LL-ITEM-NO
     ELSE
         MOVE SPACE TO LL-ITEM-NO.
     MOVE IL-SEQUENCE-NO          TO LL-SEQUENCE-NO.
     MOVE IL-WAREHOUSE-NO         TO LL-WAREHOUSE-NO.
     MOVE IL-LOCATION-NO          TO LL-LOCATION-NO.
     MOVE IL-BIN-NO               TO LL-BIN-NO.
     MOVE IL-CAPACITY             TO LL-CAPACITY.
     MOVE IL-QUANTITY-STORED      TO LL-QUANTITY-STORED.
     MOVE IL-QUANTITY-AVAILABLE TO LL-QUANTITY-AVAILABLE.
     MOVE LOCATION-LINE TO PRINT-AREA.
     PERFORM 380-WRITE-REPORT-LINE.
     MOVE 1 TO SPACE-CONTROL.
*
```

Figure 3-18   The report preparation program that uses dynamic access (part 4 of 5)

```
370-PRINT-HEADING-LINES.
*
     PERFORM 390-WRITE-PAGE-TOP-LINE.
     MOVE HEADING-LINE-2 TO PRINT-AREA.
     MOVE 2 TO SPACE-CONTROL.
     PERFORM 380-WRITE-REPORT-LINE.
     MOVE HEADING-LINE-3 TO PRINT-AREA.
     MOVE 1 TO SPACE-CONTROL.
     PERFORM 380-WRITE-REPORT-LINE.
     MOVE 2 TO SPACE-CONTROL.
*
 380-WRITE-REPORT-LINE.
*
     WRITE PRINT-AREA
         AFTER ADVANCING SPACE-CONTROL LINES.
     ADD SPACE-CONTROL TO LINE-COUNT.
*
 390-WRITE-PAGE-TOP-LINE.
*
     WRITE PRINT-AREA FROM HEADING-LINE-1
         AFTER ADVANCING PAGE.
     MOVE 1 TO LINE-COUNT.
*
 400-PRINT-ERROR-LINE.
*
     MOVE IT-ITEM-NO          TO LEL-ITEM-NO.
     MOVE LOCATION-ERROR-LINE TO PRINT-AREA.
     PERFORM 380-WRITE-REPORT-LINE.
```

Figure 3-18   The report preparation program that uses dynamic access (part 5 of 5)

specified by the key, but if this record can't be found, it turns LOCATION-FOUND-SWITCH off. When the module finishes its execution, LOCATION-FOUND-SWITCH will indicate whether or not the program was able to find the first record for the transaction.

After the first location record for a transaction has been processed, the program switches from random to sequential access. Module 350 is used to read the subsequent location records on a sequential basis. Note that the word NEXT must be used in the READ statement to indicate sequential access; otherwise, random access is assumed. After the next record has been read, the module compares the item number in the transaction record with the item number in the location record. If they're equal, LOCATION-FOUND-SWITCH remains on. If they're not or if there are no more records in the file, this switch is turned off so the program can continue with the next transaction record.

The report preparation program without dynamic access

As I've already said, all of the records in the location file could be read on a random basis so dynamic access isn't necessary in this program. In addition, this program could be written using sequential processing only. In this case, the program would use the START statement to position the file at the first location record for each transaction. Then, it would read the subsequent records for the transaction using sequential processing. This type of processing is sometimes referred to as *skip-sequential processing* because it skips from one point to another in the file as it reads the records on a sequential basis.

Figure 3-19 presents the structure chart for the report preparation program when skip-sequential processing is used. Here, module 320 is used to position the location file for each transaction. Then, module 340 is used to read the records for each transaction on a sequential basis.

Figure 3-20 presents the code for this program. In module 320, the key for the location file is set up much as it is before a random I/O operation. Then, the START statement positions the file at the key that has been established. If there's no matching key, the INVALID KEY clause turns the LOCATION-FOUND-SWITCH off so an error message will be printed on the listing.

In module 340, a sequential READ statement is used to read the next record in the location file. If there are no more records in the file or if the item number in the next record isn't equal to the item number in the transaction record, LOCATION-FOUND-SWITCH is turned off. Then, the program continues by reading the next transaction record.

DISCUSSION

If you use a microcomputer or minicomputer in your shop, you will probably make frequent use of indexed files, both for batch and interactive programs. On the other hand, if you use an IBM mainframe, you most likely will use COBOL for indexed files when you develop batch programs, but you'll probably use a facility like CICS when you use indexed files in interactive programs.

In almost all shops, though, you will need to know how to process indexed files on both a sequential and random basis. But whether or not you need to know how to use dynamic access will depend upon the shop. As I said, dynamic access is frequently used in interactive programs, but it's rarely needed in batch programs.

Terminology

dynamic access   skip-sequential processing
dynamic processing

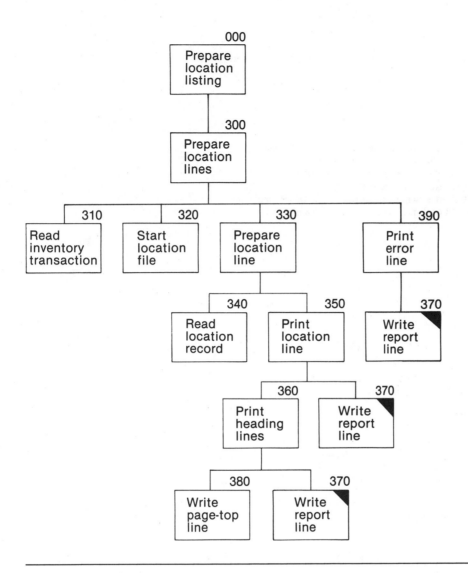

Figure 3-19   The structure chart for the report preparation program when skip-sequential processing is used

Objective

Given program specifications for a program that processes indexed files with only primary indexes, develop a COBOL program that satisfies the specifications. The program may involve any of the following: creating a file, adding records to a file, deleting records from a file, sequentially or randomly updating a file, and sequentially or randomly retrieving records from a file.

```
 IDENTIFICATION DIVISION.
*
 PROGRAM-ID.  INV3100.
*
 ENVIRONMENT DIVISION.
*
 INPUT-OUTPUT SECTION.
*
 FILE-CONTROL.
     SELECT VALTRAN   ASSIGN TO SYS020-AS-VALTRAN.
     SELECT INVLOC    ASSIGN TO SYS021-INVLOC
                      ORGANIZATION IS INDEXED
                      ACCESS IS SEQUENTIAL
                      RECORD KEY IS LR-RECORD-KEY.
     SELECT LOCLIST   ASSIGN TO SYS006-UR-1403-S.
*
 DATA DIVISION.
*
 FILE SECTION.
*
 FD  VALTRAN
     LABEL RECORDS ARE STANDARD
     RECORD CONTAINS 21 CHARACTERS.
*
 01  VALID-TRANSACTION-AREA     PIC X(21).
*
 FD  INVLOC
     LABEL RECORDS ARE STANDARD
     RECORD CONTAINS 80 CHARACTERS.
*
 01  LOCATION-RECORD-AREA.
*
     05  LR-RECORD-KEY.
         10  LR-ITEM-NO       PIC X(5).
         10  LR-SEQUENCE-NO   PIC XX.
     05  FILLER               PIC X(73).
*
 FD  LOCLIST
     LABEL RECORDS ARE OMITTED
     RECORD CONTAINS 132 CHARACTERS.
*
 01  PRINT-AREA               PIC X(132).
*
 WORKING-STORAGE SECTION.
*
 01  SWITCHES.
*
     05  VALTRAN-EOF-SWITCH          PIC X     VALUE 'N'.
         88  VALTRAN-EOF                       VALUE 'Y'.
     05  LOCATION-FOUND-SWITCH       PIC X.
         88  LOCATION-FOUND                    VALUE 'Y'.
*
 01  PRINT-FIELDS             COMP-3.
*
     05  SPACE-CONTROL        PIC S9.
```

Figure 3-20   The report preparation program that uses skip-sequential processing (part 1 of 4)

```
    05   LINES-ON-PAGE              PIC S999    VALUE +55.
    05   LINE-COUNT                 PIC S999    VALUE +99.
*
 01   INVENTORY-TRANSACTION.
*
    05   IT-ITEM-NO                 PIC X(5).
    05   IT-VENDOR-NO               PIC X(5).
    05   IT-RECEIPT-DATE            PIC X(6).
    05   IT-RECEIPT-QUANTITY        PIC S9(5).
*
 01   INVENTORY-LOCATION-RECORD.
*
    05   IL-RECORD-KEY.
       10    IL-ITEM-NO             PIC X(5).
       10    IL-SEQUENCE-NO         PIC XX.
    05   IL-LOCATION-DATA.
       10    IL-WAREHOUSE-NO        PIC X(2).
       10    IL-LOCATION-NO         PIC X(4).
       10    IL-BIN-NO              PIC X(2).
       10    IL-CAPACITY            PIC S9(5).
       10    IL-QUANTITY-STORED     PIC S9(5).
       10    IL-QUANTITY-AVAILABLE  PIC S9(5).
    05   FILLER                     PIC X(50).
*
 01   HEADING-LINE-1.
*
       .
       .
       .
*
 01   LOCATION-LINE.
*
    05   LL-ITEM-NO                 PIC X(5).
    05   FILLER                     PIC X(2)       VALUE SPACE.
    05   LL-SEQUENCE-NO             PIC X(2).
    05   FILLER                     PIC X(4)       VALUE SPACE.
    05   LL-WAREHOUSE-NO            PIC Z9.
    05   FILLER                     PIC X(2)       VALUE SPACE.
    05   LL-LOCATION-NO             PIC ZZZ9.
    05   FILLER                     PIC X(3)       VALUE SPACE.
    05   LL-BIN-NO                  PIC Z9.
    05   FILLER                     PIC X(4)       VALUE SPACE.
    05   LL-CAPACITY                PIC ZZZZ9.
    05   FILLER                     PIC X(4)       VALUE SPACE.
    05   LL-QUANTITY-STORED         PIC ZZZZ9.
    05   FILLER                     PIC X(5)       VALUE SPACE.
    05   LL-QUANTITY-AVAILABLE      PIC ZZZZ9.
    05   FILLER                     PIC X(78)      VALUE SPACE.
*
 01   LOCATION-ERROR-LINE.
*
    05   LEL-ITEM-NO                PIC X(5).
    05   FILLER                     PIC XX         VALUE SPACE.
    05   FILLER                     PIC X(24)
                                    VALUE 'NO LOCATION RECORD FOUND'.
    05   FILLER                     PIC X(101)     VALUE SPACE.
*
```

Figure 3-20   The report preparation program that uses skip-sequential processing (part 2 of 4)

```
 PROCEDURE DIVISION.
*
 000-PREPARE-LOCATION-LISTING.
*
     OPEN INPUT   VALTRAN
                  INVLOC
          OUTPUT LOCLIST.
     PERFORM 300-PREPARE-LOCATION-LINES
         UNTIL VALTRAN-EOF.
     CLOSE VALTRAN
           INVLOC
           LOCLIST.
     DISPLAY 'INV3100  I  1  NORMAL EOJ'.
     STOP RUN.
*
 300-PREPARE-LOCATION-LINES.
*
     PERFORM 310-READ-INVENTORY-TRAN.
     IF NOT VALTRAN-EOF
         MOVE 'Y' TO LOCATION-FOUND-SWITCH
         PERFORM 320-START-LOCATION-FILE
         IF LOCATION-FOUND
             PERFORM 330-PREPARE-LOCATION-LINE
                 UNTIL NOT LOCATION-FOUND
         ELSE
             PERFORM 390-PRINT-ERROR-LINE.
*
 310-READ-INVENTORY-TRAN.
*
     READ VALTRAN INTO INVENTORY-TRANSACTION
         AT END
             MOVE 'Y' TO VALTRAN-EOF-SWITCH.
*
 320-START-LOCATION-FILE.
*
     MOVE IT-ITEM-NO TO LR-ITEM-NO.
     MOVE '01'        TO LR-SEQUENCE-NO.
     START INVLOC
         KEY IS = LR-RECORD-KEY
         INVALID KEY
             MOVE 'N' TO LOCATION-FOUND-SWITCH.
*
 330-PREPARE-LOCATION-LINE.
*
     PERFORM 340-READ-LOCATION-RECORD.
     IF LOCATION-FOUND
         PERFORM 350-PRINT-LOCATION-LINE.
*
 340-READ-LOCATION-RECORD.
*
     READ INVLOC INTO INVENTORY-LOCATION-RECORD
         AT END
             MOVE 'N' TO LOCATION-FOUND-SWITCH.
     IF IT-ITEM-NO NOT = IL-ITEM-NO
         MOVE 'N' TO LOCATION-FOUND-SWITCH.
*
```

Figure 3-20   The report preparation program that uses skip-sequential processing (part 3 of 4)

```
 350-PRINT-LOCATION-LINE.
*
     IF LINE-COUNT > LINES-ON-PAGE
         PERFORM 360-PRINT-HEADING-LINES.
     IF LR-SEQUENCE-NO = '01'
         MOVE 2                   TO SPACE-CONTROL
         MOVE IT-ITEM-NO          TO LL-ITEM-NO
     ELSE
         MOVE SPACE               TO LL-ITEM-NO.
     MOVE IL-SEQUENCE-NO          TO LL-SEQUENCE-NO.
     MOVE IL-WAREHOUSE-NO         TO LL-WAREHOUSE-NO.
     MOVE IL-LOCATION-NO          TO LL-LOCATION-NO.
     MOVE IL-BIN-NO               TO LL-BIN-NO.
     MOVE IL-CAPACITY             TO LL-CAPACITY.
     MOVE IL-QUANTITY-STORED      TO LL-QUANTITY-STORED.
     MOVE IL-QUANTITY-AVAILABLE TO LL-QUANTITY-AVAILABLE.
     MOVE LOCATION-LINE TO PRINT-AREA.
     PERFORM 370-WRITE-REPORT-LINE.
     MOVE 1 TO SPACE-CONTROL.
*
 360-PRINT-HEADING-LINES.
*
     PERFORM 380-WRITE-PAGE-TOP-LINE.
     MOVE HEADING-LINE-2 TO PRINT-AREA.
     MOVE 2 TO SPACE-CONTROL.
     PERFORM 370-WRITE-REPORT-LINE.
     MOVE HEADING-LINE-3 TO PRINT-AREA.
     MOVE 1 TO SPACE-CONTROL.
     PERFORM 370-WRITE-REPORT-LINE.
     MOVE 2 TO SPACE-CONTROL.
*
 370-WRITE-REPORT-LINE.
*
     WRITE PRINT-AREA
         AFTER ADVANCING SPACE-CONTROL LINES.
     ADD SPACE-CONTROL TO LINE-COUNT.
*
 380-WRITE-PAGE-TOP-LINE.
*
     WRITE PRINT-AREA FROM HEADING-LINE-1
         AFTER ADVANCING PAGE.
     MOVE 1 TO LINE-COUNT.
*
 390-PRINT-ERROR-LINE.
*
     MOVE 2                       TO SPACE-CONTROL.
     MOVE IT-ITEM-NO              TO LEL-ITEM-NO.
     MOVE LOCATION-ERROR-LINE TO PRINT-AREA.
     PERFORM 370-WRITE-REPORT-LINE.
```

Figure 3-20   The report preparation program that uses skip-sequential processing (part 4 of 4)

Topic 3   COBOL for indexed files with alternate indexes

As you'll recall from topic 1, alternate indexes make it possible to access records in an indexed file by a field other than the primary key. In this topic, I'll present the COBOL you need to know to process indexed files using alternate indexes. First, I'll show you what you need to know for any access mode. Then, I'll show you the code for sequential processing followed by the code for random processing.

The SELECT statement

When you use an alternate index to access an indexed file, you must specify the alternate index in the SELECT statement for the file. Figure 3-21 shows the format of the SELECT statement when an alternate index is used. As you can see, you use an ALTERNATE RECORD KEY clause for each alternate key used by a file.

The ALTERNATE RECORD KEY clause specifies the name of an alternate key field for the file. The field specified must be defined in the record description for the file in the File Section of the program along with the primary key.

The WITH DUPLICATES phrase is coded when the keys in the alternate index aren't unique. It simply means that duplicate keys are okay for that index. If this phrase is omitted, it's assumed that the keys are unique.

If a file has more than one alternate index, you can code one ALTERNATE RECORD KEY clause for each of them. However, you don't have to specify all of the alternate keys in every program that uses the file. In general, you only have to specify the alternate keys that your program is going to use. If a program retrieves records from or updates records in a file, you only have to specify the alternate keys that are going to be used for accessing the records. Similarly, if a program creates a file or adds records to it, you only have to specify the alternate keys that you want maintained by the WRITE operations. Often, though, this means that you will specify all of a file's alternate keys so all of the alternate indexes will include the keys for all of the records in the file. More about this in topic 4.

FILE STATUS codes

Before I go on, I'd like to mention one of the FILE STATUS codes that you encounter when processing files with alternate indexes. If you refer back to figure 3-5, you can see that code 02 means that the I/O

```
SELECT file-name

    ASSIGN TO system-name

    ORGANIZATION IS INDEXED

                        (SEQUENTIAL)
    [ACCESS MODE IS     {RANDOM    }    ]
                        (DYNAMIC   )

    RECORD KEY IS data-name-1

    [ALTERNATE RECORD KEY IS data-name-2 [WITH DUPLICATES]] ...

    [FILE STATUS IS data-name-3]
```

Figure 3-21   The SELECT statement for indexed files with alternate keys

operation was completed successfully but a duplicate key was detected. This status only results when WITH DUPLICATES has been specified for the key in question.

In many programs, this status code won't have much effect on your code, assuming that you check FILE STATUS codes at all. To make sure an I/O operation was successful, all you have to do is check for code 02 as well as for code 00. In other programs, though, you may need to take some special action when the 02 status is encountered.

When you issue a WRITE or REWRITE statement, you'll get the 02 status code if a duplicate key is created for any of the alternate keys you named, provided they have been defined WITH DUPLICATES. This is a normal condition, so your program probably doesn't need to take any special action because of it. Note, however, that status code 22 is the result if a WRITE or REWRITE statement tries to write a record with a duplicate key when duplicates aren't allowed. In this case, the I/O operation isn't successful.

When you issue a random READ statement using an alternate key, the record retrieved is the first record written to the file with the key value you specify. If there are additional records with the same alternate key value, you'll get the 02 FILE STATUS code. The only way to retrieve those additional records is by issuing sequential READ statements via dynamic access.

When you issue a sequential READ statement using an alternate key that allows duplicates, the 02 status code is returned if there is at least one more record in the file that has the same alternate key value as the record being read. When you read the last, or only, record that has a particular alternate key value, status code 00 is returned.

To illustrate, suppose a file has three records with alternate key 10001. When the first record is read (either by a random or sequential READ statement), status code 02 is returned because there are more records with the same alternate key. When the second record is read (only by a sequential READ statement), status code 02 is returned again. But when the third record is read, status code 00 is returned because there are no more records in the file with the same alternate key value.

Depending on the application, you may need to test for status code 02 during sequential retrieval using an alternate index. If, for example, you need to retrieve all of the records that have a particular alternate key value, you can issue a START statement to position the file at the first record that has the desired key. I'll show you how to do that in a minute. Then, you can issue sequential READ statements repeatedly until status code 00 is returned. As long as status code 02 is returned, you know there's at least one more record in the file with the desired alternate key value.

Sequential processing

Sequential processing of an indexed file by an alternate key is similar to the processing of an indexed file by its primary key. The only difference is that you must specify the key you want to use before you begin processing. You do this by issuing a START statement.

The START statement   The START statement for alternate indexes has the same format I presented in figure 3-4. Instead of specifying the primary key in the KEY clause, though, you specify the alternate key. For example, to begin processing a file of employee records along an alternate index that represents social security numbers, you can code two statements like these:

```
MOVE ZERO TO PR-SOCIAL-SECURITY-NUMBER.
START EMPMAST
    KEY > PR-SOCIAL-SECURITY-NUMBER
    INVALID KEY
        MOVE 'Y' TO EMPMAST-EOF-SWITCH.
```

Then, the file will be positioned at the record with the first social security number greater than zero, and subsequent READ statements will retrieve the records from the file in alternate key sequence.

A sequential retrieval program   Figure 3-22 presents the program specifications for a program that prints a listing of a file of open item records. As you can see in the program overview, the open item file is indexed by invoice number, and it has one alternate index (customer number) with non-unique keys. Since the records are to be listed in customer number sequence, they must be retrieved by the alternate key. As a result, the file is started along the alternate index and is read sequentially. For each customer open item, a line is printed on the listing. After all the records for a customer have been processed, a customer total line is printed. And after all the records in the file have

---

Program: AR4100   Prepare open item listing   Page: 1

Designer: Anne Prince   Date: 09-03-86

Input/output specifications

File	Description	Use
OPENITM	Open item master file	Input
OILIST	Print file: Open item listing	Output

Process specifications

This program prints a listing of all records in the open item master file (OPENITM). This file's primary index is invoice number. However, the listing is to be printed in customer number sequence, so the file must be accessed sequentially by its non-unique alternate key, customer number.

Totals should be printed for each customer. At the end of the listing, grand totals should be printed.

The basic processing requirements follow:

Start the open item file along the alternate key, customer number.

For each record in the file:

1. Read an open item record.

2. Print a report line on the listing.

3. Accumulate the customer and grand totals.

4. If the record is the last one for a customer,
        print a customer total line.

Print a grand total line.

Figure 3-22   The program specifications for a sequential retrieval program that uses non-unique alternate keys (part 1 of 2)

The record layout for the open item record

```
01   OPEN-ITEM-RECORD.
*
     05   OI-INVOICE-NUMBER          PIC X(6).
     05   OI-INVOICE-DATE            PIC X(6).
     05   OI-CUSTOMER-NUMBER         PIC X(6).
     05   OI-INVOICE-AMOUNTS.
          10   OI-PRODUCT-TOTAL      PIC S9(5)V99.
          10   OI-SALES-TAX          PIC S9(5)V99.
          10   OI-FREIGHT            PIC S9(5)V99.
          10   OI-INVOICE-TOTAL      PIC S9(5)V99.
     05   OI-PAYMENT-CREDIT-DATA.
          10   OI-SUM-OF-PAYMENTS     PIC S9(5)V99.
          10   OI-SUM-OF-CREDITS      PIC S9(5)V99.
          10   OI-BALANCE-DUE         PIC S9(5)V99.
     05   FILLER                     PIC X(13).
```

The print chart for the open item listing

Figure 3-22   The program specifications for a sequential retrieval program that uses non-unique alternate keys (part 2 of 2)

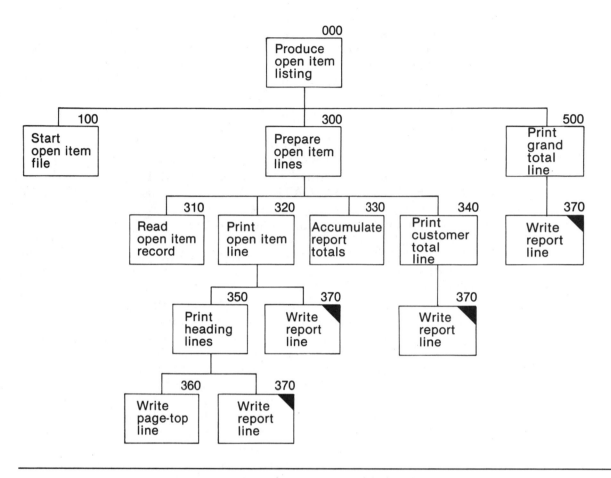

Figure 3-23   The structure chart for the sequential retrieval program that uses non-unique alternate keys

been processed, a grand total line is printed.

Figure 3-23 presents the structure chart for this program, and figure 3-24 shows the program listing. In the SELECT statement, I have coded an ALTERNATE RECORD KEY clause to define the alternate key, OI-CUSTOMER-NUMBER. Notice that this field is also defined in the record description for the file in the File Section. Because there can be more than one open item for the same customer number, I have coded the WITH DUPLICATES phrase for this key. I've also specified a FILE STATUS field that I'll use for processing the file. You'll see how that works in a minute.

Now take a look at the Procedure Division. To start the open item file along the alternate index, I moved LOW-VALUE to the key field and then issued the START statement in module 100. Because I specified the alternate key in the KEY clause, this START statement positions the file at the first record in the alternate index. Then, subsequent READ statements will retrieve the records in alternate key sequence.

Next, look at the definition of the FILE STATUS field for the open item file in working storage. It is named OPENITM-FILE-STATUS. Here, I defined two 88 conditions: LAST-CUSTOMER-INVOICE and DUPLICATE-KEY. These conditions will be turned on and off as the I/O operations for this file are performed during the execution of the program. When the file status code is 00, LAST-CUSTOMER-INVOICE will be turned on. When the code is 02, DUPLICATE-KEY will be turned on. (Although I don't use the DUPLICATE-KEY condition in the program, I thought it helped clarify what I was testing for.)

The LAST-CUSTOMER-INVOICE condition is used in module 300 to determine when the total line for a customer should be printed. As I described earlier, code 02 is returned to the program after a READ statement if there are more records with the same key. In this case, LAST-CUSTOMER-INVOICE is turned off, so the program doesn't print a customer total line. However, when there aren't any more records for the customer, LAST-CUSTOMER-INVOICE is turned on so module 300 prints a total line for the customer.

Although this program could have been written without using the FILE STATUS field, I wanted to illustrate how it can be used to control processing. If you use FILE STATUS codes in your shop, you'll probably want to code your programs using this method. If you don't normally use FILE STATUS codes, you'll probably code a program like this using traditional report preparation logic. Without the use of the FILE STATUS codes, the program must read the first record for the next customer in order to determine that there aren't any more records for the last customer. As a result, the program requires the use of a control field and more complex code in the module that controls the report printing (module 300 in figure 3-24).

```
 IDENTIFICATION DIVISION.
*
 PROGRAM-ID.  AR4100.
*
 ENVIRONMENT DIVISION.
*
 INPUT-OUTPUT SECTION.
*
 FILE-CONTROL.
     SELECT OPENITM   ASSIGN TO SYS020-OPENITM
                      ORGANIZATION IS INDEXED
                      ACCESS IS SEQUENTIAL
                      RECORD KEY IS OI-INVOICE-NUMBER
                      ALTERNATE RECORD KEY IS OI-CUSTOMER-NUMBER
                          WITH DUPLICATES
                      FILE STATUS IS OPENITM-FILE-STATUS.
     SELECT OILIST    ASSIGN TO SYS006-UR-1403-S.
*
 DATA DIVISION.
*
 FILE SECTION.
*
 FD  OPENITM
     LABEL RECORDS ARE STANDARD
     RECORD CONTAINS 80 CHARACTERS.
*
 01  OPEN-ITEM-RECORD.
*
     05  OI-INVOICE-NUMBER          PIC X(6).
     05  OI-INVOICE-DATE            PIC X(6).
     05  OI-CUSTOMER-NUMBER         PIC X(6).
     05  OI-INVOICE-AMOUNTS.
         10  OI-PRODUCT-TOTAL       PIC S9(5)V99.
         10  OI-SALES-TAX           PIC S9(5)V99.
         10  OI-FREIGHT             PIC S9(5)V99.
         10  OI-INVOICE-TOTAL       PIC S9(5)V99.
     05  OI-PAYMENT-CREDIT-DATA.
         10  OI-SUM-OF-PAYMENTS     PIC S9(5)V99.
         10  OI-SUM-OF-CREDITS      PIC S9(5)V99.
         10  OI-BALANCE-DUE         PIC S9(5)V99.
     05  FILLER                     PIC X(13).
*
 FD  OILIST
     LABEL RECORDS ARE OMITTED
     RECORD CONTAINS 132 CHARACTERS.
*
 01  PRINT-AREA           PIC X(132).
*
 WORKING-STORAGE SECTION.
*
 01  SWITCHES.
*
     05  OPENITM-EOF-SWITCH         PIC X      VALUE 'N'.
         88  OPENITM-EOF                       VALUE 'Y'.
     05  NEW-CUSTOMER-SWITCH        PIC X      VALUE 'Y'.
```

Figure 3-24   The sequential retrieval program that uses non-unique alternate keys (part 1 of 5)

```
          88   NEW-CUSTOMER                              VALUE 'Y'.
*
 01   FILE-STATUS-FIELDS.
*
      05   OPENITM-FILE-STATUS        PIC XX.
           88   LAST-CUSTOMER-INVOICE                 VALUE '00'.
           88   DUPLICATE-KEY                         VALUE '02'.
*
 01   PRINT-FIELDS               COMP-3.
*
      05   SPACE-CONTROL              PIC S9.
      05   LINE-COUNT                 PIC S9(3)     VALUE +99.
      05   LINES-ON-PAGE             PIC S9(3)     VALUE +55.
*
 01   TOTAL-FIELDS              COMP-3.
*
      05   CUSTOMER-INVOICE-TOTAL    PIC S9(7)V99   VALUE ZERO.
      05   CUSTOMER-PAYMENTS         PIC S9(7)V99   VALUE ZERO.
      05   CUSTOMER-CREDITS          PIC S9(7)V99   VALUE ZERO.
      05   CUSTOMER-BALANCE-DUE      PIC S9(7)V99   VALUE ZERO.
      05   TOTAL-INVOICE-TOTAL       PIC S9(7)V99   VALUE ZERO.
      05   TOTAL-PAYMENTS            PIC S9(7)V99   VALUE ZERO.
      05   TOTAL-CREDITS             PIC S9(7)V99   VALUE ZERO.
      05   TOTAL-BALANCE-DUE         PIC S9(7)V99   VALUE ZERO.
*
 01   HEADING-LINE-1.
*
      05   FILLER   PIC X(20)   VALUE 'OPEN ITEM LISTING'.
      05   FILLER   PIC X(112) VALUE SPACE.
*
 01   HEADING-LINE-2.
*
      05   FILLER        PIC X(20)   VALUE 'CUSTOMER   INVOICE  '.
      05   FILLER        PIC X(20)   VALUE '           INVOICE  '.
      05   FILLER        PIC X(20)   VALUE '                    '.
      05   FILLER        PIC X(20)   VALUE '           BALANC'.
      05   FILLER        PIC X(20)   VALUE 'E                   '.
      05   FILLER        PIC X(32)   VALUE SPACE.
*
 01   HEADING-LINE-3.
*
      05   FILLER        PIC X(20)   VALUE ' NUMBER    NUMBER   '.
      05   FILLER        PIC X(20)   VALUE '               TOTAL '.
      05   FILLER        PIC X(20)   VALUE '       PAYMENTS     '.
      05   FILLER        PIC X(20)   VALUE 'CREDITS          DU'.
      05   FILLER        PIC X(20)   VALUE 'E                   '.
      05   FILLER        PIC X(32)   VALUE SPACE.
*
 01   INVOICE-LINE.
*
      05   FILLER                    PIC X         VALUE SPACE.
      05   IL-CUSTOMER-NUMBER        PIC X(6).
      05   FILLER                    PIC X(3)      VALUE SPACE.
      05   IL-INVOICE-NUMBER         PIC X(6).
      05   FILLER                    PIC X(14)     VALUE SPACE.
      05   IL-INVOICE-TOTAL          PIC ZZ,ZZ9.99-.
```

Figure 3-24   The sequential retrieval program that uses non-unique alternate keys (part 2 of 5)

```
      05   FILLER                      PIC X(4)      VALUE SPACE.
      05   IL-PAYMENTS                 PIC ZZ,ZZ9.99-.
      05   FILLER                      PIC X(4)      VALUE SPACE.
      05   IL-CREDITS                  PIC ZZ,ZZ9.99-.
      05   FILLER                      PIC X(4)      VALUE SPACE.
      05   IL-BALANCE-DUE              PIC ZZ,ZZ9.99-.
      05   FILLER                      PIC X(50)     VALUE SPACE.
 *
  01   CUSTOMER-TOTAL-LINE.
 *
      05   FILLER                 PIC X(10)    VALUE SPACE.
      05   FILLER                 PIC X(19)
                                  VALUE 'CUSTOMER TOTALS:'.
      05   CTL-INVOICE-TOTAL      PIC ZZZ,ZZ9.99-.
      05   FILLER                 PIC X(3)     VALUE SPACE.
      05   CTL-PAYMENTS           PIC ZZZ,ZZ9.99-.
      05   FILLER                 PIC X(3)     VALUE SPACE.
      05   CTL-CREDITS            PIC ZZZ,ZZ9.99-.
      05   FILLER                 PIC X(3)     VALUE SPACE.
      05   CTL-BALANCE-DUE        PIC ZZZ,ZZ9.99-.
      05   FILLER                 PIC X(50)    VALUE SPACE.
 *
  01   GRAND-TOTAL-LINE.
 *
      05   FILLER                 PIC X(13)    VALUE SPACE.
      05   FILLER                 PIC X(14)    VALUE 'GRAND TOTALS:'.
      05   GTL-INVOICE-TOTAL      PIC Z,ZZZ,ZZ9.99-.
      05   FILLER                 PIC X        VALUE SPACE.
      05   GTL-PAYMENTS           PIC Z,ZZZ,ZZ9.99-.
      05   FILLER                 PIC X        VALUE SPACE.
      05   GTL-CREDITS            PIC Z,ZZZ,ZZ9.99-.
      05   FILLER                 PIC X        VALUE SPACE.
      05   GTL-BALANCE-DUE        PIC Z,ZZZ,ZZ9.99-.
      05   FILLER                 PIC X(50)    VALUE SPACE.
 *
  PROCEDURE DIVISION.
 *
  000-PRODUCE-OPEN-ITEM-LISTING.
 *
      OPEN INPUT   OPENITM
           OUTPUT OILIST.
      PERFORM 100-START-OPEN-ITEM-FILE.
      IF NOT OPENITM-EOF
          PERFORM 300-PREPARE-OPEN-ITEM-LINES
              UNTIL OPENITM-EOF
          PERFORM 500-PRINT-GRAND-TOTAL-LINE.
      CLOSE OPENITM
            OILIST.
      DISPLAY 'AR4100  I  1  NORMAL EOJ'.
      STOP RUN.
```

Figure 3-24   The sequential retrieval program that uses non-unique alternate keys (part 3 of 5)

```
*
 100-START-OPEN-ITEM-FILE.
*
     MOVE LOW-VALUE TO OI-CUSTOMER-NUMBER.
     START OPENITM
         KEY IS NOT < OI-CUSTOMER-NUMBER
         INVALID KEY
             MOVE 'Y' TO OPENITM-EOF-SWITCH.
*
 300-PREPARE-OPEN-ITEM-LINES.
*
     PERFORM 310-READ-OPEN-ITEM-RECORD.
     IF NOT OPENITM-EOF
         PERFORM 320-PRINT-OPEN-ITEM-LINE
         PERFORM 330-ACCUMULATE-REPORT-TOTALS
         IF LAST-CUSTOMER-INVOICE
             PERFORM 340-PRINT-CUSTOMER-TOTAL-LINE
             MOVE 'Y' TO NEW-CUSTOMER-SWITCH.
*
 310-READ-OPEN-ITEM-RECORD.
*
     READ OPENITM
         AT END
             MOVE 'Y' TO OPENITM-EOF-SWITCH.
*
 320-PRINT-OPEN-ITEM-LINE.
*
     IF LINE-COUNT > LINES-ON-PAGE
         PERFORM 350-PRINT-HEADING-LINES.
     IF NEW-CUSTOMER
         MOVE OI-CUSTOMER-NUMBER TO IL-CUSTOMER-NUMBER
         MOVE 'N' TO NEW-CUSTOMER-SWITCH
     ELSE
         MOVE SPACE TO IL-CUSTOMER-NUMBER.
     MOVE OI-INVOICE-NUMBER  TO IL-INVOICE-NUMBER.
     MOVE OI-INVOICE-TOTAL    TO IL-INVOICE-TOTAL.
     MOVE OI-SUM-OF-PAYMENTS TO IL-PAYMENTS.
     MOVE OI-SUM-OF-CREDITS   TO IL-CREDITS.
     MOVE OI-BALANCE-DUE       TO IL-BALANCE-DUE.
     MOVE INVOICE-LINE         TO PRINT-AREA.
     PERFORM 370-WRITE-REPORT-LINE.
     MOVE 1 TO SPACE-CONTROL.
*
 330-ACCUMULATE-REPORT-TOTALS.
*
     ADD OI-INVOICE-TOTAL     TO CUSTOMER-INVOICE-TOTAL
                                 TOTAL-INVOICE-TOTAL.
     ADD OI-SUM-OF-PAYMENTS TO CUSTOMER-PAYMENTS
                                 TOTAL-PAYMENTS.
     ADD OI-SUM-OF-CREDITS   TO CUSTOMER-CREDITS
                                 TOTAL-CREDITS.
     ADD OI-BALANCE-DUE       TO CUSTOMER-BALANCE-DUE
                                 TOTAL-BALANCE-DUE.
*
```

Figure 3-24   The sequential retrieval program that uses non-unique alternate keys (part 4 of 5)

```
 340-PRINT-CUSTOMER-TOTAL-LINE.
*
      MOVE CUSTOMER-INVOICE-TOTAL  TO CTL-INVOICE-TOTAL.
      MOVE CUSTOMER-PAYMENTS       TO CTL-PAYMENTS.
      MOVE CUSTOMER-CREDITS        TO CTL-CREDITS.
      MOVE CUSTOMER-BALANCE-DUE    TO CTL-BALANCE-DUE.
      MOVE CUSTOMER-TOTAL-LINE     TO PRINT-AREA.
      MOVE 2 TO SPACE-CONTROL.
      PERFORM 370-WRITE-REPORT-LINE.
      MOVE ZERO TO CUSTOMER-INVOICE-TOTAL
                   CUSTOMER-PAYMENTS
                   CUSTOMER-CREDITS
                   CUSTOMER-BALANCE-DUE.
*
 350-PRINT-HEADING-LINES.
*
      MOVE HEADING-LINE-1 TO PRINT-AREA.
      PERFORM 360-WRITE-PAGE-TOP-LINE.
      MOVE HEADING-LINE-2 TO PRINT-AREA.
      MOVE 2 TO SPACE-CONTROL.
      PERFORM 370-WRITE-REPORT-LINE.
      MOVE HEADING-LINE-3 TO PRINT-AREA.
      MOVE 1 TO SPACE-CONTROL.
      PERFORM 370-WRITE-REPORT-LINE.
      MOVE 2 TO SPACE-CONTROL.
*
 360-WRITE-PAGE-TOP-LINE.
*
      WRITE PRINT-AREA AFTER ADVANCING PAGE.
      MOVE 1 TO LINE-COUNT.
*
 370-WRITE-REPORT-LINE.
*
      WRITE PRINT-AREA AFTER ADVANCING SPACE-CONTROL LINES.
      ADD SPACE-CONTROL TO LINE-COUNT.
*
 500-PRINT-GRAND-TOTAL-LINE.
*
      MOVE TOTAL-INVOICE-TOTAL TO GTL-INVOICE-TOTAL.
      MOVE TOTAL-PAYMENTS       TO GTL-PAYMENTS.
      MOVE TOTAL-CREDITS        TO GTL-CREDITS.
      MOVE TOTAL-BALANCE-DUE    TO GTL-BALANCE-DUE.
      MOVE GRAND-TOTAL-LINE     TO PRINT-AREA.
      MOVE 3 TO SPACE-CONTROL.
      PERFORM 370-WRITE-REPORT-LINE.
```

Figure 3-24   The sequential retrieval program that uses non-unique alternate keys (part 5 of 5)

Random processing

There are two things you need to be aware of when you process an indexed file randomly using an alternate key. First, each time you retrieve a record you must specify what key is to be used. Second, unlike a primary key, you *can* change the value of an alternate key.

The READ statement   To specify the key to be used for retrieving a record randomly, you code the KEY clause on the READ statement. Figure 3-25 shows the format of the READ statement that you use for this type of processing. As you can see, all you need to do is code the name of the field to be used as the key in the KEY clause. If this clause is omitted, the primary key is used as a default.

The REWRITE statement   If you want to change the primary key of a record in an indexed file, you have to delete the existing record and write a new record with the new key. In contrast, you can change the alternate key of a record by simply rewriting the record with the new key. Although you probably won't need to change an alternate key very often, it's good to know that you can do it if you need to.

A random update program   Figure 3-26 presents the program overview for a random update program. Its structure and logic are like the structure and logic of the random update program presented in the last topic: a transaction record is read and the associated master record is read and updated. The only difference is that this program retrieves records by an alternate key.

The master file used in this program is a file of employee records. The file is indexed by employee number, and it has two alternate keys: social security number and employee last name. The transactions used to update the master records don't contain the employee number, so the social security number must be used to access the records.

Figure 3-27 presents the code for this program. In the SELECT statement, you can see how I coded the ALTERNATE RECORD KEY clause. Since the alternate key is unique, I didn't code the WITH DUPLICATES phrase. Because the program doesn't require the use of the second alternate key (last name), I didn't specify it in the SELECT statement.

In the READ statement for the master file, I coded the KEY clause so the social security number field will be used as the key. When the READ statement is executed, it will try to read the record with the social security number that is stored in the key field. If that record can't be found, the INVALID KEY clause will be executed.

```
READ file-name RECORD

    [INTO identifier]

    [KEY IS data-name]

    [INVALID KEY imperative-statement]
```

Figure 3-25   The READ statement for random processing of indexed files with alternate keys

Discussion

There are both advantages and disadvantages to using alternate indexes. One advantage is that they make it possible to retrieve records from a file in more than one sequence without having to sort the file. Since sorting a large file is time consuming, using alternate indexes can improve the efficiency of a system. Another advantage is that alternate keys allow records to be retrieved from a file on a random basis using more than one key, which can be extremely useful in an interactive program. The main disadvantage of alternate keys is that it takes additional time to maintain these indexes as a file is processed, so the overall efficiency of a system may be reduced.

When you use alternate keys, you can design data structures that are quite complex. And using dynamic access, you can retrieve records from these structures in a wide variety of ways. Both of these facilities, though, are more useful in an interactive system than they are in a batch system. To what extent you'll use them in COBOL will depend upon your computer system and your shop.

Terminology

None

Objective

Given program specifications for a program that processes indexed files with alternate indexes, develop a COBOL program that satisfies the specifications.

Program: PR1100 Update employee master file	Page: 1
Designer: **Anne Prince**	Date: 09-03-86

Input/output specifications

File	Description	Use
EMPTRAN	**Employee transaction file**	Input
EMPMAST	**Employee master file**	Update
ERRTRAN	**Error transaction file**	Output

Process specifications

This program maintains the employee master file (EMPMAST) based on data in a file of valid employee transactions (EMPTRAN). The primary key of the master file is employee number. The file has two alternate keys: (1) social security number, which is a unique key; and (2) employee last name, which is a non-unique key.

Since the transaction file doesn't contain the employee number, the master file is accessed using an alternate key, social security number. If a master record with the same social security number as the transaction isn't found, a transaction is written in the error file. If a master record is found, the transaction data is used to update the master record: If a field in the transaction record is non-blank, the value in the field is moved to the corresponding field in the master record.

The basic processing requirements follow:

1. Read a transaction record.

2. Read the related master record.

3. If the master record is found,
        update the master record.

4. If the master record isn't found,
        write a record on the file of error transactions.

Figure 3-26   The program overview for a random update program that uses unique alternate keys

```
 IDENTIFICATION DIVISION.
*
 PROGRAM-ID.   PR1100.
*
 ENVIRONMENT DIVISION.
*
 INPUT-OUTPUT SECTION.
*
 FILE-CONTROL.
      SELECT EMPTRAN    ASSIGN TO SYS020-AS-EMPTRAN.
      SELECT EMPMAST    ASSIGN TO SYS021-EMPMAST
                        ORGANIZATION IS INDEXED
                        ACCESS IS RANDOM
                        RECORD KEY IS MR-EMPLOYEE-NUMBER
                        ALTERNATE RECORD KEY
                            IS MR-SOCIAL-SECURITY-NUMBER.
      SELECT ERRTRAN    ASSIGN TO SYS022-AS-ERRTRAN.
*
 DATA DIVISION.
*
 FILE SECTION.
*
 FD   EMPTRAN
      LABEL RECORDS ARE STANDARD
      RECORD CONTAINS 98 CHARACTERS.
*
 01   TRANSACTION-AREA    PIC X(98).
*
 FD   EMPMAST
      LABEL RECORDS ARE STANDARD
      RECORD CONTAINS 103 CHARACTERS.
*
 01   MASTER-RECORD-AREA.
*
      05   MR-EMPLOYEE-NUMBER        PIC X(5).
      05   FILLER                    PIC X(31).
      05   MR-SOCIAL-SECURITY-NUMBER PIC X(9).
      05   FILLER                    PIC X(58).
*
 FD   ERRTRAN
      LABEL RECORDS ARE STANDARD
      RECORD CONTAINS 98 CHARACTERS.
*
 01   ERROR-TRANSACTION       PIC X(98).
*
 WORKING-STORAGE SECTION.
*
 01   SWITCHES.
*
      05   EMPTRAN-EOF-SWITCH    PIC X    VALUE 'N'.
           88   EMPTRAN-EOF               VALUE 'Y'.
      05   MASTER-FOUND-SWITCH   PIC X.
           88   MASTER-FOUND              VALUE 'Y'.
*
 01   EMPLOYEE-MAINTENANCE-TRAN.
```

Figure 3-27   The random update program that uses unique alternate keys (part 1 of 3)

```
*
      05   EMT-SOCIAL-SECURITY-NUMBER      PIC X(9).
      05   EMT-EMPLOYEE-NAME.
           10   EMT-FIRST-NAME             PIC X(10).
           10   EMT-INITIAL                PIC X.
           10   EMT-LAST-NAME              PIC X(20).
      05   EMT-ADDRESS                     PIC X(30).
      05   EMT-CITY                        PIC X(21).
      05   EMT-STATE                       PIC XX.
      05   EMT-ZIP-CODE                    PIC X(5).
*
  01  EMPLOYEE-MASTER-RECORD.
*
      05   EMR-EMPLOYEE-NUMBER             PIC X(5).
      05   EMR-EMPLOYEE-NAME.
           10   EMR-FIRST-NAME             PIC X(10).
           10   EMR-INITIAL                PIC X.
           10   EMR-LAST-NAME              PIC X(20).
      05   EMR-SOCIAL-SECURITY-NUMBER      PIC X(9).
      05   EMR-ADDRESS                     PIC X(30).
      05   EMR-CITY                        PIC X(21).
      05   EMR-STATE                       PIC XX.
      05   EMR-ZIP-CODE                    PIC X(5).
*
  PROCEDURE DIVISION.
*
  000-UPDATE-EMPLOYEE-FILE.
*
      OPEN INPUT   EMPTRAN
           I-O     EMPMAST
           OUTPUT ERRTRAN.
      PERFORM 300-PROCESS-EMPLOYEE-TRAN
          UNTIL EMPTRAN-EOF.
      CLOSE EMPTRAN
            EMPMAST
            ERRTRAN.
      DISPLAY 'PR1100  I  1  NORMAL EOJ'.
      STOP RUN.
*
  300-PROCESS-EMPLOYEE-TRAN.
*
      PERFORM 310-READ-EMPLOYEE-TRAN.
      IF NOT EMPTRAN-EOF
          PERFORM 320-READ-EMPLOYEE-MASTER
          IF MASTER-FOUND
              PERFORM 330-UPDATE-EMPLOYEE-MASTER
              PERFORM 340-REWRITE-EMPLOYEE-MASTER
          ELSE
              PERFORM 350-WRITE-ERROR-TRAN.
*
  310-READ-EMPLOYEE-TRAN.
*
      READ EMPTRAN INTO EMPLOYEE-MAINTENANCE-TRAN
          AT END
              MOVE 'Y' TO EMPTRAN-EOF-SWITCH.
*
```

Figure 3-27   The random update program that uses unique alternate keys (part 2 of 3)

```
 320-READ-EMPLOYEE-MASTER.
*
     MOVE EMT-SOCIAL-SECURITY-NUMBER
         TO MR-SOCIAL-SECURITY-NUMBER.
     MOVE 'Y' TO MASTER-FOUND-SWITCH.
     READ EMPMAST INTO EMPLOYEE-MASTER-RECORD
         KEY IS MR-SOCIAL-SECURITY-NUMBER
         INVALID KEY
             MOVE 'N' TO MASTER-FOUND-SWITCH.
*
 330-UPDATE-EMPLOYEE-MASTER.
*
     IF EMT-FIRST-NAME NOT EQUAL SPACE
         MOVE EMT-FIRST-NAME TO EMR-FIRST-NAME.
     IF EMT-INITIAL NOT EQUAL SPACE
         MOVE EMT-INITIAL TO EMR-INITIAL.
     IF EMT-LAST-NAME NOT EQUAL SPACE
         MOVE EMT-LAST-NAME TO EMR-LAST-NAME.
     IF EMT-ADDRESS NOT EQUAL SPACE
         MOVE EMT-ADDRESS TO EMR-ADDRESS.
     IF EMT-CITY NOT EQUAL SPACE
         MOVE EMT-CITY TO EMR-CITY.
     IF EMT-STATE NOT EQUAL SPACE
         MOVE EMT-STATE TO EMR-STATE.
     IF EMT-ZIP-CODE NOT EQUAL SPACE
         MOVE EMT-ZIP-CODE TO EMR-ZIP-CODE.
*
 340-REWRITE-EMPLOYEE-MASTER.
*
     REWRITE MASTER-RECORD-AREA FROM EMPLOYEE-MASTER-RECORD
         INVALID KEY
             DISPLAY 'PR1100  A  2  REWRITE ERROR FOR EMPMAST'
             DISPLAY 'PR1100  A  2  SOC SEC NUMBER = '
                 MR-SOCIAL-SECURITY-NUMBER
             MOVE 'Y' TO EMPTRAN-EOF-SWITCH.
*
 350-WRITE-ERROR-TRAN.
*
     WRITE ERROR-TRANSACTION FROM EMPLOYEE-MAINTENANCE-TRAN.
```

Figure 3-27   The random update program that uses unique alternate keys (part 3 of 3)

Topic 4   Compiler dependent code

With only a couple of changes, the programs presented in topic 2 of this chapter will run on any system that uses 1974 or 1985 ANS COBOL. In general, you have to change the system names so they are acceptable to your compiler. You have to change the single quotation marks to double marks if they are required by your compiler. And you have to change COMP-3 usage to COMP usage if COMP is appropriate for your compiler.

The programs presented in topic 3, however, will only run on compilers that support alternate indexes. And, even if your compiler does support alternate indexes, there may be some differences in the way they're handled. As a result, you should check the COBOL manuals for your compiler to find out whether it puts any limitations on your use of alternate indexes and whether the code for using them is standard.

In this topic, I'll introduce you to some typical system names for indexed files. And I'll present some compiler dependent code related to alternate indexes.

System names in SELECT statements

If you haven't used indexed files before, you'll need to find out how to code system names for them on your system. In general, their formats are similar to those for sequential files. Figure 3-28 presents the system names for disk files when you're using Microsoft COBOL, Wang VS COBOL, IBM VS COBOL, or IBM VS COBOL II.

Code for alternate indexes

As I've mentioned, the code for processing alternate indexes on the compiler you're using may be different than that given in the 1974 or 1985 COBOL standards. Some compilers may provide additional flexibility; some may restrict the ways in which files with alternate indexes can be processed. So, be sure to check the COBOL manuals for your compiler to see what your compiler provides.

For example, on the Wang VS compiler, you have to code a number after ALTERNATE RECORD KEY in the SELECT statement to indicate which key is being used. Also, in the START statement, you code the name of the alternate key field right after the word KEY and before the relational operator. Finally, all of the records in a file don't have to be indexed in an alternate index for the file. If, for example, a file consists of two different types of records, one set of records can be indexed by an alternate index, even though

Microsoft COBOL

> Format: "D I S K"
>
> Example: "D I S K"

Wang VS COBOL

> Format: "p a r a m e t e r – r e f e r e n c e – n a m e" "D I S K"
>
> Example: "I N V M A S T" "D I S K"

Note: The *parameter-reference-name* must be eight or fewer letters or digits, starting with a letter. For consistency, this can be the same name as the file name.

IBM VS COBOL on a DOS/VSE system

> Format: S Y S n n n – n a m e
>
> Example: S Y S 0 2 0 – I N V M A S T

Notes: 1. The SYS number is a number between SYS000 and SYS240 that is used to identify a specific I/O device. Find out what numbers you should use on your system.

2. The *name* consists of from three to seven letters or digits, starting with a letter. For consistency, this can be the same name as the file name. This name is used to relate the file description in the program with a file on a disk.

IBM VS COBOL or COBOL II on an OS/MVS system

> Format: [c o m m e n t s –] d d n a m e
>
> Example: I N V M A S T

Note: The *ddname* is made up of eight or fewer letters or digits, starting with a letter. For consistency, this name can be the same as the file name. This name is used to relate the file description in the program with a file on an I/O device outside of the program.

Figure 3-28   The formats of system names for indexed disk files on some common compilers

the other set of records isn't contained in the index. To do this, you use special coding in the ALTERNATE RECORD KEY clause that associates a key with specific record descriptions.

Beyond this, the requirements for the use of the ALTERNATE RECORD KEY clause may vary from one system to another. On some systems, for example, you may have to specify this clause for all of the alternate keys when you develop a program that creates or adds records to a file. On other systems, you can use utilities to keep alternate indexes up to date, so you don't have to specify all of the indexes in your COBOL programs. If, for example, you omit an alternate index from a program that adds records to a file, the new keys won't be added to the alternate index, but this can be done by a utility program later on. Because of these variations, you should find out what's expected of you in your shop.

Using alternate indexes on IBM mainframes   On an IBM mainframe, only VSAM files support alternate indexes. To create a VSAM indexed file with alternate keys, you must perform three steps. First, you define the file, its indexes, and its access paths using the DEFINE functions of the Access Method Services program (AMS). Second, you run a COBOL file creation program to create the file and build its primary index. Third, you run the BLDINDEX function of the AMS utility to create (or build) the alternate indexes required by the file.

When you update or maintain a VSAM indexed file using a COBOL program, the program may or may not update all of the alternate indexes. It depends on how you defined the alternate indexes using AMS. If a COBOL program doesn't update an alternate index, you can run the BLDINDEX function later on to bring the index up-to-date. In fact, whether or not an index is kept up-to-date by the COBOL programs that process the file, you should run the BLDINDEX function periodically to reorganize the index—especially if it allows duplicate keys.

In summary, you can't do an adequate job of writing COBOL programs for files with alternate indexes unless you know how VSAM works and how the VSAM files have been defined. If you would like to know more about VSAM, we recommend a book called *VSAM: Access Method Services and Application Programming* by Doug Lowe.

Discussion

All I/O operations are dependent to some extent on the system and compiler you're using. As a result, it's your job to find out what the requirements of your system are. In particular, find out whether your compiler handles alternate indexes using standard COBOL.

Terminology

None

Objective

Find out how to use the compiler dependent code for indexed files on your system.

Chapter 4

Relative file handling

Because relative files are used infrequently, it's possible that you won't ever use them. On the other hand, relative files can be useful in some applications, so you should at least know what they are. In this chapter, topic 1 presents the concepts you should know for relative file handling. Topic 2 presents the COBOL for relative file handling. And topic 3 presents compiler dependent code for relative file handling.

Topic 1   Relative file handling concepts

Like a record in a file with indexed organization, a record in a relative file can be accessed both sequentially and randomly. However, unlike a file with indexed organization, a file with relative organization doesn't have an index. Instead, relative organization depends on a direct relationship between the data in each record and its relative position in the file.

Relative file organization

A *relative file* consists of a specified number of areas, each of which can contain one record. Each of these areas is identified by a *relative record number* that indicates its relative position in the file. For example, the record in the first area in a relative file is identified by relative record number 1 and the record in the tenth area in the file is identified by relative record number 10, whether or not areas 2 through 9 contain records. Records in the file can then be accessed using these relative record numbers. This is referred to as *relative file organization*.

Figure 4-1 illustrates a relative file. Within each record are fields for social security number, name, and employee number. However, the records aren't accessed based on the data in these fields. Instead, the records are accessed by relative record number, which is *not* a field stored in the record.

Accessing records in a relative file

When relative files are processed sequentially, areas that don't contain records are automatically skipped. As a result, sequential processing of a relative file is similar to sequential processing of a sequential file. The program accesses the records in sequence starting with the first record in the file and continuing until the last record has been read.

When processed randomly, the relative record numbers are used to locate specific records. For instance, to locate the employee record for COLLINS in figure 4-1, the program needs to know that the relative record number is 4. Often, though, the main problem in using relative files is determining what the relative record number for a record should be. That's where the relationship between the data in the records and the relative record number comes in.

In the simplest case, a field in the file can be used as the relative record number. This is illustrated by the file in figure 4-1. As you can see, each record in this file is directly related to its position in the file

Relative record number	Social security number	First name	Middle initial	Last name	Employee number
1	499-35-5079	Stanley	L	Abbott	00001
2	279-00-1210	William	J	Colline	00002
3	899-16-9235	Alice		Crawford	00003
4	703-47-5748	Paul	M	Collins	00004
5	558-12-6168	Marie	A	Littlejohn	00005
6	559-35-2479	E	R	Siebart	00006
7	334-96-8721	Constance	M	Harris	00007
8	213-64-9290	Thomas	T	Bluestone	00008
9	572-68-3100	Jean	B	Glenning	00009
10	498-27-6117	Ronald	W	Westbrook	00010

Figure 4-1   An employee file with relative organization

by the employee number: employee number 1 has relative record number 1; employee number 2 has relative record number 2; and so on.

In other cases, however, this relationship isn't so apparent. For example, suppose the employee numbers in figure 4-1 started with 10001. Then, you could derive the relative record number by subtracting 10000 from the employee number. But what if the employee numbers range from 10001 to 90000 and there are only 2000 employees in the file? Since you wouldn't want to have 78,000 empty record areas in the file, you would have to use a more sophisticated method to convert each employee number to a relative record number.

A routine that converts a field in a record to a relative record number is sometimes called a *randomizing routine*. Its purpose is to convert a field like employee number to a relative record number that falls between one and the number of areas allocated to the file. The problem is that it's difficult to come up with a randomizing routine that will convert the field in each record to a relative record number without encountering some *duplicates*. Duplicates are two or more records that are randomized to the same relative record number. When a duplicate is encountered, the file creation program must provide a routine that puts it in an unfilled record area. And a related routine must be used in every program that accesses the file randomly. In brief, the process of handling duplicates can get quite complicated.

Discussion

Because of the difficulty involved with randomizing routines, relative files aren't used very much. Instead, indexed files are used since the programmer doesn't have to worry about where each record is stored in the file. However, there are programs in which the use of relative files is appropriate. In general, relative files are most practical when there is a simple relationship between one of the fields in each record and the relative record number of the record.

Terminology

relative file
relative record number
relative file organization
randomizing routine
duplicate

Objective

Explain how the records in a relative file are accessed on both a sequential and a random basis.

Topic 2   COBOL for relative files

In this topic, I'll present the COBOL you need to know for relative files. First, I'll show you the code for sequential processing. Then, I'll show you the code for random processing.

SEQUENTIAL PROCESSING

Figure 4-2 summarizes the COBOL code you use when you write programs that process relative files sequentially. If you've read the chapter on indexed files, most of the statements should look familiar to you. However, since you aren't required to read the chapter on indexed files before you read this chapter, I won't assume you've read it. As a result, some of the information in the indexed chapter has been duplicated in this chapter.

The SELECT statement

When you code the SELECT statement for a relative file, you have to indicate that the file is relative. You do this by coding the ORGANIZATION clause like this:

```
ORGANIZATION IS RELATIVE
```

If you don't code this clause, the compiler will assume the file is sequential.

When you process a relative file sequentially, you should code the ACCESS MODE clause like this:

```
ACCESS MODE IS SEQUENTIAL
```

Although sequential processing is assumed when this clause is omitted, it's a good idea to include it because it helps document the program.

If you refer to the summary in figure 4-2, you can see that the ACCESS MODE clause can be coded SEQUENTIAL or DYNAMIC for sequential processing. When you specify *dynamic access*, it means that the file can be accessed either sequentially or randomly. Unless you need to access a file both ways, though, it's usually best to code the specific access you'll be using. In this chapter, I'll only mention dynamic access when it affects the way a statement is coded.

The RELATIVE KEY clause in the SELECT statement for a relative file specifies the field that will contain the relative record number for a record in the file. For a sequential file, this clause is optional; you only need to code it if you're using a START statement to position the file.

SELECT statement

```
SELECT file-name

    ASSIGN TO system-name

    ORGANIZATION IS RELATIVE

    [ACCESS MODE IS {SEQUENTIAL}]
                    {DYNAMIC   }

    [RELATIVE KEY IS data-name-1]

    [FILE STATUS IS data-name-2]
```

FD statement

```
FD  file-name

    [LABEL RECORDS ARE STANDARD]

    [RECORD CONTAINS integer-1 CHARACTERS]

    [BLOCK CONTAINS integer-2 RECORDS]
```

Figure 4-2   COBOL formats for sequential processing of relative files (part 1 of 2)

Unlike the key field for an indexed file, the RELATIVE KEY field must *not* be defined within the record description for the file in the File Section of the program. Instead, it must be defined in working storage as an unsigned integer. Even if a field in each record in the file is used as the relative record number, the RELATIVE KEY clause can't refer to a field in the File Section of the program.

The last clause in the SELECT statement is the FILE STATUS clause. As you learned in chapter 2, the FILE STATUS clause specifies a field that is updated by the system after each I/O statement for a file is executed. This field is a two-digit field that is defined in working storage. If necessary, you can use the FILE STATUS field to identify the specific status that results from an I/O operation for a file.

Procedure Division statements

```
OPEN {INPUT    file-name-1 ...
      OUTPUT   file-name-2 ...
      I-O      file-name-3 ...
      EXTEND   file-name-4 ...}


START file-name [KEY IS {EQUAL TO
                         =
                         GREATER THAN
                         >
                         NOT LESS THAN
                         NOT <
                         GREATER THAN OR EQUAL TO
                         >=                        } data-name]

    [INVALID KEY imperative-statement]


READ file-name [NEXT] RECORD

    [INTO identifier]

    [AT END imperative-statement]


WRITE record-name

    [FROM identifier]

    [INVALID KEY imperative-statement]


REWRITE record-name

    [FROM identifier]

    [INVALID KEY imperative-statement]


DELETE file-name RECORD

    [INVALID KEY imperative-statement]


CLOSE  file-name-1 ...
```

Note: All 1985 COBOL elements are shaded.

Figure 4-2   COBOL formats for sequential processing of relative files (part 2 of 2)

FILE STATUS codes

Figure 4-3 summarizes the FILE STATUS codes for relative files, both for sequential and random processing. The first code, 00, indicates that the last I/O operation was successful. The second code, 10, indicates that the AT END condition occurred during a sequential reading operation. The third code, 14, indicates that the size of the relative record number of a record retrieved from the file by a READ statement is larger than the size of the field specified in the RELATIVE KEY clause. The next three codes (22, 23, and 24) all indicate invalid key conditions. The rest of the codes indicate more serious error conditions that usually lead to program termination.

The INVALID KEY clause of an I/O statement is executed when one of the invalid key conditions in figure 4-3 occurs. Although these three codes are somewhat self-explanatory, let me describe them briefly.

Code 22 indicates that a duplicate key was found. This means that the program tried to write a new record in an area that was already filled. This can occur when a file is being created or when records are being added to a file.

Code 23 indicates that the desired record wasn't found during a random I/O operation. This status can't result from a sequential I/O operation. It occurs any time a program tries to read a record with a key that isn't in a file. As a result, it indicates a problem with only one record, and it occurs fairly often in programs that randomly access the records in a file.

Code 24 indicates that the program tried to perform an operation on an area of the disk that is beyond the space assigned to a file. For example, code 24 will result when a program tries to write relative record number 3001 on a relative file that has only 3000 record areas allocated to it. This can happen when a sequential file creation program tries to write a record on the file or when a random file maintenance program tries to add a record to a file. As a result, code 24 indicates a type of error that normally shouldn't occur during the execution of a relative file handling program. When it does occur, a program usually has to terminate.

Procedure Division statements

The OPEN statement   Note in figure 4-2 that the EXTEND option has been shaded indicating that it is a part of the 1985 COBOL standards. In the 1974 standards, a relative file couldn't be opened in extend mode. However, the EXTEND option can only be used if the file is opened for sequential access; it can't be specified if the file is opened for dynamic access, even if the file is only accessed sequentially.

FILE STATUS codes	Meaning
00	Successful completion of I/O operation
10	End-of-file condition during read operation (AT END condition)
14	For a read operation, the size of the relative record number is larger than the size of the relative key field for the file
22	Invalid key condition: Duplicate key
23	Invalid key condition: Record not found
24	Invalid key condition: Boundary violation
30-39	Permanent error condition with unsuccessful completion of I/O operation
40-49	Logical error condition with unsuccessful completion of I/O operation
90-99	Defined by implementor

Figure 4-3   FILE STATUS codes for I/O operations on relative files

The INVALID KEY clause   You can code the INVALID KEY clause on START, WRITE, REWRITE, or DELETE statements when you're processing relative files sequentially. This clause is executed whenever an invalid key condition occurs. As I explained earlier, there are three conditions that can cause the execution of the INVALID KEY clause. They are represented by codes 22 through 24 in the summary in figure 4-3.

The INVALID KEY clause is optional because you can control the four invalid key conditions by analyzing the FILE STATUS field after each I/O operation. However, you'll often find that it's more efficient to use the INVALID KEY clause. In general, we recommend that you code the INVALID KEY clause, at least as the first step in your error processing routines.

The START statement   The START statement can be used for a file that is opened as INPUT or I-O. It specifies the key (relative record number) at which sequential processing should begin. When you use this statement, the starting key must be placed in the key field before the START statement is executed. Then, the KEY clause of the START statement can be used to establish the first record to be processed in the file.

To start processing at the first relative record number equal to or greater than the value in the RELATIVE KEY field, you can use the START statement like this:

```
MOVE '1000' TO INV-RR-NUMBER.
START INVMAST
     KEY IS NOT < INV-RR-NUMBER.
```

Then, the file is positioned to read the first record whose relative record number is greater than or equal to 1000. Note that the record isn't actually read; the file is simply positioned so the next READ statement will retrieve that record.

If you refer back to figure 4-2, you can see that the 1985 standards provide for a relational operator stated as GREATER THAN OR EQUAL TO. Although this means the same as NOT LESS THAN, I think it makes the relationship a little more apparent. More about the 1985 relational operators in chapter 10.

As you can see in figure 4-2, the KEY clause of the START statement is optional. If it's omitted, the file will be positioned at the first record whose key value is equal to the value placed in the RELATIVE KEY field. However, if that record doesn't exist, a record not found condition will occur (code 23). Since that usually won't be what you intended, it's a good idea to code the KEY clause so you can specify the exact relationship you want.

The READ statement   Although the READ statement has the same format for accessing relative files sequentially as it does for accessing sequential files, there is one point I would like to make. If you specify dynamic access, you must code the word NEXT on the READ statement to access the records sequentially. If you don't, random processing is assumed. When you use sequential processing, remember that the READ statement skips any empty record areas in the file.

Since you normally don't need to use dynamic access for relative files, I won't present an example of it in this chapter. If you want to see how this works, though, you can refer to the example presented in topic 2 of the last chapter. Although it uses an indexed file, the logic of dynamic processing is the same whether you're using an indexed or a relative file.

The REWRITE statement   REWRITE statements can only be used on files that are opened as I-O. When a REWRITE statement is executed for a relative file in sequential access, the record is rewritten in the area for the last record read from the file. In other words, a READ statement must be executed before a REWRITE statement is executed.

The DELETE statement   The DELETE statement is used to delete records from a file. It can only be used on a file that is opened as I-O. When it's used in sequential access mode, it deletes the record that was read by the last READ statement. In this case, the INVALID KEY clause should never be executed because the record to be deleted is obviously on the file.

When the DELETE statement is used in dynamic access mode, however, it deletes the record indicated by the value in the key field for the file. In other words, it deletes a record on a random rather than a sequential basis. As a result, you should code the INVALID KEY clause with it in case the record to be deleted can't be found in the file.

A sequential update program

Sequential processing of relative files is so similar to the processing of sequential files that you shouldn't have any problems with it. In fact, the sequential update program that I'm about to present is almost identical to the update-in-place program that I presented in the chapter on sequential file handling.

Figure 4-4 presents a program overview for the sequential update program. In this program, the records in an inventory master file are updated based on the data in a file of valid inventory transactions. After all the transactions for an item have been processed, the master record is rewritten on the file.

For this program, the inventory master file is a relative file. To compute the relative record address for any record in the file, you simply subtract 10000 from the item number of the record. Since the item numbers range from 10001 through 50000, the relative record numbers range from 1 through 40000. However, since the company has only 20,000 different items, that means half the record areas in the file are empty. In the random processing section of this topic, I'll show you the program that created this file.

If you look at the structure chart for this program in figure 4-5, you'll see that it's the same as the structure chart for the sequential update-in-place program in chapter 2 (figure 2-13). If you look at the code for this program in figure 4-6, you can see that it's very similar to the code for the sequential update program in chapter 2 (figure 2-14). However, there are a few differences that you should be aware of.

First, the SELECT statement for the inventory master file specifies relative record organization. In this case, I didn't code the RELATIVE KEY clause since the file is being accessed sequentially starting with the first record.

Second, I used the INVALID KEY clause on the REWRITE

Program: INV1200 Update inventory file (sequential)	Page: 1
Designer: Mike Murach	Date: 09-03-86

Input/output specifications

File	Description	Use
VALTRAN	Valid inventory transaction file	Input
INVMAST	Inventory master file	Update
ERRTRAN	Unmatched inventory transaction file	Output

Process specifications

This program updates an inventory master file (INVMAST) based on the
data in a file of valid inventory transaction records (VALTRAN). The
master file should be read on a sequential basis, and the updated
records should be rewritten to the master file.

To compute the relative record number for a master record, you
subtract 10000 from the record's item number. As a result, the
records in the master file are in sequence by item number. That's why
they can be updated on a sequential basis. VALTRAN is also in item
number sequence.

If a transaction has the same item number as a master record, the
transaction matches the master record. Then, the transaction data
should be used to update the master record: The on hand quantity in
the master record should be increased by the receipt quantity in the
transaction record.

If a matching master record can't be found for a transaction, the
transaction is unmatched. Then, the transaction record should be
written on the file of error transactions (ERRTRAN). The record
formats for VALTRAN and ERRTRAN are the same.

The basic processing requirements follow:

1. Read a transaction record.

2. If necessary, get inventory master records until a record with a
   matching or greater item number is found. This includes rewriting
   the last master record that was updated.

3. If the transaction is matched,
      the matching master record should be updated.

4. If the transaction is unmatched,
      the record should be written on the file of error transactions.

Figure 4-4   The program overview for a program that sequentially updates a relative file

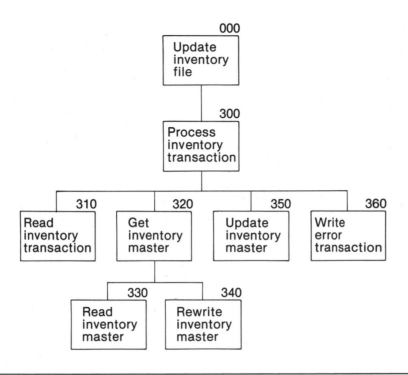

Figure 4-5   The structure chart for the sequential update program

statement instead of checking a FILE STATUS field. Remember, though, that some shops will require that you use file status codes to check the execution of each I/O operation.

Third, although the READ statement in module 330 is coded just as you would code any sequential READ statement, it doesn't work quite the same. For a relative file, the READ statement reads the records in sequence by relative record number. If a record area is empty, it is skipped, so each READ statement in this program reads one inventory master record until there are no more records in the file.

```
 IDENTIFICATION DIVISION.
*
 PROGRAM-ID.  INV1200.
*
 ENVIRONMENT DIVISION.
*
 INPUT-OUTPUT SECTION.
*
 FILE-CONTROL.
     SELECT VALTRAN    ASSIGN TO SYS020-AS-VALTRAN.
     SELECT INVMAST    ASSIGN TO SYS021-INVMAST
                       ORGANIZATION IS RELATIVE
                       ACCESS IS SEQUENTIAL.
     SELECT ERRTRAN    ASSIGN TO SYS022-AS-ERRTRAN.
*
 DATA DIVISION.
*
 FILE SECTION.
*
 FD  VALTRAN
     LABEL RECORDS ARE STANDARD
     RECORD CONTAINS 21 CHARACTERS.
*
 01  VALID-TRANSACTION-AREA    PIC X(21).
*
 FD  INVMAST
     LABEL RECORDS ARE STANDARD
     RECORD CONTAINS 80 CHARACTERS.
*
 01  MASTER-RECORD-AREA        PIC X(80).
*
 FD  ERRTRAN
     LABEL RECORDS ARE STANDARD
     RECORD CONTAINS 21 CHARACTERS.
*
 01  ERROR-TRANSACTION         PIC X(21).
*
 WORKING-STORAGE SECTION.
*
 01  SWITCHES.
*
     05  ALL-RECORDS-PROCESSED-SWITCH  PIC X      VALUE 'N'.
         88  ALL-RECORDS-PROCESSED                VALUE 'Y'.
     05  MASTER-UPDATED-SWITCH         PIC X      VALUE 'N'.
         88  MASTER-UPDATED                       VALUE 'Y'.
*
 01  INVENTORY-TRANSACTION.
*
     05  IT-ITEM-NO           PIC 9(5).
     05  IT-VENDOR-NO         PIC X(5).
     05  IT-RECEIPT-DATE      PIC X(6).
     05  IT-RECEIPT-QUANTITY  PIC S9(5).
*
 01  INVENTORY-MASTER-RECORD.
*
```

Figure 4-6   The sequential update program (part 1 of 3)

```
       05    IM-DESCRIPTIVE-DATA.
             10    IM-ITEM-NO              PIC 9(5).
             10    IM-ITEM-DESC            PIC X(20).
             10    IM-UNIT-COST            PIC S999V99.
             10    IM-UNIT-PRICE           PIC S999V99.
       05    IM-INVENTORY-DATA.
             10    IM-REORDER-POINT        PIC S9(5).
             10    IM-ON-HAND              PIC S9(5).
             10    IM-ON-ORDER             PIC S9(5).
       05    FILLER                        PIC X(30).
*
 PROCEDURE DIVISION.
*
 000-UPDATE-INVENTORY-FILE.
*
     OPEN INPUT   VALTRAN
          I-O     INVMAST
          OUTPUT  ERRTRAN.
     MOVE ZERO TO IM-ITEM-NO.
     PERFORM 300-PROCESS-INVENTORY-TRAN
         UNTIL ALL-RECORDS-PROCESSED.
     CLOSE VALTRAN
           INVMAST
           ERRTRAN.
     DISPLAY 'INV1200 I 1  NORMAL EOJ'.
     STOP RUN.
*
 300-PROCESS-INVENTORY-TRAN.
*
     PERFORM 310-READ-INVENTORY-TRAN.
     PERFORM 320-GET-INVENTORY-MASTER
         UNTIL IM-ITEM-NO NOT < IT-ITEM-NO.
     IF        IM-ITEM-NO = 99999
           AND IT-ITEM-NO = 99999
         MOVE 'Y' TO ALL-RECORDS-PROCESSED-SWITCH
     ELSE
         IF IM-ITEM-NO = IT-ITEM-NO
             PERFORM 350-UPDATE-INVENTORY-MASTER
         ELSE
             PERFORM 360-WRITE-ERROR-TRAN.
*
 310-READ-INVENTORY-TRAN.
*
     READ VALTRAN INTO INVENTORY-TRANSACTION
         AT END
             MOVE 99999 TO IT-ITEM-NO.
*
 320-GET-INVENTORY-MASTER.
*
     IF MASTER-UPDATED
         PERFORM 340-REWRITE-INVENTORY-MASTER
         PERFORM 330-READ-INVENTORY-MASTER
     ELSE
         PERFORM 330-READ-INVENTORY-MASTER.
*
```

Figure 4-6   The sequential update program (part 2 of 3)

```
 330-READ-INVENTORY-MASTER.
*
     READ INVMAST INTO INVENTORY-MASTER-RECORD
         AT END
             MOVE 99999 TO IM-ITEM-NO.
*
 340-REWRITE-INVENTORY-MASTER.
*
     REWRITE MASTER-RECORD-AREA FROM INVENTORY-MASTER-RECORD
         INVALID KEY
             DISPLAY 'INV1200  A  2   REWRITE ERROR FOR INVMAST'
             DISPLAY 'INV1200   A  2   ITEM NUMBER = ' IM-ITEM-NO
             MOVE 'Y' TO ALL-RECORDS-PROCESSED-SWITCH.
     MOVE 'N' TO MASTER-UPDATED-SWITCH.
*
 350-UPDATE-INVENTORY-MASTER.
*
     ADD IT-RECEIPT-QUANTITY TO IM-ON-HAND.
     MOVE 'Y' TO MASTER-UPDATED-SWITCH.
*
 360-WRITE-ERROR-TRAN.
*
     WRITE ERROR-TRANSACTION FROM INVENTORY-TRANSACTION.
```

Figure 4-6   The sequential update program (part 3 of 3)

RANDOM PROCESSING

Figure 4-7 summarizes the COBOL code you use when you write programs that process relative files randomly. There are no new statements here, but there are a few variations you should be aware of. After I discuss these variations, I will present two programs that use some of these COBOL elements.

The SELECT statement

The main difference between the SELECT statement for a relative file processed sequentially and one processed randomly is in the ACCESS MODE clause. For a randomly accessed file, you must specify either RANDOM or DYNAMIC. Random access means that records will be accessed depending on their key values (relative record numbers). Dynamic access means that records in the file can be accessed both sequentially and randomly. If a program is only going to process a file on a random basis, though, we recommend that you specify RANDOM in this clause, not DYNAMIC. Note in figure 4-7 that the RELATIVE KEY clause isn't optional when you use random access.

Procedure Division statements

The OPEN statement   If you look at the OPEN statement in figure 4-7, you'll notice that there isn't an EXTEND option. That makes sense because records don't have to be added at the end of a file when you use random access. Similarly, you can't use the EXTEND option on a dynamic access file, even if the records are going to be added sequentially.

The READ statement   The only difference in the READ statement is that the INVALID KEY clause can be coded for random access. Before a READ statement is executed, the relative record number of the desired record must be placed in the field specified in the RELATIVE KEY clause. Then, if no record exists with that record number, an invalid key condition occurs.

The WRITE, REWRITE, and DELETE statements   Although the formats of the WRITE, REWRITE, and DELETE statements are the same for random access as they are for sequential access, the way these statements are processed is different. For sequential access, the record processed depends on the location of the record pointer when the statement is issued. For random access, the record processed depends on the value in the key field for the file. As a result, you don't have to issue a READ statement for a record before you issue a REWRITE or DELETE statement for it.

SELECT statement

<u>SELECT</u> file-name

    <u>ASSIGN</u> TO system-name

    <u>ORGANIZATION</u> IS <u>RELATIVE</u>

    <u>ACCESS</u> MODE IS { <u>RANDOM</u> }
                  { <u>DYNAMIC</u> }

    <u>RELATIVE</u> KEY IS data-name-1

    [FILE <u>STATUS</u> IS data-name-2]

FD statement

<u>FD</u>   file-name

    [<u>LABEL</u> <u>RECORDS</u> ARE <u>STANDARD</u>]

    [<u>RECORD</u> CONTAINS integer-1 CHARACTERS]

    [<u>BLOCK</u> CONTAINS integer-2 RECORDS]

Figure 4-7   COBOL formats for random processing of relative files (part 1 of 2)

When the WRITE statement is executed, it adds a record to a file. As a result, the INVALID KEY clause should only be executed if a record is already stored in the record area addressed by the relative record number (a duplicate key) or if the relative record number is greater than the number of record areas allocated to the file (a boundary violation). When the REWRITE statement is executed, it writes a record on the file in the relative record number addressed by the RELATIVE KEY field. As a result, its INVALID KEY clause should only be executed if a record with that relative record number doesn't already exist on the file (record not found). Similarly, the DELETE statement tries to delete a record with a specific relative record number from the file. As a result, its INVALID KEY clause should only be executed if a record with that relative record number doesn't already exist on the file (record not found). In most programs, a record is read before a REWRITE or DELETE statement is executed for a relative record number so the program knows that the record already exists.

Procedure Division statements

```
OPEN {INPUT    file-name-1 ...}
     {OUTPUT   file-name-2 ...}
     {I-O      file-name-3 ...}

READ file-name RECORD

    [INTO identifier]

    [INVALID KEY imperative-statement]

WRITE record-name

    [FROM identifier]

    [INVALID KEY imperative-statement]

REWRITE record-name

    [FROM identifier]

    [INVALID KEY imperative-statement]

DELETE file-name RECORD

    [INVALID KEY imperative-statement]

CLOSE  file-name-1 ...
```

Note: All 1985 COBOL elements are shaded.

Figure 4-7   COBOL formats for random processing of relative files (part 2 of 2)

Two illustrative programs

Now I'd like to present two programs that illustrate some of the code used for random processing of relative files. The first program creates a relative file. The second program updates it on a random basis.

```
┌─────────────────────────────────────────────────────────────────────────┐
│                                                                           │
│  Program: INV1100    Create inventory file          Page: 1              │
│                                                                           │
├─────────────────────────────────────────────────────────────────────────┤
│                                                                           │
│  Designer: Anne Prince                              Date: 09-03-86       │
│                                                                           │
└─────────────────────────────────────────────────────────────────────────┘
```

Input/output specifications

```
┌─────────────────────────────────────────────────────────────────────────┐
│                                                                           │
│  File              Description                       Use                  │
│                                                                           │
├─────────────────────────────────────────────────────────────────────────┤
│                                                                           │
│  INVMAST           Sequential inventory master file  Input               │
│  INVMSTR           Relative inventory master file    Output              │
│                                                                           │
│                                                                           │
│                                                                           │
│                                                                           │
│                                                                           │
└─────────────────────────────────────────────────────────────────────────┘
```

Process specifications

```
┌─────────────────────────────────────────────────────────────────────────┐
│                                                                           │
│  This program creates a relative file of inventory master records from   │
│  a sequential file of master records.  The records are written in the    │
│  relative file on a random basis.  To calculate the relative record      │
│  number for each master record, subtract 10000 from the item number.     │
│                                                                           │
│  The basic processing requirements follow:                               │
│                                                                           │
│  1.  Read a sequential inventory record.                                 │
│                                                                           │
│  2.  Write a relative inventory record.                                  │
│                                                                           │
│                                                                           │
│                                                                           │
│                                                                           │
│                                                                           │
│                                                                           │
│                                                                           │
└─────────────────────────────────────────────────────────────────────────┘
```

Figure 4-8   The program overview for a program that creates a relative file

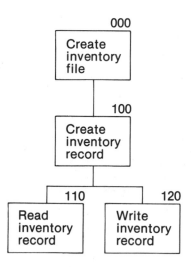

Figure 4-9   The structure chart for the file creation program

A file creation program   Figure 4-8 presents the program overview for a program that creates a relative file of inventory master records from a sequential file of inventory records. Although the sequential file is in sequence by item number, the program will work the same way no matter what sequence this file is in because the relative records are written on the new file on a random basis. To find the relative record number for an inventory master record, the program simply subtracts 10000 from the item number. Since the item numbers range from 10001 through 50000, the file has to provide for 40,000 record areas. However, only half of these record areas will be used since there are only 20,000 records in the file.

Figure 4-9 presents the structure chart for this program. Here, module 110 reads one inventory record from the sequential file, and module 120 writes the inventory record on the relative file. Because the randomizing routine in this case is so simple, I didn't need to provide a separate module for it. But sometimes a routine like this is quite complex so it should be coded in its own module.

Figure 4-10 presents the code for this program. In the SELECT statement for the relative file, I specified RANDOM access and a RELATIVE KEY named INVMAST-RR-NUMBER. Then, in working storage, I described the relative key field as 9(5) since the relative record number must be an unsigned integer.

In module 120, I coded the WRITE statement with the INVALID KEY clause. However, this clause should only be executed if the program tries to write a record at a relative record number that already has a record stored in it. Since this should only happen if the input file has two inventory records with the same item number, the INVALID KEY clause shouldn't ever be executed in this program.

```
IDENTIFICATION DIVISION.
*
PROGRAM-ID.  INV1100.
*
ENVIRONMENT DIVISION.
*
INPUT-OUTPUT SECTION.
*
FILE-CONTROL.
     SELECT INVMAST   ASSIGN TO SYS020-AS-INVMAST.
     SELECT INVMSTR   ASSIGN TO SYS021-INVMSTR
                      ORGANIZATION IS RELATIVE
                      ACCESS IS RANDOM
                      RELATIVE KEY IS INVMAST-RR-NUMBER.
*
DATA DIVISION.
*
FILE SECTION.
*
FD   INVMAST
     LABEL RECORDS ARE STANDARD
     RECORD CONTAINS 80 CHARACTERS.
*
01   SEQUENTIAL-RECORD-AREA  PIC X(80).
*
FD   INVMSTR
     LABEL RECORDS ARE STANDARD
     RECORD CONTAINS 80 CHARACTERS.
*
01   RELATIVE-RECORD-AREA    PIC X(80).
*
WORKING-STORAGE SECTION.
*
01   SWITCHES.
*
     05   INVMAST-EOF-SWITCH    PIC X     VALUE 'N'.
          88   INVMAST-EOF                VALUE 'Y'.
*
01   KEY-FIELDS.
*
     05   INVMAST-RR-NUMBER     PIC 9(5).
*
01   INVENTORY-MASTER-RECORD.
*
     05   IM-DESCRIPTIVE-DATA.
          10   IM-ITEM-NUMBER     PIC 9(5).
          10   IM-ITEM-DESC       PIC X(20).
          10   IM-UNIT-COST       PIC S999V99.
          10   IM-UNIT-PRICE      PIC S999V99.
     05   IM-INVENTORY-DATA.
          10   IM-REORDER-POINT   PIC S9(5).
          10   IM-ON-HAND         PIC S9(5).
          10   IM-ON-ORDER        PIC S9(5).
     05   FILLER                  PIC X(30).
*
```

Figure 4-10   The random file creation program (part 1 of 2)

```
PROCEDURE DIVISION.
*
000-CREATE-INVENTORY-FILE.
*
    OPEN INPUT   INVMAST
         OUTPUT INVMSTR.
    PERFORM 100-CREATE-INVENTORY-RECORD
        UNTIL INVMAST-EOF.
    CLOSE INVMAST
          INVMSTR.
    DISPLAY 'INV1100  I  1   NORMAL EOJ'.
    STOP RUN.
*
100-CREATE-INVENTORY-RECORD.
*
    PERFORM 110-READ-INVENTORY-RECORD.
    IF NOT INVMAST-EOF
        PERFORM 120-WRITE-INVENTORY-RECORD.
*
110-READ-INVENTORY-RECORD.
*
    READ INVMAST INTO INVENTORY-MASTER-RECORD
        AT END
            MOVE 'Y' TO INVMAST-EOF-SWITCH.
*
120-WRITE-INVENTORY-RECORD.
*
    SUBTRACT 10000 FROM IM-ITEM-NUMBER GIVING INVMAST-RR-NUMBER.
    WRITE RELATIVE-RECORD-AREA FROM INVENTORY-MASTER-RECORD
        INVALID KEY
            DISPLAY 'INV1100  A  2   WRITE ERROR FOR INVMSTR'
            DISPLAY 'INV1100  A  2   ITEM NO. = ' IM-ITEM-NUMBER
            MOVE 'Y' TO INVMAST-EOF-SWITCH.
```

Figure 4-10   The random file creation program (part 2 of 2)

A random update program   Figure 4-11 presents a program over-view for a program that updates a relative file of inventory records based on the data in a sequential file of valid inventory transactions. This program is just like the sequential update program I presented earlier in this chapter, except that the records are processed on a random, rather than a sequential, basis.

As you can see in the program overview, I have assumed that the transaction file is in no particular sequence, so the program reads a transaction, reads the master record with the same item number, changes the master record, and then rewrites it. If the transaction file were in sequence by item number, however, this would be inefficient. In that case, the program should check to make sure that all the trans-actions for a record have been processed before the master record is rewritten on the file.

Program: INV1200   Update inventory file (random)   Page: 1

Designer: **Anne Prince**   Date: 09-03-86

Input/output specifications

File	Description	Use
VALTRAN	Valid inventory transaction file	Input
INVMAST	Inventory master file	Update
ERRTRAN	Unmatched inventory transaction file	Output

Process specifications

This program updates an inventory master file (INVMAST) based on the data in a file of valid inventory transaction records (VALTRAN). The file should be updated on a random basis. To calculate the relative record number for a master record, subtract 10000 from its item number.

If a master record is found for a transaction, the transaction data should be used to update the master record: The on hand quantity in the master record should be increased by the receipt quantity in the transaction record.

If a master record is not found for a transaction, the transaction record should be written on the file of error transactions (ERRTRAN). The record format for ERRTRAN is the same as for VALTRAN.

The basic processing requirements follow:

1. Read a transaction record.

2. Read the master record with the same item number as in the transaction record.

3. If a master record is found,
        the master record should be updated.

4. If a master record is not found,
        the transaction record should be written on the file of error transactions.

Figure 4-11   The program overview for a program that randomly updates a relative file

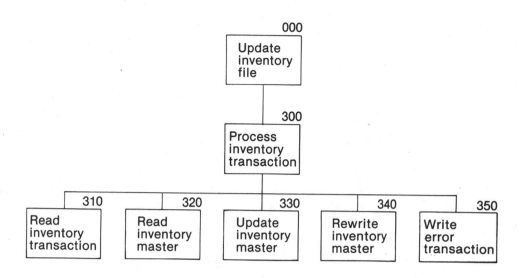

Figure 4-12   The structure chart for the random update program

Figure 4-12 presents the structure chart for this program. It has modules to read an inventory transaction, to read a master record on a random basis, to update the data in the master record, to rewrite the master record, and to write an error transaction. All of these modules are controlled by module 300.

Figure 4-13 presents the code for this program. It should be easy enough to understand. In the SELECT statement for the relative file, I specified random access and a relative key named INVMAST-RR-NUMBER. Just as in the file creation program, the relative key field is described in working storage as 9(5).

In module 300, if a master record is found to match an inventory transaction, modules 330 and 340 are called to update the master record and rewrite it on the file. Otherwise, module 350 is called to write the transaction record on the error file.

In module 320, which is designed to read an inventory master record, the item number in the transaction record is first converted to a relative record number by subtracting 10000 from it. This number is placed in the RELATIVE KEY field, INVMAST-RR-NUMBER. Next, MASTER-FOUND-SWITCH is turned on. Then, the READ statement tries to read the master record with the relative record number specified in INVMAST-RR-NUMBER. If it can't find this record, the INVALID KEY clause is executed so MASTER-FOUND-SWITCH is turned off. The result of this code is to turn the MASTER-FOUND condition on if the record is found and to turn it off if it isn't found. This condition is used in module 300 to control the processing of the program.

```
 IDENTIFICATION DIVISION.
*
 PROGRAM-ID.  INV1200.
*
 ENVIRONMENT DIVISION.
*
 INPUT-OUTPUT SECTION.
*
 FILE-CONTROL.
     SELECT VALTRAN   ASSIGN TO SYS020-AS-VALTRAN.
     SELECT INVMAST   ASSIGN TO SYS021-INVMAST
                      ORGANIZATION IS RELATIVE
                      ACCESS IS RANDOM
                      RELATIVE KEY IS INVMAST-RR-NUMBER.
     SELECT ERRTRAN   ASSIGN TO SYS022-AS-ERRTRAN.
*
 DATA DIVISION.
*
 FILE SECTION.
*
 FD  VALTRAN
     LABEL RECORDS ARE STANDARD
     RECORD CONTAINS 21 CHARACTERS.
*
 01  VALID-TRANSACTION-AREA    PIC X(21).
*
 FD  INVMAST
     LABEL RECORDS ARE STANDARD
     RECORD CONTAINS 80 CHARACTERS.
*
 01  MASTER-RECORD-AREA        PIC X(80).
*
 FD  ERRTRAN
     LABEL RECORDS ARE STANDARD
     RECORD CONTAINS 21 CHARACTERS.
*
 01  ERROR-TRANSACTION         PIC X(21).
*
 WORKING-STORAGE SECTION.
*
 01  SWITCHES.
*
     05   VALTRAN-EOF-SWITCH       PIC X     VALUE 'N'.
          88   VALTRAN-EOF                   VALUE 'Y'.
     05   MASTER-FOUND-SWITCH      PIC X.
          88   MASTER-FOUND                  VALUE 'Y'.
*
 01  KEY-FIELDS.
*
     05   INVMAST-RR-NUMBER        PIC 9(5).
*
 01  INVENTORY-TRANSACTION.
*
     05   IT-ITEM-NO            PIC 9(5).
     05   IT-VENDOR-NO          PIC X(5).
```

Figure 4-13   The random update program (part 1 of 3)

```
    05   IT-RECEIPT-DATE          PIC X(6).
    05   IT-RECEIPT-QUANTITY      PIC S9(5).
*
 01  INVENTORY-MASTER-RECORD.
*
    05   IM-DESCRIPTIVE-DATA.
         10   IM-ITEM-NO          PIC 9(5).
         10   IM-ITEM-DESC        PIC X(20).
         10   IM-UNIT-COST        PIC S999V99.
         10   IM-UNIT-PRICE       PIC S999V99.
    05   IM-INVENTORY-DATA.
         10   IM-REORDER-POINT    PIC S9(5).
         10   IM-ON-HAND          PIC S9(5).
         10   IM-ON-ORDER         PIC S9(5).
    05   FILLER                   PIC X(30).
*
 PROCEDURE DIVISION.
*
 000-UPDATE-INVENTORY-FILE.
*
    OPEN INPUT  VALTRAN
         I-O    INVMAST
         OUTPUT ERRTRAN.
    PERFORM 300-PROCESS-INVENTORY-TRAN
        UNTIL VALTRAN-EOF.
    CLOSE VALTRAN
          INVMAST
          ERRTRAN.
    DISPLAY 'INV1200 I 1  NORMAL EOJ'.
    STOP RUN.
*
 300-PROCESS-INVENTORY-TRAN.
*
    PERFORM 310-READ-INVENTORY-TRAN.
    IF NOT VALTRAN-EOF
        PERFORM 320-READ-INVENTORY-MASTER
        IF MASTER-FOUND
            PERFORM 330-UPDATE-INVENTORY-MASTER
            PERFORM 340-REWRITE-INVENTORY-MASTER
        ELSE
            PERFORM 350-WRITE-ERROR-TRAN.
*
 310-READ-INVENTORY-TRAN.
*
    READ VALTRAN INTO INVENTORY-TRANSACTION
        AT END
            MOVE 'Y' TO VALTRAN-EOF-SWITCH.
*
 320-READ-INVENTORY-MASTER.
*
    SUBTRACT 10000 FROM IT-ITEM-NO GIVING INVMAST-RR-NUMBER.
    MOVE 'Y' TO MASTER-FOUND-SWITCH.
    READ INVMAST INTO INVENTORY-MASTER-RECORD
        INVALID KEY
            MOVE 'N' TO MASTER-FOUND-SWITCH.
*
```

Figure 4-13   The random update program (part 2 of 3)

```
 330-UPDATE-INVENTORY-MASTER.
✿
     ADD IT-RECEIPT-QUANTITY TO IM-ON-HAND.
✿
 340-REWRITE-INVENTORY-MASTER.
✿
     REWRITE MASTER-RECORD-AREA FROM INVENTORY-MASTER-RECORD
         INVALID KEY
             DISPLAY 'INV1200  A  2  REWRITE ERROR FOR INVMAST'
             DISPLAY 'INV1200  A  2  ITEM NUMBER = ' IM-ITEM-NO
             MOVE 'Y' TO VALTRAN-EOF-SWITCH.
✿
 350-WRITE-ERROR-TRAN.
✿
     WRITE ERROR-TRANSACTION FROM INVENTORY-TRANSACTION.
```

Figure 4-13   The random update program (part 3 of 3)

DISCUSSION

When compared to indexed files, relative files have three main disadvantages. First, it's often difficult to convert a field in a master record to a unique relative record number, a difficulty you don't have when you use indexed files. Second, a relative file is likely to use disk space inefficiently due to the number of empty record areas it contains. Third, a relative file can't use alternate keys.

Because of these disadvantages, relative files are used infrequently. Because relative files can sometimes be processed more efficiently than indexed files, though, they do have an occasional use.

Terminology

dynamic access

Objective

Given program specifications for a program that processes relative files, develop a COBOL program that satisfies the specifications. The program may involve any of the following: creating a file, adding records to a file, deleting records from a file, sequentially or randomly updating a file, and sequentially or randomly retrieving records from a file.

Topic 3   Compiler dependent code

With only a couple of changes, the programs presented in topic 2 of this chapter will run on any system that uses 1974 or 1985 ANS COBOL, provided that it supports relative files. In general, you have to change the system names so they are acceptable to your compiler. You have to change the single quotation marks to double marks if they are required by your compiler. And you have to change COMP-3 usage to COMP usage if COMP is appropriate for your compiler. But most important, you have to be sure that your system supports relative files, since not all systems do.

System names in SELECT statements

In most cases, the system names for relative files are the same as for indexed files. If you haven't read the chapter on indexed files, you might want to refer to figure 3-28. It presents the system names for disk files on some common systems when you're using Microsoft COBOL, Wang VS COBOL, IBM VS COBOL, or IBM VS COBOL II. If you're using some other compiler, you'll need to find out how to code the system names on your own.

Relative file support

Because you can do anything with an indexed file that you can do with a relative file, some systems don't fully support relative files. And some don't support relative files at all.

Terminology

None

Objective

Find out if your system supports relative files. If it does, find out how to use the compiler dependent code for relative files on your system.

Chapter 5

The sort/merge feature

In this chapter, you'll learn how to write COBOL programs that sort and merge files. Topic 1 presents the concepts you need to know for sorting and merging files. Topic 2 presents the COBOL for programs that sort and merge files. And topic 3 presents some compiler dependent code related to the sort and merge functions.

Topic 1   Sorting and merging concepts

In any computer installation, much of the processing requires that the records in a file be arranged in certain sequences. For example, before you can run the sequential update program that I've referred to throughout this section, both the input file of transactions and the master file of inventory records have to be in sequence by item number. Similarly, before a report preparation program can be run, the input file or files must be in the reporting sequence.

To arrange the records in a file into an appropriate sequence, the records can be *sorted*. Similarly, to combine the records in two or more sorted files into one sorted file, the records can be *merged*. To provide for these functions, most operating systems provide a general-purpose program called a *sort/merge program*. This program can be used for all of the sorting and merging required by an installation. To use it, you supply the specifications for the factors that vary from one sort or merge job to the next. Because a sort/merge program is used for sorting far more frequently than it is used for merging, it's often re-ferred to simply as a *sort program*.

Today, most mainframe COBOL compilers and some minicom-puter compilers allow you to use the system's sort/merge program within a COBOL program. This allows you to sort or merge a file in the same program that performs other processing functions. When a compiler provides for this feature, there are some advantages to using it, so some COBOL shops use this feature frequently.

In this topic, I will present the concepts related to the use of the sort/merge feature of COBOL. First, I'll present the concepts related to programs that sort files. Then, I'll present the concepts related to programs that merge files. Last, I'll explain how the use of this feature can improve processing efficiency.

Sorting concepts

When you use the sort/merge program within a COBOL program, the sort function takes place in three steps. First, the records to be sorted are released to the sort program by the COBOL program. Second, the records are sorted by the sort/merge program. Third, the sorted records are either written to a new file or are made available to the COBOL program for further processing.

In the first step, the COBOL program doesn't have to release all of the records in a file to the sort/merge program. Often, in fact, a COBOL program selects records from one or more input files before passing them on to the sort/merge program. Then, only the selected records are sorted.

Under the 1974 standards, the input file used by the sort/merge program has to have sequential organization. Under the 1985 standards, however, the input file can have sequential, indexed, or relative organization. However, the input file can only be accessed sequentially by the program. Also, under both sets of standards, the records in the input file can be fixed- or variable-length, but the keys used to sort the records must be in the same position in each record.

Before the sort/merge program is executed, the COBOL program must tell it what the key fields are going to be. The *key fields* are those fields that contain the data that the file is supposed to be sequenced by. The COBOL program must also tell the sort/merge program whether the records are supposed to be sorted into ascending or descending sequence based on each key field. Although most sort programs provide for eight or more keys to be specified, it's common for only one or two to be used. For instance, a sort by invoice number within customer number, both in ascending sequence, is a sort based on only two keys.

The exact sequence of the sorted file depends on the *collating sequence* of a computer. Two of the most commonly-used collating sequences, EBCDIC and ASCII, are summarized in figure 5-1. This summary doesn't present all of the special characters, but it presents those that you are most likely to use. In general, EBCDIC is used on all IBM mainframes, and ASCII is used on all other systems. As you can see, the EBCDIC special characters have lower values than the alphabetic characters, which have lower values than the decimal digits. In contrast, the ASCII digits have lower values than the letters.

One of the problems with both the EBCDIC and ASCII collating sequences is that alphabetic fields may not get sorted properly if they contain both lowercase and uppercase letters. Using the EBCDIC sequence, for example, *Murach* has a lower value than *MANNING*; using the ASCII sequence, *MURACH* has a lower value than *Manning*. Usually, though, you would like Manning to have a lower value than Murach no matter what combinations of lowercase and uppercase letters the names consist of. As a result, some systems allow you to specify your own collating sequences so you can get around problems like this.

After the records have been sorted, they can be written to a file specified by the COBOL program, or they can be returned to the program in sorted sequence for further processing. Like the input file, a file used for output can have fixed- or variable-length records. Under the 1974 standards, though, the output file must have sequential organization. Under the 1985 standards, the file can have sequential, indexed, or relative organization. Records written to a relative file will be written in relative record number sequence, beginning with 1. Records written to an indexed file will be written in primary key sequence, so the file must have been sorted into primary key sequence. However, alternate keys may be specified for an indexed output file.

EBCDIC collating sequence	ASCII collating sequence
LOW-VALUE	LOW-VALUE
(space)	(space)
. (period)	" (quotation mark)
((left parenthesis)	$ (dollar sign)
+ (plus)	& (ampersand)
& (ampersand)	' (apostrophe, single quotation mark)
$ (dollar sign)	((left parenthesis)
* (asterisk)	) (right parenthesis)
) (right parenthesis)	* (asterisk)
; (semicolon)	+ (plus)
– (hyphen, minus, dash)	, (comma)
/ (slash)	– (hyphen, minus, dash)
, (comma)	. (period)
: (colon)	/ (slash)
' (apostrophe, single quotation mark)	0 through 9
" (quotation mark)	: (colon)
a through z (lowercase)	; (semicolon)
A through Z (uppercase)	A through Z (uppercase)
0 through 9	a through z (lowercase)
HIGH-VALUE	HIGH-VALUE

Figure 5-1   The ASCII and EBCDIC collating sequence for some commonly-used characters in ascending sequence

Merging concepts

When you use the sort/merge program to merge files, the merge function takes place in two steps. First, the input files are merged. Second, the merged file is either processed by the COBOL program, or it is written to an output file.

You probably have a clear view of what merging is, but in case you don't, figure 5-2 presents a schematic illustration of merging. Here, two sorted input files are merged to create one sorted output file. In general, a sort/merge program can be used to merge many input files in one execution of the program, but this usually isn't necessary.

In 1974 COBOL, the input and output files in a merge function can have only sequential organization. Under the 1985 standards, though, the input and output files can have sequential, indexed, or relative organization. Under both the 1974 and 1985 standards, the input and output files can be fixed- or variable-length. The only restriction is that the key fields be in the same positions in all of the records in all of the files.

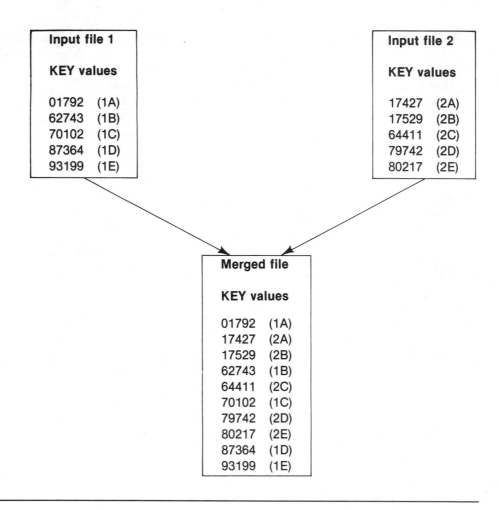

Figure 5-2   Example of the merge function

Why sorts and merges within a COBOL program can improve processing efficiency

When you use the sort/merge program within a COBOL program, it is referred to as an *internal sort*. When the sort/merge program is used by itself, it is referred to as a *standalone sort*. On most systems, a COBOL program with an internal sort is more efficient than a COBOL program plus a standalone sort.

To illustrate, figure 5-3 shows two ways in which a report can be prepared from a file of invoice records. Using a standalone sort, the invoice file is first sorted, thus producing a sorted invoice file. Then, the sorted file is read and processed by a COBOL program to prepare the required sales report. Using an internal sort, one COBOL program reads the invoice file, sorts it, and prepares the required sales report.

Sorting with a standalone sort

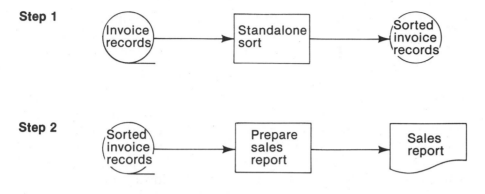

Sorting with an internal sort

Figure 5-3 A standalone sort vs. an internal sort

On most systems, the second way will run more efficiently because the COBOL program with the internal sort never takes the time to produce the file of sorted invoice records. Instead, the sort/merge program presents the records to the COBOL program in sequence before they have been written onto a final output file. As a result, the COBOL program with the internal sort doesn't require as many I/O operations as the system with the standalone sort followed by the COBOL program. If, for example, the invoice file consists of 500 blocks of records, the first method in figure 5-3 will require 1000 more I/O operations than the program with the internal sort—500 extra output operations to produce the sorted invoice file and 500 extra input operations when the COBOL program reads the sorted invoice file.

For the same reason, *internal merges* can be more efficient than *standalone merges*. That is, the merged file is never actually created when an internal merge is used so fewer I/O operations are required to get the job done.

Before a merge can be run, however, the input files have to be in the appropriate sequence, which often means that they have to be sorted first. In this case, it's more efficient to sort all of the files in one sort operation than it is to first sort the files and then merge them. I'll explain how you can do this in the next topic.

Discussion

The main reason for using an internal sort is to improve processing efficiency. That's why many companies make frequent use of internal sorts. On the other hand, some companies never use internal sorts, either because the sort/merge feature of COBOL isn't available on their compiler or because the use of it doesn't lead to improved efficiency on their system.

Internal merges are used much less frequently than internal sorts, because it's often more efficient to sort the data from several files into a single file than it is to sort the data in each of the files separately and then merge the separate files into one file. There are times, though, when the files to be merged are already in the appropriate sequence so an internal merge does lead to improved processing efficiency. As a result, you should know how to use internal merges as well as internal sorts if you work for a company that uses them.

Terminology

sorting
merging
sort/merge program
sort program
key field
collating sequence
internal sort
standalone sort
internal merge
standalone merge

Objective

Explain why a COBOL program with an internal sort is usually more efficient than a COBOL program plus a standalone sort.

Topic 2   COBOL for sorting and merging

Figure 5-4 summarizes the COBOL you use when you write programs that sort or merge files. As you can see, there are few differences between the language used for sorting and the language used for merging. In this topic, I'll start by presenting the COBOL for sorting. Then, I'll present the COBOL for merging. I'll finish by presenting some 1985 COBOL considerations that apply to both sorting and merging.

COBOL FOR SORTING

As you can see in figure 5-4, the Procedure Division contains most of the code for an internal sort. However, you do need to define a file that is used for the sort. This file, called the *sort work file*, is the work space that the sort/merge program uses for sorting the records so it can pass the sorted records back to the COBOL program in the proper sequence. Actually, *sort work file* is a misleading term because a sort program usually uses more than one file for this work space. In COBOL, though, you're only required to code a SELECT statement and file description for one sort work file, no matter how many work files the sort/merge program actually uses.

The SELECT statement for the sort work file

The sort work file, like any other file, requires a SELECT statement in the Environment Division. Its format is the same as for any sequential file.

The SD statement for the sort work file

Up to now, you've always defined a file in the File Section using an FD statement. For sort work files, however, you use an SD (Sort work Description) statement. Its format is like the format of an FD statement except that you don't code the LABEL RECORDS or BLOCK CONTAINS clauses. These characteristics are controlled by the sort/merge program.

The record description for the sort work file

Like other files, a sort work file requires a record description in the Data Division. The only requirement for the record description is that

SELECT statement

<u>SELECT</u> sort/merge-file-name

    <u>ASSIGN</u> TO system-name.

SD statement and sort/merge record description

<u>SD</u>   sort/merge-file-name

    [<u>RECORD</u> CONTAINS integer-1 CHARACTERS].

01   sort-work-record-name.

Note: The keys to be used in the sort or merge must be defined in the sort-work record area.

Figure 5-4   COBOL statement formats for sorting and merging (part 1 of 2)

it contain the key fields that the sort will be based upon. These fields will be named in the SORT statement, as you'll see in a moment.

If you're sorting several types of records, you can code one record description for each record format. In this case, you only have to define the key fields in one of the descriptions. However, the keys must be present in the same positions in all of the records.

The SORT statement

The SORT statement controls the processing in a program that uses an internal sort. It specifies the name of the sort file, the sequence that the records are to be sorted into, the input file or input processing procedure, and the output file or output processing procedure.

The ASCENDING/DESCENDING KEY clause   The KEY clause specifies the order in which the records in the sort file are to be sorted. It specifies one or more of the key fields defined in the sort record description. If you look at the statement format in figure 5-4, you'll see that a file can be arranged in key sequence in either ascending or descending order.

If you have more than one key field in a file, you can mix ASCENDING and DESCENDING in the same SORT statement. For example, let's say you want to print an accounts receivable report showing the balance due for each unpaid invoice (INV-BAL-DUE) in descending order. However, if invoices for two or more different customers have the same amount, these are to be shown in ascending

Procedure Division statements

SORT sort-file-name

$$\left\{ON \begin{Bmatrix} \underline{ASCENDING} \\ \underline{DESCENDING} \end{Bmatrix} KEY \{data\text{-}name\text{-}1\} \dots \right\} \dots$$

[WITH <u>DUPLICATES IN ORDER</u>]

[COLLATING <u>SEQUENCE</u> IS alphabet-name]

$$\begin{Bmatrix} \underline{INPUT} \ \underline{PROCEDURE} \ IS \ procedure\text{-}name\text{-}1 \\ \underline{USING} \ \{file\text{-}name\text{-}1\} \dots \end{Bmatrix}$$

$$\begin{Bmatrix} \underline{OUTPUT} \ \underline{PROCEDURE} \ IS \ procedure\text{-}name\text{-}2 \\ \underline{GIVING} \ \{file\text{-}name\text{-}2\} \ \dots \end{Bmatrix}$$

MERGE merge-file-name

$$\left\{ON \begin{Bmatrix} \underline{ASCENDING} \\ \underline{DESCENDING} \end{Bmatrix} KEY \{data\text{-}name\text{-}1\} \dots \right\} \dots$$

[COLLATING <u>SEQUENCE</u> IS alphabet-name]

<u>USING</u> file-name-1 {file-name-2} ...

$$\begin{Bmatrix} \underline{OUTPUT} \ \underline{PROCEDURE} \ IS \ procedure\text{-}name\text{-}1 \\ \underline{GIVING} \ \{file\text{-}name\text{-}3\} \ \dots \end{Bmatrix}$$

<u>RELEASE</u> sort-work-record-name [<u>FROM</u> identifier]

<u>RETURN</u> sort/merge-file-name RECORD [<u>INTO</u> identifier]

    Aᵀ <u>END</u> imperative-statement

paragraph-name. <u>EXIT</u>.

Notes: 1. The 1985 COBOL elements are shaded.

       2. In 1974 COBOL, an input or output procedure has to be a section, and a RELEASE or RETURN statement has to be coded in the section that represents the related input or output procedure.

       3. In 1985 COBOL, an input or output procedure can be a section or a paragraph, and a RELEASE or RETURN statement doesn't have to be coded in the related input or output procedure.

Figure 5-4   COBOL statement formats for sorting and merging (part 2 of 2)

customer-number (INV-CUST-NO) sequence. To accomplish this sorting task, you code a SORT statement that starts like this:

```
SORT SORTFILE
    ON DESCENDING KEY INV-BAL-DUE
       ASCENDING KEY  INV-CUST-NO
```

The records will then be arranged in ascending customer-number sequence within descending balance-due sequence.

The WITH DUPLICATES IN ORDER clause The WITH DUPLICATES clause is a new feature under 1985 COBOL. It tells the sort program what to do if there are multiple records with the same keys. In the example above, for instance, there may be two or more records with the same balance due and customer number. In this case, if the WITH DUPLICATES clause is coded, the records with the duplicate keys will be returned from the sort program in the same order that they were released to it. If the WITH DUPLICATES clause isn't coded, the order in which the records will be returned is unpredictable. Since it takes additional processing time to keep the duplicate records in order, you shouldn't code this clause unless you definitely need it.

The COLLATING SEQUENCE clause The COLLATING SEQUENCE clause lets you use a collating sequence for the sort that is different than the collating sequence used for other operations within the program. Within this clause, the alphabet name refers to a name that has been established in the SPECIAL-NAMES paragraph of the Configuration Section in the Environment Division. Although I've included this clause in figure 5-4 so the formats for the SORT and MERGE statements are complete, it's likely that you'll never use it.

I'm not going to show you how to establish an alphabet name and a new collating sequence in the Environment Division for several reasons. First, the Environment Division code for establishing an alphabet is somewhat compiler dependent. Second, as I just mentioned, it's likely that you will never have to change the sequence on your system. Third, if you do have to change the sequence, it's likely that your shop will have an established procedure for doing so.

The input and output procedures An *input procedure* is a procedure that processes one or more input files before the sort work file is sorted. An *output procedure* is a procedure that processes the data in a sort work file after the file has been sorted. The SORT statement passes control to its input procedure before the sort function takes place and to its output procedure after the sort function has taken place. It does this much like a PERFORM statement passes control to a COBOL paragraph.

Using 1974 COBOL, the input and output procedures of a SORT statement had to be sections. A *section* is a portion of a COBOL program that starts with a *section name*. A section name is just like a paragraph name except that it is followed by the word SECTION as in this example:

```
100-SELECT-CUSTOMER-RECORDS SECTION.
```

Here, the section name is 100-SELECT-CUSTOMER-RECORDS. Note that a space separates the section name and the word SECTION. One section ends when the next section begins or when the end of the program is reached. You'll see sections used in the first two programs in this topic, because most people are still using 1974 COBOL compilers.

Under the 1985 standards, though, the input and output procedures in an internal sort don't have to be sections. They can be paragraphs. Since the use of paragraphs is more in keeping with our style of structured programming, we recommend that you use paragraphs instead of sections if you're using a 1985 COBOL compiler. I'll explain this in more detail later on in this topic.

The USING clause   If you don't need to process the input file before it's sorted, you don't need to code an input procedure or specify one in the SORT statement. Instead, all you need to do is name the input file that's to be sorted in the USING clause. Since the sort program will automatically open and close the file, the input file shouldn't be open when the SORT statement is executed.

The GIVING clause   Just as a USING clause can replace an input procedure, a GIVING clause can replace an output procedure if the sorted records don't have to be processed by your program. When you use the GIVING clause, the sorted records are written directly to the output file named in this clause. This file can then be used as input to another program.

To illustrate, suppose that I wanted to select all of the customers with non-zero balances from an accounts receivable file and write the selected records to a new file in ascending balance-due order. Then, the SORT statement might look like this:

```
SORT SORTFILE
    ON ASCENDING KEY INV-BAL-DUE
    INPUT PROCEDURE IS 100-SELECT-CUSTOMER-RECORDS
    GIVING SELCUST.
```

Here, the input procedure is used to select the appropriate records from the customer file. Then, the file is sorted into ascending balance-due sequence, and the sorted records are written to a file named SELCUST.

There are two other things you should know when you use the GIVING clause. First, the output file must not be open when the SORT statement is executed because the sort/merge program will automatically open and close the file. Second, under the 1985 standards, you can specify more than one output file in the GIVING clause. Then, each sorted record is written in each of the output files specified.

Incidentally, you should never code both a USING and a GIVING clause in the same SORT statement. If you do this, there's no reason for using an internal sort. A standalone sort will accomplish the same thing more efficiently.

The RELEASE statement

The RELEASE statement is similar to the WRITE statement in that it is an output verb. It passes a record to the sort work area so it's ready for sorting. Under the 1974 standards, the RELEASE statement must be coded in an input procedure, which must be a section, but that's not required by the 1985 standards. Also, since it is an output verb like the WRITE statement, we recommend that it be coded in its own module.

If you look at the statement format in figure 5-4, you'll see you can use the FROM option in a RELEASE statement just as you can in a WRITE statement. This causes a record to be moved to the sort work area before it is released for sorting.

The RETURN statement

The RETURN statement is similar to the READ statement in that it is an input verb. After a file has been sorted, the RETURN verb makes the next sorted record available to the program. Under the 1974 standards, the RETURN verb must be coded in an output procedure, which must be a section, but that's not required by the 1985 standards. Also, since RETURN is an input verb like the READ statement, we recommend that it be coded in its own module.

If you look at the format in figure 5-4, you'll see that you can code an INTO option with a RETURN statement just as you can with a READ statement. This causes the sorted record to be moved to an output or working-storage area. You must also use the AT END clause with the RETURN statement so your program can tell when there aren't any more records in the sort work file.

The EXIT statement

You may already be familiar with the EXIT statement. It's a one-word statement that doesn't cause any processing to take place. However, it does provide a way for a program to reach the end of an input or output procedure. As shown in the format in figure 5-4, it must be the only statement in a paragraph when it's used.

Under the 1974 COBOL standards, an exit paragraph is normally the last paragraph of an input or output procedure. When an exit paragraph is reached, the sort program knows that the input or output procedure has completed its processing. As a result, the program continues with its next function. That function is either the sort portion of the SORT statement (following an input procedure) or the first statement after the SORT statement (following an output procedure).

To get to the exit paragraph of an input or output procedure, a GOTO statement is used. This is one of the special cases in which you have to use a GOTO statement whether you want to or not. You'll see this illustrated in a moment. Under the 1985 standards, though, you don't have to use exit paragraphs or GOTO statements, and I'll illustrate that too.

Two illustrative programs

Now I'd like to show you two programs that illustrate the COBOL code for an internal sort. The first program shows how the SORT statement works when both an input and output procedure are used. The second program shows a SORT statement with the USING clause instead of an input procedure.

An edit-sort-and-update program　　　Figure 5-5 presents a program overview for a program that edits a file of inventory transactions, sorts the valid transactions into item number sequence, and updates the sequential master file based on the data in the valid transactions. In other words, the functions of an edit program, a sort program, and an update program are combined in one program. If you refer back to chapter 2, you'll find that the program described in these specifications combines the functions of the edit and update programs presented in figures 2-7 through 2-12.

Figure 5-6 is a structure chart for this program. Here, modules 100, 300, and 400 reflect the three main jobs of the program: (1) editing the inventory transactions; (2) sorting the valid transactions into item number sequence; and (3) updating the inventory master records. Note that module 240, which writes an invalid transaction to the error file, is a common module. It will be called by both the input and output procedures of the SORT statement.

Figure 5-7 presents the COBOL code for this program. Take a minute to look it over and get acquainted with the new statements. I think you'll understand most of it.

The first thing I want you to notice in the program is the SELECT statement for the sort work file, named SORTWRK.

Because it's a sequential file, its format is like the format of the input file. I'll discuss the system names used for sort work files in topic 3 of this chapter.

Instead of coding an FD statement for the sort work file, I've coded an SD statement. In the record description that follows, I've only coded one field and the rest is filler. The field I've coded, SW-ITEM-NO, is the key field for the sort, so it must be defined in this record description.

Now take a look at the Procedure Division. First, let's look at the SORT statement in module 000. It specifies that the sort work file (SORTWRK) is to be sorted by the key field (SW-ITEM-NO) in ascending sequence. Before the sort is executed, the input procedure named 100-EDIT-INVENTORY-TRANS is to be executed. After the sort, the output procedure named 400-UPDATE-INVENTORY-MASTERS is to be executed.

To provide for the input and output procedures, which must be sections in 1974 COBOL, the entire program is divided into sections. The first section, named 000-UPDATE-INVENTORY-FILE, starts with a paragraph named 000-UPDATE-INVENTORY-FILE-P. The P is added to the paragraph name to distinguish it from the section name, since it can't be the same as the section name. When using some compilers, this paragraph name can be omitted, but other compilers require that all sections be divided into paragraphs so a paragraph name like this is required. The rest of the program consists of a section that represents the input procedure of the SORT statement and a section that represents its output procedure.

In module 100, the top-level module of the input procedure, module 200 is executed repeatedly until the end of the transaction file is reached. Module 200 performs module 210 to read each transaction record and module 220 to edit each record. Then, if a transaction is valid, module 200 performs module 230 to release a record for sorting; otherwise, it performs module 240 to write an invalid transaction on the error file.

When the end of the transaction file is reached, module 100 uses a GO TO statement to branch to the last paragraph in this section, 100-EXIT. Without the GOTO, the program would fall through to module 200. When 100-EXIT is executed, the SORT statement knows that the input procedure is finished because the EXIT statement is the last statement in this section. The only code required in the exit paragraph is the EXIT statement.

After the valid transactions have been sorted, the output procedure is executed. Module 400, the top-level module of this procedure, executes module 500 repeatedly until all of the records in the transaction file and the old master file have been processed. Module 500, in turn, performs module 510, which returns the sorted records from the sort program; then, it performs modules 520 through 550 to update the master record that is affected by each transaction. If a

Program:	INV1200 Update inventory file	Page: 1
Designer:	Mike Murach	Date: 09-03-86

Input/output specifications

File	Description	Use
INVTRAN	Inventory transaction file	Input
INVMAST	Old inventory master file	Input
NEWMAST	New inventory master file	Output
ERRTRAN	Invalid inventory transaction file	Output

Process specifications

This program does three major functions: (1) it edits a file of inventory transactions (INVTRAN); (2) it sorts the valid transactions into sequence by item number; and (3) it sequentially updates an inventory master file (INVMAST) based on the data in the valid inventory transactions, thus creating a new master file that contains the updated master records (NEWMAST). If the program discovers any invalid transactions, either during the editing function or the update function, it writes the error transactions in the invalid transaction file (ERRTRAN).

To edit the inventory transactions, the program simply checks the item number, vendor number, and receipt quantity fields to make sure they're numeric. If they are, the transaction record is considered valid.

If a valid transaction has the same item number as a master record, the transaction matches the master record. Then, the transaction data should be used to update the master record: The on hand quantity in the master record should be increased by the receipt quantity in the transaction record.

Both INVTRAN and INVMAST are sequential files, but only INVMAST is in sequence by item number. Also, the record formats for INVTRAN and ERRTRAN are the same, and the record formats for INVMAST and NEWMAST are the same.

Figure 5-5   The program specifications for an update program with an internal sort

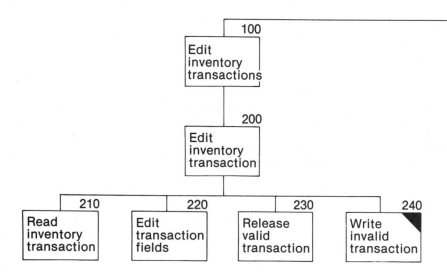

Figure 5-6   The structure chart for an edit-sort-and-update program

transaction isn't matched by a master record, module 500 performs module 240 to write the record on the error file. When all of the sorted records have been processed, module 400 passes control back to the SORT statement by using a GO TO statement that branches to the last paragraph in the section, 400-EXIT. Again, this module contains only an EXIT statement.

If you've compared the coding in figure 5-7 to the structure chart in figure 5-6, you may be wondering why the SORT statement is coded in module 000. Why isn't it in module 300, "sort valid transactions"?

The SORT statement must be coded in module 000, because it controls the execution of the rest of the program. In other words, the SORT statement controls all three of the functions defined by modules 100, 300, and 400 in figure 5-6. However, module 300 is empty because the actual sorting is done by the system's sort/merge program, which is called by the SORT statement. In terms of COBOL, then,

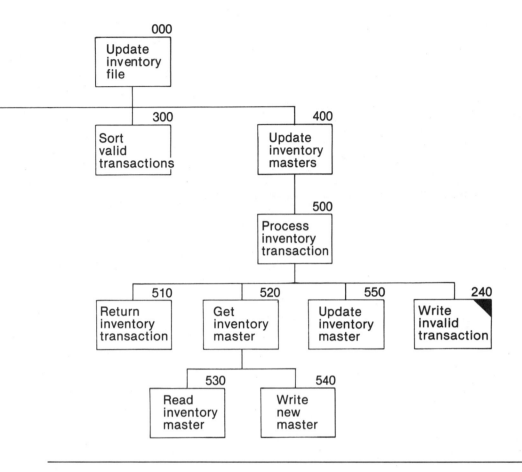

module 300 is a *dummy module*, so it's coded as a comment in figure 5-7. If the SORT statement contained a USING clause instead of an input procedure, module 100 would be a dummy module too. And, if it contained a GIVING clause instead of an output procedure, module 400 would be a dummy module. However, you would never code an internal sort with both USING and GIVING clauses because it would be more efficient to use a standalone sort.

Although dummy modules don't have to be included on the structure chart for a program, we recommend that you include them to indicate the processing that's done by the SORT statement. This will make your structure charts conceptually correct. Similarly, it can't hurt to put a comment line or two in your COBOL code for each dummy module that results from a SORT statement, as we did in the program in figure 5-7. That way it will be clear to anybody who has to modify the program that a module in the structure chart is actually a dummy module done by the sort/merge program.

```
IDENTIFICATION DIVISION.
*
 PROGRAM-ID.  INV1200.
*
 ENVIRONMENT DIVISION.
*
 INPUT-OUTPUT SECTION.
*
 FILE-CONTROL.
      SELECT INVTRAN ASSIGN SYS020-AS-SORTIN.
      SELECT INVMAST ASSIGN SYS021-AS-INVMAST.
      SELECT NEWMAST ASSIGN SYS022-AS-NEWMAST.
      SELECT ERRTRAN ASSIGN SYS023-AS-ERRTRAN.
      SELECT SORTWRK ASSIGN SYS001-UT-FBA1-S-SORTWK1.
*
 DATA DIVISION.
*
 FILE SECTION.
*
 FD   INVTRAN
      LABEL RECORDS ARE STANDARD
      RECORD CONTAINS 21 CHARACTERS.
*
 01   INVENTORY-TRANSACTION-AREA    PIC X(21).
*
 FD   INVMAST
      LABEL RECORDS ARE STANDARD
      RECORD CONTAINS 80 CHARACTERS.
*
 01   MASTER-RECORD-AREA        PIC X(80).
*
 FD   NEWMAST
      LABEL RECORDS ARE STANDARD
      RECORD CONTAINS 80 CHARACTERS.
*
 01   NEW-MASTER-AREA           PIC X(80).
*
 FD   ERRTRAN
      LABEL RECORDS ARE STANDARD
      RECORD CONTAINS 21 CHARACTERS.
*
 01   ERROR-TRANSACTION         PIC X(21).
*
 SD   SORTWRK
      RECORD CONTAINS 21 CHARACTERS.
*
 01   SORT-WORK-AREA.
*
      05   SW-ITEM-NO           PIC X(5).
      05   FILLER               PIC X(16).
*
 WORKING-STORAGE SECTION.
*
 01   SWITCHES.
*
```

Figure 5-7   The edit-sort-and-update program using 1974 COBOL (part 1 of 4)

```
        05    INVTRAN-EOF-SWITCH                  PIC X      VALUE 'N'.
              88   INVTRAN-EOF                                VALUE 'Y'.
        05    VALID-TRAN-SWITCH                   PIC X.
              88   VALID-TRAN                                 VALUE 'Y'.
        05    ALL-RECORDS-PROCESSED-SWITCH   PIC X      VALUE 'N'.
              88   ALL-RECORDS-PROCESSED                      VALUE 'Y'.
        05    FIRST-EXECUTION-SWITCH              PIC X      VALUE 'Y'.
              88   FIRST-EXECUTION                            VALUE 'Y'.
*
  01    INVENTORY-TRANSACTION.
*
        05    IT-ITEM-NO            PIC X(5).
        05    IT-VENDOR-NO          PIC X(5).
        05    IT-RECEIPT-DATE       PIC X(6).
        05    IT-RECEIPT-QUANTITY-X PIC X(5).
        05    IT-RECEIPT-QUANTITY REDEFINES IT-RECEIPT-QUANTITY-X
                                    PIC 9(5).
*
  01    INVENTORY-MASTER-RECORD.
*
        05    IM-DESCRIPTIVE-DATA.
              10    IM-ITEM-NO               PIC X(5).
              10    IM-ITEM-DESC             PIC X(20).
              10    IM-UNIT-COST             PIC 999V99.
              10    IM-UNIT-PRICE            PIC 999V99.
        05    IM-INVENTORY-DATA.
              10    IM-REORDER-POINT         PIC S9(5).
              10    IM-ON-HAND               PIC S9(5).
              10    IM-ON-ORDER              PIC S9(5).
        05    FILLER                         PIC X(30).
*
 PROCEDURE DIVISION.
*
 000-UPDATE-INVENTORY-FILE SECTION.
*
 000-UPDATE-INVENTORY-FILE-P.
*
        OPEN INPUT    INVTRAN
                      INVMAST
             OUTPUT   NEWMAST
                      ERRTRAN.
        SORT SORTWRK
            ON ASCENDING KEY SW-ITEM-NO
            INPUT PROCEDURE IS 100-EDIT-INVENTORY-TRANS
            OUTPUT PROCEDURE IS 400-UPDATE-INVENTORY-MASTERS.
        CLOSE INVTRAN
              INVMAST
              NEWMAST
              ERRTRAN.
        DISPLAY 'INV1200  I  1   NORMAL EOJ'.
        STOP RUN.
```

Figure 5-7   The edit-sort-and-update program using 1974 COBOL (part 2 of 4)

```
*
 100-EDIT-INVENTORY-TRANS SECTION.
*
 100-EDIT-INVENTORY-TRANS-P.
*
     PERFORM 200-EDIT-INVENTORY-TRAN
         UNTIL INVTRAN-EOF.
     GO TO 100-EXIT.
*
 200-EDIT-INVENTORY-TRAN.
*
     PERFORM 210-READ-INVENTORY-TRAN.
     IF NOT INVTRAN-EOF
         PERFORM 220-EDIT-TRANSACTION-FIELDS
         IF VALID-TRAN
             PERFORM 230-RELEASE-VALID-TRAN
         ELSE
             PERFORM 240-WRITE-INVALID-TRAN.
*
 210-READ-INVENTORY-TRAN.
*
     READ INVTRAN INTO INVENTORY-TRANSACTION
         AT END
             MOVE 'Y' TO INVTRAN-EOF-SWITCH.
*
 220-EDIT-TRANSACTION-FIELDS.
*
     MOVE 'Y' TO VALID-TRAN-SWITCH.
     IF        IT-ITEM-NO NOT NUMERIC
         OR IT-VENDOR-NO NOT NUMERIC
         OR IT-RECEIPT-QUANTITY-X NOT NUMERIC
         MOVE 'N' TO VALID-TRAN-SWITCH.
*
 230-RELEASE-VALID-TRAN.
*
     RELEASE SORT-WORK-AREA FROM INVENTORY-TRANSACTION.
*
 240-WRITE-INVALID-TRAN.
*
     WRITE ERROR-TRANSACTION FROM INVENTORY-TRANSACTION.
*
 100-EXIT.
*
     EXIT.
*
*300-SORT-VALID-TRANSACTIONS.  DUMMY MODULE DONE BY SORT PROGRAM.
*
 400-UPDATE-INVENTORY-MASTERS SECTION.
*
 400-UPDATE-INVENTORY-MASTERS-P.
*
     MOVE LOW-VALUE TO IM-ITEM-NO.
     PERFORM 500-PROCESS-INVENTORY-TRAN
         UNTIL ALL-RECORDS-PROCESSED.
     GO TO 400-EXIT.
*
```

Figure 5-7   The edit-sort-and-update program using 1974 COBOL (part 3 of 4)

```
500-PROCESS-INVENTORY-TRAN.
*
    PERFORM 510-RETURN-INVENTORY-TRAN.
    PERFORM 520-GET-INVENTORY-MASTER
        UNTIL IM-ITEM-NO NOT < IT-ITEM-NO.
    IF          IM-ITEM-NO = HIGH-VALUE
          AND IT-ITEM-NO = HIGH-VALUE
        MOVE 'Y' TO ALL-RECORDS-PROCESSED-SWITCH
    ELSE
        IF IM-ITEM-NO = IT-ITEM-NO
            PERFORM 550-UPDATE-INVENTORY-MASTER
        ELSE
            PERFORM 240-WRITE-INVALID-TRAN.
*
510-RETURN-INVENTORY-TRAN.
*
    RETURN SORTWRK INTO INVENTORY-TRANSACTION
        AT END
            MOVE HIGH-VALUE TO IT-ITEM-NO.
*
520-GET-INVENTORY-MASTER.
*
    IF FIRST-EXECUTION
        PERFORM 530-READ-INVENTORY-MASTER
        MOVE 'N' TO FIRST-EXECUTION-SWITCH
    ELSE
        PERFORM 540-WRITE-NEW-MASTER
        PERFORM 530-READ-INVENTORY-MASTER.
*
530-READ-INVENTORY-MASTER.
*
    READ INVMAST INTO INVENTORY-MASTER-RECORD
        AT END
            MOVE HIGH-VALUE TO IM-ITEM-NO.
*
540-WRITE-NEW-MASTER.
*
    WRITE NEW-MASTER-AREA FROM INVENTORY-MASTER-RECORD.
*
550-UPDATE-INVENTORY-MASTER.
*
    ADD IT-RECEIPT-QUANTITY TO IM-ON-HAND.
*
400-EXIT.
*
    EXIT.
```

Figure 5-7   The edit-sort-and-update program using 1974 COBOL (part 4 of 4)

You may have noticed in figure 5-6 that modules 200 and 500 are multiples of 100s, instead of 10s, even though they're at the third level of the structure chart. We did this because modules 100 and 400, the top-level modules in the input and output procedures, are roughly equivalent to 000 modules in other programs. As a result, the modules that they call should be numbered by 100s. Perhaps you can understand this better if you review the structure charts for the edit and update programs in figures 2-8 and 2-11. These are the structure charts that the chart in figure 5-6 is based upon.

By the way, you can have more than one SORT statement in the same program, although you probably won't find many programs in which you need that capability. In the edit-and-update program, for example, you could sort the error file and list the contents of it after module 000 finishes executing the first SORT statement. However, only one sort can be executed at a time. In other words, you can't code a SORT statement in the input or output procedure of another SORT statement.

A three-level report preparation program   To give you a little more feel for the COBOL sort structure and language, let me show you another example. Figure 5-8 presents the progam overview and print chart for a program that reads an invoice file indexed by invoice number and prints a summary report showing total sales at three levels: branch, salesman, and customer. In order to produce this report, the invoice records have to be sorted by customer number within salesman number within branch number.

Since sorting an indexed file is a new feature under the 1985 standards, you can't develop this program using a 1974 COBOL compiler. Also, if you haven't read chapter 3 yet, don't worry about my reference to the indexed file in this program. Just concentrate on the sort logic.

Figure 5-9 is a structure chart for this program. Here again, the modules at the second level of the chart reflect the processing that is done by the SORT statement in module 000. In this case, however, there is no need to process the records before sorting them, so module 100 will be a dummy module. Also, the sort module will be empty because the actual sorting is done by the system's sort/merge program under the control of the SORT statement. After the sort has been completed, module 300 will control the processing that prepares the sales report from the sorted records.

Figure 5-10 gives the program listing for this report preparation program. Although this program contains the same sort elements as the edit-sort-and-update program, there are a couple of differences you should notice.

First, because the invoice file is indexed, the ORGANIZATION, ACCESS, and RECORD KEY clauses must all be coded for this file. Since an indexed file in a sort operation must have sequential access, that's what I've specified in the ACCESS clause.

```
+-----------------------------------------------------------------------+
| Program: MKTG1100  Prepare sales report        Page: 1                |
+-----------------------------------------------------------------------+
| Designer: Anne Prince                          Date: 09-03-86         |
+-----------------------------------------------------------------------+
```

Input/output specifications

```
+-----------------------------------------------------------------------+
| File            Description                         Use               |
|                                                                       |
| INVOICE         Invoice file                        Input             |
| SALESRPT        Print file:  Sales report           Output            |
|                                                                       |
|                                                                       |
|                                                                       |
|                                                                       |
+-----------------------------------------------------------------------+
```

Process specifications

```
+-----------------------------------------------------------------------+
| This program prepares a sales report from data in the invoice file    |
| (INVOICE).  The invoice file is indexed by invoice number.            |
|                                                                       |
| The report should be printed in sequence by customer number within    |
| salesrep number within branch number.  As a result, the invoice file  |
| has to be sorted into this sequence.  Then, one line is printed on the |
| report for each customer; total lines are printed for each salesrep    |
| and branch; and a grand total line is printed at the end of the report.|
|                                                                       |
| To calculate the sales amount for each invoice record, the program     |
| must multiply unit price times quantity.                              |
|                                                                       |
+-----------------------------------------------------------------------+
```

Figure 5-8   The program specifications for a report preparation program with an internal sort (part 1 of 2)

The print chart for the sales report

Record Name	Line	Content
HD4-LINE-1	1	`SALES REPORT OF 99/99/99    PAGE 999`
	2	
HD4-LINE-2	3	`BRANCH  SALESREP   CUSTOMER    SALES`
HD4-LINE-3	4	`NUMBER  NUMBER     NUMBER      AMOUNT`
	5	
CUSTOMER-TOTAL-LINE	6	`X       XX        XXXXX       ZZZZ9.99`
	7	`                   XXXXX       ZZZZ9.99`
SALESREP-TOTAL-LINE	8	`                              ZZZZZZ9.99 *`
	9	
	10	`        XX        XXXXX       ZZZZ9.99`
	11	`                   XXXXX       ZZZZ9.99`
	12	`                   XXXXX       ZZZZ9.99`
	13	`                   XXXXX       ZZZZ9.99`
	14	`                   XXXXX       ZZZZ9.99`
	15	`                              ZZZZZZ9.99 *`
	16	
BRANCH-TOTAL-LINE	17	`                              ZZZZZZ9.99 * *`
	18	
	19	`X       XX        XXXXX       ZZZZ9.99`
	20	`                   XXXXX       ZZZZ9.99`
	21	`                   XXXXX       ZZZZ9.99`
	22	`                              ZZZZZZ9.99 *`
	23	
	24	`        XX        XXXXX       ZZZZ9.99`
	25	`                   XXXXX       ZZZZ9.99`
	26	`                   XXXXX       ZZZZ9.99`
	27	`                              ZZZZZZ9.99 *`
	28	
	29	`        XX        XXXXX       ZZZZ9.99`
	30	`                   XXXXX       ZZZZ9.99`
	31	`                              ZZZZZZ9.99 *`
	32	
	33	`                              ZZZZZZ9.99 * *`
	34	
	35	
GRAND-TOTAL-LINE	36	`              GRAND TOTAL $ZZZZZZ9.99 * * *`
	37–50	

Figure 5-8   The program specifications for a report preparation program with an internal sort (part 2 of 2)

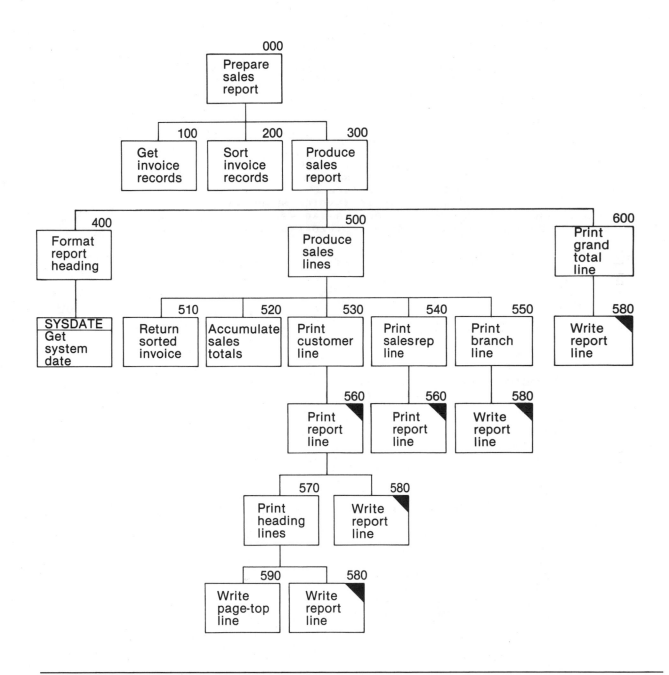

Figure 5-9   The structure chart for the report preparation program with an internal sort

```
 IDENTIFICATION DIVISION.
*
 PROGRAM-ID.       MKTG1100.
*
 ENVIRONMENT DIVISION.
*
 INPUT-OUTPUT SECTION.
*
 FILE-CONTROL.
     SELECT INVOICE   ASSIGN TO SYS020-INVOICE
                      ORGANIZATION IS INDEXED
                      ACCESS IS SEQUENTIAL
                      RECORD KEY IS IA-INVOICE-NUMBER.
     SELECT SALESRPT ASSIGN TO SYS006-UR-1403-S.
     SELECT SORTWRK   ASSIGN TO SYS001-UT-FBA1-S-SORTWK1.
*
 DATA DIVISION.
*
 FILE SECTION.
*
 FD  INVOICE
     LABEL RECORDS ARE STANDARD
     RECORD CONTAINS 80 CHARACTERS.
*
 01  INVOICE-AREA.
*
     05  IA-INVOICE-NUMBER    PIC X(5).
     05  FILLER               PIC X(75).
*
 FD  SALESRPT
     LABEL RECORDS ARE OMITTED
     RECORD CONTAINS 132 CHARACTERS.
*
 01  PRINT-AREA            PIC X(132).
*
 SD  SORTWRK
     RECORD CONTAINS 80 CHARACTERS.
*
 01  SORT-WORK-AREA.
*
     05  FILLER           PIC X(11).
     05  SW-BRANCH-NO      PIC X.
     05  SW-SALESREP-NO    PIC XX.
     05  SW-CUSTOMER-NO    PIC X(5).
     05  FILLER           PIC X(61).
*
 WORKING-STORAGE SECTION.
*
 01  SWITCHES.
*
     05  INVOICE-EOF-SWITCH      PIC X      VALUE 'N'.
         88  INVOICE-EOF                    VALUE 'Y'.
     05  FIRST-RECORD-SWITCH     PIC X      VALUE 'Y'.
         88  FIRST-RECORD                   VALUE 'Y'.
     05  NEW-BRANCH-SWITCH       PIC X      VALUE 'Y'.
```

Figure 5-10   The report preparation program with an internal sort (part 1 of 6)

```
              88   NEW-BRANCH                              VALUE 'Y'.
        05   NEW-SALESREP-SWITCH         PIC X            VALUE 'Y'.
              88   NEW-SALESREP                            VALUE 'Y'.
*
   01   CONTROL-FIELDS.
*
        05   OLD-CUSTOMER-NO        PIC X(5).
        05   OLD-SALESREP-NO        PIC XX.
        05   OLD-BRANCH-NO          PIC X.
*
   01   PRINT-FIELDS              COMP-3.
*
        05   SPACE-CONTROL          PIC S9.
        05   LINE-COUNT             PIC S999      VALUE +99.
        05   LINES-ON-PAGE          PIC S999      VALUE +55.
        05   PAGE-COUNT             PIC S999      VALUE ZERO.
*
   01   DATE-FIELDS.
*
        05   PRESENT-DATE           PIC 9(6).
*
   01   TOTAL-FIELDS             COMP-3.
*
        05   INVOICE-TOTAL          PIC S9(5)V99.
        05   CUSTOMER-SALES-TOTAL   PIC S9(5)V99    VALUE ZERO.
        05   SALESREP-SALES-TOTAL   PIC S9(7)V99    VALUE ZERO.
        05   BRANCH-SALES-TOTAL     PIC S9(7)V99    VALUE ZERO.
        05   GRAND-SALES-TOTAL      PIC S9(7)V99    VALUE ZERO.
*
   01   INVOICE-RECORD.
*
        05   FILLER                PIC X(11).
        05   IR-BRANCH-NO          PIC X.
        05   IR-SALESREP-NO        PIC XX.
        05   IR-CUSTOMER-NO        PIC X(5).
        05   IR-QUANTITY           PIC S9(3).
        05   FILLER                PIC X(5).
        05   IR-UNIT-PRICE         PIC S9(3)V99.
        05   FILLER                PIC X(48).
*
   01   NEXT-REPORT-LINE          PIC X(132).
*
   01   HEADING-LINE-1.
*
        05   FILLER                PIC X(6)      VALUE SPACE.
        05   FILLER                PIC X(16)     VALUE 'SALES REPORT OF'.
        05   HDG1-DATE             PIC XX/XX/XX.
        05   FILLER                PIC X(9)      VALUE '    PAGE'.
        05   HDG1-PAGE-NO          PIC ZZ9.
        05   FILLER                PIC X(90)     VALUE SPACE.
*
   01   HEADING-LINE-2.
*
        05   FILLER           PIC X(20)    VALUE 'BRANCH    SALESREP   CU'.
        05   FILLER           PIC X(20)    VALUE 'STOMER     SALES       '.
        05   FILLER           PIC X(92)    VALUE SPACE.
```

Figure 5-10   The report preparation program with an internal sort (part 2 of 6)

```
*
 01   HEADING-LINE-3.
*
     05   FILLER              PIC X(20)    VALUE 'NUMBER    NUMBER     N'.
     05   FILLER              PIC X(20)    VALUE 'UMBER       AMOUNT   '.
     05   FILLER              PIC X(92)    VALUE SPACE.
*
 01   CUSTOMER-TOTAL-LINE.
*
     05   FILLER              PIC X(2)     VALUE SPACE.
     05   CTL-BRANCH-NO       PIC X.
     05   FILLER              PIC X(8)     VALUE SPACE.
     05   CTL-SALESREP-NO     PIC XX.
     05   FILLER              PIC X(7)     VALUE SPACE.
     05   CTL-CUSTOMER-NO     PIC X(5).
     05   FILLER              PIC X(5)     VALUE SPACE.
     05   CTL-SALES-AMOUNT    PIC ZZZZ9.99.
     05   FILLER              PIC X(94)    VALUE SPACE.
*
 01   SALESREP-TOTAL-LINE.
*
     05   FILLER              PIC X(28)    VALUE SPACE.
     05   STL-SALES-AMOUNT    PIC ZZZZZZ9.99.
     05   FILLER              PIC X(94)    VALUE ' *'.
*
 01   BRANCH-TOTAL-LINE.
*
     05   FILLER              PIC X(28)    VALUE SPACE.
     05   BTL-SALES-AMOUNT    PIC ZZZZZZ9.99.
     05   FILLER              PIC X(94)    VALUE ' * *'.
*
 01   GRAND-TOTAL-LINE.
*
     05   FILLER              PIC X(28)    VALUE SPACE.
     05   GTL-SALES-AMOUNT    PIC ZZZZZZ9.99.
     05   FILLER              PIC X(94)    VALUE ' * * *'.
*
 PROCEDURE DIVISION.
*
 000-PREPARE-SALES-REPORT SECTION.
*
 000-PREPARE-SALES-REPORT-P.
*
     OPEN OUTPUT SALESRPT.
     SORT SORTWRK
         ON ASCENDING KEY SW-BRANCH-NO
                          SW-SALESREP-NO
                          SW-CUSTOMER-NO
         USING INVOICE
         OUTPUT PROCEDURE IS 300-PRODUCE-SALES-REPORT.
     CLOSE SALESRPT.
     DISPLAY 'MKTG1100  I  1  NORMAL EOJ'.
     STOP RUN.
*
*100-GET-INVOICE-RECORDS.  DUMMY MODULE DONE BY SORT PROGRAM.
*
```

Figure 5-10   The report preparation program with an internal sort (part 3 of 6)

```
*200-SORT-INVOICE-RECORDS.  DUMMY MODULE DONE BY SORT PROGRAM.
*
 300-PRODUCE-SALES-REPORT SECTION.
*
 300-PRODUCE-SALES-REPORT-P.
*
     PERFORM 400-FORMAT-REPORT-HEADING.
     PERFORM 500-PRODUCE-SALES-LINES
         UNTIL INVOICE-EOF.
     PERFORM 600-PRINT-GRAND-TOTAL-LINE.
     GO TO 300-EXIT.
*
 400-FORMAT-REPORT-HEADING.
*
     CALL 'SYSDATE' USING PRESENT-DATE.
     MOVE PRESENT-DATE TO HDG1-DATE.
*
 500-PRODUCE-SALES-LINES.
*
     PERFORM 510-RETURN-SORTED-INVOICE.
     IF NOT INVOICE-EOF
         IF FIRST-RECORD
             PERFORM 520-ACCUMULATE-SALES-TOTALS
             MOVE IR-BRANCH-NO    TO OLD-BRANCH-NO
             MOVE IR-SALESREP-NO TO OLD-SALESREP-NO
             MOVE IR-CUSTOMER-NO TO OLD-CUSTOMER-NO
             MOVE 'N' TO FIRST-RECORD-SWITCH
         ELSE
             IF IR-BRANCH-NO > OLD-BRANCH-NO
                 PERFORM 530-PRINT-CUSTOMER-LINE
                 PERFORM 540-PRINT-SALESREP-LINE
                 PERFORM 550-PRINT-BRANCH-LINE
                 MOVE IR-BRANCH-NO    TO OLD-BRANCH-NO
                 MOVE IR-SALESREP-NO TO OLD-SALESREP-NO
                 MOVE IR-CUSTOMER-NO TO OLD-CUSTOMER-NO
                 PERFORM 520-ACCUMULATE-SALES-TOTALS
             ELSE
                 IF IR-SALESREP-NO > OLD-SALESREP-NO
                     PERFORM 530-PRINT-CUSTOMER-LINE
                     PERFORM 540-PRINT-SALESREP-LINE
                     MOVE IR-SALESREP-NO TO OLD-SALESREP-NO
                     MOVE IR-CUSTOMER-NO TO OLD-CUSTOMER-NO
                     PERFORM 520-ACCUMULATE-SALES-TOTALS
                 ELSE
                     IF IR-CUSTOMER-NO > OLD-CUSTOMER-NO
                         PERFORM 530-PRINT-CUSTOMER-LINE
                         MOVE IR-CUSTOMER-NO TO OLD-CUSTOMER-NO
                         PERFORM 520-ACCUMULATE-SALES-TOTALS
                     ELSE
                         PERFORM 520-ACCUMULATE-SALES-TOTALS
     ELSE
         PERFORM 530-PRINT-CUSTOMER-LINE
         PERFORM 540-PRINT-SALESREP-LINE
         PERFORM 550-PRINT-BRANCH-LINE.
*
```

Figure 5-10 The report preparation program with an internal sort (part 4 of 6)

```
 510-RETURN-SORTED-INVOICE.
*
     RETURN SORTWRK INTO INVOICE-RECORD
         AT END
             MOVE HIGH-VALUE TO IR-BRANCH-NO
             MOVE 'Y' TO INVOICE-EOF-SWITCH.
*
 520-ACCUMULATE-SALES-TOTALS.
*
     COMPUTE INVOICE-TOTAL = IR-UNIT-PRICE
                           * IR-QUANTITY.
     ADD INVOICE-TOTAL TO CUSTOMER-SALES-TOTAL.
     ADD INVOICE-TOTAL TO SALESREP-SALES-TOTAL.
     ADD INVOICE-TOTAL TO BRANCH-SALES-TOTAL.
     ADD INVOICE-TOTAL TO GRAND-SALES-TOTAL.
*
 530-PRINT-CUSTOMER-LINE.
*
     IF NEW-BRANCH
         MOVE OLD-BRANCH-NO TO CTL-BRANCH-NO
     ELSE
         MOVE SPACE TO CTL-BRANCH-NO.
     IF NEW-SALESREP
         MOVE OLD-SALESREP-NO TO CTL-SALESREP-NO
     ELSE
         MOVE SPACE TO CTL-SALESREP-NO.
     MOVE OLD-CUSTOMER-NO TO CTL-CUSTOMER-NO.
     MOVE CUSTOMER-SALES-TOTAL TO CTL-SALES-AMOUNT.
     MOVE CUSTOMER-TOTAL-LINE TO NEXT-REPORT-LINE.
     PERFORM 560-PRINT-REPORT-LINE.
     MOVE 1 TO SPACE-CONTROL.
     MOVE ZERO TO CUSTOMER-SALES-TOTAL.
     MOVE 'N' TO NEW-SALESREP-SWITCH
                 NEW-BRANCH-SWITCH.
*
 540-PRINT-SALESREP-LINE.
*
     MOVE SALESREP-SALES-TOTAL TO STL-SALES-AMOUNT.
     MOVE SALESREP-TOTAL-LINE TO NEXT-REPORT-LINE.
     PERFORM 560-PRINT-REPORT-LINE.
     MOVE 2 TO SPACE-CONTROL.
     MOVE ZERO TO SALESREP-SALES-TOTAL.
     MOVE 'Y' TO NEW-SALESREP-SWITCH.
*
 550-PRINT-BRANCH-LINE.
*
     MOVE BRANCH-SALES-TOTAL TO BTL-SALES-AMOUNT.
     MOVE BRANCH-TOTAL-LINE TO PRINT-AREA.
     PERFORM 580-WRITE-REPORT-LINE.
     MOVE ZERO TO BRANCH-SALES-TOTAL.
     MOVE 'Y' TO NEW-BRANCH-SWITCH.
*
```

Figure 5-10   The report preparation program with an internal sort (part 5 of 6)

```
 560-PRINT-REPORT-LINE.
*

     IF LINE-COUNT > LINES-ON-PAGE
         PERFORM 570-PRINT-HEADING-LINES.
     MOVE NEXT-REPORT-LINE TO PRINT-AREA.
     PERFORM 580-WRITE-REPORT-LINE.
*
 570-PRINT-HEADING-LINES.
*

     ADD 1 TO PAGE-COUNT.
     MOVE PAGE-COUNT TO HDG1-PAGE-NO.
     MOVE HEADING-LINE-1 TO PRINT-AREA.
     PERFORM 590-WRITE-PAGE-TOP-LINE.
     MOVE HEADING-LINE-2 TO PRINT-AREA.
     MOVE 2 TO SPACE-CONTROL.
     PERFORM 580-WRITE-REPORT-LINE.
     MOVE HEADING-LINE-3 TO PRINT-AREA.
     MOVE 1 TO SPACE-CONTROL.
     PERFORM 580-WRITE-REPORT-LINE.
     MOVE 2 TO SPACE-CONTROL.
*
 580-WRITE-REPORT-LINE.
*

     WRITE PRINT-AREA
         AFTER ADVANCING SPACE-CONTROL LINES.
     ADD SPACE-CONTROL TO LINE-COUNT.
*
 590-WRITE-PAGE-TOP-LINE.
*

     WRITE PRINT-AREA
         AFTER ADVANCING PAGE.
     MOVE 1 TO LINE-COUNT.
*
 600-PRINT-GRAND-TOTAL-LINE.
*

     MOVE GRAND-SALES-TOTAL TO GTL-SALES-AMOUNT.
     MOVE GRAND-TOTAL-LINE TO PRINT-AREA.
     MOVE 3 TO SPACE-CONTROL.
     PERFORM 580-WRITE-REPORT-LINE.
*
 300-EXIT.
*

     EXIT.
```

Figure 5-10   The report preparation program with an internal sort (part 6 of 6)

Next, notice that the record description for the sort work file (SORT-WORK-AREA) includes three key fields: SW-BRANCH-NO, SW-SALESMAN-NO, and SW-CUSTOMER-NO. These fields are specified in the SORT statement in module 000 of the program. When this statement is executed, the invoice records will be sorted into ascending customer-number sequence within ascending salesman-number sequence within ascending branch-number sequence.

Finally, since the invoice records don't require any processing before they're sorted, the SORT statement contains a USING clause, not an input procedure. Because the USING clause does the function of module 100 in the structure chart, module 100 is a dummy module, so it's coded as a comment. Because the sort/merge program opens a USING file before it begins processing its records and closes it when it finishes processing its records, the OPEN and CLOSE statements don't specify the invoice file.

The output procedure is similar to the one in the edit-sort-and-update program. The top-level module, module 300, executes module 500 repeatedly until the end of the invoice file is reached. Then, it performs module 600, after which it branches to the exit module so control returns to the SORT statement.

COBOL FOR MERGING

The COBOL for merging files is almost identical to the COBOL for sorting a file. A SELECT statement must be coded for the *merge work file*, and the file must be defined by an SD statement and record description. In the record description, you must define one or more key fields that will be used for the merge function. The only coding differences are in the MERGE statement itself. Because this statement is so similar to the SORT statement, though, I'm not going to present a program that illustrates its use.

The MERGE statement

The format for the MERGE statement is given in figure 5-4. Notice that the MERGE statement doesn't allow for an input procedure, so there are no RELEASE statements in COBOL merge programs. Instead, every COBOL MERGE statement must contain a USING clause. This clause causes the input files to be opened and closed and input records to be made available to the merge operation. You should also notice that the WITH DUPLICATES clause of 1985 COBOL can't be used in a MERGE statement, although it can be used in a SORT statement.

Under 1974 COBOL, if the MERGE statement specifies an output procedure, the program should consist of two sections: one for the output procedure and one for the rest of the program. Within the output procedure, the top-level module should end with a GO TO statement that branches to an exit paragraph at the end of the section. Also, the output procedure must contain a RETURN statement that returns the merged records to the program.

Except for the WITH DUPLICATES clause, 1985 COBOL provides the same features for the MERGE statement that it does for the SORT statement. First, multiple GIVING files can be specified. Second, indexed and relative files can be used as input to the merge function. Third, the output procedure can be a paragraph instead of a section, and the RETURN statement doesn't have to be coded within the paragraph or section that represents the output procedure. I'll explain the significance of this in just a moment.

Like the SORT statement, more than one MERGE statement can be coded in the same program. However, only one merge function can be done at a time. In other words, you can't code a MERGE statement in the output procedure of another MERGE statement.

Another method for merging files

When a MERGE statement is executed, the files that are being merged have to already be in the proper sequence. As a result, it's often more efficient to sort the records in more than one file into a single file than it is to first sort the records in the files and then merge them. To sort the records from several files using only one SORT statement, you code the SORT statement just as you would in any sorting operation, but you code it with an input procedure. Then, in the input procedure, you read the records from all of the files that you want to merge together, and you release them to the sort program. As a result, the sort work file will contain the records from all of the files to be merged, and the sort/merge program will sort them into a single file.

To illustrate, suppose that the program in figure 5-9 prepares the report from the data in several invoice files. As a result, the invoice files have to be merged before the report can be prepared. In this case, the SORT statement would be coded with an input procedure, so module 100 wouldn't be a dummy module. It would be the top-level module in the input procedure, and it would contain statements like these:

```
PERFORM 200-GET-1ST-INVOICE-FILE
    UNTIL INVOICE1-EOF.
PERFORM 230-GET-2ND-INVOICE-FILE
    UNTIL INVOICE2-EOF.
PERFORM 260-GET-3RD-INVOICE-FILE
    UNTIL INVOICE3-EOF.
```

Then, modules 200, 230, and 260 would call modules to read the three input files (INVOICE1, INVOICE2, and INVOICE3) and to release their records to the sort work file. When the input procedure finished executing, the SORT statement would call the sort/merge module to sort all of the records in the sort file, after which the output procedure would prepare the required report from the single sort work file.

1985 COBOL FOR SORTING AND MERGING

I've already mentioned the new features for the SORT/MERGE statement that are provided by 1985 COBOL. These include the WITH DUPLICATES clause, the use of multiple GIVING files, and the use of indexed and relative input and output files. I hope by now that you understand how they are used.

In addition, I want to make sure that you understand how to use paragraphs instead of sections for input and output procedures under the 1985 standards. Because we think this is an important improvement for COBOL compilers, I'd like to present it in more detail.

When you use the 1974 standards, the procedures referred to by a SORT statement have to be sections. Also, RELEASE and RETURN statements can only be coded within the sections that represent the input and output procedures. Finally, the execution of a section ends when its last statement is executed. That's why GO TO statements and exit paragraphs are required by the 1974 standards.

Under the 1985 standards, though, the input and output procedures can be coded as single paragraphs. In addition, the RETURN and RELEASE statements can be coded outside of the input or output procedure. Then, when a paragraph that represents an input or output procedure finishes its execution, control is returned to the SORT statement.

Although this may sound complex, it simplifies the coding for input and output procedures. To illustrate, figure 5-11 presents the edit-sort-and-update program of figure 5-7 when the 1985 features are used. This program was tested using Wang VS COBOL, which provides these 1985 features, even though it's a 1974 compiler.

As you can see, the program in figure 5-11 doesn't use sections or exit paragraphs. Similarly, it doesn't use GO TO statements that branch to the exit paragraphs. Instead, the input and output procedures are coded as paragraphs so control returns to the SORT statement when these paragraphs finish their execution. In other words, the input procedure returns control to the SORT statement when paragraph 100 finishes its execution; the output procedure returns control to the SORT statement when paragraph 400 finishes its execution. As you can see, module 100 calls module 200, which calls module 230, which contains the RELEASE statement for the sort. And module 400 calls module 500, which calls module 510, which contains the RETURN statement for the sort.

```
IDENTIFICATION DIVISION.
*
PROGRAM-ID.  INV1200.
*
ENVIRONMENT DIVISION.
*
INPUT-OUTPUT SECTION.
*
FILE-CONTROL.
    SELECT INVTRAN   ASSIGN TO "INVTRAN" "DISK".
    SELECT INVMAST   ASSIGN TO "INVMAST" "DISK".
    SELECT NEWMAST   ASSIGN TO "NEWMAST" "DISK".
    SELECT ERRTRAN   ASSIGN TO "ERRTRAN" "DISK".
    SELECT SORTWRK   ASSIGN TO "SORTWRK" "DISK".
*
DATA DIVISION.
*
FILE SECTION.
*
FD  INVTRAN
    LABEL RECORDS ARE STANDARD
    RECORD CONTAINS 21 CHARACTERS.
*
01  INVENTORY-TRANSACTION-AREA    PIC X(21).
*
FD  INVMAST
    LABEL RECORDS ARE STANDARD
    RECORD CONTAINS 80 CHARACTERS.
*
01  MASTER-RECORD-AREA            PIC X(80).
*
FD  NEWMAST
    LABEL RECORDS ARE STANDARD
    RECORD CONTAINS 80 CHARACTERS.
*
01  NEW-MASTER-AREA               PIC X(80).
*
FD  ERRTRAN
    LABEL RECORDS ARE STANDARD
    RECORD CONTAINS 21 CHARACTERS.
*
01  ERROR-TRANSACTION             PIC X(21).
*
SD  SORTWRK
    RECORD CONTAINS 21 CHARACTERS.
*
01  SORT-WORK-AREA.
*
    05  SW-ITEM-NO                PIC X(5).
    05  FILLER                    PIC X(16).
*
WORKING-STORAGE SECTION.
*
01  SWITCHES.
*
```

Figure 5-11   The edit-sort-and-update program using 1985 COBOL (part 1 of 4)

```
     05   INVTRAN-EOF-SWITCH              PIC X     VALUE "N".
          88   INVTRAN-EOF                          VALUE "Y".
     05   VALID-TRAN-SWITCH              PIC X.
          88   VALID-TRAN                           VALUE "Y".
     05   ALL-RECORDS-PROCESSED-SWITCH  PIC X     VALUE "N".
          88   ALL-RECORDS-PROCESSED                VALUE "Y".
     05   FIRST-EXECUTION-SWITCH         PIC X     VALUE "Y".
          88   FIRST-EXECUTION                      VALUE "Y".
*
 01  INVENTORY-TRANSACTION.
*
     05   IT-ITEM-NO            PIC X(5).
     05   IT-VENDOR-NO          PIC X(5).
     05   IT-RECEIPT-DATE       PIC X(6).
     05   IT-RECEIPT-QUANTITY-X PIC X(5).
     05   IT-RECEIPT-QUANTITY REDEFINES IT-RECEIPT-QUANTITY-X
                               PIC S9(5).
*
 01  INVENTORY-MASTER-RECORD.
*
     05   IM-DESCRIPTIVE-DATA.
          10   IM-ITEM-NO               PIC X(5).
          10   IM-ITEM-DESC             PIC X(20).
          10   IM-UNIT-COST             PIC S999V99.
          10   IM-UNIT-PRICE            PIC S999V99.
     05   IM-INVENTORY-DATA.
          10   IM-REORDER-POINT         PIC S9(5).
          10   IM-ON-HAND               PIC S9(5).
          10   IM-ON-ORDER              PIC S9(5).
     05   FILLER                        PIC X(30).
*
 PROCEDURE DIVISION.
*
 000-UPDATE-INVENTORY-FILE.
*
     OPEN INPUT   INVTRAN
                  INVMAST
          OUTPUT  NEWMAST
                  ERRTRAN.
     SORT SORTWRK
         ON ASCENDING KEY SW-ITEM-NO
         INPUT PROCEDURE IS 100-EDIT-INVENTORY-TRANS
         OUTPUT PROCEDURE IS 400-UPDATE-INVENTORY-MASTERS.
     CLOSE INVTRAN
           INVMAST
           NEWMAST
           ERRTRAN.
     DISPLAY "INV1200  I  1   NORMAL EOJ".
     STOP RUN.
*
 100-EDIT-INVENTORY-TRANS.
*
     PERFORM 200-EDIT-INVENTORY-TRAN
         UNTIL INVTRAN-EOF.
*
```

Figure 5-11   The edit-sort-and-update program using 1985 COBOL (part 2 of 4)

```
 200-EDIT-INVENTORY-TRAN.
*
     PERFORM 210-READ-INVENTORY-TRAN.
     IF NOT INVTRAN-EOF
         PERFORM 220-EDIT-TRANSACTION-FIELDS
         IF VALID-TRAN
             PERFORM 230-RELEASE-VALID-TRAN
         ELSE
             PERFORM 240-WRITE-INVALID-TRAN.
*
 210-READ-INVENTORY-TRAN.
*
     READ INVTRAN INTO INVENTORY-TRANSACTION
         AT END
             MOVE "Y" TO INVTRAN-EOF-SWITCH.
*
 220-EDIT-TRANSACTION-FIELDS.
*
     MOVE "Y" TO VALID-TRAN-SWITCH.
     IF      IT-ITEM-NO NOT NUMERIC
         OR IT-VENDOR-NO NOT NUMERIC
         OR IT-RECEIPT-QUANTITY-X NOT NUMERIC
         MOVE "N" TO VALID-TRAN-SWITCH.
*
 230-RELEASE-VALID-TRAN.
*
     RELEASE SORT-WORK-AREA FROM INVENTORY-TRANSACTION.
*
 240-WRITE-INVALID-TRAN.
*
     WRITE ERROR-TRANSACTION FROM INVENTORY-TRANSACTION.
*
*300-SORT-VALID-TRANSACTIONS.  DUMMY MODULE DONE BY SORT PROGRAM.
*
 400-UPDATE-INVENTORY-MASTERS.
*
     MOVE LOW-VALUE TO IM-ITEM-NO.
     PERFORM 500-PROCESS-INVENTORY-TRAN
         UNTIL ALL-RECORDS-PROCESSED.
*
 500-PROCESS-INVENTORY-TRAN.
*
     PERFORM 510-RETURN-INVENTORY-TRAN.
     PERFORM 520-GET-INVENTORY-MASTER
         UNTIL IM-ITEM-NO NOT < IT-ITEM-NO.
     IF      IM-ITEM-NO = HIGH-VALUE
         AND IT-ITEM-NO = HIGH-VALUE
         MOVE "Y" TO ALL-RECORDS-PROCESSED-SWITCH
     ELSE
         IF IM-ITEM-NO = IT-ITEM-NO
             PERFORM 550-UPDATE-INVENTORY-MASTER
         ELSE
             PERFORM 240-WRITE-INVALID-TRAN.
*
```

Figure 5-11   The edit-sort-and-update program using 1985 COBOL (part 3 of 4)

```
510-RETURN-INVENTORY-TRAN.
*
    RETURN SORTWRK INTO INVENTORY-TRANSACTICN
        AT END
            MOVE HIGH-VALUE TO IT-ITEM-NO.
*
 520-GET-INVENTORY-MASTER.
*
    IF FIRST-EXECUTION
        PERFORM 530-READ-INVENTORY-MASTER
        MOVE "N" TO FIRST-EXECUTION-SWITCH
    ELSE
        PERFORM 540-WRITE-NEW-MASTER
        PERFORM 530-READ-INVENTORY-MASTER.
*
 530-READ-INVENTCRY-MASTER.
*
    READ INVMAST INTO INVENTORY-MASTER-RECORD
        AT END
            MOVE HIGH-VALUE TO IM-ITEM-NO.
*
 540-WRITE-NEW-MASTER.
*
    WRITE NEW-MASTER-AREA FROM INVENTORY-MASTER-RECORD.
*
 550-UPDATE-INVENTORY-MASTER.
*
    ADD IT-RECEIPT-QUANTITY TO IM-ON-HAND.
*
```

Figure 5-11   The edit-sort-and-update program using 1985 COBOL (part 4 of 4)

EFFICIENCY CONSIDERATIONS

When you develop a program that is going to sort hundreds or thousands of records, you have to consider the efficiency of the resulting program. Two of the most important factors for sorting efficiency are (1) the number of records to be sorted, and (2) the length of the records to be sorted. For maximum efficiency, you should write your programs so they sort as few records as possible and so the records to be sorted are as short as possible. This means that most programs with an internal sort should select or reformat records in the input procedure.

To illustrate, refer back to the program in figure 5-10. If you review the record descriptions, you can see that both the input record and the sort work record are 80 bytes long. However, the output procedure only requires 16 bytes of data in each record. As a result, the efficiency of the program could be improved by using an input procedure that moves only the required data into a 16-byte sort work record.

Of course, few programs are as simple as the one in figure 5-10. Nevertheless, you should always keep these two factors in mind as you develop a program with an internal sort. In many programs, you can adjust one or both of these factors so the program runs more efficiently. This is particularly true for programs that prepare reports from the sorted records.

DISCUSSION

As you have seen, the COBOL sort/merge feature under the 1974 standards presents some problems for the structured programmer. Specifically, the SORT and MERGE statements force you to use sections, GO TO statements, and EXIT statements in your code. Nevertheless, if you pattern your programs after the programs presented in this topic, you should be able to develop effective programs that use the sort/merge feature of 1974 COBOL.

To its credit, the 1985 standards have removed some of the restrictions of the 1974 standards. As a result, you no longer have to divide your programs into sections and you no longer have to use GO TO and EXIT statements. That's why we feel the 1985 standards for the sort/merge feature are a significant improvement over the 1974 standards.

Terminology

sort work file
input procedure
output procedure
section
section name
dummy module
merge work file

Objective

Given the program specifications for a program that requires an internal sort or merge, write a COBOL program that satisfies the specifications. The specifications may require an input procedure, an output procedure, or both.

Topic 3   Compiler dependent code

With only a couple of changes, the programs presented in topic 2 of this chapter will run on any system that uses 1974 or 1985 ANS COBOL. In general, you have to change the system names so they are acceptable to your compiler. You have to change the single quotation marks to double marks if they are required by your compiler. And you have to change COMP-3 usage to COMP usage if COMP is appropriate for your compiler. Also, remember that the program in figure 5-10 uses an indexed input file, which is only acceptable to a 1985 compiler.

Beyond this, there are some special considerations you should be aware of when you use the sort/merge feature on some systems. In this topic, I'll present a few of these that pertain to compilers for IBM mainframes so you'll know what to look for when you use the sort/merge feature of your compiler.

System names in SELECT statements

On many systems, the SELECT statements for sort and merge work files have the same format as for any other sequential file. However, some systems require you to use special names in the ASSIGN clause. That's because they have to be the same as the names used by the sort/merge program.

For example, when you use the VS COBOL compiler on an IBM mainframe running under DOS, the ASSIGN clause for a sort file must look like this:

```
ASSIGN TO SYS001-UT-device-S-SORTWK1
```

Here, SYS001 must identify the I/O device for the work file, and SORTWK1 must be the name of the sort work file.

When you use the VS COBOL or VS COBOL II compiler under OS, the compiler treats the entire ASSIGN clause for the sort work file as comments. However, it does check to make sure that it's coded correctly. Thus, the SELECT statement for a sort work file can be coded just as it is for any other file.

Sorting or merging files that contain variable-length records

If your system supports files of variable-length records and allows you to sort or merge them using the sort/merge feature of COBOL, you should read your reference manuals to see whether there are any special requirements for their use. For instance, when you use IBM's VS COBOL or VS COBOL II compiler, you can't code USING or GIVING clauses for the variable-length files. Instead, you must process the variable-length files by using input or output procedures.

In addition, the use of variable-length records in sort/merge programs has many of the same requirements that I described in the topic on variable-length records in chapter 2. If a variable-length file consists of record formats with different lengths, you must let the system know which record format a RELEASE or RETURN statement applies to so the system can determine the length of the record. If a file consists of records that contain the OCCURS DEPENDING ON clause, you have to make sure that the DEPENDING ON field is set to the proper value before a RELEASE or RETURN statement is issued for a record so the system can determine the length of the record. And you shouldn't use RELEASE FROM or RETURN INTO statements for files with OCCURS DEPENDING ON.

Another method for merging files in OS programs

At the end of the last topic, I showed you a way to merge files by coding an input procedure that reads records from more than one input file and releases them to the sort program. Under OS, though, you can do this more easily by treating the files as a *concatenated data set* (*concatenate* means to link together). To do this, you code the COBOL program just as you would if it were sorting only one file. Then, in your JCL for running the program, you code the files to be merged as a concatenated data set. When you do this, the program reads the concatenated files one after another just as if they were all one file.

Using the IBM special registers

Under IBM COBOL, *special registers* are provided as a means of communication between your COBOL program and the sort/merge program. They are used to pass information to and receive information from the sort/merge program. In general, this information is designed to improve the efficiency of sort and merge functions. Often, these registers are referred to as *sort registers*, even though some of them can also be used for merge functions.

Figure 5-12 presents the two sort registers we feel you should be using with the VS COBOL or VS COBOL II compilers on IBM mainframes. Both registers are extensions to standard COBOL. When you use these registers, you don't define them in working storage. Because they're reserved words, they have fixed meanings defined by the COBOL compiler. For instance, you can see in figure 5-12 that the SORT-RETURN register has an implied picture of S9(4).

Sort register	Picture	Contents	Compiler	Recommendation
SORT-RETURN	S9(4)	The return code of the sort/ merge program	VS COBOL VS COBOL II	You should use this so the program can test to make sure the sort or merge worked properly. On OS systems, you should move 16 into this register when you want the sort or merge to end after the next RELEASE or RETURN statement.
SORT-CONTROL	X(8)	A ddname for the file that contains the sort/merge control statements	VS COBOL II (OS only)	You should use this so parameters can be supplied that can improve the efficiency of the sort/merge program.

Figure 5-12   The IBM special registers for the sort/merge program

In general, you should use the SORT-RETURN register in all of your programs to make sure that the sort or merge function worked properly. If you're using the VS COBOL II compiler, you should also use the SORT-CONTROL register so control statements can be supplied outside of the COBOL program that can improve the efficiency of the sort or merge function.

SORT-RETURN   When the sort/merge program finishes its execution, it places a return code in this register that tells whether the sort/merge program terminated normally or abnormally. If SORT-RETURN contains zero, the sort/merge worked properly; if it contains 16, it failed. We recommend that you use this register in all of your programs to check on the operation of the sort/merge function. Then, you can do whatever error processing is necessary if there's a problem.

Figure 5-13 presents some typical code for the top-level module of a COBOL program that uses the SORT-RETURN register. In this case, if the return code isn't zero, the program displays an error message.

When using the VS COBOL or COBOL II compiler under OS, you can also *send* the sort/merge program a code of 16 by moving this value to the SORT-RETURN register. Then, the sort/merge program will end after the next RETURN or RELEASE statement is executed.

```
000-UPDATE-INVENTORY-FILE.
*
    OPEN INPUT   INVTRAN
                 INVMAST
         OUTPUT  NEWMAST
                 ERRTRAN.
    SORT SORTWRK
        ON ASCENDING KEY SW-ITEM-NO
        INPUT PROCEDURE IS 100-EDIT-INVENTORY-TRANS
        OUTPUT PROCEDURE IS 400-UPDATE-INVENTORY-MASTERS.
    IF SORT-RETURN NOT = ZERO
        DISPLAY 'INV1200  A  2  SORT FAILED'.
    CLOSE INVTRAN
          INVMAST
          NEWMAST
          ERRTRAN.
    DISPLAY 'INV1200  I  1  NORMAL EOJ'.
    STOP RUN.
*
```

Figure 5-13   The use of the SORT-RETURN register on an IBM mainframe

If, for example, one of your programs detects that something has gone haywire, you can code a statement like this:

```
    IF ERROR-CONDITION
        MOVE 16 TO SORT-RETURN.
```

Then, when the program executes the next RETURN or RELEASE statement, the sort/merge function will end, and control will return to the statement following the SORT/MERGE statement.

SORT-CONTROL   When you use the COBOL II compiler, you can use sort control statements outside of the COBOL program to supply values like the size of the file to be sorted or the amount of core storage to be used for the sort. Information like this can improve the efficiency of a sort or merge operation. When you use sort control statements, you can put the ddname of the file that contains these control statements in a register named SORT-CONTROL. If you don't use this register, IGZSRTCD is used as the default name for the file of control statements.

Changing the collating sequence

As I mentioned in topic 2, you can change the collating sequence for a sort or a merge operation on some systems. However, the code that you use to do this in the Environment Division is to some extent compiler dependent. For instance, on the Wang VS system, you can't change the collating sequence at all. On IBM mainframes, you can easily change the sequence from EBCDIC to ASCII, but it takes time to establish a new collating sequence. In any event, if you ever have to change the collating sequence on your system, you'll have to study your reference manuals to figure out what you should code in the Environment Division.

Discussion

In large shops, the sort/merge feature of COBOL is used frequently. As a result, it's important that you write your programs so they will be executed efficiently. To do this, you have to make use of any COBOL extensions that help you improve a program's efficiency. As a result, before you begin using the sort/merge feature, you should find out what support your compiler provides for it and what the standards are for its use in your shop.

Terminology

concatenated data set
special register
sort register

Objective

Find out how to use the compiler dependent code for the COBOL sort/merge feature on your system.

COBOL by function or feature

This section consists of five chapters that show you how to use functions or features that are available within standard COBOL. Since you don't have to read these chapters in sequence, you can skip from one chapter to another as you read this section. However, a professional programmer should be able to use all of the functions and features presented in this section, so you should eventually read all of the chapters. Although you may not have a 1985 COBOL compiler available to you right now, you should read chapter 10 anyway so you will know how 1985 COBOL will affect your programming in the future.

Chapter 6

How to use the COPY library

This chapter is divided into three topics. Topic 1 shows you how to use the COPY library at a basic level. Topic 2 shows you how to use it at an advanced level as done in some shops, even though we don't recommend this use of the COPY library. And topic 3 presents some compiler dependencies that are related to the use of the COPY library. If you've read the topic on the COPY library in *Structured ANS COBOL, Part 1*, you can skip topic 1 of this chapter because it presents the same information.

Topic 1   Basic use of the COPY library

Since a large portion of a typical COBOL program consists of routine descriptions for files, records, and fields, a lot of effort would be wasted if each programmer had to code the same descriptions for each program. Also, there would probably be minor differences in the way each programmer defined the files and records...differences that could lead to errors.

Fortunately, though, segments of COBOL code can be written just once and stored in a *source statement library*. Then, you can copy the segments of code into your programs using COPY statements. This saves coding time, promotes consistency between programs, and reduces errors.

The COPY library

Normally, you can have one or more source statement libraries for each language you use on your system. These libraries are stored on disk devices so the segments of code within them can be accessed rapidly. Since you use the COPY statement in COBOL to copy segments of code from a library into your program, a COBOL source statement library is often referred to as a *COPY library*. From now on, I'll refer to COBOL source statement libraries as COPY libraries.

Each segment of code in the COPY library can be called a *COPY member*. On IBM mainframes, COPY members are also called *COPY books*. And on other systems, they may be called by other names.

Each COPY member in a library is identified by a unique name that can be called a *member name*, *book name*, or *text name*. In this chapter, we'll use the term *text name* to refer to the name that identifies a COPY member. That is consistent with most COBOL manuals.

The COPY statement

Figure 6-1 illustrates the use of a COPY library. Here, a COPY member contains the record and field descriptions for a transaction record. The text name for this COPY member is TRANREC. In the Data Division, the following COPY statement specifies that the member named TRANREC should be copied into the program:

```
COPY TRANREC.
```

Then, when the source program is compiled, the statements from the COPY library are copied into the program and printed on the source

TRANREC member in the COPY library

```
*
 01   INVENTORY-TRANSACTION-RECORD.
*
        05   ITR-CODE            PIC X.
        05   ITR-ITEM-NO         PIC X(5).
        05   ITR-QUANTITY        PIC S9(5).
        05   ITR-REF-NO          PIC X(6).
        05   ITR-REF-DATE        PIC X(6).
```

COPY statement in the Data Division

```
COPY TRANREC.
```

Resulting source code as printed on the source listing

```
            COPY TRANREC.
C           *
C            01   INVENTORY-TRANSACTION-RECORD.
C           *
C                   05   ITR-CODE            PIC X.
C                   05   ITR-ITEM-NO         PIC X(5).
C                   05   ITR-QUANTITY        PIC S9(5).
C                   05   ITR-REF-NO          PIC X(6).
C                   05   ITR-REF-DATE        PIC X(6).
```

Figure 6-1   Using the COPY statement to copy a record description into the Data Division of a program

listing. Usually, the letter C or some other character like a plus sign is printed to the left of each copied statement on the source listing to show that it has been copied into the program.

A COPY statement can be used wherever a programmer-defined word (name), a reserved word, a literal, a PICTURE character string, or a comment entry can be used. It can also be used wherever a separator like a space or a period can be used. In other words, a COPY statement can generally be used in any logical place within a program. Its basic format is simply the word COPY followed by the text name of the member that you want to copy into the program.

Once a COPY member has been copied into a program, it is treated as a part of the program. In the case of a record description like the one in figure 6-1, the programmer can use any of the names in the COPY member in statements in the Procedure Division. For instance, she can use the name INVENTORY-TRANSACTION-RECORD to refer to the entire record, and she can use ITR-CODE and ITR-ITEM-NO to refer to two of the fields within the record.

Incidentally, you'll have to check whether your system allows you to begin a COPY member with a blank comment line like the one used in figure 6-1. For example, the interactive editor on the Wang VS system won't let you start a COPY member in this way. However, if you can start each COPY member with a comment line on your system, I think it makes the compiled listing easier to read.

Guidelines for using the COPY library

So far, I've shown you how to use the COPY library and COPY statement. Now, let me give you some ideas about where in a program you should use COPY statements.

File and record descriptions   Storing file and record descriptions is the most important job of the COPY library. Besides saving programmer time by eliminating repetitive coding, this ensures that all the programs within an installation will use the same names for the records and fields within a file. This, in turn, reduces confusion, program bugs, and interface problems between programs written by different programmers.

At the least, then, the COPY library should contain a COPY member for each record description used within each file of a system. And you should always copy these descriptions into your programs. Then, if a change must be made to a description, a change to one COPY member makes it possible for all programs using the COPY member to be changed simply by recompiling them. In addition, unless system limitations make this impossible, you may want to use COPY members for the SELECT and FD statements of the files within your system.

If you're writing the first program that processes a file, you should see to it that the file and record descriptions are stored in the COPY library. On the other hand, if your program is going to use files that have already been stored in the COPY library, you should get listings of the members so you'll know what code is going to be copied into your program.

Tables   Another common use of the COPY library is to store commonly used tables that aren't subject to a lot of change. For example, suppose a table contains the names of the 50 states as well as their two-letter abbreviations. This table shouldn't ever need to be changed, and it should be used frequently by programmers who want to convert a state code to the expanded state name or vice versa.

Procedure Division paragraphs   In general, we don't recommend that you use COPY members for code in the Procedure Division because the paragraph names and data names usually have to be changed to suit your program. However, some shops do use COPY members in the Procedure Division, and there is a REPLACING clause that you can use with the COPY statement to modify code as it's copied into your program. In case your shop requires it, we'll show you how to use the REPLACING clause in the next topic.

For the most part, though, we recommend that you copy the Procedure Division code you want from a previous program using the copy facility of your system's editor. Or, you can copy the code you need by entering it into the system manually. Then, you can change the names to suit your program, and the code becomes a permanent part of your program. In contrast, the COPY statement copies code into your program every time the program is compiled.

Discussion

A professional programmer uses COPY statements in almost every program. Usually, right after you get complete specifications for a program, you should get listings of all the COPY members that might be applicable to your program. In fact, in a modern COBOL shop, the program specifications should include listings of the COPY members that define the files and records that the program uses.

Terminology

source statement library
COPY library
COPY member
COPY book
member name
book name
text name

Objective

Given program specifications and listings of related members in a COPY library, use the COPY statement to copy the members into your program.

Topic 2   Advanced use of the COPY library

In many COBOL shops, you will use the COPY statement only as described in topic 1. In some shops, though, you will need to use an expanded form of the COPY statement. In this topic, I'll first show you the complete format of the COPY statement. Then, I'll present some guidelines for its use.

The complete format of the COPY statement

Figure 6-2 presents the complete format of the COPY statement. As you can see, the statement has two optional clauses: the OF/IN clause and the REPLACING clause.

The OF/IN clause   It's common for an installation to have more than one COBOL COPY library. When that's the case, you can use the OF/IN clause to specify the library name as well as the text name of a COPY member. As a result, a single program can copy members from more than one library. For instance, the statement

```
COPY TRANREC OF INVCLIB
```

will copy the member named TRANREC in the library named INVCLIB into your program. When you use the OF/IN clause, you can use either OF or IN because they mean the same thing.

The REPLACING clause   The REPLACING clause allows you to change a COPY member as you copy it into your program. When it's used, the compiler searches the COPY member for the specified text, identifier, literal, or word and replaces each occurrence with the value given in the BY clause. The COPY library itself, however, is not changed.

To illustrate, suppose the TRANREC member in figure 6-1 were copied using this statement:

```
COPY TRANREC REPLACING ==05== BY ==10==.
```

Then, all of the 05 levels would be changed to 10 levels in the compiled program.

Figure 6-3 gives another example of the REPLACING clause. In this case, the identifier INVENTORY-TRANSACTION-RECORD is changed to TRANSACTION-WORK-AREA as the COPY member is copied into the source program. Also, the pseudo-text option is used to change one of the pictures from S9(5) to X(5).

When you use the pseudo-text option, the compiler searches the COPY member for the text between the first pair of double equals signs. Whenever it finds a matching portion of text, it replaces what it

```
COPY text-name    [{OF}  library-name]
                   {IN}

    [REPLACING  {(==pseudo-text-1==)}
                {(identifier-1    )}
                {(literal-1       )}
                {(word-1          )}

          BY    {==pseudo-text-2==}}}  ...
                {identifier-2    }
                {literal-2       }
                {word-2          }
```

Figure 6-2   The complete format of the COPY statement

finds with the text between the second pair of double equals signs. As it searches for text, it treats more than one blank the same as one blank, so the blanks don't have to match up exactly for the REPLACING clause to operate as intended. Also, you can replace a pseudo-text string of one or more words with zero, one, or more words. This means you can remove a pseudo-text string from a COPY member if you use a statement like this:

```
COPY TRANREC
     REPLACING ==USAGE IS== BY ====.
```

Here, USAGE IS is replaced by zero words. In effect, then, it's deleted from the COPY member.

Guidelines for using the REPLACING clause

One of the main benefits of using the COPY library is that you can coordinate data names and descriptions in all the programs that use the same files and records. But when you use the REPLACING clause, you encourage variations from one program to another. And this, of course, increases the chance of confusion and error...just what you were trying to avoid. That's why we recommend that you avoid the use of the REPLACING clause.

On the other hand, if your shop standards allow you to use REPLACING clauses, an occasional REPLACING clause for a COPY member in the Data Division is harmless enough. If, for example, you want to make a minor change to a record description, you can copy its COPY member using a REPLACING clause like the one in figure 6-3.

Sometimes, your shop standards will require you to use COPY members for some of the modules in your Procedure Divisions. For instance, some shops use COPY members for all I/O modules. In some of these shops, you have to copy the members into your Procedure

TRANREC member in the COPY library

```
*
 01    INVENTORY-TRANSACTION-RECORD.
*
       05   ITR-CODE           PIC X.
       05   ITR-ITEM-NO        PIC X(5).
       05   ITR-QUANTITY       PIC S9(5).
       05   ITR-REF-NO         PIC X(6).
       05   ITR-REF-DATE       PIC X(6).
```

COPY statement in the Data Division

```
COPY TRANREC REPLACING INVENTORY-TRANSACTION-RECORD
                  BY UNEDITED-INVENTORY-TRANSACTION
     ==S9(5)== BY ==X(5)==.
```

Resulting source code as printed on the source listing

```
        COPY TRANREC REPLACING INVENTORY-TRANSACTION-RECORD
                          BY UNEDITED-INVENTORY-TRANSACTION
             ==S9(5)== BY ==X(5)==.
C       *
C          01   UNEDITED-INVENTORY-TRANSACTION.
C       *
C               05   ITR-CODE           PIC X.
C               05   ITR-ITEM-NO        PIC X(5).
C               05   ITR-QUANTITY       PIC X(5).
C               05   ITR-REF-NO         PIC X(6).
C               05   ITR-REF-DATE       PIC X(6).
```

Figure 6-3   Using the COPY statement with the REPLACING clause in the Data Division

Division without replacing any of the code, so you have to accept the module numbers and data names that are coded in the members. In other shops, you can use the REPLACING clause so you can adjust the module numbers and data names to your program.

Figure 6-4 illustrates the use of the REPLACING clause in a COPY statement that copies a read module into a program. Here, the paragraph name in the COPY member is changed so it is consistent with the structure chart of the program. In effect, though, only the module number is changed. Nevertheless, you have to code the REPLACING clause as shown because you can only replace full words with this clause, not character strings like 999.

I think the example in figure 6-4 helps illustrate why we don't recommend the use of COPY statements with REPLACING clauses. In the time that it takes to code the COPY statement correctly, you can probably code the read module itself. So what do you gain by using the COPY library? This is also true when you use REPLACING clauses to modify longer COPY members. Often, it takes longer to get

RDIMSTSQ member in the COPY library

```
*
 999-READ-INVENTORY-MASTER.
*
     READ INVMAST INTO INVENTORY-MASTER-RECORD
         AT END
             MOVE 'Y' TO INVMAST-EOF-SWITCH.
```

COPY statement in the Procedure Division

```
COPY RDIMSTSQ
    REPLACING 999-READ-INVENTORY-MASTER
        BY 330-READ-INVENTORY-MASTER.
```

Resulting source code as printed on the source listing

```
         COPY RDIMSTSQ
             REPLACING 999-READ-INVENTORY-MASTER
                 BY 330-READ-INVENTORY-MASTER.
C        *
C         330-READ-INVENTORY-MASTER.
C        *
C             READ INVMAST INTO INVENTORY-MASTER-RECORD
C                 AT END
C                     MOVE 'Y' TO INVMAST-EOF-SWITCH.
```

Figure 6-4   Using the COPY statement with the REPLACING clause in the Procedure Division

the COPY statement to work the way you want it to than it would to copy what you want from another program and modify it to suit your program using your interactive editor.

Terminology

None

Objective

If you use the REPLACING clause in your shop, code a COPY statement with a REPLACING clause that will copy a specified COPY member into your program so it is suitable for your program.

Topic 3   Compiler dependent code

Since the COPY statement is so simple, the compiler dependent code is relatively trivial. You should be aware, however, that the OF/IN clause isn't required on all systems; that the REPLACING clause isn't available on all compilers; and that some systems provide other copy facilities that are used instead of the COBOL copy facility.

The OF/IN clause

We sometimes use the OF/IN clause on our Wang VS system because we keep COBOL COPY members in several different libraries. It isn't necessary on the Wang system, though, because you can identify the libraries you're using in other ways.

On most systems, in fact, this facility isn't needed. On an IBM PC, for example, libraries aren't supported at all, so the text name in a COPY statement identifies a file that contains one COPY member. In contrast, on IBM mainframes, you don't need to identify the libraries in your COPY statements because you can set up a chain of COPY libraries to be searched using job control language.

So check your shop standards. In some shops, you may be expected to identify the libraries you're using in COPY statements. In other shops, you may be prohibited from identifying them, even if this facility is available to you.

The REPLACING clause

This clause isn't available on all compilers. In particular, it's not likely to be available on the compilers for microcomputers or minicomputers. For instance, this clause isn't available with Microsoft COBOL or Wang VS COBOL. As a result, you should find out whether it's available on your system before you try to use it.

Other copy facilities

In some shops, the copy facility of COBOL is replaced by the copy facility of an interactive editor or program development system. If that's the case in your shop, you may be using a statement like an INCLUDE statement to copy code from a source library into your program. Most copy facilities, though, are similar in concept to the COBOL copy facility.

Terminology

None

Objective

Find out if you use the COBOL copy facility in your shop. If so, find out what your shop standards are for its use.

Chapter 7

How to use subprograms

This chapter is divided into three topics. Topic 1 explains what subprograms are and shows you how to call them. Topic 2 shows you how to code COBOL subprograms. And topic 3 discusses some compiler dependent code, even though you probably won't ever use any of it. If you've read the material on calling subprograms in *Structured ANS COBOL, Part 1*, you can skip topic 1 of this chapter because it presents the same information.

Topic 1   How to call subprograms

Some processing routines are so general that they can be used in many different programs. In our shop, for example, all of our edit programs check state codes and zip codes to make sure that they're valid. And all our report preparation programs get the date and time so they can be printed in the report headings. Needless to say, it would be a waste of programming effort to develop routines like this from scratch each time they were needed.

Fortunately, though, a commonly used routine can be coded, compiled, and tested, after which it can be stored in a *subprogram library*. Then, this *subprogram* can be called by any COBOL programs that need to use its function. This saves coding, compiling, and testing time, and it reduces programming errors.

To call a subprogram, you only need to know how to use the CALL statement. Before I present this statement, though, I'm going to describe how subprograms are stored. After I present this statement, I'll discuss the problems that you may encounter when testing and debugging programs that call subprograms.

The subprogram library

Normally, you can have one or more subprogram libraries on your system. These libraries are stored on disk devices so the segments of code within them can be accessed rapidly. On IBM mainframes, these libraries are called *relocatable libraries* because the modules within them must be relocated by the linkage editor before they can be executed. On other systems, these libraries are called *object libraries* to distinguish them from source libraries.

The subprograms in a subprogram library have already been compiled and tested, so they consist of object code. As a result, each subprogram can also be called an *object module*. Before a subprogram can be executed, the linkage editor must link it with the program that uses it.

Each subprogram in a library is identified by a unique name that can be called a *subprogram name*. On IBM mainframes, you'll also hear these names referred to as *module names*.

The CALL statement

To execute a subprogram, a COBOL program issues a CALL statement, as shown in figure 7-1. The program that contains the CALL statement is referred to as the *calling program* (or *calling module*).

Statement format

```
CALL 'subprogram-name' [USING identifier-1 ...]
```

Example

```
 DATA DIVISION.
*
     .
     .
     05   DEVIATION-TOTAL               PIC S9(5)      COMP-3.
     05   DEVIATION-TOTAL-SQ-ROOT       PIC S9(5)V99   COMP-3.
     .
     .
*
 PROCEDURE DIVISION.
*
     .
     .
     CALL 'SQROOT' USING DEVIATION-TOTAL
                         DEVIATION-TOTAL-SQ-ROOT.
     MOVE DEVIATION-TOTAL-SQ-ROOT TO SL-DEVIATION-TOTAL-SQ-ROOT.
     .
     .
```

Figure 7-1   Calling a subprogram that takes the square root of the first field passed to it and puts the result in the second field

When it passes control to the subprogram, it *calls* the subprogram. Sometimes, you'll hear the subprogram referred to as the *called module*, or the *called program*.

As you can see in the CALL statement format in figure 7-1, the name of the subprogram can be followed by a USING clause that identifies one or more data items that are *passed* to the subprogram. If more than one data item is used, the order in which they are listed must correspond to the order in which the subprogram expects to receive them. Also, the pictures and usages of the fields must correspond to the expectations of the subprogram. As a result, you must get detailed specifications about the subprogram so you can pass it the fields it needs in the order and with the formats it expects.

In figure 7-1, the subprogram calculates the square root of the number in the first field that is passed to it and puts the result in the second field. As a result, the CALL statement in the calling program is coded as follows:

```
     CALL 'SQROOT' USING DEVIATION-TOTAL
                         DEVIATION-TOTAL-SQ-ROOT.
```

Here, the name of the subprogram is SQROOT; the name of the field to be operated upon is DEVIATION-TOTAL; and the name of the field that should receive the result is DEVIATION-TOTAL-SQ-ROOT. After the subprogram has calculated the square root of DEVIATION-TOTAL, it moves the result to DEVIATION-TOTAL-SQ-ROOT and returns control to the first statement after the CALL statement in the calling program. In figure 7-1, that statement is a MOVE statement.

Notice that nothing has been said about the language in which the subprogram is written. It may have been written in COBOL, but it may also have been written in another language. Since the object module for the calling program is linked with the object module for the subprogram, it doesn't matter what language the subprogram was written in.

Testing and debugging problems

When you write a program that calls one or more subprograms, you should get the specifications for each subprogram before you code your program. That way you'll know how to define the records or fields that each subprogram requires. You'll also know in what sequence to code the data names in the USING portion of the CALL statement.

When you're testing a program that calls one or more subprograms, you may encounter some problems that are difficult to debug. If, for example, a program is cancelled during the execution of one of the subprograms, which module caused the problem: the calling program or the subprogram?

When a subprogram fails or returns incorrect data to the calling program, the first thing to do is make sure that the fields were passed to the subprogram in the right sequence and with the right formats. Most of the time, you'll find that the calling program passed data in a form that wasn't expected by the subprogram. This is particularly true if the subprogram has been used so long that it has been thoroughly tested.

If you're sure that your program has passed data to the subprogram properly and you're not sure that the subprogram has been thoroughly tested, it's possible that the problem is in the subprogram. In this case, you should pass the problem on to the person who is responsible for maintaining the subprogram. In the next topic, you will learn how to write and maintain COBOL subprograms yourself.

Discussion

A professional programmer uses CALL statements in almost every program. Usually, right after you get complete specifications for a program, you should check your subprogram library to see whether it offers any functions that you might find useful in your program. Then, when you design the structure chart for your program, you include a striped box for each subprogram that you'll use. This is illustrated by the program in appendix A, which calls two subprograms named SYSDATE and SYSTIME.

Terminology

subprogram library
subprogram
relocatable library
object library
object module
subprogram name
module name
calling program
calling module
calling a subprogram
called module
called program
passing data to a subprogram

Objective

Given program specifications and subprogram specifications, use CALL statements to call the required subprograms whenever needed by your program.

Topic 2   How to write subprograms

As I said in the last topic, subprograms that are called by COBOL programs don't have to be written in COBOL. In fact, some sub-programs perform functions that can't be coded in COBOL. On the other hand, most of the subprogams in a typical COBOL shop are written in COBOL.

To write a subprogram in COBOL, some additional language elements are required. These elements are summarized in figure 7-2. As you can see, you have to code a Linkage Section in a subprogram; you have to code a USING clause on the Procedure Division header within a subprogram; and you have to use the EXIT PROGRAM statement to end the subprogram and return control to the calling program.

To help you understand these elements, figure 7-3 presents a sub-program for calculating the square root of a number. This figure also shows the code that is used to call the subprogram so you can see how the calling program and the called subprogram are related. In prac-tice, you normally wouldn't have a subprogram for a function that can be coded in one COBOL statement, but this example does illustrate the elements of a subprogram. Also, you should realize that the COMPUTE statement in this subprogram won't compile on all compilers, because many don't allow exponentiation (**) to a frac-tional power (.5). This subprogram works when the compiler allows fractional exponents because raising a number to the .5 power is the same as taking the square root of the number.

The Linkage Section

When a subprogram is called, one or more fields are usually passed to the subprogram. In this case, the passed fields must be described in the Linkage Section in the subprogram. For instance, two fields are passed to the SQROOT subprogram whenever it is called. As a result, two fields are described in the Linkage Section in figure 7-3.

The Linkage Section is coded in the Data Division after the Working-Storage Section. Within the Linkage Section, the fields that are passed to the subprogram must be described at the 01 or 77 level. Since we recommend that you avoid 77 levels in all of your programs, we suggest that you code these fields with 01 levels. In the subprogram in figure 7-3, two fields are described at the 01 level: VALUE-RECEIVED and SQUARE-ROOT. Notice that the pictures and usages of these fields correspond exactly to the pictures and usages of the fields that are passed by the CALL statement in the calling pro-gram.

You should realize that the fields that are described in the

Statement formats

```
LINKAGE SECTION.

01  data-name ...

PROCEDURE DIVISION USING data-name-1 ...

    EXIT PROGRAM.
```

Figure 7-2   COBOL code for writing subprograms

Linkage Section aren't actually a part of the subprogram. Instead, they are part of the calling program. As a result, you can't code VALUE clauses for any of the fields in the Linkage Section, except at the 88 level (condition names). When a subprogram operates on the fields that are passed to it, it actually operates on the fields in the calling program.

Sometimes, it's practical for the calling program to use the same names for the passed fields that are used in the subprogram. If you can do this and it's logical, it's a good idea to use the same names. Often, though, it's illogical or impractical. For instance, when you develop a calling program, you usually don't know what names are used in the Linkage Section of a subprogram because you don't have easy access to the source code for the subprogram. Similarly, when you develop a subprogram, you may not know what programs are going to be calling your subprogram.

In the case of the SQROOT subprogram in figure 7-3, the subprogram uses general names because it performs a general-purpose function that can be called by many different types of programs. As a result, the calling program uses different names for the passed fields than the subprogram does.

The Procedure Division header

A subprogram, like any other program structure, should have one *entry point* and one *exit point*. The entry point is always the start of the Procedure Division. In other words, the subprogram begins with the first statement in the Procedure Division.

When data is passed to a subprogram, the Procedure Division header must identify that data in a USING clause. The data items referred to by the USING clause must be in the same order as the items listed in the CALL statement in the calling program. In figure 7-3, note that the field names listed in the Procedure Division header are the same as the names of the fields described in the Linkage Section.

Calling program

```
 DATA DIVISION.
*
     .
     .
     05   DEVIATION-TOTAL              PIC S9(5)      COMP-3.
     05   DEVIATION-TOTAL-SQ-ROOT      PIC S9(5)V99   COMP-3.
     .
     .
*
 PROCEDURE DIVISION.
*
     .
     .
     CALL 'SQROOT' USING DEVIATION-TOTAL
                         DEVIATION-TOTAL-SQ-ROOT.
     MOVE DEVIATION-TOTAL-SQ-ROOT TO SL-DEVIATION-TOTAL-SQ-ROOT.
     .
     .
```

Subprogram

```
 IDENTIFICATION DIVISION.
*
 PROGRAM-ID.  SQROOT.
*
 ENVIRONMENT DIVISION.
*
 DATA DIVISION.
*
 LINKAGE SECTION.
*
 01  VALUE-RECEIVED              PIC S9(5)      COMP-3.
*
 01  SQUARE-ROOT                 PIC S9(5)V99   COMP-3.
*
 PROCEDURE DIVISION USING VALUE-RECEIVED
                         SQUARE-ROOT.
*
 000-CALCULATE-SQUARE-ROOT.
*
     COMPUTE SQUARE-ROOT = VALUE-RECEIVED ** .5.
*
 000-EXIT.
*
     EXIT PROGRAM.
```

Figure 7-3   A subprogram that calculates the square root of a number

The EXIT PROGRAM statement

To indicate the exit point of a subprogram, the EXIT PROGRAM statement is used. When it's executed, the program returns to the first statement following the CALL statement of the calling program. In figure 7-3, the subprogram returns control to the MOVE statement in the calling program.

If you use a 1974 compiler, the EXIT PROGRAM statement has to be coded in a paragraph by itself as illustrated in figure 7-3. Here, after all of the statements in module 000 have been executed, control "falls through" to the exit paragraph. Normally, you shouldn't let your program fall through from one paragraph to another because it's a questionable programming practice, but in this case it is acceptable.

If you use a 1985 compiler, though, the EXIT PROGRAM statement doesn't have to be coded in its own paragraph. As a result, it can be coded as the last statement in a paragraph. For instance, module 000 in the subprogram in figure 7-3 can be coded like this:

```
000-CALCULATE-SQUARE-ROOT.
*
    COMPUTE SQUARE-ROOT = VALUE-RECEIVED ** .5.
    EXIT PROGRAM.
```

Since this is consistent with effective structured programming practices, we recommend that you code the EXIT PROGRAM statement like this if it's supported by your compiler.

The SYSTIME subprogram

Figure 7-4 illustrates another subprogram. It is a SYSTIME subprogram like the one that is called by the program in appendix A. It gets the current time from the system and formats it so it can be printed in a report heading or displayed on a screen. We call a subprogram like this from all of the report preparation programs that we develop in our shop because the time is part of our standard report heading.

Although this subprogram doesn't illustrate any new coding elements, I would like you to notice a few things in it. First, note that this subprogram requires a 1985 COBOL compiler because the EXIT PROGRAM statement isn't coded in a separate paragraph. Second, as required, VALUE clauses are *not* coded for any of the fields in the Linkage Section. Instead, literals like 'TIME:' are moved into the fields named in the Linkage Section. Third, although each of the fields in the formatted time could be passed individually to the subprogram, it is more efficient to treat them all as part of one record description. Thus, only one record name is listed in the Procedure Division header, and only one record name needs to be listed in a CALL statement that calls this subprogram.

```
IDENTIFICATION DIVISION.
*
PROGRAM-ID.  SYSTIME.
*
ENVIRONMENT DIVISION.
*
DATA DIVISION.
*
WORKING-STORAGE SECTION.
*
01  TIME-FIELD              PIC 9(8).
*
01  TIME-FIELD-PARTS REDEFINES TIME-FIELD.
*
    05  TIME-HOURS-AND-MINUTES.
        10  TIME-HOURS    PIC S99.
        10  TIME-MINUTES  PIC XX.
    05  FILLER            PIC X(4).
*
LINKAGE SECTION.
*
01  TIME-DATA.
*
    05  TD-CAPTION         PIC X(7).
    05  TD-HOURS           PIC Z9.
    05  TD-COLON           PIC X.
    05  TD-MINUTES         PIC XX.
    05  FILLER             PIC X.
    05  TD-TIME-SUFFIX     PIC XX.
*
PROCEDURE DIVISION USING TIME-DATA.
*
000-FORMAT-SYSTEM-TIME.
*
    MOVE SPACE TO TIME-DATA.
    MOVE 'TIME:' TO TD-CAPTION.
    ACCEPT TIME-FIELD FROM TIME.
    MOVE ':' TO TD-COLON.
    MOVE TIME-MINUTES TO TD-MINUTES.
    IF TIME-HOURS < 12
        MOVE 'AM' TO TD-TIME-SUFFIX
    ELSE
        MOVE 'PM' TO TD-TIME-SUFFIX.
    PERFORM 100-FORMAT-HOURS.
    EXIT PROGRAM.
*
100-FORMAT-HOURS.
*
    IF TIME-HOURS > 12
        SUBTRACT 12 FROM TIME-HOURS.
    IF TIME-HOURS = ZERO
        MOVE 12 TO TD-HOURS
    ELSE
        MOVE TIME-HOURS TO TD-HOURS.
```

Figure 7-4   The SYSTIME subprogram with a 1985 EXIT PROGRAM statement

Nested subprograms

In some cases, a main program calls a subprogram that calls another subprogram. In this case, the subprograms are referred to as *nested subprograms*. Because the relationship between a called subprogram and a calling program is the same no matter how many levels of nesting are used, no additional coding techniques are involved. Just be aware that one subprogram can call another subprogram.

Testing and debugging subprograms

Often, when you write a subprogram, none of the programs that call it have been developed yet. In this case, you can write a simple calling program to test your subprogram. In general, the simpler you make this calling program, the better, so you can concentrate on the code in your subprogram.

When you debug a subprogram, remember that the first thing to do is make sure that the fields were passed to the subprogram in the right sequence and with the right formats. If you wrote both the calling program and the subprogram, you shouldn't have a problem with this. However, a simple clerical error in one of the definitions can cause problems that appear to be quite complex.

1985 COBOL for using subprograms

In the 1974 standards, the section on the use of subprograms is only eight pages long; in the 1985 standards, it is 35 pages long. That should tell you that the 1985 standards provide a number of enhancements to the 1974 standards for using subprograms. In general, these enhancements are designed to let you have more control over the ways in which data and files are used by programs and subprograms.

Because some of these enhancements look like they will be difficult to implement, we don't expect them to be supported by the compilers for microcomputers or minicomputers. On the other hand, the 1985 enhancements probably will be supported by the compilers for most mainframes.

Whether or not the 1985 enhancements are supported by your compiler, we believe that they give you a level of control over data and files that you don't need for application programming. As a result, we don't think the enhancements will be used in the typical COBOL shop. Instead, we believe that subprograms will continue to be called and coded as described in topics 1 and 2 of this chapter. That's why we're *not* going to present the 1985 enhancements for subprogram use in this book or in this COBOL training series.

Discussion

Coding a subprogram in COBOL is similar to coding a main program. In general, the only differences are: (1) that you have to define passed fields in the Linkage Section; (2) that you have to code a USING clause on the Procedure Division header to identify the passed fields; and (3) that you code an EXIT PROGRAM statement instead of a STOP RUN statement to return control to the calling program. Once you become familiar with these COBOL elements, you should have no problem coding your own subprograms.

Terminology

entry point
exit point
nested subprograms

Objective

Given the description of a subprogram, write the subprogram in COBOL.

Topic 3   Compiler dependent code

The subprograms presented in the last topic will run on any system with only a couple of changes. First, the single quotes should be changed to double quotes if that's appropriate for your system. Second, the usages should be coded so they're appropriate for your system. Third, if you're not using a 1985 COBOL compiler, the EXIT PROGRAM statement in figure 7-4 should be coded in its own paragraph.

Beyond this, there is some other compiler dependent code related to the use of subprograms that you should be aware of. First, if you're using an IBM mainframe, you should know what the GOBACK and ENTRY statements do in case you have to modify subprograms that use them. Second, in case it's available on your system, you should know what dynamic access is and how the CANCEL statement is used in conjunction with it.

The GOBACK statement

The GOBACK statement is an IBM extension to the VS COBOL and VS COBOL II compilers for IBM mainframes. It works just like the EXIT PROGRAM statement in that it returns control to the calling program. The difference is that the GOBACK statement doesn't require its own paragraph as the EXIT PROGRAM statement does under the 1974 standards. As a result, the GOBACK statement is widely used in IBM shops. However, since the EXIT PROGRAM statement no longer has to be coded in its own paragraph under the 1985 standards, we expect to see less use of the GOBACK statement in the future.

The ENTRY statement

The ENTRY statement is another IBM extension to the VS COBOL and VS COBOL II compilers. This statement can be used to provide entry points in a subprogram in places other than the start of the Procedure Division. When you use ENTRY statements, a subprogram can be coded so it has one entry point for one function, a second entry point for a second function, and so on.

As we see it, though, a subprogram should only do one function, and it should only have one entry and one exit point. This is consistent with modern structured programming practices. As a result, we don't recommend the use of this statement.

Dynamic access and the CANCEL statement

Throughout this chapter we've made the assumption that a sub-program is compiled and linked with a calling program. As a result, the calling program and its subprograms are loaded and executed as a single load module. This is referred to as *static access* of a subprogram.

Some systems, however, provide for *dynamic access* of a sub-program. When dynamic access is used, the subprogram is *not* linked with the calling program until it is called by the CALL statement. How it is linked at that time is done in different ways on different systems. On some systems, a subprogram is actually linked to the calling program when a CALL statement for it is executed; on other systems, the subprogram is only "logically" linked to the calling program. In either case, the intent of dynamic access is to improve the efficiency of the system.

When you use dynamic access, you can use a CANCEL statement in the calling program to cancel the link to the subprogram, although you don't have to do this. Once a subprogram is cancelled, it is no longer linked (actually or logically) to the calling program. However, it can be linked again to the calling program by issuing another CALL statement for it. Obviously, a program shouldn't cancel a subprogram before it calls one, so a CANCEL statement for a subprogram should only be issued after a CALL statement for the subprogram.

To illustrate the use of the CANCEL statement, suppose the sub-program in figure 7-4 were accessed dynamically. Then, this CANCEL statement could be coded after the CALL statement:

```
CANCEL 'SYSTIME'.
```

Here, the operand of the CANCEL statement names only óne sub-program, but a series of subprograms can be cancelled by a single statement. The CANCEL statement is supported by both the 1974 and the 1985 COBOL standards.

When a subprogram is cancelled by a CANCEL statement, it is returned to its *initial state*. This means that all of the fields in working storage are restored to the values given them by their VALUE clauses. This also means that all files are returned to the status they had when the subprogram was first called. Then, the next time the subprogram is called, it will be executed as if it were being executed for the first time. Since most subprograms don't need to be returned to their initial states, though, you usually don't need to code the CANCEL statement for this purpose. For instance, the subprograms in both figures 7-3 and 7-4 can be repeatedly executed without returning them to their initial state.

On most systems, you will never need to use the CANCEL state-ment because dynamic access isn't provided by the system and the CANCEL statement isn't supported by the compiler. This is true for the Microsoft compiler on an IBM PC, the Wang VS compiler on a

Wang VS system, and the VS COBOL compiler on an IBM main-frame running under DOS/VSE. On the other hand, dynamic access and the CANCEL statement are supported on an IBM mainframe under OS/MVS when using VS COBOL or VS COBOL II.

If you're using some other system, you should find out if it supports dynamic access. If it does, you should find out whether it requires the use of the CANCEL statement. In some cases, the use of this statement can improve the performance of the dynamic access facility; on other systems, it has little or no effect on performance.

Terminology

static access
dynamic access
initial state

Objective

Find out what compiler dependent code (if any) you should use in your shop for calling and writing subprograms.

Chapter 8

How to handle tables

Many programs require the use of tables. That's why the COBOL standards provide language for handling tables. In fact, the 1974 COBOL standards provide language for tables of up to three levels, and the 1985 standards provide for tables of up to seven levels.

The tables you'll probably use most often are one-level tables. Those are tables that tabulate data based on only one variable factor. I'll show you how to handle one-level tables using indexes in topic 1. In topic 2, I'll show you how to handle multilevel tables using indexes. These tables are based on more than one variable factor. Then, in topic 3, I'll show you how to handle any table using subscripts. Finally, in topic 4, I'll present some compiler dependent code related to table handling.

Topic 1 How to handle one-level tables using indexes

This topic presents the COBOL code for handling one-level tables. If you've read *Part 1* of this series, you should be familiar with most of the material this topic presents. However, it does cover a couple of new items. Specifically, it presents relative indexing, index usage, and the use of the VARYING clause in a SEARCH statement. Since table handling can be quite difficult, we recommend that you review this topic whether or not you've read the topic on table handling in *Part 1*. At the least, you should read the material on relative indexing, index usage, and the VARYING clause in the SEARCH statement; all three are identified by headings.

The COBOL elements for table handling

Figure 8-1 presents a subset of the COBOL elements for table handling. These are the only elements you'll need for the vast majority of tables that your programs will operate upon. As you can see, the table handling elements include four clauses for defining a table in the Data Division. They provide for a new kind of usage (INDEX). They provide two statements: the SET and the SEARCH statements. And they provide an expanded form of the PERFORM statement.

As you read through this topic, please refer to the formats in figure 8-1. I'll explain each of them as I present examples of table handling code. By the time you complete this topic, you should be able to use any of the elements in figure 8-1.

How to define a table in the Data Division

Figures 8-2 and 8-3 present two tables and their COBOL definitions. Both tables are defined by using the OCCURS clause and the INDEXED BY clause. For most tables, those are the only clauses you'll need. To put constant values in the table in figure 8-2, the REDEFINES clause is also used.

The tables in figures 8-2 and 8-3 are *one-level tables* because they tabulate data based on only one variable factor. The table in figure 8-2 varies based on the month number. The table in figure 8-3 varies based on item number. As you get more experience, you'll realize that most of the tables you work with are one-level tables.

Although the tables in figures 8-2 and 8-3 are similar in form, you can see that I coded them differently. In the COBOL code, the month table has only one field that is repeated, but the price table has two fields that are repeated. In figure 8-2, I didn't code the month numbers as part of the table because they are simply the numbers from 1 through 12. By the time you complete this topic, you should

Data Division code for table definitions

Format 1

```
level-number  data-name-1  OCCURS integer TIMES

                           [ ⎰ASCENDING ⎱  KEY IS data-name-2]
                             ⎱DESCENDING⎰

                           INDEXED BY {index-name-1} ...
```

Format 2 (for a binary search of a variable-length table)

```
level-number  data-name-1  OCCURS integer-1 TO integer-2 TIMES

                           DEPENDING ON data-name-2

                           [ ⎰ASCENDING ⎱  KEY IS data-name-3]
                             ⎱DESCENDING⎰

                           INDEXED BY {index-name-1} ...
```

Data Division code for index data items

```
level-number data-name   [USAGE IS] INDEX
```

Procedure Division code for referring to an entry in a table

```
data-name   ⎰(index-name)[± literal]        ⎱
            ⎱(literal-occurrence-number)⎰
```

Figure 8-1   A subset of the COBOL elements for table handling (part 1 of 2)

understand why it isn't necessary to code the month numbers in this table.

The OCCURS clause   The OCCURS clause can be used to describe any data item that is at a level from 02 through 49. It can be used with an elementary item as in figure 8-2. It can be used with a group item as in figure 8-3.

The integer in the OCCURS clause tells how many times a field or group of fields is to be repeated in storage. As a result, the table in figure 8-2 requires 108 bytes of storage since the 9-byte field is repeated 12 times. Similarly, the table in figure 8-3 requires 112 bytes of storage since the 7-byte group consisting of item number and item price is repeated 16 times.

The SET statement

Format 1

$$\underline{SET} \quad \begin{Bmatrix} \text{identifier-1} \\ \text{index-name-1} \end{Bmatrix} \quad \underline{TO} \quad \begin{Bmatrix} \text{identifier-2} \\ \text{index-name-2} \\ \text{literal-1} \end{Bmatrix}$$

Format 2

$$\underline{SET} \quad \text{index-name} \quad \begin{Bmatrix} \underline{UP} \ \underline{BY} \\ \underline{DOWN} \ \underline{BY} \end{Bmatrix} \quad \begin{Bmatrix} \text{identifier} \\ \text{literal} \end{Bmatrix}$$

The SEARCH statement

Format 1 (sequential search)

$$\underline{SEARCH} \quad \text{identifer-1} \quad \left[\text{VARYING} \quad \begin{Bmatrix} \text{identifier-2} \\ \text{index-name} \end{Bmatrix} \right]$$

[AT $\underline{END}$ imperative-statement-1]

$\underline{WHEN}$ condition-1 $\begin{Bmatrix} \text{imperative-statement-2} \\ \underline{NEXT} \ \underline{SENTENCE} \end{Bmatrix}$

[$\underline{WHEN}$ condition-2 $\begin{Bmatrix} \text{imperative-statement-3} \\ \underline{NEXT} \ \underline{SENTENCE} \end{Bmatrix}$] ...

Format 2 (binary search)

$\underline{SEARCH} \ \underline{ALL}$ identifier

[AT $\underline{END}$ imperative-statement-1]

$\underline{WHEN}$ equal-condition

$\begin{Bmatrix} \text{imperative-statement-2} \\ \underline{NEXT} \ \underline{SENTENCE} \end{Bmatrix}$

The PERFORM VARYING statement

$\underline{PERFORM}$ paragraph-name

$\underline{VARYING}$ index-name-1 $\underline{FROM}$ $\begin{Bmatrix} \text{identifier-1} \\ \text{index-name-2} \\ \text{literal-1} \end{Bmatrix}$ $\underline{BY}$ $\begin{Bmatrix} \text{identifer-2} \\ \text{literal-2} \end{Bmatrix}$

$\underline{UNTIL}$ condition

Figure 8-1 A subset of the COBOL elements for table handling (part 2 of 2)

Month table

Number	Month	Number	Month
1	JANUARY	7	JULY
2	FEBRUARY	8	AUGUST
3	MARCH	9	SEPTEMBER
4	APRIL	10	OCTOBER
5	MAY	11	NOVEMBER
6	JUNE	12	DECEMBER

Table definition in COBOL

```
01   MONTH-TABLE.
*
     05   MONTH-NAME            PIC X(9)
                                OCCURS 12 TIMES
                                INDEXED BY MONTH-INDEX.
```

Table definition in COBOL with constant values

```
01   MONTH-TABLE-VALUES.
*
     05   FILLER               PIC  X(9)   VALUE 'JANUARY  '.
     05   FILLER               PIC  X(9)   VALUE 'FEBRUARY '.
     05   FILLER               PIC  X(9)   VALUE 'MARCH    '.
     05   FILLER               PIC  X(9)   VALUE 'APRIL    '.
     05   FILLER               PIC  X(9)   VALUE 'MAY      '.
     05   FILLER               PIC  X(9)   VALUE 'JUNE     '.
     05   FILLER               PIC  X(9)   VALUE 'JULY     '.
     05   FILLER               PIC  X(9)   VALUE 'AUGUST   '.
     05   FILLER               PIC  X(9)   VALUE 'SEPTEMBER'.
     05   FILLER               PIC  X(9)   VALUE 'OCTOBER  '.
     05   FILLER               PIC  X(9)   VALUE 'NOVEMBER '.
     05   FILLER               PIC  X(9)   VALUE 'DECEMBER '.
*
 01  MONTH-TABLE REDEFINES MONTH-TABLE-VALUES.
*
     05   MONTH-NAME           PIC X(9)
                               OCCURS 12 TIMES
                               INDEXED BY MONTH-INDEX.
```

Statement that refers to an entry in the month table

```
MOVE MONTH-NAME (MONTH-INDEX) TO HDG3-MONTH-NAME.
```

Figure 8-2   A month table and its COBOL definitions

Price table

Item number	Price	Item number	Price
101	12.50	277	1.11
107	50.00	297	7.77
111	7.70	305	.10
158	5.55	341	15.00
161	62.50	342	57.50
192	25.00	343	65.00
201	.40	347	22.50
213	6.66	351	.35

Table definition in COBOL

```
 01   PRICE-TABLE.
*
      05   PRICE-GROUP          OCCURS 16 TIMES
                                INDEXED BY PRICE-TABLE-INDEX.
           10   ITEM-NUMBER     PIC X(3).
           10   ITEM-PRICE      PIC S99V99.
*
```

Statement that refers to a price in the price table

```
MULTIPLY TR-QUANTITY BY ITEM-PRICE (PRICE-TABLE-INDEX)
    GIVING LINE-ITEM-EXTENSION ROUNDED.
```

Figure 8-3   A price table and its COBOL definition

The INDEXED BY clause   The INDEXED BY clause follows the OCCURS clause and assigns an *index name* to the *index* for the table entries. In figure 8-2, MONTH-INDEX is the index for the 12 MONTH-NAME entries. To refer to any of the 12 entries in the Procedure Division, you can code the data name followed by the index name in parentheses as in this statement:

```
MOVE MONTH-NAME (MONTH-INDEX) TO HDG3-MONTH-NAME.
```

Here, the value of MONTH-INDEX determines which of the 12 month values will be moved to HDG3-MONTH-NAME. If, for example, MONTH-INDEX has a value equivalent to 3, the third MONTH-NAME in the table is moved to HDG3-MONTH-NAME.

In figure 8-3, PRICE-TABLE-INDEX is the index name for the 16 occurrences of PRICE-GROUP. Then, either of the fields within each of the 16 groups can be referred to using this index name, as in these examples:

```
ITEM-NUMBER (PRICE-TABLE-INDEX)
ITEM-PRICE (PRICE-TABLE-INDEX)
```

Here again, the actual entries referred to depend upon the value of PRICE-TABLE-INDEX at the time of the referral. If, for example, the index value is 10, the coding above refers to the tenth item number (297) and the tenth price (7.77).

You can also use the index name to refer to PRICE-GROUP as a whole:

```
PRICE-GROUP (PRICE-TABLE-INDEX)
```

In most cases, though, you'll want to refer to the individual fields, not to the group item.

When you index a table as illustrated in figures 8-2 and 8-3, you don't define the index as a field in storage elsewhere in the program. Instead, the INDEXED BY clause automatically defines the index, giving it a size and usage that is appropriate for the system you're using.

The REDEFINES clause　　When a table isn't likely to be changed, you will often code its values in the Data Division. This is illustrated by the second table definition in figure 8-2. Since the month values aren't going to change, they may as well be coded as part of the program.

To code constant values for a table in the Data Division, you need to use the REDEFINES clause as shown in figure 8-2. Because VALUE clauses are illegal in statements that redefine a storage area, you must first code the values of the table. Then, you redefine the storage area as a table by using the REDEFINES, OCCURS, and INDEXED BY clauses.

Since a price table like the one in figure 8-3 is likely to change, you normally wouldn't code its values as part of the Data Division. Instead, you would read the values into storage at the start of any program that uses the table. Nevertheless, figure 8-4 shows you two ways to define the data in the price table. Although this table has data that's likely to be changed, other tables with the same form may have data that won't be changed.

In the first method in figure 8-4, one VALUE clause is used for each of the 32 fields within the table. First, an item number; next, an item price; then, another item number; and so on. In the second method, one VALUE clause gives the values for a group of values consisting of one item number and one item price. You could also define

Method 1

```
01    PRICE-TABLE-VALUES.
*
      05    FILLER              PIC X(3)        VALUE '101'.
      05    FILLER              PIC S99V99      VALUE +12.50.
      05    FILLER              PIC X(3)        VALUE '107'.
      05    FILLER              PIC S99V99      VALUE +50.00.
            .
            .
      05    FILLER              PIC X(3)        VALUE '351'.
      05    FILLER              PIC S99V99      VALUE +.35.
*
 01    PRICE-TABLE REDEFINES PRICE-TABLE-VALUES.
*
      05    PRICE-GROUP         OCCURS 16 TIMES
                                INDEXED BY PRICE-TABLE-INDEX.
         10    ITEM-NUMBER      PIC X(3).
         10    ITEM-PRICE       PIC S99V99.
*
```

Method 2

```
 01    PRICE-TABLE-VALUES.
*
      05    FILLER              PIC X(7)        VALUE '1011250'.
      05    FILLER              PIC X(7)        VALUE '1075000'.
            .
            .
      05    FILLER              PIC X(7)        VALUE '3510035'.
*
 01    PRICE-TABLE REDEFINES PRICE-TABLE-VALUES.
*
      05    PRICE-GROUP         OCCURS 16 TIMES
                                INDEXED BY PRICE-TABLE-INDEX.
         10    ITEM-NUMBER      PIC X(3).
         10    ITEM-PRICE       PIC S99V99.
*
```

Figure 8-4   Two ways to define the price table in figure 8-3 with constant values

more than one group in a single VALUE clause, but the more you combine fields and groups, the more difficult your coding is to read.

If you define your table fields with computational usages, you have to code one VALUE clause for each field as shown in method 1 in figure 8-4, or the values won't be stored properly. Also, if some of the fields in the table have signs, you have to use method 1.

How to refer to the entries in a table

I've already shown you the most common way to refer to entries in a table. That is, you code the name of the field you want to refer to followed by the index name for the table, as in this example:

```
ITEM-PRICE (PRICE-TABLE-INDEX)
```

Then, the value of the index determines the specific table element that the code refers to.

Sometimes, however, you may know which entry you want to refer to at the time that you code the program. If so, you can code the index value as a literal, as in this example:

```
MONTH-NAME (1)
```

Here, the code refers to the first month in the table.

When you use a literal instead of an index name, it represents an *occurrence number*. As a result, it must be an integer between one and the number of times the element occurs in the table. For the month table, the occurrence number must be from one through 12; for the price table, the occurrence number must be from one through 16.

Although you can use either an index name or an occurrence number to identify an entry in a table, you should realize that the values aren't the same. In contrast to an occurrence number, an index represents a *displacement value* from the start of the table. For instance, the index value for the first month in the month table is a displacement value of 0 (the first month is zero positions from the start of the table), but the occurrence number is 1. Similarly, the index value is 9 for the second month and 18 for the third month, but the corresponding occurrence numbers are 2 and 3. Fortunately, you don't have to worry about this when you handle tables in COBOL, because the compiler handles the conversions between occurrence numbers and displacement values. In fact, as you'll see in a moment, you use occurrence numbers rather than displacement values to assign a value to an index.

Relative indexing   Another way to refer to an entry in a table is by using *relative indexing*. When you use relative indexing, you follow the name of the field by an index name increased or decreased by some literal value. For example, if you coded

```
MONTH-NAME (MONTH-INDEX + 1)
```

one would be converted to its corresponding index value and added to the index value of MONTH-INDEX. In other words, the occurrence number of MONTH-INDEX would be increased by one. In the example above, if the occurrence value of MONTH-INDEX is 8, MONTH-NAME (MONTH-INDEX + 1) is the ninth entry in the table (SEPTEMBER).

Although you can accomplish the same thing using the SET statement, as you'll see later in this topic, relative indexing requires less code and is just as clear. So, we recommend you use it whenever it's appropriate. Keep in mind when you use relative indexing that the resulting occurrence number must fall between one and the number of elements specified in the OCCURS clause for the table. Also, notice that you must leave a space on both sides of the plus or minus sign.

How to load a fixed-length table into storage

When the values in a table are likely to change, you normally load the table into storage from a disk file at the start of any program that uses the table. As a result, you normally load a price table like the one in figure 8-3 from a disk file.

A routine for loading this table is illustrated in figure 8-5. This routine assumes that each group of table entries is stored in one record in a sequential file that contains all of the values for the table. If you study this code, you should be able to understand it without too much trouble. The only new statement is the PERFORM VARYING statement.

The PERFORM VARYING statement   To load a table, a PERFORM VARYING statement is often useful. This is illustrated by the statement in figure 8-5:

```
PERFORM 110-LOAD-PRICE-TABLE-ENTRY
    VARYING PRICE-TABLE-INDEX FROM 1 BY 1
    UNTIL PTABLE-EOF
        OR PRICE-TABLE-INDEX > 16.
```

This statement executes module 110 until the end of the table file has been reached or until the occurrence value represented by the index is greater than 16 (the number of entries defined for the table). The VARYING clause in this statement gives the index a starting value equivalent to an occurrence value of one (FROM 1). That means that the index points to the first price group in the table the first time module 110 is executed. Then, each time module 110 is executed, the index is increased by an occurrence value of one (BY 1).

Figure 8-6 illustrates the flow of control for the PERFORM VARYING statement. Note that the index is increased by the BY value right after the called module is performed but before the condition is tested again. And, as always when the UNTIL clause is used, the condition is tested *before* the called module is performed.

```
WORKING-STORAGE SECTION.
*
 01   SWITCHES.
*
      05   PTABLE-EOF-SWITCH    PIC X             VALUE 'N'.
           88   PTABLE-EOF                        VALUE 'Y'.
*
 01   PRICE-TABLE.
*
      05   PRICE-GROUP          OCCURS 16 TIMES
                                INDEXED BY PRICE-TABLE-INDEX.
           10   ITEM-NUMBER     PIC X(3).
           10   ITEM-PRICE      PIC S99V99.
*
 01   PRICE-TABLE-RECORD.
*
      05   PT-ITEM-NUMBER       PIC X(3).
      05   PT-ITEM-PRICE        PIC S99V99.
      05   FILLER               PIC X(13).
*
      .
      .
      .
*
 PROCEDURE DIVISION.
*
      .
      .
 100-LOAD-PRICE-TABLE.
*
      PERFORM 110-LOAD-PRICE-TABLE-ENTRY
          VARYING PRICE-TABLE-INDEX FROM 1 BY 1
          UNTIL PTABLE-EOF
              OR PRICE-TABLE-INDEX > 16.
*
 110-LOAD-PRICE-TABLE-ENTRY.
*
      PERFORM 120-READ-PRICE-TABLE-RECORD.
      IF NOT PTABLE-EOF
          MOVE PT-ITEM-NUMBER TO ITEM-NUMBER (PRICE-TABLE-INDEX)
          MOVE PT-ITEM-PRICE  TO ITEM-PRICE (PRICE-TABLE-INDEX).
*
 120-READ-PRICE-TABLE-RECORD.
*
      READ PTABLE RECORD INTO PRICE-TABLE-RECORD
          AT END
              MOVE 'Y' TO PTABLE-EOF-SWITCH.
      .
      .
```

Figure 8-5   Loading a price table with 16 entries

Statement format

```
PERFORM paragraph-name
    VARYING index-name FROM value-1 BY value-2
    UNTIL condition
```

Flow of control

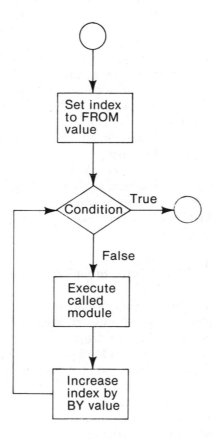

Figure 8-6   Flowchart for the logic of the PERFORM VARYING statement

With this as background, I hope you can understand the OR portion of the condition in the PERFORM VARYING statement in figure 8-5:

```
OR PRICE-TABLE-INDEX > 16
```

This stops the loading of the table if the number of entries in the table file is greater than the number of entries provided for by the OCCURS clause for the table. The condition isn't coded as

```
PRICE-TABLE-INDEX = 16
```

because the index is increased by a value of one after each execution of module 110 but *before* the condition is checked. So PRICE-TABLE-INDEX will be increased to a value of 16 right after the fifteenth entry is loaded into the table. As a result, a greater-than condition has to be used, or the program will exit the PERFORM statement without loading the sixteenth table entry.

One final point I want to mention is that I've simplified this routine to illustrate the essential table handling elements. In a production program, you'd have to do some kind of error processing if the end of the PTABLE file were reached before 16 values had been loaded into the table.

How to load a variable-length table into storage

In actual practice, the number of entries in a table like the price table is usually variable. As new items are added to the product line, the number increases. As items are dropped, the number decreases. Normally, then, a table like this is loaded as a variable-length table.

Figure 8-7 illustrates the code for loading a variable-length price table into storage. Here, the OCCURS clause for the table gives an occurrence value of 100. That means that the table may hold a maximum of 100 groups of item number and item price. However, the actual number of entries loaded into this table will depend upon the number of entries in the table file. This number will be stored in a count field named PT-ENTRY-COUNT.

The PERFORM VARYING statement in figure 8-7 is much like the one in figure 8-5. This time, the statement says that module 110 should be repeatedly executed until the end of the table file has been reached or until the index value represents an occurrence number greater than 100. After each time that module 110 is executed, the occurrence number represented by the index is increased by one.

The SET statement   In module 110, two SET statements are used:

```
SET PRICE-TABLE-INDEX DOWN BY 1
SET PT-ENTRY-COUNT TO PRICE-TABLE-INDEX
```

```
WORKING-STORAGE SECTION.
*
 01   SWITCHES.
*
     05   PTABLE-EOF-SWITCH   PIC X          VALUE 'N'.
          88   PTABLE-EOF                    VALUE 'Y'.
*
 01   COUNT-FIELDS.
*
     05   PT-ENTRY-COUNT      INDEX.
*
 01   PRICE-TABLE.
*
     05   PRICE-GROUP         OCCURS 100 TIMES
                              INDEXED BY PRICE-TABLE-INDEX.
          10   ITEM-NUMBER    PIC X(3).
          10   ITEM-PRICE     PIC S99V99.
*
 01   PRICE-TABLE-RECORD.
*
     05   PT-ITEM-NUMBER      PIC X(3).
     05   PT-ITEM-PRICE       PIC S99V99.
     05   FILLER              PIC X(13).
*
     .
     .
     .
*
 PROCEDURE DIVISION.
*
     .
     .
     .
 100-LOAD-PRICE-TABLE.
*
     PERFORM 110-LOAD-PRICE-TABLE-ENTRY
         VARYING PRICE-TABLE-INDEX FROM 1 BY 1
         UNTIL PTABLE-EOF
             OR PRICE-TABLE-INDEX > 100.
*
 110-LOAD-PRICE-TABLE-ENTRY.
*
     PERFORM 120-READ-PRICE-TABLE-RECORD.
     IF NOT PTABLE-EOF
         MOVE PT-ITEM-NUMBER TO ITEM-NUMBER (PRICE-TABLE-INDEX)
         MOVE PT-ITEM-PRICE  TO ITEM-PRICE (PRICE-TABLE-INDEX)
     ELSE
         SET PRICE-TABLE-INDEX DOWN BY 1
         SET PT-ENTRY-COUNT TO PRICE-TABLE-INDEX.
*
 120-READ-PRICE-TABLE-RECORD.
*
     READ PTABLE RECORD INTO PRICE-TABLE-RECORD
         AT END
             MOVE 'Y' TO PTABLE-EOF-SWITCH.
     .
     .
```

Figure 8-7   Loading a price table with a variable number of entries

They are executed when the end of the table file has been reached
(PTABLE-EOF). The first one reduces the index for the table by the
equivalent of one occurrence number. The second one sets PT-
ENTRY-COUNT equal to PRICE-TABLE-INDEX. I'll have more to
say about that in a minute.

Remember that index values are not the same as occurrence
numbers. That's why you have to use SET statements when you
operate upon indexes. They make the appropriate conversions
between displacement values and occurrence numbers.

Do you understand why the index value has to be reduced by an
occurrence number of one before it represents the number of entries in
the table? Remember that the index value is increased after the called
module is performed. As a result, if 16 values have been loaded into
the table, the index is increased to an occurrence value of 17 before
module 110 is executed again. So when the end-of-file condition for
the table file occurs during the execution of module 110, no new
values are loaded into the table, and the index value represents an
occurrence number that is one more than the number of table entries.
That's why it has to be reduced by one before the value of PT-
ENTRY-COUNT can be set.

Index usage   In figure 8-7, notice that the field used to keep track
of the number of entries in the table, PT-ENTRY-COUNT, is defined
with *index usage*:

```
05  PT-ENTRY-COUNT      INDEX.
```

This field is called an *index data item*, and it can contain the actual
displacement value of any index. When you define an index data
item, the compiler sets up a field large enough to store any index
value, so PICTURE and VALUE clauses aren't allowed. If you refer
back to figure 8-1, you can see that USAGE and IS are optional words
in the USAGE clause, so index usage can be specified with just the
word INDEX.

An index data item can only be specified in a SET statement or in
a relation test with an index or another index data item. In figure 8-7,
for example, the SET statement

```
SET PT-ENTRY-COUNT TO PRICE-TABLE-INDEX
```

sets PT-ENTRY-COUNT to the current displacement value of the
index. In this case, the displacement value represents the last entry in
the table.

Although the count field in this example doesn't have to be
defined with index usage, it will make your program run more efficiently if it is. That's because no conversion is necessary since both PT-
ENTRY-COUNT and PRICE-TABLE-INDEX contain displacement
values. In contrast, if you were to use a count field with computational usage, the displacement value in the index would have to be

converted to an occurrence number before it could be stored in the count field.

How to search a table in sequence

Once a table has been loaded into storage, you can search it to find the entries your program requires. For a simple table like the month table, you can find the entry you want by setting the index to the appropriate value. If, for example, you want to move the name of the current month into a heading line, you can code statements like this:

```
SET MONTH-INDEX TO CURRENT-MONTH.
MOVE MONTH-NAME (MONTH-INDEX) TO HDG3-MONTH-NAME.
```

Here, the SET statement sets the index value to the equivalent of the occurrence value represented by CURRENT-MONTH. This assumes, of course, that CURRENT-MONTH is a value from 01 through 12. Technically, this isn't a search, because the program gets the entry you want without searching through the other entries in the table first. Nevertheless, this code has the same effect as a search.

To illustrate a true search, figure 8-8 illustrates a routine that searches the variable-length price table that was loaded by the code in figure 8-7. This assumes that the code in figure 8-7 and figure 8-8 are parts of the same program. First, the table is loaded into storage. Then, it is searched as part of the processing of the program. You should be able to understand this routine without too much difficulty because the only new statement it presents is the SEARCH statement.

The SEARCH statement   The SEARCH statement in figure 8-8 is coded as follows:

```
SEARCH PRICE-GROUP
    AT END
        MOVE 'N' TO PRICE-FOUND-SWITCH
    WHEN PRICE-TABLE-INDEX > PT-ENTRY-COUNT
        MOVE 'N' TO PRICE-FOUND-SWITCH
    WHEN ITEM-NUMBER (PRICE-TABLE-INDEX) = TR-ITEM-NO
        MOVE ITEM-PRICE (PRICE-TABLE-INDEX) TO UNIT-PRICE
        MOVE 'Y' TO PRICE-FOUND-SWITCH.
```

When this statement is executed, it searches the item numbers in the table until the index displacement value is greater than the displacement value of the last entry in the table (PT-ENTRY-COUNT) or until the item number in the table is equal to TR-ITEM-NO. In other words, the search ends when the condition in either WHEN clause becomes true. If neither condition ever becomes true, the search ends when all 100 entries in the table have been searched (AT END).

In figure 8-8, the SET statement sets the index to the equivalent of an occurrence value of one before the SEARCH statement is executed. As a result, the search starts with the first item number in the table. Then, it continues in sequence from the first item to the last. Note that a SET statement must always give a starting value to an index before a sequential SEARCH statement is executed, but the value doesn't have to be one.

Since the SEARCH statement searches the entries in sequence from the first to the last, the entries themselves don't have to be in sequence. In the price table, for example, the item numbers could be in reversed sequence or in no sequence at all and the search in figure 8-8 would still work.

However, the sequence of the entries can have a major effect on the processing efficiency of the program. Since you usually search a table from the first entry to the last (that is, you set the search index to one before starting), the most used entries should be the first ones in the table and the least used entries should be the last ones. If, for example, 60 percent of the transactions in the price table involve item numbers 305, 347, and 351, these entries should be the first ones in the table.

Since the search routine in figure 8-8 is for a variable-length table, the SEARCH statement uses two WHEN clauses and an AT END clause. You should realize, though, that coding a SEARCH statement is simpler when the table has a fixed number of entries. If, for example, the price table always had 16 occurrences, the SEARCH statement could be coded as follows:

```
SEARCH PRICE-GROUP
    AT END
        MOVE 'N' TO PRICE-FOUND-SWITCH
    WHEN ITEM-NUMBER (PRICE-TABLE-INDEX) = TR-ITEM-NO
        MOVE ITEM-PRICE (PRICE-TABLE-INDEX) TO UNIT-PRICE
        MOVE 'Y' TO PRICE-FOUND-SWITCH.
```

Here, the search either finds the right item number in the table or it ends when it has searched all of the item numbers in the table.

How to search a table with a binary search

Figure 8-9 shows how you can use a *binary search* to search the variable-length price table. For a binary search, the item numbers have to be in sequence in the table. Then, the search starts with an item number near the middle of the table, and that number's compared to the desired item number. Based on this comparison, the search continues in either the first half or the second half of the table. The next comparison is near the middle of the half just selected, and the search continues by successively halving the portion of the table remaining. Eventually, the condition in the WHEN clause of the SEARCH statement is satisfied or the AT END clause is executed.

```
WORKING-STORAGE SECTION.
*
 01  SWITCHES.
*
     .
     .
     05  PRICE-FOUND-SWITCH          PIC X.
         88  PRICE-FOUND                         VALUE 'Y'.
*
 01  COUNT-FIELDS.
*
     05  PT-ENTRY-COUNT     INDEX.
*
 01  PRICE-TABLE.
*
     05  PRICE-GROUP            OCCURS 100 TIMES
                               INDEXED BY PRICE-TABLE-INDEX.
         10  ITEM-NUMBER    PIC X(3).
         10  ITEM-PRICE     PIC S99V99.
*
 01  WORK-FIELDS            COMP-3.
*
     05  UNIT-PRICE         PIC S999V99.
*
 01  TRANSACTION-RECORD.
*
     05  TR-REFERENCE-CODE  PIC X(6).
     05  TR-REFERENCE-DATE  PIC X(6).
     05  TR-CUSTOMER-NO     PIC X(5).
     05  TR-ITEM-NO         PIC X(3).
     .
     .
*
 PROCEDURE DIVISION.
*
     .
     .
 350-SEARCH-PRICE-TABLE.
*
     SET PRICE-TABLE-INDEX TO 1.
     SEARCH PRICE-GROUP
         AT END
             MOVE 'N' TO PRICE-FOUND-SWITCH
         WHEN PRICE-TABLE-INDEX > PT-ENTRY-COUNT
             MOVE 'N' TO PRICE-FOUND-SWITCH
         WHEN ITEM-NUMBER (PRICE-TABLE-INDEX) = TR-ITEM-NO
             MOVE ITEM-PRICE (PRICE-TABLE-INDEX) TO UNIT-PRICE
             MOVE 'Y' TO PRICE-FOUND-SWITCH.
*
     .
     .
```

Figure 8-8   Searching a price table with a variable number of entries

The advantage of a binary search is its speed. In a table of 16 occurrences, any entry can be found with a maximum of just four comparisons. In contrast, a sequential search requires an average of eight comparisons to find an entry if the frequency of use is distributed evenly over the 16 entries. For large tables, say tables of 128 or more entries, a binary search is likely to be far more efficient than a sequential search. As a rule of thumb, you should use a binary search whenever you're searching a table that contains 50 or more entries in an even distribution.

If you study the coding in figure 8-9, you can see that it's just like the coding in figure 8-8 with a few exceptions: (1) the OCCURS clause specifies a range of values; (2) the DEPENDING ON clause and the ASCENDING KEY clause are used to define the table; (3) no SET statement is required; and (4) a SEARCH ALL statement is used.

The OCCURS clause   When you use a binary search with a variable-length table, the OCCURS clause gives the range of occurrences that can be searched. Normally, this clause is coded so the range is from the first occurrence to the last, as in figure 8-9:

```
OCCURS 1 TO 100 TIMES
```

Here, the first integer says that the search should include the entries of the table starting with the first occurrence. The second integer says that the table may have a maximum of 100 occurrences. Then, as you will see in a moment, the DEPENDING ON clause names a field that specifies the actual number of occurrences to be searched.

This clause can be coded so the range of the search doesn't include all of the entries in the table, but you'll rarely, if ever, want to do this. If, for example, the clause in figure 8-9 were coded as

```
OCCURS 11 TO 100 TIMES
```

the first ten entries in the table wouldn't be included in the search. Usually, though, if you didn't want to include these entries in the search, you wouldn't bother to define them or load them into the table.

The DEPENDING ON clause   Because the price table is variable in length, the DEPENDING ON clause must be used. It tells the SEARCH ALL statement how many entries are actually in the table. In contrast, the OCCURS clause gives the maximum number of entries that might be in the table. For the SEARCH ALL statement to work properly, the proper value must be moved into the field named in the DEPENDING ON clause before the SEARCH statement is executed. Thus, PT-ENTRY-COUNT must have the proper occurrence value in figure 8-9.

```
     WORKING-STORAGE SECTION.
*
 01   SWITCHES.
*
        .
        .
     05   PRICE-FOUND-SWITCH PIC X.
          88   PRICE-FOUND                    VALUE 'Y'.
*
 01   COUNT-FIELDS.
*
     05   PT-ENTRY-COUNT      PIC S9(3)  COMP-3.
*
 01   PRICE-TABLE.
*
     05   PRICE-GROUP          OCCURS 1 TO 100 TIMES
                               DEPENDING ON PT-ENTRY-COUNT
                               ASCENDING KEY IS ITEM-NUMBER
                               INDEXED BY PRICE-TABLE-INDEX.
          10   ITEM-NUMBER     PIC X(3).
          10   ITEM-PRICE      PIC S99V99.
*
 01   WORK-FIELDS             COMP-3.
*
     05   UNIT-PRICE          PIC S999V99.
*
 01   TRANSACTION-RECORD.
*
     05   TR-REFERENCE-CODE  PIC X(6).
     05   TR-REFERENCE-DATE  PIC X(6).
     05   TR-CUSTOMER-NO     PIC X(5).
     05   TR-ITEM-NO         PIC X(3).
        .
        .
*
 PROCEDURE DIVISION.
*
        .
        .
 350-SEARCH-PRICE-TABLE.
*
     SEARCH ALL PRICE-GROUP
         AT END
             MOVE 'N' TO PRICE-FOUND-SWITCH
         WHEN ITEM-NUMBER (PRICE-TABLE-INDEX) = TR-ITEM-NO
             MOVE ITEM-PRICE (PRICE-TABLE-INDEX) TO UNIT-PRICE
             MOVE 'Y' TO PRICE-FOUND-SWITCH.
*
        .
        .
```

Figure 8-9   Searching a variable-length price table with a binary search

If a table has a fixed number of occurrences or you're not using a binary search, you don't have to code this clause when you define it. However, if a table has a variable number of occurrences and you are using a binary search, you should code this clause. If you don't, the binary search will search all of the occurrences in the table, whether or not they are used, so the search won't be as efficient as it could be.

Notice in this example that the count field, PT-ENTRY-COUNT, isn't defined with index usage. That's because any field specified in the DEPENDING ON clause must contain an occurrence number. And since a field defined with index usage contains a displacement value, it can't be the object of a DEPENDING ON clause.

The ASCENDING/DESCENDING KEY clause   In the price table, the item number is the *key* for the search. In a binary search, the keys must be in either ascending or descending sequence in the table. As a result, this clause tells the SEARCH statement what the *key field* is and what sequence it's in.

The SEARCH ALL statement   When the SEARCH ALL statement is executed, it performs a binary search on the key field defined for the table. Since the binary search figures out its own starting point, you don't have to set the index value using a SET statement before the SEARCH ALL statement is executed.

If you compare the SEARCH ALL statement in figure 8-9 with the SEARCH statement in figure 8-8, you can see that the second WHEN clause isn't used in the SEARCH ALL statement. It isn't needed, because the DEPENDING ON clause limits the binary search to the actual number of entries in the table. If you check the statement format in figure 8-1, you can see that two WHEN clauses are illegal in a SEARCH ALL statement. In addition, you can only code equal conditions in the one WHEN clause; greater-than or less-than conditions are illegal.

How to use the VARYING clause in the SEARCH statement

If you refer back to the table handling summary in figure 8-1, you can see that you can code more than one index name in an INDEXED BY clause. If you do, you can use more than one index to refer to the entries in the table. Then, you can use the VARYING clause in the SEARCH statement to specify the index that you want to be used when the statement is executed. If you omit the VARYING clause, the compiler assumes that you want the first index listed in the INDEXED BY clause to be used.

For most of the table handling routines you'll ever write, you won't need to use more than one index for a table. As a result, you won't need to use the VARYING clause in the SEARCH statement. If you don't need these elements, you shouldn't use them because they can only lead to confusion. Occasionally, though, you may need to search a table two or more times in succession with a different index for each search, so I want you to be aware that the code for doing this is available.

Discussion

By using the table handling elements presented in this topic, you should be able to handle the one-level tables required by most of the programs you are assigned. You should realize, however, that tables of two or three levels are fairly common in business programs. I'll show you how to handle these tables in the next topic.

When you code table handling routines, you should be on guard for debugging problems. Three of the most common coding errors are (1) failing to set an index to a starting value before a SEARCH statement is executed, (2) using an index that is beyond the acceptable number of occurrences for a table, and (3) specifying the wrong index name in the VARYING clause of a SEARCH statement. These errors can lead to program cancellation and difficult debugging problems, so it's best to avoid these problems by watching for these errors when you code.

As you might guess, commonly used tables are often supplied as COPY members. For instance, a constant table like the month table is likely to be available as a COPY member. Similarly, a routine for loading a commonly used table like the price table may be available as a subprogram. Then, you can load the table by issuing a single CALL statement.

Terminology

one-level table
index name
index
occurrence number
displacement value
relative indexing

index usage
index data item
binary search
key
key field

Objective

Given program specifications involving a one-level table, code the required COBOL routines.

Topic 2   How to handle multilevel tables using indexes

For many table handling problems, single-level tables are either inadequate or inconvenient. For instance, income tax withholdings vary based on two factors: amount of pay and number of dependents. To handle a problem like this using single-level tables, you would have to define a separate table for each number of dependents. If, for example, there could be from zero to ten dependents, you would have to define eleven single-level tables. Then, you would look up the amount to be withheld in the appropriate table.

An easier way to handle this kind of problem is to use a two-level table. With a table like this, two indexes are used to refer to the correct table entry. For example, figure 8-10 illustrates a two-level insurance rating table. In this case, two variable factors, age and job class, determine the premium to be charged.

Three-level tables are also relatively common. Figure 8-11, for example, is a three-level insurance rating table similar to the two-level table in figure 8-10. Here, one more variable factor, the applicant's sex, has been added. Thus, age, sex, and job class are used to determine the premium.

A table that varies based on two or more factors is called a *multilevel table*. If you're using the 1974 standards, you can code tables of up to three levels. The 1985 standards, however, provide for tables of up to seven levels. Since tables of more than three levels are rare, though, I won't show any examples of them in this book. If you understand the code for handling two- and three-level tables, you should have no problem extending it to tables with more than three levels if you ever need to.

How to define a multilevel table

To define a multilevel table in COBOL, you code OCCURS clauses within OCCURS clauses. If you look at the table description in figure 8-10, you can see that a field named AGE-GROUP occurs six times. Then, within each AGE-GROUP field are fields named HIGH-AGE and INSURANCE-RATE. (You'll see why the table contains the HIGH-AGE field when I show you a search routine for the table.) As you can see, the field named INSURANCE-RATE occurs four times. As a result, the area named RATE-TABLE consists of 24 rate fields, four for each of the six age groups.

The definition of the three-level table in figure 8-11 is similar. Here, however, there are three levels of OCCURS clauses. At the first level is the field AGE-GROUP, which occurs six times. This time, the

Rate table

Age	Class 1	Class 2	Class 3	Class 4
18-34	23.50	27.05	35.25	52.90
35-39	24.00	27.55	35.75	53.40
40-44	24.60	28.15	36.35	54.00
45-49	25.30	28.85	37.05	54.70
50-54	26.30	29.85	38.05	55.70
55-59	28.00	31.55	39.75	57.40

Table definition in COBOL

```
01   RATE-TABLE.
*
     05   AGE-GROUP            OCCURS 6 TIMES
                              INDEXED BY AGE-INDEX.
         10   HIGH-AGE        PIC XX.
         10   INSURANCE-RATE  OCCURS 4 TIMES
                              INDEXED BY CLASS-INDEX
                              PIC S99V99.
*
```

Statement that refers to a rate in the rate table

```
ADD INSURANCE-RATE (AGE-INDEX CLASS-INDEX) TO POLICY-RATE.
```

Figure 8-10   A two-level rate table and its COBOL definition

age group contains both the low and high age limits. (Again, you'll see why this is necessary when I show you the search routine for the table.) At the second level, the field SEX-GROUP occurs two times within each age group. Finally, at the third level, the field INSURANCE-RATE occurs two times within each sex group. As a result, this table also consists of 24 rate fields (6 x 2 x 2).

How to refer to the entries in a multilevel table

As with one-level tables, indexes can be used to refer to individual fields or groups of fields in multilevel tables. In the two-level table in figure 8-10, for example, any of the 24 rates can be referred to by the code

```
INSURANCE-RATE (AGE-INDEX CLASS-INDEX)
```

depending on the values of AGE-INDEX and CLASS-INDEX.

Rate table

Age	Men Class 1	Men Class 2	Women Class 1	Women Class 2
18-34	23.50	27.05	24.75	28.45
35-39	24.00	27.55	25.80	29.50
40-44	24.60	28.15	27.10	30.80
45-49	25.30	28.85	29.10	32.80
50-54	26.30	29.85	31.55	35.25
55-59	28.00	31.55	35.00	38.70

Table definition in COBOL

```
01   RATE-TABLE.
*
     05   AGE-GROUP                OCCURS 6 TIMES
                                   INDEXED BY AGE-INDEX.
          10   LOW-AGE             PIC XX.
          10   HIGH-AGE            PIC XX.
          10   SEX-GROUP           OCCURS 2 TIMES
                                   INDEXED BY SEX-INDEX.
               15   INSURANCE-RATE OCCURS 2 TIMES
                                   INDEXED BY CLASS-INDEX
                                   PIC S99V99.
*
```

Statement that refers to a rate in the rate table

```
ADD INSURANCE-RATE (AGE-INDEX SEX-INDEX CLASS-INDEX)
    TO POLICY-RATE.
```

Figure 8-11   A three-level rate table and its COBOL definition

Another way to refer to the table entries is by occurrence number. For example, INSURANCE-RATE (1 1) refers to the rate corresponding to age group 1 and class 1 and INSURANCE-RATE (3 4) refers to age group 3 and class 4. Finally, relative indexing can be used to refer to the table entries. If, for example, the value of AGE-INDEX is 6 and the value of CLASS-INDEX is 2, then the code

```
INSURANCE-RATE (AGE-INDEX CLASS-INDEX - 1)
```

refers to class 1 in age group 6.

Notice in all of these examples that the indexes or occurrences must be specified in the order in which they're defined in the table. Also, the indexes or occurrences must be separated by at least one space. Although a comma may be coded to separate indexes or occurrences, commas are not required and we don't use them in our shop. Since commas are ignored by COBOL compilers, you must code one or more spaces after each comma that you use.

The code for referring to entries in a three-level table follows the same format. For example, to refer to the rate for a person in age group 4, sex group 1, and class 5, you could use indexes as in this code

```
INSURANCE-RATE (AGE-INDEX SEX-INDEX CLASS-INDEX)
```

when AGE-INDEX is 4, SEX-INDEX is 1, and CLASS-INDEX is 5. Or, you could use occurrence numbers like this:

```
INSURANCE-RATE (4 1 5)
```

Finally, you could use relative indexing in a number of ways, including this one:

```
INSURANCE-RATE (AGE-INDEX - 1 SEX-INDEX CLASS-INDEX + 2)
```

Here, INSURANCE-RATE (4 1 5) is referred to if AGE-INDEX is 5, SEX-INDEX is 1, and CLASS-INDEX is 3.

```
WORKING-STORAGE SECTION.
*
 01  SWITCHES.
*
     05  RATE-TABLE-EOF-SWITCH     PIC X     VALUE 'N'.
         88  RATE-TABLE-EOF                  VALUE 'Y'.
*
 01  RATE-TABLE.
*
     05  AGE-GROUP                 OCCURS 6 TIMES
                                   INDEXED BY AGE-INDEX.
         10  HIGH-AGE              PIC XX.
         10  INSURANCE-RATE        OCCURS 4 TIMES
                                   INDEXED BY CLASS-INDEX
                                   PIC S99V99.
*
 01  RATE-TABLE-RECORD.
*
     05  RT-HIGH-AGE               PIC XX.
     05  RT-INSURANCE-RATE         OCCURS 4 TIMES
                                   INDEXED BY RT-CLASS-INDEX
                                   PIC S99V99.
     05  FILLER                    PIC X(2).
*
     .
     .
     .
```

Figure 8-12   Loading a two-level rate table with 24 entries (part 1 of 2)

How to load a fixed-length, multilevel table into storage

When the values in a multilevel table are likely to change, you normally load the table into storage from a disk file at the start of any program that uses the table. For example, the rates in the rate tables in figures 8-10 and 8-11 are likely to change periodically. As a result, these tables should be stored on disk so they can be modified as needed.

Figure 8-12 shows a program for loading the two-level table in figure 8-10. As you can see in the figure, two PERFORM VARYING statements are used to load the table since the table has two levels. The first PERFORM statement in module 100 executes module 110 while it varies the value of AGE-INDEX from one to six. As a result, module 110 is executed six times. Each time it is executed, it reads a new table record, moves the high age in the record to the proper position in RATE-TABLE according to the value of AGE-INDEX, and executes the second PERFORM VARYING statement. This statement varies the RT-CLASS-INDEX from one to four while it executes

```
PROCEDURE DIVISION.
*
       .
       .
       .
 100-LOAD-RATE-TABLE.
*
     PERFORM 110-LOAD-RATE-TABLE-ENTRY
         VARYING AGE-INDEX FROM 1 BY 1
         UNTIL AGE-INDEX > 6
            OR RATE-TABLE-EOF.
*
 110-LOAD-RATE-TABLE-ENTRY.
*
     PERFORM 120-READ-RATE-TABLE-RECORD.
     IF NOT RATE-TABLE-EOF
         MOVE RT-HIGH-AGE TO HIGH-AGE (AGE-INDEX)
         PERFORM 130-LOAD-INSURANCE-RATE
             VARYING RT-CLASS-INDEX FROM 1 BY 1
             UNTIL RT-CLASS-INDEX > 4.
*
 120-READ-RATE-TABLE-RECORD.
*
     READ RTABLE RECORD INTO RATE-TABLE-RECORD
         AT END
             MOVE 'Y' TO RATE-TABLE-EOF-SWITCH.
*
 130-LOAD-INSURANCE-RATE.
*
     SET CLASS-INDEX TO RT-CLASS-INDEX.
     MOVE RT-INSURANCE-RATE (RT-CLASS-INDEX)
         TO INSURANCE-RATE (AGE-INDEX CLASS-INDEX).
       .
       .
```

Figure 8-12   Loading a two-level rate table with 24 entries (part 2 of 2)

module 130. Thus, the four class rates within each age group are stored in the table area. Note that CLASS-INDEX is set to RT-CLASS-INDEX in module 130 so it will be varied along with RT-CLASS-INDEX as the rates are stored.

The code to load the fixed-length, three-level rate table in figure 8-11 would be similar. The actual code would depend on how the table is defined and what the format is for the records that are used to load the table. However, the main difference would be that three levels of PERFORM VARYING statements would be used: one to vary AGE-INDEX, one to vary SEX-INDEX, and one to vary CLASS-INDEX.

```
WORKING-STORAGE SECTION.
*
 01   SWITCHES.
*
      05   RATE-TABLE-EOF-SWITCH    PIC X     VALUE 'N'.
           88   RATE-TABLE-EOF                VALUE 'Y'.
*
 01   COUNT-FIELDS.
*
      05   AGE-GROUP-COUNT          INDEX.
*
 01   RATE-TABLE.
*
      05   AGE-GROUP                OCCURS 10 TIMES
                                    INDEXED BY AGE-INDEX.
           10   LOW-AGE            PIC XX.
           10   HIGH-AGE           PIC XX.
           10   SEX-GROUP          OCCURS 2 TIMES
                                    INDEXED BY SEX-INDEX.
                15   INSURANCE-RATE OCCURS 2 TIMES
                                    INDEXED BY CLASS-INDEX
                                    PIC S99V99.
*
 01   RATE-TABLE-RECORD.
*
      05   RT-LOW-AGE               PIC XX.
      05   RT-HIGH-AGE              PIC XX.
      05   RT-SEX-GROUP             OCCURS 2 TIMES
                                    INDEXED BY RT-SEX-INDEX.
           10   RT-INSURANCE-RATE   OCCURS 2 TIMES
                                    INDEXED BY RT-CLASS-INDEX
                                    PIC S99V99.
*
```

Figure 8-13   Loading a three-level rate table with a variable number of entries (part 1 of 2)

How to load a variable-length, multilevel table into storage

In the example in figure 8-12, we assumed that there were always six age groups. But what if there could be a variable number of age groups? Then, the rate table would have to be defined to provide for these variances.

Figure 8-13 illustrates the code for loading a variable-length rate table into storage. Here, I'm using the three-level table described in figure 8-11. Notice that the OCCURS clause for AGE-GROUP gives an occurrence value of 10. That means the table may hold a maximum of ten age groups. However, the actual number of entries loaded into this table will depend upon the number of entries in the table file. This number will be stored in a field named AGE-GROUP-COUNT. Notice in the table definition that both the low age limit and high age limit are stored in each age group since these limits may change.

```
PROCEDURE DIVISION.
*
       .
       .
       .
 100-LOAD-RATE-TABLE.
*
     PERFORM 110-LOAD-RATE-TABLE-ENTRY
         VARYING AGE-INDEX FROM 1 BY 1
         UNTIL AGE-INDEX > 10
            OR RATE-TABLE-EOF.
*
 110-LOAD-RATE-TABLE-ENTRY.
*
     PERFORM 120-READ-RATE-TABLE-RECORD.
     IF NOT RATE-TABLE-EOF
         MOVE RT-LOW-AGE  TO LOW-AGE (AGE-INDEX)
         MOVE RT-HIGH-AGE TO HIGH-AGE (AGE-INDEX)
         PERFORM 130-LOAD-SEX-GROUP-RATE
             VARYING RT-SEX-INDEX FROM 1 BY 1
             UNTIL RT-SEX-INDEX > 2
     ELSE
         SET AGE-INDEX DOWN BY 1
         SET AGE-GROUP-COUNT TO AGE-INDEX.
*
 120-READ-RATE-TABLE-RECORD.
*
     READ RTABLE RECORD INTO RATE-TABLE-RECORD
         AT END
             MOVE 'Y' TO RATE-TABLE-EOF-SWITCH.
*
 130-LOAD-SEX-GROUP-RATE.
*
     SET SEX-INDEX TO RT-SEX-INDEX.
     PERFORM 140-LOAD-INSURANCE-RATE
         VARYING RT-CLASS-INDEX FROM 1 BY 1
         UNTIL RT-CLASS-INDEX > 2.
*
 140-LOAD-INSURANCE-RATE.
*
     SET CLASS-INDEX TO RT-CLASS-INDEX.
     MOVE RT-INSURANCE-RATE (RT-SEX-INDEX RT-CLASS-INDEX)
         TO INSURANCE-RATE (AGE-INDEX SEX-INDEX CLASS-INDEX).
       .
       .
```

Figure 8-13   Loading a three-level rate table with a variable number of entries (part 2 of 2)

If you understand how to load a fixed-length, multilevel table, you shouldn't have any trouble understanding the code in figure 8-13. Since the table being loaded is three levels, you have to use three PERFORM VARYING statements. The first one varies the age index, the second one varies the sex index, and the third one varies the class index. Also, since the table is variable length, when the end of the table file is reached, you have to code two SET statements to store the number of age group entries in the file. The first SET statement reduces the index for the age groups by the equivalent of one occurrence number so it contains a value that corresponds to the actual number of entries in the table. The second SET statement sets AGE-GROUP-COUNT to the displacement value of the index. Notice that I have defined AGE-GROUP-COUNT with index usage. Then, no conversion is necessary when the second SET statement is executed.

How to search a multilevel table using a single-level search

Once a table has been loaded into storage, you can search it to find the entries your program requires. In general, when you search multilevel tables, you can think of them as tables within tables. Then, you can treat each level as a single-level table.

Figure 8-14 shows a routine that searches the table that was loaded by the routine in figure 8-13. Since the applicant record, which provides the input used to search the table, contains both the applicant's sex and class, only the age group needs to be searched. Before the search takes place, however, the program tests the applicant's age (AR-AGE), sex (AR-SEX), and class (AR-CLASS) to make sure they are within valid limits. To check AR-AGE, the program makes sure that it isn't less than the lowest age limit in the table or greater than the highest age limit in the table. To check the sex and class, the program simply tests to be sure they aren't less than one or greater than two. If all three fields are valid, the program executes the search module.

At the beginning of the search module, three SET statements are issued. These set the age index to an occurrence value of one and set the class and sex indexes to the values indicated by the input fields. When the SEARCH statement is executed, it does a single-level search of the high-age field. When the applicant's age is less than or equal to the table age, AGE-INDEX represents the proper age index value, and Y is moved to AGE-GROUP-FOUND-SWITCH. Then,

```
INSURANCE-RATE (AGE-INDEX SEX-INDEX CLASS-INDEX)
```

refers to the desired entry.

Even though the table searched in figure 8-14 is a three-level table, only a single-level search is needed since two of the index values are given in the input data. When this is *not* the case, the search routine is a little more complex. Then, more than one SEARCH statement can be used to search the table.

How to search a multilevel table using a multilevel search

To illustrate a multilevel search, take a look at the two-level table definition in the program in figure 8-15. This table is similar to the price table presented in the last topic except that it contains a variable number of item groups for a variable number of stores. As you can see, there can be a maximum of 20 store groups, each of which can contain a maximum of 100 items, but the number of stores and the number of item groups for each store are variable. As a result, STORE-COUNT represents the actual number of stores loaded in the table, and ITEM-COUNT, which has index usage, represents the actual number of item groups for each store.

Now take a look at the search routine for this table. As you can see in module 350, the search takes place in two steps. First, the store group is searched by module 360. In this module, the store index is set to one and the store group is searched for a store with the same number as in the input record. If all of the stores that were loaded into the table are searched and no matching entry is found or if the end of the file is reached, N is moved to STORE-FOUND-SWITCH and the search is cancelled. However, if a matching store entry is found, Y is moved to STORE-FOUND-SWITCH. In either case, control is returned to module 350 when the search is completed.

If the store is found, module 370 is executed to search the item group for an item number that matches the item number in the input record. The format of this search is the same as the search for the store number, but there are a couple things you should notice. First, this search is performed on ITEM-GROUP, which is the second level of the table. In other words, the search is not performed on all of the stores. Since STORE-INDEX is already set to the location of the correct store, the search is only performed on the item groups for that store. Second, to test if the last item loaded in the table for that store has been reached, the item index is compared to the item count for that store. Since the store index has already been set, ITEM-COUNT (STORE-INDEX) refers to the item count for the selected store.

If you understand how to do this two-level search, you should have no trouble coding routines that do searches for three or more levels. One thing to keep in mind when you do a multilevel search is that you have to start by searching the highest level first. Then, you work your way down to the lowest level. If you don't, the higher-level indexes won't be set properly, and the search routine won't work right.

```
WORKING-STORAGE SECTION.
*
 01   SWITCHES.
*
        .
        .
        .
     05   VALID-APPLICANT-SWITCH      PIC X    VALUE 'N'.
          88  VALID-APPLICANT                  VALUE 'Y'.
     05   AGE-GROUP-FOUND-SWITCH      PIC X    VALUE 'N'.
          88  AGE-GROUP-FOUND                  VALUE 'Y'.
*
 01   COUNT-FIELDS.
*
     05   AGE-GROUP-COUNT      INDEX.
*
 01   WORK-FIELDS            COMP-3.
*
     05   POLICY-RATE        PIC S999V99.
        .
        .
 01   RATE-TABLE.
*
     05   AGE-GROUP                OCCURS 10 TIMES
                                   INDEXED BY AGE-INDEX.
          10   LOW-AGE             PIC XX.
          10   HIGH-AGE            PIC XX.
          10   SEX-GROUP           OCCURS 2 TIMES
                                   INDEXED BY SEX-INDEX.
               15   INSURANCE-RATE OCCURS 2 TIMES
                                   INDEXED BY CLASS-INDEX
                                   PIC S99V99.
*
 01   APPLICANT-RECORD.
*
     05   AR-AGE      PIC XX.
     05   AR-SEX      PIC X.
     05   AR-CLASS    PIC X.
        .
        .
```

Figure 8-14   Searching a three-level, variable-length rate table with a single-level search (part 1 of 2)

```
PROCEDURE DIVISION.
*
    .
    .
    IF AR-AGE < LOW-AGE (1)
        MOVE 'N' TO VALID-APPLICANT-SWITCH
    ELSE
        SET AGE-INDEX TO AGE-GROUP-COUNT
        IF AR-AGE > HIGH-AGE (AGE-INDEX)
            MOVE 'N' TO VALID-APPLICANT-SWITCH.
    IF        AR-SEX < 1
        OR AR-SEX > 2
        MOVE 'N' TO VALID-APPLICANT-SWITCH.
    IF        AR-CLASS < 1
        OR AR-CLASS > 2
        MOVE 'N' TO VALID-APPLICANT-SWITCH.
    IF VALID-APPLICANT
        PERFORM 220-SEARCH-RATE-TABLE
        IF AGE-GROUP-FOUND
            MOVE INSURANCE-RATE (AGE-INDEX SEX-INDEX CLASS-INDEX)
                TO POLICY-RATE
        ELSE
    .
    .
*
 220-SEARCH-RATE-TABLE.
*
    SET AGE-INDEX   TO 1.
    SET SEX-INDEX   TO AR-SEX.
    SET CLASS-INDEX TO AR-CLASS.
    SEARCH AGE-GROUP
        AT END
            MOVE 'N' TO AGE-GROUP-FOUND-SWITCH
        WHEN AR-AGE NOT > HIGH-AGE (AGE-INDEX)
            MOVE 'Y' TO AGE-GROUP-FOUND-SWITCH.
*
    .
    .
```

Figure 8-14   Searching a three-level, variable-length rate table with a single-level search (part 2 of 2)

```
WORKING-STORAGE SECTION.
*
 01  SWITCHES.
*
     .
     .
     05  STORE-FOUND-SWITCH      PIC X    VALUE 'N'.
         88  STORE-FOUND                  VALUE 'Y'.
     05  ITEM-FOUND-SWITCH       PIC X    VALUE 'N'.
         88  ITEM-FOUND                   VALUE 'Y'.
*
 01  COUNT-FIELDS.
*
     05  STORE-COUNT                 INDEX.
*
 01  PRICE-TABLE.
*
     05  STORE-GROUP                 OCCURS 20 TIMES
                                     INDEXED BY STORE-INDEX.
         10  STORE-NUMBER            PIC XX.
         10  ITEM-COUNT              INDEX.
         10  ITEM-GROUP              OCCURS 100 TIMES
                                     INDEXED BY ITEM-INDEX.
             15  ITEM-NUMBER         PIC X(3).
             15  ITEM-PRICE          PIC S99V99.
*
 01  WORK-FIELDS          COMP-3.
*
     05  UNIT-PRICE       PIC S999V99.
*
 01  SALES-TRANSACTION.
*
     05  ST-STORE-NUMBER     PIC XX.
     05  ST-ITEM-NUMBER      PIC X(3).
     05  ST-QUANTITY         PIC S9(3).
     .
     .
```

Figure 8-15   Searching a two-level, variable-length table with a multilevel search (part 1 of 2)

```
 PROCEDURE DIVISION.
*
     .
     .
     .
 350-SEARCH-PRICE-TABLE.
*
     PERFORM 360-SEARCH-STORE-GROUP.
     IF STORE-FOUND
         PERFORM 370-SEARCH-ITEM-GROUP.
*
 360-SEARCH-STORE-GROUP.
*
     SET STORE-INDEX TO 1.
     SEARCH STORE-GROUP
         AT END
             MOVE 'N' TO STORE-FOUND-SWITCH
         WHEN STORE-INDEX > STORE-COUNT
             MOVE 'N' TO STORE-FOUND-SWITCH
         WHEN STORE-NUMBER (STORE-INDEX) = ST-STORE-NUMBER
             MOVE 'Y' TO STORE-FOUND-SWITCH.
*
 370-SEARCH-ITEM-GROUP.
*
     SET ITEM-INDEX TO 1.
     SEARCH ITEM-GROUP
         AT END
             MOVE 'N' TO ITEM-FOUND-SWITCH
         WHEN ITEM-INDEX > ITEM-COUNT (STORE-INDEX)
             MOVE 'N' TO ITEM-FOUND-SWITCH
         WHEN ITEM-NUMBER (STORE-INDEX ITEM-INDEX)
                 = ST-ITEM-NUMBER
             MOVE ITEM-PRICE (STORE-INDEX ITEM-INDEX)
                 TO UNIT-PRICE
             MOVE 'Y' TO ITEM-FOUND-SWITCH.
     .
     .
```

Figure 8-15   Searching a two-level, variable-length table with a multilevel search (part 2 of 2)

```
PERFORM procedure-name

    VARYING   {identifier-1}   FROM   {identifier-2}
              {index-name-1}          {index-name-2}
                                      {literal-1   }


         BY   {identifier-3}   UNTIL   condition-1
              {literal-2   }


   [AFTER   {identifier-4}   FROM   {identifier-5}
            {index-name-3}          {index-name-4}
                                    {literal-3   }


       BY   {identifier-6}   UNTIL   condition-2 ]  ...
            {literal-4   }
```

Figure 8-16   An expanded form of the PERFORM statement

The PERFORM statement VARYING more than one index

Generally, when a multilevel table is used in a program, it's searched for a particular entry as I just described. However, there are occasions when you need to manipulate all of the values in a table. To do this, an expanded form of the PERFORM statement can be used. Its format is given in figure 8-16. As you can see, this format allows more than one index to be varied by the same statement. The first index to be varied is specified in the VARYING clause. Then, other indexes to be varied are specified in the AFTER clauses that follow. Usually, the indexes are specified in sequence from the highest to the lowest level index for a table, but you can specify the indexes in whatever sequence is appropriate for the problem you're handling.

Under the 1974 standards, the PERFORM statement can vary up to three indexes, one in the VARYING clause and two in AFTER clauses. Since a table can only have three levels under the 1974 standards, that's all that's needed. Under the 1985 standards, however, the PERFORM has been expanded to accommodate up to seven indexes, one in the VARYING clause and six in AFTER clauses. That way, it can accommodate all seven levels of a table.

To illustrate how to use this expanded PERFORM, suppose all the rates in the two-level insurance table are to be added together. Figure 8-17 shows how the PERFORM statement can be used for this purpose. Here, the PERFORM statement varies AGE-INDEX from an occurrence value of one through six and CLASS-INDEX from one through four. As a result, 210-ACCUMULATE-RATE-TOTAL is executed 24 times. The first time it is executed, INSURANCE-RATE (1 1) is added to RATE-TOTAL; the second time, INSURANCE-RATE (1 2) is added; then INSURANCE-RATE (1 3); then

```
WORKING-STORAGE SECTION.
*
        .
        .
*
 01   WORK-FIELDS          COMP-3.
*
      05   RATE-TOTAL       PIC S9(3)V99.
        .
        .
*
 01   RATE-TABLE.
*
      05   AGE-GROUP              OCCURS 6 TIMES
                                 INDEXED BY AGE-INDEX.
           10   HIGH-AGE         PIC XX.
           10   INSURANCE-RATE   OCCURS 4 TIMES
                                 INDEXED BY CLASS-INDEX
                                 PIC S99V99.
*
        .
        .
*
 PROCEDURE DIVISION.
*
        .
        .
      PERFORM 210-ACCUMULATE-RATE-TOTAL
          VARYING AGE-INDEX FROM 1 BY 1
          UNTIL AGE-INDEX > 6
              AFTER CLASS-INDEX FROM 1 BY 1
              UNTIL CLASS-INDEX > 4.
        .
        .
*
 210-ACCUMULATE-RATE-TOTAL.
*
      ADD INSURANCE-RATE (AGE-INDEX CLASS-INDEX) TO RATE-TOTAL.
        .
        .
```

Figure 8-17   Using a two-level PERFORM statement

INSURANCE-RATE (1 4); then INSURANCE-RATE (2 1); and so on.

Since all of the rates in the table are being operated upon in this example, you get the same result if you reverse the sequence in which the indexes are specified in the PERFORM statement. In this case, the first rate to be accumulated is INSURANCE-RATE (1 1); the second one is INSURANCE-RATE (2 1); and so on. The result is that all 24 rates get added to RATE-TOTAL.

Of course, you could also get the same result by using nested PERFORM statements like the ones used in the two load programs presented earlier in this topic. In general, though, the use of the PERFORM VARYING statement with one or more AFTER clauses leads to code that is easy to follow. As a result, there's no reason to use nested PERFORM statements when you can accomplish the same thing in a single statement.

Discussion

By now, you should realize that handling multilevel tables is simply an extension of the principles for handling one-level tables. Table descriptions, index notation, the SEARCH statement, and even the PERFORM statement can all be seen as defining or operating upon one-level tables within one-level tables.

You should also realize that some of the programs in this topic have been simplified in order to show the basic table handling elements. In actual practice, you won't always use indexes for a table with only two or three elements. For example, in the three-level insurance table, you probably wouldn't index the sex code. Instead, you would use condition names in the input record. Then, you would set up two two-level tables, one for men and one for women, and process them according to the value of AR-SEX.

In general, if there are only a few elements in some level of a table, you shouldn't handle them using table handling code because other COBOL code will run more efficiently. As a result, I think you'll find that two levels of OCCURS clauses are all you'll need in the vast majority of your programs. Usually, you can handle a table in more than one way, so you have to decide which way leads to the most efficient code and the code that is easiest to understand.

Terminology

multilevel table

Objective

Apply the COBOL elements presented in this topic to your application programs.

Topic 3   How to use subscripts

In the last two topics, I showed you how to handle tables using indexes. You should realize, though, that you can also handle tables using *subscripts* instead of indexes. Although you probably won't use them much because they aren't as efficient as indexes, this topic will show you how to use subscripts to handle tables.

How to define a table and its subscripts

The definition for a table that uses subscripts is similar to a table definition that uses indexes. For example, figure 8-18 shows the definition for a one-level price table that uses subscripts. This is the same table that is defined in figure 8-3 using indexes. As you can see, the only difference is that the INDEXED BY clause isn't used when you're using subscripts. Instead, the subscript for the table must be defined in working storage.

When you define a subscript, you should realize that it represents an occurrence number, not a displacement value. Therefore, it should be defined as an integer, and it should be large enough to contain the highest occurrence in the table. For example, in figure 8-18, I've defined the subscript as

```
05  PRICE-TABLE-SUB     PIC S99.
```

Since the table contains only 16 entries, two digits are sufficient in this case.

Note, too, that I've coded COMP at the 01 level for the subscript in figure 8-18. Because a subscript with computational usage usually leads to more efficient object code than a subscript with display usage, you should define all subscripts with the computational usage that is appropriate for them. You should also define them as signed (S in the picture).

You can also code constant values for a table that uses subscripts just as you can for a table that uses indexes. To do that, you code the values of the table and then redefine the area as a table using the REDEFINES and OCCURS clauses. Figure 8-19 shows one way this can be done for the price table in figure 8-18. Again, this definition is identical to the definition for a price table using indexes except that the INDEXED BY clause isn't used.

To define a multilevel table using subscripts, you use OCCURS clauses within OCCURS clauses, just as you do for indexed tables. For example, figure 8-20 shows the same table presented in figure 8-15 except that subscripts are used. As you can see, the only differences are that the subscripts associated with the table are defined in working storage, and no INDEXED BY clauses are coded.

Subscript definition

```
01    SUBSCRIPTS                COMP.
*
      05   PRICE-TABLE-SUB      PIC S99.
*
```

Table definition

```
01   PRICE-TABLE.
*
     05   PRICE-GROUP           OCCURS 16 TIMES.
          10   ITEM-NUMBER      PIC X(3).
          10   ITEM-PRICE       PIC S99V99.
*
```

Statement that refers to a price in the price table

```
MULTIPLY TR-QUANTITY BY ITEM-PRICE (PRICE-TABLE-SUB)
    GIVING LINE-ITEM-EXTENSION ROUNDED.
```

Figure 8-18   A price table that uses subscripts

```
01   PRICE-TABLE-VALUES.
*
     05   FILLER               PIC X(7)  .    VALUE '1011250'.
     05   FILLER               PIC X(7)       VALUE '1075000'.
     .
     .
     05   FILLER               PIC X(7)       VALUE '3510035'.
*
01   PRICE-TABLE REDEFINES PRICE-TABLE-VALUES.
*
     05   PRICE-GROUP          OCCURS 16 TIMES.
          10   ITEM-NUMBER     PIC X(3).
          10   ITEM-PRICE      PIC S99V99.
*
```

Figure 8-19   One way to define the price table in figure 8-18 with constant values

How to refer to the entries in a table

Under the 1974 standards, you can refer to the entries in a table that uses subscripts in two ways. First, you can code the name of the field

Subscript definition

```
 01    SUBSCRIPTS              COMP.
 *
       05   STORE-SUB          PIC S99.
       05   ITEM-SUB           PIC S9(3).
 *
```

Table definition

```
 01    PRICE-TABLE.
 *
       05   STORE-GROUP              OCCURS 20 TIMES.
            10   STORE-NUMBER        PIC XX.
            10   ITEM-COUNT          PIC S9(3)              COMP.
            10   ITEM-GROUP          OCCURS 100 TIMES.
                 15   ITEM-NUMBER    PIC X(3).
                 15   ITEM-PRICE     PIC S99V99.
 *
```

Figure 8-20   A two-level price table and its subscripts

you want to refer to followed by the subscript, as in these examples:

```
    ITEM-PRICE (PRICE-TABLE-SUB)
    ITEM-PRICE (STORE-SUB ITEM-SUB)
```

Then, the values of the subscripts determine the specific table element that the code refers to.

Second, if you know which entries you want to refer to at the time you code a program, you can code the subscripts as literals, as in these examples:

```
    ITEM-PRICE (1)
    ITEM-PRICE (1 1)
```

These examples refer to the first price in a one-level and a two-level table.

Under the 1985 standards, you can also refer to a table entry with a relative subscript value, as in these examples:

```
    ITEM-PRICE (PRICE-TABLE-SUB + 1)
    ITEM-PRICE (STORE-SUB - 2 ITEM-SUB)
```

Here, one subscript is increased by one, while another subscript is decreased by two. This can be referred to as *relative subscripting*, and it is analogous to relative indexing when indexes are used.

When you use subscripts to refer to the elements in a table, they represent occurrence numbers. As a result, a subscript must be an integer between one and the number of times an element can occur in the table. For the one-level price table, the occurrence number must be from one to 16. For the two-level price table, the occurrence numbers must be from one to 20 and from one to 100, respectively.

One more thing you should know about using subscripts is that you can use the same subscript to refer to items in different tables. This makes sense because a subscript represents an occurrence number. In contrast, an index can only be associated with one table. In this sense, subscripts are more flexible than indexes.

How to load a fixed-length table into storage

You can load a fixed-length table that uses subscripts into storage using the same techniques you use for tables with indexes. The only difference in the code is that you have to vary a subscript instead of an index in the PERFORM VARYING statement. For example, assuming that each group of table entries is stored in one record in a sequential file that contains all of the values for the table, you can use the routine in figure 8-21 to load the one-level price table. As you can see, the PERFORM VARYING statement causes module 110 to be executed until the end of the table file has been reached or until the subscript is greater than 16. Module 110 then reads a record from the table file and moves the entries into the proper places in the price table.

Again, this routine has been simplified to illustrate the essential table handling elements. In a production program, you'd have to do some kind of error processing if the end of the PTABLE file were reached before 16 values had been loaded into the table.

To load a multilevel table into storage, you use nested PERFORM VARYING statements just as you do with indexes. Then, the first PERFORM VARYING statement varies the subscript associated with the first level of the table, the second PERFORM VARYING statement varies the subscript associated with the second level of the table, and so on. You can refer back to figure 8-12 to see how this is done with indexes. Then, if you're using subscripts instead of indexes, you simply vary the subscripts associated with a table instead of the indexes.

How to load a variable-length table into storage

You'll remember from the sections in the last two topics on loading variable-length tables that after the last record in the table file was reached, the index had to be reduced by one before the count field was set. To reduce the index and to set the count field to the value in the index, the SET statement was used. Because a subscript represents an

```
WORKING-STORAGE SECTION.
*
 01  SWITCHES.
*
     05  PTABLE-EOF-SWITCH    PIC X        VALUE 'N'.
         88  PTABLE-EOF                    VALUE 'Y'.
*
 01  SUBSCRIPTS           COMP.
*
     05  PRICE-TABLE-SUB     PIC S99.
*
 01  PRICE-TABLE.
*
     05  PRICE-GROUP         OCCURS 16 TIMES.
         10  ITEM-NUMBER     PIC X(3).
         10  ITEM-PRICE      PIC S99V99.
*
 01  PRICE-TABLE-RECORD.
*
     05  PT-ITEM-NUMBER      PIC X(3).
     05  PT-ITEM-PRICE       PIC S99V99.
     05  FILLER              PIC X(13).
*
        .
        .
        .
*
 PROCEDURE DIVISION.
*
        .
        .
 100-LOAD-PRICE-TABLE.
*
     PERFORM 110-LOAD-PRICE-TABLE-ENTRY
         VARYING PRICE-TABLE-SUB FROM 1 BY 1
         UNTIL PTABLE-EOF
             OR PRICE-TABLE-SUB > 16.
*
 110-LOAD-PRICE-TABLE-ENTRY.
*
     PERFORM 120-READ-PRICE-TABLE-RECORD.
     IF NOT PTABLE-EOF
         MOVE PT-ITEM-NUMBER TO ITEM-NUMBER (PRICE-TABLE-SUB)
         MOVE PT-ITEM-PRICE  TO ITEM-PRICE (PRICE-TABLE-SUB).
*
 120-READ-PRICE-TABLE-RECORD.
*
     READ PTABLE RECORD INTO PRICE-TABLE-RECORD
         AT END
             MOVE 'Y' TO PTABLE-EOF-SWITCH.
        .
        .
```

Figure 8-21   Loading a price table with 16 entries using subscripts

```
WORKING-STORAGE SECTION.
*
 01   SWITCHES.
*
     05   PTABLE-EOF-SWITCH     PIC X        VALUE 'N'.
          88   PTABLE-EOF                    VALUE 'Y'.
*
 01   SUBSCRIPTS             COMP.
*
     05   PRICE-TABLE-SUB      PIC S9(3).
*
 01   COUNT-FIELDS          COMP.
*
     05   PT-ENTRY-COUNT      PIC S9(3).
*
 01   PRICE-TABLE.
*
     05   PRICE-GROUP           OCCURS 100 TIMES.
          10   ITEM-NUMBER      PIC X(3).
          10   ITEM-PRICE       PIC S99V99.
*
 01   PRICE-TABLE-RECORD.
*
     05   PT-ITEM-NUMBER        PIC X(3).
     05   PT-ITEM-PRICE         PIC S99V99.
     05   FILLER                PIC X(13).
*
     .
     .
     .
```

Figure 8-22   Loading a price table with a variable number of entries using subscripts (part 1 of 2)

occurrence value instead of a displacement value, however, no conversion is necessary so the SET statement isn't used with subscripts.

Figure 8-22 illustrates a routine for loading the one-level price table, assuming it can contain up to 100 entries. Notice in module 110 that when the end of the table file is reached, the value of the subscript is reduced by one using a SUBTRACT statement and PT-ENTRY-COUNT is set to the value in the subscript using a MOVE statement. Also notice that PT-ENTRY-COUNT is not defined with index usage. Since index usage implies that a displacement value is to be stored in the field, it shouldn't be used with subscripts. Instead, the count field should be defined with the same size and usage as the subscript it's associated with. In this example, it's defined with a picture of S9(3) and COMP usage since that's how PRICE-TABLE-SUB is defined.

If you understand the procedure for loading variable-length, multilevel tables into storage using indexes, you should have no problem loading a variable-length, multilevel table using subscripts. If you need to, you can refer to figure 8-13 to see how it's done using indexes.

```
  PROCEDURE DIVISION.
 *
        .
        .
        .
  100-LOAD-PRICE-TABLE.
 *
     PERFORM 110-LOAD-PRICE-TABLE-ENTRY
        VARYING PRICE-TABLE-SUB FROM 1 BY 1
        UNTIL PTABLE-EOF
           OR PRICE-TABLE-SUB > 100.
 *
  110-LOAD-PRICE-TABLE-ENTRY.
 *
     PERFORM 120-READ-PRICE-TABLE-RECORD.
     IF NOT PTABLE-EOF
        MOVE PT-ITEM-NUMBER TO ITEM-NUMBER (PRICE-TABLE-SUB)
        MOVE PT-ITEM-PRICE  TO ITEM-PRICE (PRICE-TABLE-SUB)
     ELSE
        SUBTRACT 1 FROM PRICE-TABLE-SUB
        MOVE PRICE-TABLE-SUB TO PT-ENTRY-COUNT.
 *
  120-READ-PRICE-TABLE-RECORD.
 *
     READ PTABLE RECORD INTO PRICE-TABLE-RECORD
        AT END
           MOVE 'Y' TO PTABLE-EOF-SWITCH.
        .
        .
        .
```

Figure 8-22   Loading a price table with a variable number of entries using subscripts (part 2 of 2)

Then, if you're using subscripts, you vary the subscripts associated with the table instead of the indexes, and you use SUBTRACT and MOVE statements to store the entry count instead of the SET statement.

How to search a table

When you search a table using subscripts, you can't use the SEARCH statement. That's because the SEARCH statement requires the use of the field specified in the INDEXED BY clause for the table. Since the INDEXED BY clause isn't coded in the definition for a table that uses subscripts, the SEARCH statement can't be used.

To search a table that uses subscripts, you have to use the PERFORM VARYING statement. This is illustrated in figure 8-23, which presents a routine for searching the price table that was loaded in figure 8-22. As you can see, before the PERFORM VARYING statement is executed, ITEM-FOUND-SWITCH must be set to N. Then, the PERFORM VARYING statement causes module 350 to be

```
WORKING-STORAGE SECTION.
*
 01   SWITCHES.
*
        .
        .
      05   ITEM-FOUND-SWITCH    PIC X.
           88   ITEM-FOUND                VALUE 'Y'.
*
 01   SUBSCRIPTS             COMP.
*
      05   PRICE-TABLE-SUB     PIC S9(3).
*
 01   COUNT-FIELDS          COMP.
*
      05   PT-ENTRY-COUNT     PIC S9(3).
*
 01   PRICE-TABLE.
*
      05   PRICE-GROUP         OCCURS 100 TIMES.
           10   ITEM-NUMBER    PIC X(3).
           10   ITEM-PRICE     PIC S99V99.
*
 01   WORK-FIELDS           COMP-3.
*
      05   UNIT-PRICE          PIC S999V99.
*
 01   TRANSACTION-RECORD.
*
      05   TR-REFERENCE-CODE   PIC X(6).
      05   TR-REFERENCE-DATE   PIC X(6).
      05   TR-CUSTOMER-NO      PIC X(5).
      05   TR-ITEM-NO          PIC X(3).
        .
        .
 PROCEDURE DIVISION.
*
        .
        .
      MOVE 'N' TO ITEM-FOUND-SWITCH.
      PERFORM 350-SEARCH-PRICE-TABLE
          VARYING PRICE-TABLE-SUB FROM 1 BY 1
          UNTIL ITEM-FOUND
             OR PRICE-TABLE-SUB > PT-ENTRY-COUNT.
      IF ITEM-FOUND
          SUBTRACT 1 FROM PRICE-TABLE-SUB
          MOVE ITEM-PRICE (PRICE-TABLE-SUB) TO UNIT-PRICE.
        .
        .
 350-SEARCH-PRICE-TABLE.
*
      IF ITEM-NUMBER (PRICE-TABLE-SUB) = TR-ITEM-NO
          MOVE 'Y' TO ITEM-FOUND-SWITCH.
```

Figure 8-23   Searching a variable-length price table using the PERFORM VARYING statement

executed until the item specified in the input record is found or until the subscript is greater than the number of occurrences in the table. Module 350 simply tests to see if the item number in the current table entry is equal to the item number in the input record. If it is, Y is moved to ITEM-FOUND-SWITCH. Because a PERFORM VARYING statement is used, one must be subtracted from the subscript after an item has been found so it refers to the correct entry.

The routine for searching a table with a fixed number of entries is only slightly different. For example, to search a price table with only 16 occurrences, the PERFORM VARYING statement is coded like this:

```
PERFORM 350-SEARCH-PRICE-TABLE
    VARYING PRICE-TABLE-SUB FROM 1 BY 1
    UNTIL PRICE-FOUND
        OR PRICE-TABLE-SUB > 16.
```

Here, PRICE-TABLE-SUB is varied until the item is found or the subscript is greater than 16.

To search a multilevel table using subscripts, you use nested PERFORM VARYING statements just as you do when you load a multilevel table. For example, to search the two-level price table defined in figure 8-20, you can use the routine in figure 8-24. The first PERFORM VARYING statement performs module 350 until a matching item is found or the store subscript is greater than the number of stores in the table. In module 350, when a matching store is found, module 360 is executed until a matching item is found or the item subscript is greater than the number of items for that store in the table. In module 360, when a matching item number is found, Y is moved to ITEM-FOUND-SWITCH.

If you'll look back at the control module in figure 8-24 that contains the first PERFORM VARYING statement, you'll see that the program tests the ITEM-FOUND condition after the search routine has finished its execution. If the condition is met, one is subtracted from both subscripts so they point to the correct table entries.

Discussion

Although subscripts and indexes provide almost identical capabilities, subscripts tend to be less efficient than indexes. Because the computer locates the entries in a table by their displacements from the beginning of the table and because subscripts represent occurrence numbers, a subscript must be converted to a displacement value each time it's used to refer to an entry in the table. Since this is inefficient, indexes should be used whenever possible.

Sometimes, though, you can't use indexes to define a table. For instance, when you're using the screen handling facilities of the Wang VS compiler, you can't use indexes for a table that is displayed on the

```
WORKING-STORAGE SECTION.
*
 01   SWITCHES.
*
         .
         .
         .
     05   ITEM-FOUND-SWITCH          PIC X.
          88   ITEM-FOUND                        VALUE 'Y'.
*
 01   SUBSCRIPTS                COMP.
*
     05   STORE-SUB            PIC S99.
     05   ITEM-SUB             PIC S9(3).
*
 01   COUNT-FIELDS             COMP.
*
     05   STORE-COUNT          PIC S9(3).
*
 01   PRICE-TABLE.
*
     05   STORE-GROUP              OCCURS 20 TIMES.
          10   STORE-NUMBER        PIC XX.
          10   ITEM-COUNT          PIC S9(3)            COMP.
          10   ITEM-GROUP          OCCURS 100 TIMES.
               15   ITEM-NUMBER    PIC X(3).
               15   ITEM-PRICE     PIC S99V99.
*
 01   WORK-FIELDS              COMP-3.
*
     05   UNIT-PRICE           PIC S999V99.
*
 01   SALES-TRANSACTION.
*
     05   ST-STORE-NUMBER      PIC XX.
     05   ST-ITEM-NUMBER       PIC X(3).
     05   ST-QUANTITY          PIC S9(3).
         .
         .
         .
```

Figure 8-24   Searching a two-level, variable-length price table using nested PERFORM VARYING statements (part 1 of 2)

screen. Instead, you must refer to the displayed items by using subscripts. Then, the same subscript can be used to refer to both the table defined for the screen and the corresponding table in working storage.

You should realize that you can use both indexes and subscripts for the same table. Normally, though, you don't want to do this because it can only lead to confusion. If you only use one index for each table, the index name is clearly documented by the INDEXED BY clause.

```
  PROCEDURE DIVISION.
*
         .
         .
      MOVE 'N' TO ITEM-FOUND-SWITCH.
      PERFORM 350-SEARCH-STORE-GROUP
          VARYING STORE-SUB FROM 1 BY 1
          UNTIL ITEM-FOUND
            OR STORE-SUB > STORE-COUNT.
      IF ITEM-FOUND
          SUBTRACT 1 FROM STORE-SUB
          SUBTRACT 1 FROM ITEM-SUB
          MOVE ITEM-PRICE (STORE-SUB ITEM-SUB) TO UNIT-PRICE.
         .
         .
  350-SEARCH-STORE-GROUP.
*
      IF STORE-NUMBER (STORE-SUB) = ST-STORE-NUMBER
          PERFORM 360-SEARCH-ITEM-GROUP
              VARYING ITEM-SUB FROM 1 BY 1
              UNTIL ITEM-FOUND
                OR ITEM-SUB > ITEM-COUNT (STORE-SUB).
*
  360-SEARCH-ITEM-GROUP.
*
      IF ITEM-NUMBER (STORE-SUB ITEM-SUB) = ST-ITEM-NO
          MOVE 'Y' TO ITEM-FOUND-SWITCH.
```

Figure 8-24   Searching a two-level, variable-length price table using nested PERFORM VARYING statements (part 2 of 2)

Terminology

subscript
relative subscripting

Objective

Apply the COBOL elements presented in this topic to your application programs, but only when subscripts are required.

Topic 4   Compiler dependent code

The programming examples presented in this chapter should run on any compiler that uses the 1974 or 1985 standards with only the few changes that I've mentioned throughout this book: system names, quotation marks, and usages. In addition, you should know what the appropriate usage is for subscripts on your system and how the SEARCH ALL statement is implemented on your system (if at all).

Subscript usages

For efficiency, a subscript should be defined as a signed integer with computational usage. On systems that support only one computational usage, this presents no problem because you define all subscripts with the computational usage that is supported by your system. Using Microsoft COBOL on the IBM PC, for example, you define subscripts with COMP-3 usage just as you define other fields that are going to be involved in computations or arithmetic comparisons. Similarly, using VS COBOL on the Wang VS system, you define subscripts with COMP usage.

IBM mainframes, however, support more than one computational usage. For most fields that are involved in computations or arithmetic comparisons, you should use COMP-3 usage. However, for subscripts, you should always use COMP usage.

SEARCH ALL statements

The ANS standards for the SEARCH ALL statement say that "a nonserial type of search operation *may* take place" during its execution "in a manner specified by the implementor." That means that the implementor (the developer of the compiler) can decide how the search will take place. It doesn't necessarily have to be a nonserial, or binary, search.

Often, then, the SEARCH ALL statement as implemented on the compilers for microcomputers or minicomputers doesn't do a binary search. Instead, it does the same kind of sequential search that a regular SEARCH statement does. In a case like this, the SEARCH ALL statement won't perform any faster than a SEARCH statement. As a result, there's no point in coding the extra clauses to define the table along with the SEARCH ALL statement unless you intend to convert your programs to a compiler with a binary search later on.

Also, the compilers for microcomputers and minicomputers don't always support the extra clauses for table definition, regardless of how they implement the SEARCH ALL statement. For example, the

Wang VS COBOL compiler doesn't support the DEPENDING ON clause, even though it implements the SEARCH ALL statement as a binary search. As a result, a binary search on that system won't be adjusted to the actual length of the variable-length table.

In contrast, the compilers for mainframes usually do implement the SEARCH ALL statement with a binary search. For instance, the VS COBOL and VS COBOL II compilers for IBM mainframes provide binary searches, and they use the value you specify in the DEPENDING ON clause to adjust the search to the actual length of the table.

The point of all this is that you should find out how the SEARCH ALL statement is implemented on your system. Then, you can decide whether it's worth using.

Terminology

None

Objective

Find out what the appropriate usage for a subscript is on your system and find out how the SEARCH ALL statement is implemented on your system.

Chapter 9

How to manipulate characters

Some programs require that operations be performed on the individual characters within a field. For instance, an editing program may change each blank within a numeric field to a zero. A function like this can be referred to as *character manipulation*.

The three COBOL statements that are commonly used for character manipulation are INSPECT, STRING, and UNSTRING. Topic 1 of this chapter will show you how to use these statements. Then, topic 2 will present some compiler dependent code that you should be aware of.

Topic 1   INSPECT, STRING, and UNSTRING

The INSPECT, STRING, and UNSTRING statements are provided for by both the 1974 and 1985 standards. Although the STRING and UNSTRING statements are the same under both standards, some new features have been added to the INSPECT statement that make it more versatile. I will mention these features as I discuss the different formats of the INSPECT statement.

THE INSPECT STATEMENT

Figure 9-1 gives the four formats of the INSPECT statement, and figure 9-2 gives some examples of it in operation. Although this statement may look complicated at first, it isn't that difficult once you understand it. When the INSPECT statement is executed, the field named as identifier-1 is examined one character at a time from left to right. During this examination, certain characters can be counted (tallied), replaced by other characters, or both counted and replaced.

The field operated upon by the INSPECT statement must have DISPLAY usage, and it can be alphabetic, alphanumeric, or numeric. Then, the literals used in the TALLYING, REPLACING, and CONVERTING clauses must be consistent with the field description. For instance, you wouldn't tally A's in a numeric field or 9's in an alphabetic field. If a numeric field is signed, the sign is ignored during the execution of the INSPECT statement.

The TALLYING clause

The TALLYING clause of the INSPECT statement allows you to keep a count of certain characters in the field being inspected. To use the TALLYING clause, you simply specify the name of the field you want the count to be accumulated in as identifier-2. Then, you must specify one of the two phrases that follow: CHARACTERS or ALL/LEADING. Notice that you can specify more than one count field with its related CHARACTERS or ALL/LEADING phrase within a single TALLYING clause. This is illustrated by examples 2, 6, and 10 in figure 9-2.

Before I describe each of the phrases you can use in the TALLYING clause, I want you to understand two factors related to the tallying function. First, the count fields named in this clause are not set to zero each time the INSPECT statement is executed. As a result, you must give your count fields starting values before the related INSPECT statements are executed. If you want a tallying function to start with a value of zero, you must set the related count

Format 1

```
INSPECT identifier-1

    TALLYING identifier-2 FOR ⎧ CHARACTERS [ {BEFORE/AFTER} INITIAL {identifier-4/literal-2} ] ... ⎫
                              ⎨ {ALL/LEADING} {identifier-3/literal-1} [ {BEFORE/AFTER} INITIAL {identifier-4/literal-2} ] ⎬ ...
                              ⎩                                                                                              ⎭
```

Format 2

```
INSPECT identifier-1

    REPLACING ⎧ CHARACTERS BY {identifier-5/literal-3} [ {BEFORE/AFTER} INITIAL {identifier-4/literal-2} ] ... ⎫
              ⎨ {ALL/LEADING/FIRST} {identifier-3/literal-1} BY {identifier-5/literal-3} [ {BEFORE/AFTER} INITIAL {identifier-4/literal-2} ] ⎬ ...
              ⎩                                                                                                                              ⎭
```

Format 3

```
INSPECT identifier-1

    TALLYING identifier-2 FOR ⎧ CHARACTERS [ {BEFORE/AFTER} INITIAL {identifier-4/literal-2} ] ... ⎫
                              ⎨ {ALL/LEADING} {identifier-3/literal-1} [ {BEFORE/AFTER} INITIAL {identifier-4/literal-2} ] ⎬ ...
                              ⎩                                                                                              ⎭

    REPLACING ⎧ CHARACTERS BY {identifier-5/literal-3} [ {BEFORE/AFTER} INITIAL {identifier-4/literal-2} ] ... ⎫
              ⎨ {ALL/LEADING/FIRST} {identifier-3/literal-1} BY {identifier-5/literal-3} [ {BEFORE/AFTER} INITIAL {identifier-4/literal-2} ] ⎬ ...
              ⎩                                                                                                                              ⎭
```

Format 4

```
INSPECT identifier-1

    CONVERTING {identifier-6/literal-4} TO {identifier-7/literal-5} [ {BEFORE/AFTER} INITIAL {identifier-4/literal-2} ] ...
```

Note: The 1985 elements are shaded.

Figure 9-1   The INSPECT statement

Statement	FIELD-1 (Before)	FIELD-1 (After)	COUNT-1 (After)	COUNT-2 (After)
1. INSPECT FIELD-1 TALLYING COUNT-1 FOR CHARACTERS BEFORE INITIAL ','.	123,1,4	123,1,4	3	N/A
2. INSPECT FIELD-1 TALLYING COUNT-1 FOR ALL '$' ALL ',' ALL '.' COUNT-2 FOR CHARACTERS.	$2,829.51	$2,829.51	3	6
3. INSPECT FIELD-1 REPLACING ALL ' ' BY '0'.	147bb21	1470021	N/A	N/A
4. INSPECT FIELD-1 TALLYING COUNT-1 FOR LEADING ' ' REPLACING LEADING ' ' BY '*'.	bbbb123	****123	4	N/A
5. INSPECT FIELD-1 REPLACING FIRST '*' BY '$'.	****123	$***123	N/A	N/A
6. INSPECT FIELD-1 TALLYING COUNT-1 FOR CHARACTERS BEFORE '.' COUNT-2 FOR CHARACTERS AFTER '.'.	12451.6	12451.6	5	1
7. INSPECT FIELD-1 REPLACING ALL 'X' BY 'Y' AFTER INITIAL 'R' 'B' BY 'Z' AFTER INITIAL 'R' 'C' BY 'Q' AFTER INITIAL 'R'.	RXXBQCY ZACDWBR ARCRXEB	RYYZQQY ZACDWBR ARQRYEZ	N/A N/A N/A	N/A N/A N/A
8. INSPECT FIELD-1 TALLYING COUNT-1 FOR ALL '012' REPLACING ALL 'N4' BY '00'.	N4012L	00012L	1	N/A
9. INSPECT FIELD-1 TALLYING COUNT-1 FOR CHARACTERS BEFORE INITIAL '.' AFTER INITIAL '$'.	$123.45	$123.45	7	N/A
10. INSPECT FIELD-1 TALLYING COUNT-1 FOR CHARACTERS FOR ALL '$' ',' '.' COUNT-2 FOR CHARACTERS.	$2,829.51	$2,829.51	3	6
11. INSPECT FIELD-1 REPLACING CHARACTERS BY ' ' BEFORE INITIAL '.' CHARACTERS BY ' ' AFTER INITIAL '.'.	ABCD.XYZ	bbbb.bbb	N/A	N/A
12. INSPECT FIELD-1 CONVERTING 'XBC' TO 'YZQ' AFTER INITIAL 'R'.	RXXBQCY ZACDWBR ARCRXEB	RYYZQQY ZACDWBR ARQRYEZ	N/A N/A N/A	N/A N/A N/A

Notes: 1. The 1985 examples are shaded.

2. A b stands for one space.

Figure 9-2 The INSPECT statement in operation

field to zero before the INSPECT statement is executed. Otherwise, the INSPECT statement tallies by ones beginning with whatever values are in the count fields. In the examples in figure 9-2, we assume that COUNT-1 and COUNT-2 have starting values of zero when the INSPECT statements are executed.

Second, you must understand that a character or group of characters is only counted once for each execution of an INSPECT statement. If a character is identified more than once in a TALLYING clause, it is only counted the first time. For instance, in example 2 in figure 9-2, COUNT-2 has a value of only six after the statement is executed, even though the CHARACTERS option means to count every character in the field and there are nine characters in the field. This is explained by the fact that the dollar sign, comma, and period were already tallied in COUNT-1 by the first portion of the TALLYING clause. Similarly, COUNT-1 in example 9 has a value of seven after the INSPECT statement is executed, not the value of ten that you might expect. In this case, the characters 1, 2, and 3 are tallied only once although they are identified twice.

The CHARACTERS phrase   When you use the CHARACTERS phrase, the INSPECT statement counts all of the characters in the specified field, unless the BEFORE/AFTER phrase is coded. For example, if you coded the statement

```
INSPECT FIELD-1
    TALLYING COUNT-1 FOR CHARACTERS
```

it would simply count the number of characters in FIELD-1. Notice that you can code more than one CHARACTERS phrase for each count field.

The BEFORE/AFTER phrase   The BEFORE/AFTER phrase is used to further select the characters to be counted in a specified field. If you specify BEFORE, all of the characters in the field before the character specified as identifier-4 or literal-2 are counted. If you specify AFTER, all of the characters after the specified character are counted.

Examples 1, 6, and 9 in figure 9-2 show three ways the BEFORE and AFTER phrases can be used. In example 1, a count of all of the characters before the first comma in FIELD-1 is accumulated in COUNT-1. In example 6, a count of all of the characters before the first period in FIELD-1 is accumulated in COUNT-1, and a count of all of the characters after the first period is accumulated in COUNT-2. Notice in this example that the INITIAL clause isn't used. Since INITIAL is always assumed, it is only coded for clarity.

Example 9 illustrates one of the new features of the 1985 INSPECT statement. This feature allows you to code both a BEFORE and an AFTER phrase for a single count field. However, only one of each phrase may be coded, and the phrases are executed separately. In this example, a count of all of the characters before the first period and then all of the characters after the first dollar sign is accumulated in COUNT-1. Under the 1974 standards, you would have to specify separate count fields in order to code both a BEFORE and AFTER phrase within a single TALLYING phrase, as in example 6. This 1985 enhancement applies wherever the BEFORE/AFTER phrase can be specified in any of the INSPECT statement formats.

The ALL/LEADING phrase   The ALL and LEADING phrases allow you to count only the characters specified by identifier-3 or literal-1. When you use the ALL phrase, all occurrences of the specified character are counted, unless the BEFORE/AFTER phrase is coded. In example 2 of figure 9-2, you can see how the ALL phrase is used to count all dollar signs, commas, and periods. When you use the LEADING phrase, only the occurrences of the specified characters before the occurrence of another character are counted. Again, if you code the BEFORE/AFTER phrase, only the occurrences before or after the occurrence of a specified character are counted.

As example 2 illustrates, you can code more than one ALL/LEADING phrase for a single count field. In addition, under the 1985 standards, you can code a single ALL/LEADING phrase that specifies more than one character to be counted. This is illustrated in example 10 of figure 9-2. Notice that this example produces the same results as example 2.

The REPLACING clause

When you use the REPLACING clause of the INSPECT statement, you replace one character in a field with another character. There are two phrases you can use within the REPLACING clause. The CHARACTERS BY phrase causes all characters in a field to be replaced, and the ALL/LEADING/FIRST phrase causes only specified characters to be replaced. The BEFORE and AFTER phrases can be used within both of these phrases.

The CHARACTERS BY phrase   If you code the CHARACTERS BY phrase, all characters in the field being inspected are replaced by the character specified by identifier-5 or literal-3, unless the BEFORE/AFTER phrase is coded. In this case, literal-3 or the size of the data item referenced by identifier-5 must be one character in length. In other words, you can't replace one character in a field with more than one character.

Example 11 in figure 9-2 illustrates the use of the CHARACTERS BY phrase. Here, all characters both before and after the first period are replaced by spaces. This example illustrates another new feature of the 1985 standards: the coding of more than one CHARACTERS BY phrase. Under the 1974 standards, one INSPECT REPLACING statement would have to be coded for each type of replacement.

The ALL/LEADING/FIRST phrase   The ALL/LEADING/FIRST phrase is used to select specific characters to be replaced in the field being inspected. The characters to be replaced are specified by identifier-3 or literal-1, and the characters they're to be replaced by are specified by identifier-5 or literal-3. In this case, literal-3 or the size of identifier-5 must be the same size as literal-1 or identifier-3.

When you code ALL, all of the characters specified are replaced. Examples 3 and 7 in figure 9-2 give examples of this. Notice in example 7 that three different identifying phrases are specified. Otherwise, with a 1985 compiler, you could code this function by using more than one ALL phrase. When you code LEADING, only the leading characters are replaced. When you code FIRST, only the first occurrence of the specified character is replaced. Example 5 in figure 9-2 gives an example of this.

The TALLYING and REPLACING clauses

When you use the third form of the INSPECT statement, you can both tally and replace characters in a field. To do this you code both the TALLYING and REPLACING clauses as I've described them. Examples 4 and 8 in figure 9-2 illustrate the use of both clauses in one statement. Notice in example 8 that literals with more than one character are used.

The CONVERTING clause

The CONVERTING clause of the INSPECT statement is a new feature of the 1985 standards. It's used to change each of the characters specified by identifier-6 or literal-4 to the associated character specified by identifier-7 or literal-5. In this case, the sizes of identifier-6 or literal-4 and identifier-7 or literal-5 must be the same.

Example 12 in figure 9-2 shows the use of the CONVERTING clause. Here, after the first occurrence of 'R', every occurrence of 'X' is changed to 'Y', every occurrence of 'B' is changed to 'Z', and every occurrence of 'C' is changed to 'Q'. In other words, it isn't the group of characters that's changed, it's each separate character.

Although the 1974 standards provide the same capability without the CONVERTING clause, the code is much more cumbersome. For instance, example 12 could be coded using three REPLACING phrases, as illustrated in example 7. As you can see, though, the CONVERTING phrase simplifies this function considerably.

Uses of the INSPECT statement

In general, there are two major uses of the INSPECT statement: (1) editing and (2) translation.

Editing *Editing*, or *input validation*, refers to the analysis or modification of input fields to be sure they are valid. For instance, a numeric field should consist only of the digits 0 through 9 and a sign. Because a blank in place of a zero is one of the most common causes of an invalid field, some editing routines convert all blanks in numeric fields to zeros. This can be done using a statement like the one in example 3 of figure 9-2. Similarly, the INSPECT statement can count or replace other invalid characters within a field.

Translation *Translation* refers to the conversion of specified characters within a field to other specified characters. For example, because of programming error or conversion from one system to another, a file of records will sometimes contain certain characters that must be translated to their proper form by using a series of INSPECT statements with the REPLACING option. Example 4 in figure 9-2, for instance, illustrates how blanks at the beginning of a field can be converted to asterisks.

THE STRING STATEMENT

Figure 9-3 gives the format of the STRING statement, and figure 9-4 presents some examples of it in operation. When the STRING statement is executed, several fields, called sending fields, are joined together to form one field, called the receiving field. This process is known as *concatenation*.

The fields to be joined together by a STRING statement are specified by one or more occurrences of identifier-1 or literal-1. The receiving field is specified by identifier-3 in the INTO phrase. The DELIMITED BY phrase allows you to specify a character (or combination of characters) to mark the end of each sending field. Only those characters in each sending field to the left of the *delimiter* are used in the STRING operation. If you want to use all of the characters in the sending fields, you specify SIZE as the delimiter.

There are two options that can be used with the STRING statement. When the POINTER option is used, the data is moved to the receiving field starting at the position indicated by the pointer field. Then, every time a character is moved to the receiving field, the pointer field is increased by one. That way, the pointer field always points to the next character in the receiving field.

When you specify an ON OVERFLOW clause with the STRING statement, the clause is executed if the pointer field doesn't contain an

```
STRING  {identifier-1}  ... DELIMITED BY  {identifier-2}  ...
        {literal-1   }                    {literal-2   }
                                          {SIZE        }

        INTO identifier-3

        [WITH POINTER identifier-4]

        [ON OVERFLOW imperative-statement]
```

Figure 9-3   The STRING statement

Statement	FIELD-1 PIC X(5)	FIELD-2 PIC X(5)	FIELD-3 PIC X(5)	RECEIVING-FIELD PIC X(20)	POINT-FIELD (Before)	(After)
1. STRING FIELD-1 FIELD-2 FIELD-3 DELIMITED BY SIZE INTO RECEIVING-FIELD.	ABC*D	EF*GH	IJKLM	ABC*DEF*GHIJKLMbbbbb	N/A	N/A
2. STRING FIELD-1 FIELD-2 FIELD-3 DELIMITED BY '*' INTO RECEIVING-FIELD.	ABC*D	EF*GH	IJKLM	ABCEFIJKLMbbbbbbbbbb	N/A	N/A
3. STRING FIELD-1 FIELD-2 DELIMITED BY SIZE INTO RECEIVING-FIELD WITH POINTER POINT-FIELD.	ABCDE	FGHIJ	N/A	bbbbABCDEFGHIJbbbbbb	5	15

Note: A *b* stands for one space.

Figure 9-4   The STRING statement in operation

acceptable value. This means its value is less than one or greater than the number of characters in the receiving field. Without the ON OVERFLOW clause, the program leaves the STRING statement and continues with the next statement in sequence. With the ON OVERFLOW clause, the program does whatever the clause tells it to do. Usually, the imperative statement in this clause is a MOVE statement that sets an appropriate switch.

Using 1985 COBOL, you can code a NOT ON OVERFLOW clause and an END-STRING delimiter as part of this statement. However, you usually don't need to code these options. As a result, I won't discuss them until chapter 10 when I present many of the other 1985 COBOL elements.

To understand the operation of the STRING statement, consider the examples given in figure 9-4. In example 1, the fields are DELIMITED BY SIZE so the fields are used in their entirety. As a result, the data from FIELD-1 is moved to the receiving field, followed by the data from FIELD-2 and FIELD-3.

In example 2, the delimiter is an asterisk (*). Thus, for FIELD-1 and FIELD-2, only the characters before the asterisk are moved. Because FIELD-3 doesn't contain an asterisk, all of its characters are moved in the STRING operation.

In example 3, the sending fields are again delimited by size, but this time only FIELD-1 and FIELD-2 are to be strung together and the WITH POINTER clause is used. Because the initial value of POINT-FIELD is 5, the first character of FIELD-1 is placed in position 5 of the receiving field, the second character is placed in position 6, and so on. When the STRING statement is completed, the value in POINT-FIELD is 15. As a result, a subsequent STRING statement can place up to six additional characters immediately to the right of those already placed in RECEIVING-FIELD.

Uses of the STRING statement

You probably won't use the STRING statement much. In our shop, we only use it in programs that create keys for indexed records from the data in several fields within each record. For instance, the key for each record in our customer file is made up of data extracted from the customer name, address, and zip code fields. After we extract the characters we want from each field using the UNSTRING statement, we string them together into one field using the STRING statement.

THE UNSTRING STATEMENT

Figure 9-5 gives the format of the UNSTRING statement, and figure 9-6 gives some examples of it in operation. Basically, the UNSTRING statement is the opposite of the STRING statement. Instead of joining

```
UNSTRING identifier-1

  [DELIMITED BY [ALL] {identifier-2}  OR [ALL] {identifier-3}  ...]
                      {literal-1  }            {literal-2  }

  INTO {identifier-4 [DELIMITER IN identifier-5] [COUNT IN identifier-6] } ...

  [WITH POINTER identifier-7]

  [TALLYING IN identifier-8]

  [ON OVERFLOW imperative-statement]
```

Figure 9-5   The UNSTRING statement

Statement	SENDING-FIELD PIC X(10)	FIELD-1 PIC X(5)	FIELD-2 PIC X(5)	COUNT-1	COUNT-2	POINT-FIELD (Before)	POINT-FIELD (After)	TALLY-FIELD
1. UNSTRING SENDING-FIELD DELIMITED BY '*' INTO FIELD-1 FIELD-2.	ABC*DEFbbb	ABCbb	DEFbb	N/A	N/A	N/A	N/A	N/A
2. UNSTRING SENDING-FIELD DELIMITED BY '*' INTO FIELD-1 COUNT IN COUNT-1 FIELD-2 COUNT IN COUNT-2 WITH POINTER POINT-FIELD TALLYING IN TALLY-FIELD.	ABC*DEFbbb	ABCbb	DEFbb	3	3	1	8	2
3. UNSTRING SENDING-FIELD DELIMITED BY '*' OR '/' INTO FIELD-1 DELIMITER IN FIELD-2.	ABC/DEF*GH	ABCbb	/bbbb	N/A	N/A	N/A	N/A	N/A
4. UNSTRING SENDING-FIELD DELIMITED BY ALL '*' INTO FIELD-1 FIELD-2.	ABC***DEFb	ABCbb	DEFbb	N/A	N/A	N/A	N/A	N/A

Note: A b stands for one space.

Figure 9-6   The UNSTRING statement in operation

several fields into one field, the UNSTRING statement separates one field into the one or more fields named in the INTO clause. When you code this statement, the DELIMITED BY clause specifies the character at which one field should end and the next should begin. Also, you can specify more than one delimiter character by coding the OR phrase. If ALL is specified for a delimiter character, successive occurrences of that character are treated as one.

For each receiving field specified, both the DELIMITER IN and COUNT IN clauses can be coded. If the DELIMITER IN clause is coded, the delimiter character for that receiving field is placed in the field specified. You can use this clause when more than one delimiter character is specified and you need to know which one has been found. If the COUNT IN clause is coded, a count of the number of characters in the receiving field is kept in the field specified.

The UNSTRING statement also allows a WITH POINTER option. If this option is specified, the UNSTRING operation begins with the position in the sending field indicated by the pointer field. If, for example, the pointer field contains a value of ten, the first nine characters of the sending field are ignored. As the UNSTRING statement is executed, the pointer field is incremented by ones so it always points to the position of the next character to be processed. When the UNSTRING statement is issued, of course, the pointer field must not be less than one or greater than the length of the sending field.

The TALLYING IN option may be used to count the number of receiving fields operated upon. This count includes all receiving fields used by the UNSTRING statement, even if no data was placed in a field. (This can happen if two delimiter characters are found next to each other in the sending field and the word ALL isn't used in the DELIMITED BY clause.) If, for example, ten receiving fields are specified and only six are used before the end of the sending field is reached, the field specified in the TALLYING IN clause will contain a value of six. As with the INSPECT statement, the field specified must be reset to zero before each execution of the UNSTRING statement if you want the tally to be accurate.

The last option of the UNSTRING statement is the ON OVERFLOW clause. The two possible causes of overflow during an UNSTRING operation are these: (1) the pointer field has a value less than one or greater than the number of characters in the sending field and the UNSTRING statement hasn't finished its execution; and (2) there are no more receiving fields and the end of the sending field hasn't been reached. Without the ON OVERFLOW clause, the program leaves the UNSTRING statement and continues with the next statement in sequence. With the ON OVERFLOW clause, the program does whatever the clause tells it to do. Usually, the imperative statement in this clause sets an appropriate switch.

Using 1985 COBOL, you can code a NOT ON OVERFLOW clause and an END-UNSTRING delimiter. However, you usually don't need to code these options. As a result, I won't discuss them until chapter 10 when I present many of the other 1985 COBOL elements.

Example 1 in figure 9-6 illustrates a simple use of the UNSTRING statement. Here, one field is divided into two, delimited by an asterisk (*). Notice that the asterisk is not a part of either of the receiving fields.

Example 2 illustrates the use of COUNT IN, WITH POINTER, and TALLYING IN. This statement uses the same fields as the first example, but (1) a count is kept of the number of characters placed in each field, (2) POINT-FIELD is used to indicate the next position that's to be processed in the sending field, and (3) TALLY-FIELD is used to accumulate the number of receiving fields used.

Example 3 illustrates the use of the DELIMITER IN clause. Here, either an asterisk or a slash can be used as a delimiter. To determine which was used, the delimiter is stored in FIELD-2. As you can see, a slash was used, so FIELD-2 contains a slash. This example also illustrates that it's possible to use only one receiving field since all of the characters in the sending field don't have to be used. Although an overflow condition will occur in this case, processing will continue with the next statement unless an ON OVERFLOW clause is coded.

Example 4 illustrates the use of the DELIMITED BY ALL option. As you can see, three successive occurrences of the asterisk delimiter are treated as one. If the ALL option hadn't been specified, spaces would have been moved to FIELD-2 since it is defined as alphanumeric. If FIELD-2 were numeric, zeros would have been moved to it.

You should also be aware that a figurative constant, such as SPACE, can be used as a delimiter. Whenever a figurative constant is used, the ALL option is automatically assumed. As a result, five consecutive spaces are treated as one delimiter.

Uses of the UNSTRING statement

The UNSTRING statement is often used for processing *free form input*. Free form input consists of records that don't have strictly defined fields. This type of input is relatively common in teleprocessing applications, but it can also be used in interactive applications.

To illustrate the use of the UNSTRING statement for processing free form input, suppose a program is to print a two-, three-, or four-line mailing label for each record in an address file. The difficult part of the program is determining where one field of the address ends and the next begins because the input is free form. Instead of fixed address fields, the fields are separated by a single slash (/). Furthermore, the last address field in the record may or may not end with a slash.

Figure 9-7 presents the COBOL listing for this program. I won't bother to present a structure chart for it because the program requires only seven modules in a standard report preparation structure. In

```
 IDENTIFICATION DIVISION.
*
 PROGRAM-ID.  PRTLABEL.
*
 ENVIRONMENT DIVISION.
*
 INPUT-OUTPUT SECTION.
*
 FILE-CONTROL.
     SELECT ADDFILE ASSIGN TO SYS020-AS-ADDFILE.
     SELECT MAILIST ASSIGN TO SYS006-UR-1403-S.
*
 DATA DIVISION.
*
 FILE SECTION.
*
 FD  ADDFILE
     LABEL RECORDS ARE STANDARD
     RECORD CONTAINS 80 CHARACTERS.
*
 01  ADDRESS-RECORD          PIC X(80).
*
 FD  MAILIST
     LABEL RECORDS ARE OMITTED
     RECORD CONTAINS 132 CHARACTERS.
*
 01  PRINT-AREA              PIC X(132).
*
 WORKING-STORAGE SECTION.
*
 01  SWITCHES.
*
     05  ADDRESS-EOF-SWITCH  PIC X    VALUE 'N'.
         88  ADDRESS-EOF              VALUE 'Y'.
*
 01  COUNT-FIELDS            COMP-3.
*
     05  NUMBER-OF-LINES     PIC S9.
*
 01  LABEL-LINES.
*
     05  LABEL-LINE-1        PIC X(132).
     05  LABEL-LINE-2        PIC X(132).
     05  LABEL-LINE-3        PIC X(132).
     05  LABEL-LINE-4        PIC X(132).
*
 PROCEDURE DIVISION.
*
 000-PREPARE-MAILING-LABELS.
*
     OPEN INPUT  ADDFILE
          OUTPUT MAILIST.
     PERFORM 100-PREPARE-MAILING-LABEL
         UNTIL ADDRESS-EOF.
```

Figure 9-7   Processing free form input data using the UNSTRING statement (part 1 of 2)

```
        CLOSE ADDFILE
               MAILIST.
        DISPLAY 'PRTLABEL  I  1  NORMAL EOJ'.
        STOP RUN.
 *
  100-PREPARE-MAILING-LABEL.
 *
        PERFORM 110-READ-ADDRESS-RECORD.
        IF NOT ADDRESS-EOF
            PERFORM 120-BUILD-LABEL-LINES
            PERFORM 130-PRINT-LABEL-LINES.
 *
  110-READ-ADDRESS-RECORD.
 *
        READ ADDFILE
            AT END
                MOVE 'Y' TO ADDRESS-EOF-SWITCH.
 *
  120-BUILD-LABEL-LINES.
 *
        MOVE ZERO TO NUMBER-OF-LINES.
        MOVE SPACE TO LABEL-LINES.
        UNSTRING ADDRESS-RECORD
            DELIMITED BY '/'
            INTO LABEL-LINE-1
                 LABEL-LINE-2
                 LABEL-LINE-3
                 LABEL-LINE-4
            TALLYING IN NUMBER-OF-LINES.
 *
  130-PRINT-LABEL-LINES.
 *
        MOVE LABEL-LINE-1 TO PRINT-AREA.
        PERFORM 140-WRITE-LABEL-TOP-LINE.
        IF NUMBER-OF-LINES > 1
            MOVE LABEL-LINE-2 TO PRINT-AREA
            PERFORM 150-WRITE-LABEL-LINE
            IF NUMBER-OF-LINES > 2
                MOVE LABEL-LINE-3 TO PRINT-AREA
                PERFORM 150-WRITE-LABEL-LINE
                IF NUMBER-OF-LINES > 3
                    MOVE LABEL-LINE-4 TO PRINT-AREA
                    PERFORM 150-WRITE-LABEL-LINE.
 *
  140-WRITE-LABEL-TOP-LINE.
 *
        WRITE PRINT-AREA
            AFTER ADVANCING PAGE.
 *
  150-WRITE-LABEL-LINE.
 *
        WRITE PRINT-AREA
            AFTER ADVANCING 1 LINE.
```

Figure 9-7   Processing free form input data using the UNSTRING statement (part 2 of 2)

brief, module 100 performs module 110 to read an address record. Then, module 100 performs module 120 to build the label lines for the record, after which it performs module 130 to print the label for the record.

In module 120, the label lines are built using a single UNSTRING statement:

```
UNSTRING ADDRESS-RECORD
    DELIMITED BY '/'
    INTO LABEL-LINE-1
         LABEL-LINE-2
         LABEL-LINE-3
         LABEL-LINE-4
    TALLYING IN NUMBER-OF-LINES.
```

Note, however, that module 120 sets NUMBER-OF-LINES to zero before this statement is executed. Then, module 130 uses the NUMBER-OF-LINES field to determine how many lines should be printed for each label.

In our shop, we wrote a COBOL program for IBM mainframes that analyzes the source code of other COBOL programs. In this program, we used the UNSTRING statement to place the words used in each COBOL line into successive fields within a table. As a result, the primary delimiter was one or more blanks. Basically, COBOL statements are another form of free form input, so you can see that the UNSTRING statement is quite useful for this type of application.

DISCUSSION

INSPECT, STRING, and UNSTRING were first defined by the 1974 COBOL standards. Until then, COBOL was extremely limited in terms of character manipulation. Today, however, these three statements make it easy for you to code most character manipulation functions.

Terminology

character manipulation
editing
input validation
translation

concatenation
delimiter
free form input

Objective

Given program specifications for a program that requires character manipulation, code the program in COBOL using the elements presented in this topic whenever they are appropriate.

Topic 2   Compiler dependent code

All of the code in topic 1 of this chapter is standard. However, all of the code may not be available on your system unless your compiler is a high-level implementation of COBOL. In addition, it's possible that your compiler still supports some of the earlier character manipulation statements like the EXAMINE and TRANSFORM statements. In this topic, then, I'm going to briefly discuss the new and the old statements in terms of compiler dependency.

The INSPECT statement

The INSPECT statement has to be implemented on any 1974 or 1985 compiler that calls itself "standard." However, if your compiler isn't a full implementation of the standards, it may not provide for the series of clauses and phrases that are indicated by ellipses (...) in the first three formats shown in figure 9-1.

In general, the mainframe compilers provide full implementations of this statement, the microcomputer compilers don't, and minicomputer compilers may or may not provide full implementations. For instance, the IBM VS and VS COBOL II compilers for mainframes provide full implementations of the INSPECT statement, and so does the Wang VS compiler. On the other hand, Microsoft COBOL for the IBM PC doesn't provide a full implementation of this statement. As a result, if you're using some other compiler, you should check your reference manuals to see how this statement has been implemented.

The STRING and UNSTRING statements

The STRING and UNSTRING statements don't have to be implemented on a standard 1974 or 1985 compiler, but they do have to be implemented on compilers that are full implementations of the standards. In general, the mainframe compilers provide these statements, but the microcomputer and minicomputer compilers may or may not provide them. Today, the IBM mainframe compilers provide for these statements, and so do the Wang VS compiler and the Microsoft COBOL compiler for an IBM PC. If you're using some other compiler, though, it's a good idea to check your reference manuals to see whether these statements are available to you.

The EXAMINE and TRANSFORM statements

The EXAMINE statement was the predecessor of the INSPECT statement. It was included in the 1968 COBOL standards but was replaced by the INSPECT statement in the 1974 standards. However, IBM continued to support it as an extension to the VS compilers for mainframes. As a result, you may discover the use of this statement in programs that are currently being maintained by the VS compiler on IBM mainframes.

Similarly, the TRANSFORM statement was originally a statement supported by IBM compilers before the acceptance of the 1968 COBOL standards. Although it was never adopted as a standard statement, IBM continued to support it as an extension to its 1968 and 1974 compilers, including its VS compilers for mainframes. As a result, you may discover the use of this statement in programs that are currently being maintained by the VS compiler on IBM mainframes.

Since these statements are no longer standard, you should replace them with INSPECT statements whenever you find them in a program that you're maintaining. Although they're still supported by the VS COBOL compiler, they are not supported by the VS COBOL II compiler. Since the EXAMINE and TRANSFORM statements are far more limited than the INSPECT statement, it's usually quite easy to replace them with INSPECT statements.

Terminology

None

Objective

1. Find out to what extent INSPECT, STRING, and UNSTRING are implemented on your system.

2. Given an EXAMINE or TRANSFORM statement in an old program, replace it with an INSPECT statement that performs the same function.

Chapter 10

The 1985 COBOL elements

Throughout this book, I've presented elements of the 1985 COBOL compilers when they've applied to the function I was explaining. For instance, I presented the VARYING IN SIZE clause of the FD statement in the topic on sequential files of variable-length records in chapter 2. I presented relative subscripting in chapter 8. And I presented some enhancements to the INSPECT statement in chapter 9.

Many of the 1985 COBOL elements, though, are general-purpose elements, so they don't apply to any of the other chapters in this book. As a result, I'm presenting those elements in this chapter. In topic 1, I'll present most of the 1985 COBOL elements that are designed for structured programming. If you've read chapter 7 in *Structured ANS COBOL, Part 1*, you can skip this topic. In topic 2, I'll present most of the other general-purpose elements that are a part of the 1985 COBOL standards. And in topic 3, I'll present some compiler dependent code related to the 1985 standards.

I am not, however, going to try to present all of the new 1985 COBOL elements in this chapter or in this book. I'm just going to present the ones that I think you should be aware of.

Topic 1   The 1985 COBOL elements for structured programming

Many of the new elements in the 1985 COBOL standards are designed to make it easier for you to code structured programs. In contrast, most of the other new elements are relatively trivial. In this topic, you will learn how to use the 1985 COBOL elements for structured programming so you can take advantage of them as soon as a 1985 compiler is available to you.

In this topic, I'll first present the most important new elements for structured coding. I'll show you how they work and give you recommendations for their use. Then, I'll show you how they can be used in the investment-listing program of appendix A. As you will see, these new elements won't have much effect on the way you design and code your programs, but they're useful at times.

Structured delimiters

Figure 10-1 shows the verbs that can have *structured delimiters* under the 1985 standards. Simply stated, the purpose of a structured delimiter is to show where a statement ends. So, in the first example in figure 10-1, the READ statement ends with the END-READ delimiter; however, the IF condition is still in effect for the MOVE statement that follows.

In general, structured delimiters are only useful when one conditional statement is used within another one. This is illustrated by the examples in figure 10-1. If a statement isn't used within another statement, it doesn't need a structured delimiter, because the period at the end of the statement is the delimiter. As a result, structured delimiters should have only a minor effect on your coding and little or no effect on the way you design programs.

Of all the structured delimiters, you'll probably use the END-IF delimiter the most. Because structured programming makes extensive use of nested IF statements, the END-IF can help you improve the readability of your modules as illustrated in figure 10-2. In the top example, the programmer had to code the IF NOT EMPLOYEE-EOF condition twice because the only way he could end the second IF statement was with a period. In the bottom example, the programmer ends the second IF statement with an END-IF so the code for the module is easier to read.

You should notice in figure 10-2 that the structured delimiter in the second example is aligned with the IF statement it ends. This makes it obvious which IF statement it's associated with. Whenever you use structured delimiters, you should align them in this way.

Input/output verbs

READ	REWRITE	RETURN
WRITE	DELETE	START

Example

```
IF CONDITION-A
    READ TRANREC
        INVALID KEY
            MOVE 'Y' TO INVALID-KEY-SWITCH
    END-READ
    MOVE TR-RECORD-KEY TO OLD-RECORD-KEY.
```

Computational verbs

ADD	MULTIPLY	COMPUTE
SUBTRACT	DIVIDE	

Example

```
IF CONDITION-A
    ADD B TO C
        ON SIZE ERROR
            MOVE ZERO TO C
    END-ADD
    ADD C TO D.
```

Miscellaneous verbs

IF	EVALUATE	STRING
PERFORM	SEARCH	UNSTRING
CALL		

Example

```
IF CONDITION-A
    IF CONDITION-B
        PERFORM 100-PROCESS-CONDITION-B
    ELSE
        PERFORM 200-PROCESS-OTHER-CONDITION
    END-IF
    PERFORM 300-PROCESS-CONDITION-A.
```

Figure 10-1   Verb list for structured delimiters

With the exception of END-IF, I don't think you'll use delimiters much. If you isolate I/O statements in their own modules as shown in this book, you won't ever need the delimiters for the I/O verbs. And

Coding without END-IF

```
*
 100-PRODUCE-EMPLOYEE-LINE.
*
     PERFORM 110-READ-EMPLOYEE-RECORD.
     IF NOT EMPLOYEE-EOF
         IF SR-ACTIVE-EMPLOYEE
             PERFORM 120-PRINT-ACTIVE-LINE
         ELSE
             PERFORM 130-PRINT-INACTIVE-LINE.
     IF NOT EMPLOYEE-EOF
         PERFORM 140-ACCUMULATE-GRAND-TOTAL.
*
```

Coding with END-IF

```
*
 100-PRODUCE-EMPLOYEE-LINE.
*
     PERFORM 110-READ-EMPLOYEE-RECORD.
     IF NOT EMPLOYEE-EOF
         IF SR-ACTIVE-EMPLOYEE
             PERFORM 120-PRINT-ACTIVE-LINE
         ELSE
             PERFORM 130-PRINT-INACTIVE-LINE
         END-IF
         PERFORM 140-ACCUMULATE-GRAND-TOTAL.
*
```

Figure 10-2   How END-IF can improve the readability of a module

you should have only an occasional need for delimiters on the computational verbs and the other miscellaneous verbs. As a general rule,
then, you should only use structured delimiters when they improve
readability...and this should be infrequently.

The inline PERFORM

The *inline PERFORM* is a structure that many structured programming advocates have wanted for years. When you use an inline
PERFORM, you code the performed function right after the
PERFORM statement, and you end the function with the END-
PERFORM delimiter. In other words, the performed function is not
coded in a separate paragraph. This is illustrated by the example in
figure 10-3.

When the inline PERFORM is used as shown in figure 10-3, we
agree that it is useful. Here, module 000 simply calls module 200 to
load the price table. Then, module 200 uses an inline PERFORM

Coding without an inline PERFORM

```
000-PREPARE-PRICE-LISTING.
*
    .
    .
    PERFORM 200-LOAD-PRICE-TABLE
        VARYING PRICE-TABLE-INDEX FROM 1 BY 1
        UNTIL PTABLE-EOF.
    .
    .
*
 200-LOAD-PRICE-TABLE.
*
    PERFORM 210-READ-PRICE-TABLE-RECORD.
    IF NOT PTABLE-EOF
        MOVE PT-ITEM-NUMBER
            TO ITEM-NUMBER (PRICE-TABLE-INDEX)
        MOVE PT-ITEM-PRICE
            TO ITEM-PRICE (PRICE-TABLE-INDEX)
    ELSE
        SET PRICE-TABLE-INDEX DOWN BY 1
        SET PT-ENTRY-COUNT TO PRICE-TABLE-INDEX.
*
```

Coding with an inline PERFORM

```
 000-PREPARE-PRICE-LISTING.
*
    .
    .
    PERFORM 200-LOAD-PRICE-TABLE.
    .
    .
*
 200-LOAD-PRICE-TABLE.
*
    PERFORM
        VARYING PRICE-TABLE-INDEX FROM 1 BY 1
        UNTIL PTABLE-EOF
            PERFORM 210-READ-PRICE-TABLE-RECORD
            IF NOT PTABLE-EOF
                MOVE PT-ITEM-NUMBER
                    TO ITEM-NUMBER (PRICE-TABLE-INDEX)
                MOVE PT-ITEM-PRICE
                    TO ITEM-PRICE (PRICE-TABLE-INDEX)
            ELSE
                SET PRICE-TABLE-INDEX DOWN BY 1
                SET PT-ENTRY-COUNT TO PRICE-TABLE-INDEX
    END-PERFORM.
```

Figure 10-3   How an inline PERFORM can improve the code of a load-table module

VARYING statement to load the table. Without the inline PERFORM, module 000 must call module 200 with a PERFORM VARYING statement. For functions like this, we believe that the coding with the inline PERFORM is preferable to the coding without it.

The problem with the inline PERFORM is that it makes it relatively easy for you to code more than one function in a single COBOL paragraph. And that can lead to complex paragraphs that are difficult to read, test, and maintain. As a result, we don't think you should use inline PERFORMs much. As we see it, you should only use them when 1974 COBOL forces you to divide a function in a way that you wouldn't otherwise divide it. Then, the use of an inline PERFORM can help you consolidate the code in a single module so you improve both the structure and coding of your program.

The PERFORM UNTIL statement WITH TEST AFTER

As you've already learned, the condition stated in a PERFORM UNTIL statement is tested before the performed module is called. Then, if the condition is true, the module isn't called. Although this is acceptable most of the time, there are times when it would be nice to have the statement test the condition after the module is called. And that is what the WITH TEST AFTER language of the 1985 standards provides for.

Figure 10-4 illustrates how this statement can be useful. Without this clause, the search module derives an index that is one larger than the index of the desired table entry. As a result, the search module has to set the index down by 1 before passing control back to its calling module. But when the WITH TEST AFTER clause is used, the index has the desired value when the table entry is found.

Figure 10-5 presents flowcharts for the operation of PERFORM statements with tests before and after. When you use a before test, the index named in the VARYING clause is increased after the called module or inline statements have been executed. In contrast, when you use an after test, the index is *not* increased if the condition is true after the called module or the inline statements have been executed. This explains why you have to reduce the index in the example in figure 10-4 by an occurrence value of one when the before test is used, but you don't have to reduce it at all when the after test is used.

Because the WITH TEST AFTER clause has limited application, you probably won't use it much. In fact, you can do anything with the traditional before test that you can do WITH TEST AFTER. Nevertheless, you should use this clause whenever it improves the clarity of your code.

Coding with test before

```
100-GENERATE-DEPT-STATISTICS.
*
        .
        .
    PERFORM 130-SEARCH-DEPT-TABLE
        VARYING DT-INDEX FROM 1 BY 1
        UNTIL DT-ENTRY-FOUND
            OR DT-INDEX > DT-TABLE-LIMIT.
    SET DT-INDEX DOWN BY 1.
        .
        .
*
 130-SEARCH-DEPT-TABLE.
*
    IF DEPT-LOOKUP = DT-ENTRY (DT-INDEX)
        MOVE 'Y' TO DT-ENTRY-FOUND-SW.
```

Coding WITH TEST AFTER

```
100-GENERATE-DEPT-STATISTICS.
*
        .
        .
    PERFORM 130-SEARCH-DEPT-TABLE
        WITH TEST AFTER
        VARYING DT-INDEX FROM 1 BY 1
        UNTIL DT-ENTRY-FOUND
            OR DT-INDEX = DT-TABLE-LIMIT.
        .
        .
*
 130-SEARCH-DEPT-TABLE.
*
    IF DEPT-LOOKUP = DT-ENTRY (DT-INDEX)
        MOVE 'Y' TO DT-ENTRY-FOUND-SW.
```

Figure 10-4   How WITH TEST AFTER can improve the code of a search function

The SET TO TRUE statement

The SET TO TRUE statement is designed to be used with condition names. By using this statement, you can set a condition to true without knowing the value required by the condition. This is illustrated in figure 10-6. As you can see, using the SET TO TRUE statement is equivalent to moving the value of a condition to a field.

If you follow the examples in this book for coding and testing switches and flags, your coding will be quite readable. As a result, the SET TO TRUE statement won't do much to improve the clarity of your code. But it may make it easier for you to write the code in your Procedure Divisions.

PERFORM VARYING with test before

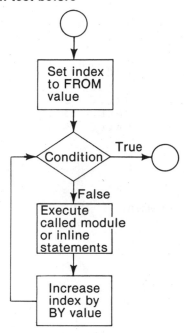

PERFORM VARYING with test after

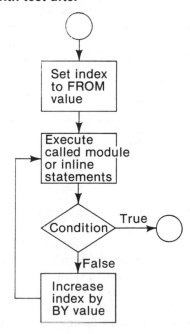

Figure 10-5 Flowcharts for the logic of PERFORM VARYING statements with before and after tests

Field description with condition names

```
DATA DIVISION.
*
        .
        .
        .
  05    COMMISSION-STATUS      PIC X.
        88    TRAINEE          VALUE '1'.
        88    ASSISTANT        VALUE '2'.
        88    ASSOCIATE        VALUE '3'.
        88    MANAGER          VALUE '4'.
*
        .
        .
```

Turning a condition on with a MOVE statement

```
PROCEDURE DIVISION.
*
      .
      .
      MOVE '3' TO COMMISSION-STATUS.
      .
      .
*
```

Turning a condition on with a SET TO TRUE statement

```
PROCEDURE DIVISION.
*
      .
      .
      SET ASSOCIATE TO TRUE.
      .
      .
*
```

Figure 10-6   The SET TO TRUE statement

In particular, you may want to use the SET TO TRUE statement when the value assigned to a condition name is not directly related to the condition name. In figure 10-6, for example, numeric values are assigned to mnemonic condition names. In a case like this, it's easier for you to remember a condition name than the value assigned to it. So it's somewhat easier for you to code the program if you use SET TO TRUE statements for turning conditions on. And this can also make your code somewhat easier to follow.

**The 1985 elements as used in the
investment-listing program of appendix A**

To give you a better idea of how you can make use of the 1985
COBOL elements in your programs, I've rewritten the investment-
listing program of appendix A using 1985 COBOL elements wherever
appropriate. This made it possible for me to improve the readability
of the coding somewhat as shown by the portion of the program in
figure 10-7.

In module 300 in figure 10-7, an END-COMPUTE delimiter is
used to end the COMPUTE statement. As a result, this statement can
be coded within a nested IF statement. Without the delimiter, this
COMPUTE statement has to end with a period and the IF NOT
INVMAST-EOF condition has to be repeated, or the COMPUTE
statement has to be coded in module 320 and performed as shown in
appendix A. In this case, I think moving the calculation of the investment amount to module 300 improves the readability and logic of the
program. In addition, it improves the efficiency of the program
because module 320 is only called when the investment amount is
greater than 10,000. In the other version of the program, module 320
is executed once for each inventory record.

In module 300, I used the SET TO TRUE statement to turn the
INVESTMENT-SIZE-ERROR condition on. I also used it in module
310. Frankly, I don't think this improves the readability of the program at all. Also, for simple switches, I think you should be able to set
a condition to false as well as to true. But why quibble? If you think
this statement improves readability, by all means use it.

The 1985 elements presented in this topic don't apply to any of
the other paragraphs in this program. As you can see, then, these
elements won't have much effect on most of your programs. Nevertheless, they can be useful at times.

Discussion

In this topic, I haven't presented all of the new code for structured
programming that is part of the 1985 standards. Instead, I have
presented what I feel is the most important code. In the next topic, I
will present a couple of other 1985 elements for structured programming. I'll also present some 1985 elements that I think you should be
aware of, even though they aren't related to structured programming.

Terminology

structured delimiter
inline PERFORM

```
300-PREPARE-INVESTMENT-LINE.
*
    PERFORM 310-READ-INVENTORY-RECORD.
    IF NOT INVMAST-EOF
        COMPUTE INVESTMENT-AMOUNT = IM-ON-HAND * IM-UNIT-PRICE
            ON SIZE ERROR
                MOVE 9999999.99 TO INVESTMENT-AMOUNT
                SET INVESTMENT-SIZE-ERROR TO TRUE
        END-COMPUTE
        IF INVESTMENT-AMOUNT > 10000
            PERFORM 320-COMPUTE-INVENTORY-FIELDS
            PERFORM 330-PRINT-INVESTMENT-LINE.
*
310-READ-INVENTORY-RECORD.
*
    READ INVMAST RECORD INTO INVENTORY-MASTER-RECORD
        AT END
            SET INVMAST-EOF TO TRUE.
    IF NOT INVMAST-EOF
        ADD 1 TO RECORD-COUNT.
*
320-COMPUTE-INVENTORY-FIELDS.
*
    IF         NOT INVESTMENT-SIZE-ERROR
        AND IM-LAST-MONTH-SALES POSITIVE
        COMPUTE NO-OF-MONTHS-STOCK ROUNDED =
            INVESTMENT-AMOUNT / IM-LAST-MONTH-SALES
            ON SIZE ERROR
                MOVE 999.9 TO NO-OF-MONTHS-STOCK
    ELSE
        MOVE 999.9 TO NO-OF-MONTHS-STOCK.
*
330-PRINT-INVESTMENT-LINE.
*
    .
    .
```

Figure 10-7   1985 coding used in the investment-listing program of appendix A

Objective

If you have a 1985 compiler available to you, apply the elements
presented in this topic to your application programs.

Topic 2   Other 1985 COBOL elements

This topic introduces you to most of the other new language provided by the 1985 COBOL standards. It begins by presenting two more elements related to structured programming. Then, it presents a selection of new elements that are unrelated to structured programming, starting with several that you probably will use and ending with a couple that you probably won't use.

Two more elements for structured programming

NOT clauses   Many of the COBOL statements provide clauses for specific conditions like the AT END condition in a sequential read statement or the ON SIZE ERROR condition in an arithmetic statement. Now, under 1985 COBOL, these statements also provide a clause that is executed when the condition doesn't occur. For instance, you can code a NOT AT END clause in a sequential read statement and a NOT ON SIZE ERROR clause in an arithmetic statement. The NOT clauses of 1985 COBOL are summarized in figure 10-8.

In general, you should find the NOT AT END and NOT INVALID KEY clauses useful when you code I/O statements. For

Clause	Statements
NOT ON SIZE ERROR	ADD SUBTRACT MULTIPLY DIVIDE COMPUTE
NOT AT END	READ RETURN
NOT INVALID KEY	READ START WRITE DELETE REWRITE
NOT ON OVERFLOW	STRING UNSTRING
NOT ON EXCEPTION	CALL

Figure 10-8   NOT clauses and the statements they apply to

A sequential read module using NOT AT END

```
310-READ-INVENTORY-RECORD.
*
     READ INVMAST RECORD INTO INVENTORY-MASTER-RECORD
         AT END
             SET INVMAST-EOF TO TRUE
         NOT AT END
             ADD 1 TO RECORD-COUNT.
```

A random read module using NOT INVALID KEY

```
310-READ-INVENTORY-RECORD.
*
     MOVE TR-PART-NO TO IM-PART-NO.
     READ INVMAST RECORD INTO INVENTORY-MASTER-RECORD
         INVALID KEY
             MOVE 'N' TO RECORD-FOUND-SWITCH
         NOT INVALID KEY
             MOVE 'Y' TO RECORD-FOUND-SWITCH.
```

Figure 10-9   Use of the NOT clauses in sequential and random read modules

instance, figure 10-9 illustrates the use of these clauses in sequential and random read statements. Without these clauses, the coding for the same functions is a bit less clear so we recommend the use of these clauses as shown. Note, in figure 10-9, that I used the SET TO TRUE statement in the AT END clause, but I didn't use it in the NOT INVALID KEY clause because I wanted the coding to parallel the coding in the INVALID KEY clause.

Similarly, you will probably find that the other NOT clauses are useful in some situations. Often, you can use the normal clause to set a switch one way and the NOT clause to set the switch the other way. For instance, you can use the ON SIZE ERROR clause to turn an error switch on, while you use the NOT ON SIZE ERROR clause to turn the error switch off.

The EVALUATE statement   One of the purposes of the EVALUATE statement is to implement the *case structure* of structured programming. This structure and its implementation in 1974 COBOL is illustrated in figure 10-10. As you can see, one function is performed for each case depending on the value of the integer field that is tested at the start of the structure. If the integer field contains a one, the function for case 1 will be performed; if the integer field contains a two, the function for case 2 will be performed; and so on. This is an acceptable structure because it has only one entry and one exit point. However, it should only be used when the situation is right for it.

The case structure

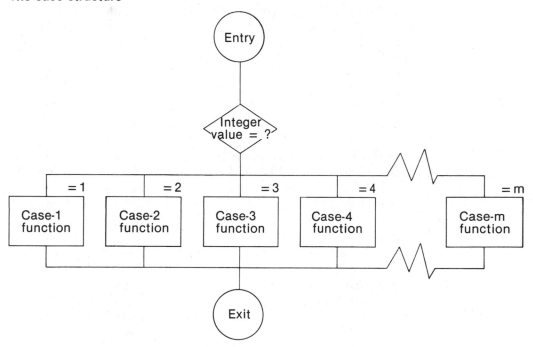

Coding for a case structure with 9 cases

```
IF TR-ACTIVITY-CODE = 1
    PERFORM CODE-1-FUNCTION
ELSE IF TR-ACTIVITY-CODE = 2
    PERFORM CODE-2-FUNCTION
ELSE IF TR-ACTIVITY-CODE = 3
    PERFORM CODE-3-FUNCTION
ELSE IF TR-ACTIVITY-CODE = 4
    PERFORM CODE-4-FUNCTION
ELSE IF TR-ACTIVITY-CODE = 5
    PERFORM CODE-5-FUNCTION
ELSE IF TR-ACTIVITY-CODE = 6
    PERFORM CODE-6-FUNCTION
ELSE IF TR-ACTIVITY-CODE = 7
    PERFORM CODE-7-FUNCTION
ELSE IF TR-ACTIVITY-CODE = 8
    PERFORM CODE-8-FUNCTION
ELSE IF TR-ACTIVITY-CODE = 9
    PERFORM CODE-9-FUNCTION
ELSE
    PERFORM DEFAULT-FUNCTION.
```

Figure 10-10   The case structure and its implementation in 1974 COBOL

In the past, it was common to code the case structure using the GOTO/DEPENDING statement. However, this statement requires an EXIT paragraph at the end of the case structure and a GOTO statement at the end of each of the other paragraphs within the case structure. As a result, we feel it is better to code the case structure with a *linear nest* of IF statements as shown in figure 10-10. As you can see, you code a linear nest so each IF statement handles one of the cases in the case structure, and you don't use the normal indentation for a nested IF statement. Instead, the indentation reflects the case structure.

Under the 1985 COBOL standards, you can also implement the case structure with an EVALUATE statement. In addition, though, the EVALUATE statement can be used to code complex logical structures including the structures for most decision tables. The format of this statement is given in figure 10-11, and, as you can see, it's cumbersome.

Rather than explain the operation of this statement in detail, I'm just going to present a couple of examples of it in use. Then, if you decide you have a need for it, you can find out how to apply it on your system. As you will see, the EVALUATE statement isn't too difficult to use if you keep its application simple. But you can code structures that are extremely difficult to read and understand.

Figure 10-12 shows how the EVALUATE statement can be used to implement a simple case structure. Notice that by using the word OTHER, you can perform a function if the field has a value other than those specified. Also, by using the word THRU, you can code conditions that are more difficult to code in a linear nest. If you compare the EVALUATE statement with the linear nest above it, I think you'll agree that the EVALUATE statement is easier to read and understand.

Figure 10-13 shows an EVALUATE statement that handles a more complex set of conditions. Here, each action depends on the values in three fields. For instance, when EXPERIENCE-CATEGORY has a value of 1, COLLEGE-DEGREE-CATEGORY has a value of B, and SALARY-REQUIREMENT-CATEGORY has a value of 1, then module 310 is performed. If the word ANY is used, it means that any value in that field is acceptable. For instance, module 350 is performed when EXPERIENCE-CATEGORY has a value of 2, COLLEGE-DEGREE-CATEGORY has a value of P, and SALARY-REQUIREMENT-CATEGORY has any value. With code like this, you can use the EVALUATE statement to specify the logic for most decision tables.

I think you can tell from these examples that the EVALUATE statement can help improve the readability of some programming functions. However, this statement is limited in application so you probably won't use it much. Also, you don't ever have to use the EVALUATE statement because you can get the same results with a

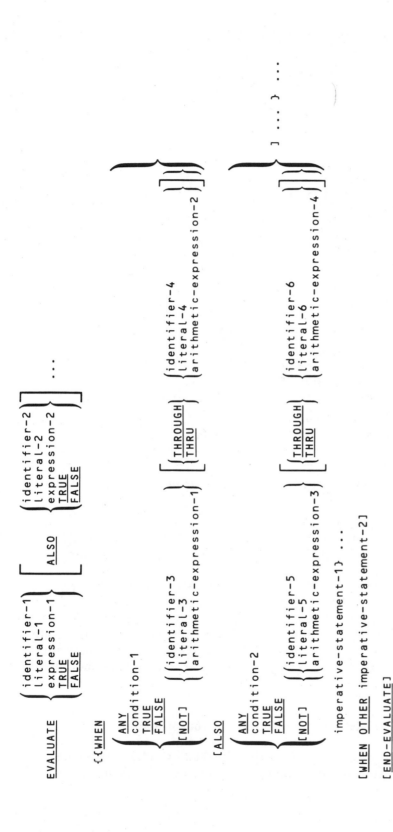

Figure 10-11 The format of the EVALUATE statement

The case structure as implemented by nested IF statements in linear form

```
IF ITR-TRAN-CODE = 1
    PERFORM 240-EDIT-CODE-1-FIELDS
ELSE IF ITR-TRAN-CODE = 2
    PERFORM 250-EDIT-CODE-2-FIELDS
ELSE IF ITR-TRAN-CODE = 3
    PERFORM 260-EDIT-CODE-3-FIELDS
ELSE IF ITR-TRAN-CODE = 4
    PERFORM 270-EDIT-CODE-4-FIELDS
ELSE IF ITR-TRAN-CODE = 5
    PERFORM 280-EDIT-CODE-5-FIELDS
ELSE IF ITR-TRAN-CODE NOT < 6 AND NOT > 10
    PERFORM 290-EDIT-COMMON-FIELDS
ELSE
    MOVE MARK TO ITL-TYPE-CODE-ERROR
    MOVE 'N' TO VALID-TRAN-SWITCH
    ADD 1 TO INVALID-TRAN-CODE-COUNT.
```

The case structure as implemented by an EVALUATE statement

```
EVALUATE ITR-TRAN-CODE
    WHEN 1           PERFORM 240-EDIT-CODE-1-FIELDS
    WHEN 2           PERFORM 250-EDIT-CODE-2-FIELDS
    WHEN 3           PERFORM 260-EDIT-CODE-3-FIELDS
    WHEN 4           PERFORM 270-EDIT-CODE-4-FIELDS
    WHEN 5           PERFORM 280-EDIT-CODE-5-FIELDS
    WHEN 6 THRU 10 PERFORM 290-EDIT-COMMON-FIELDS
    WHEN OTHER       MOVE MARK TO ITL-TYPE-CODE-ERROR
                     MOVE 'N' TO VALID-TRAN-SWITCH
                     ADD 1 TO INVALID-TRAN-CODE-COUNT.
```

Figure 10-12   A simple case structure as implemented by nested IF statements and an EVALUATE statement

sequence of IF statements or nested IF statements. Finally, the EVALUATE statement shouldn't have any effect on the design of your programs.

One danger in using the EVALUATE statement is that you can create code with it that is extremely difficult to understand . In fact, I haven't begun to show you all the different ways that this statement can be coded. Our general recommendation, then, is to use this statement when it improves the clarity of your code, but don't hesitate to replace an EVALUATE statement with IF statements should the EVALUATE statement become confusing.

Some other 1985 COBOL elements that you probably will use

Figure 10-14 summarizes some other 1985 COBOL elements that you will probably find useful in one program or another. With just a few

```
WORKING-STORAGE SECTION.
*
01  APPLICANT-CATEGORY-FIELDS.
*
    05  EXPERIENCE-CATEGORY        (  PIC X.
        88  NO-EXPERIENCE                           VALUE '1'.
        88  UNDER-5-YEARS                           VALUE '2'.
        88  5-AND-OVER-YEARS                        VALUE '3'.
    05  COLLEGE-DEGREE-CATEGORY       PIC X.
        88  NO-DEGREE                               VALUE 'N'.
        88  BACHELORS-DEGREE                        VALUE 'B'.
        88  MASTERS-DEGREE                          VALUE 'M'.
        88  DOCTORAL-DEGREE                         VALUE 'P'.
    05  SALARY-REQUIREMENT-CATEGORY   PIC X.
        88  UNDER-20-THOUSAND                       VALUE '1'.
        88  FROM-20-TO-35-THOUSAND                  VALUE '2'.
        88  OVER-35-THOUSAND                        VALUE '3'.
*
    .
    .
*
PROCEDURE DIVISION.
*
    .
    .
*
300-EVALUATE-APPLICANT-DATA.
*
    EVALUATE EXPERIENCE-CATEGORY
        ALSO COLLEGE-DEGREE-CATEGORY
        ALSO SALARY-REQUIREMENT-CATEGORY
    WHEN '1'     ALSO 'B'     ALSO '1'        PERFORM 310-ACTION-1
    WHEN '1'     ALSO 'M'     ALSO '2'        PERFORM 320-ACTION-2
    WHEN '1'     ALSO 'P'     ALSO '3'        PERFORM 330-ACTION-3
    WHEN '2'     ALSO NOT 'P' ALSO NOT '3'    PERFORM 340-ACTION-4
    WHEN '2'     ALSO 'P'     ALSO ANY        PERFORM 350-ACTION-5
    WHEN '3'     ALSO NOT 'P' ALSO ANY        PERFORM 360-ACTION-6
    WHEN '3'     ALSO 'P'     ALSO ANY        PERFORM 370-ACTION-7
    WHEN OTHER                                PERFORM 380-DEFAULT.
```

Figure 10-13   An EVALUATE statement that operates on three fields so it can direct the processing of a decision table

exceptions, none of these elements allow you to do anything you couldn't do with 1974 COBOL. In fact, all of them represent rather trivial improvements to the 1974 standards. Nevertheless, you should be aware that these elements are available to you.

New usages   Under the 1974 standards, USAGE clauses could specify only one form of computational usage (COMPUTATIONAL, or COMP). Many systems, though, offer more than one form of computational usage. As a result, the compilers for these systems used

New usages

$$[\underline{USAGE}\ IS]\ \left\{\begin{array}{l}\text{BINARY}\\ \text{COMPUTATIONAL}\\ \text{COMP}\\ \text{DISPLAY}\\ \text{INDEX}\\ \text{PACKED-DECIMAL}\end{array}\right\}$$

New relational operators

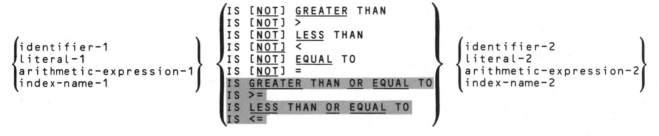

$$\left\{\begin{array}{l}\text{identifier-1}\\ \text{literal-1}\\ \text{arithmetic-expression-1}\\ \text{index-name-1}\end{array}\right\} \left\{\begin{array}{l}\text{IS [NOT] GREATER THAN}\\ \text{IS [NOT] >}\\ \text{IS [NOT] LESS THAN}\\ \text{IS [NOT] <}\\ \text{IS [NOT] EQUAL TO}\\ \text{IS [NOT] =}\\ \text{IS GREATER THAN OR EQUAL TO}\\ \text{IS >=}\\ \text{IS LESS THAN OR EQUAL TO}\\ \text{IS <=}\end{array}\right\} \left\{\begin{array}{l}\text{identifier-2}\\ \text{literal-2}\\ \text{arithmetic-expression-2}\\ \text{index-name-2}\end{array}\right\}$$

Reference modification

```
data-name [(leftmost-character-position: [length])]
```

Omission of FILLER

```
level-number [FILLER] defining-clauses
```

Expanded class tests

$$\text{identifier IS [NOT]} \left\{\begin{array}{l}\text{NUMERIC}\\ \text{ALPHABETIC}\\ \text{ALPHABETIC-LOWER}\\ \text{ALPHABETIC-UPPER}\\ \text{class-name}\end{array}\right\}$$

Figure 10-14   Some other 1985 COBOL elements you probably will use (part 1 of 2)

extensions to provide for these other usages. On an IBM mainframe, for example, COMP is used for one form of computational usage, while COMP-3 is an extension that is used for another form.

To remove this shortcoming of the 1974 standards, the 1985 standards provide for two new usages. BINARY usage indicates a form of data representation that is based on the binary numbering system. PACKED-DECIMAL usage indicates a form of representation that is based on the decimal numbering system. Then, if the compiler developer wants, COMP can be used for a third form of data representation. Today, when you use the VS COBOL or VS COBOL II compiler on an IBM mainframe, COMP is equivalent to BINARY in

New ADD statement format

```
ADD {identifier-1} ... TO {identifier-2} GIVING {identifier-3 [ROUNDED]} ...
    {literal-1   }       {literal-2   }
```

The ACCEPT DAY-OF-WEEK statement

```
ACCEPT identifier FROM DAY-OF-WEEK
```

The CONTINUE statement

```
CONTINUE
```

The INITIALIZE statement

```
INITIALIZE {identifier-1} ...

    [                  {(ALPHABETIC        )}              {identifier-2}    ]
    [ REPLACING        {(ALPHANUMERIC      )} DATA BY      {literal-1   } ...]
    [                  {(NUMERIC           )}                               ]
    [                  {(ALPHANUMERIC-EDITED)}                              ]
    [                  {(NUMERIC-EDITED     )}                              ]
```

Note: In the formats that combine 1974 and 1985 elements, the 1985 elements are shaded.

Figure 10-14   Some other 1985 COBOL elements you probably will use (part 2 of 2)

---

the 1985 standards, and COMP-3 is equivalent to PACKED-DECIMAL.

New relational operators   The last four relational operators in the summary in figure 10-14 represent 1985 operators. Although GREATER THAN OR EQUAL TO is equivalent to NOT LESS THAN, it can improve readability in some cases. Similarly, LESS THAN OR EQUAL TO is equivalent to NOT GREATER THAN, but it can improve readability in some cases. Using these operators, you can code any relation so it represents the condition you're trying to express.

Reference modification   Under the 1974 standards, you can only refer to the entire record or field that is represented by a record name or a field name. Under the 1985 standards, though, you can use *reference modification* to refer to a portion of a record or field. For instance, this code

```
EMPLOYEE-NAME (3: 2)
```

refers to two characters in the field named EMPLOYEE-NAME,

starting with the third character from the left. Similarly,

```
EMPLOYEE-NAME (2)
```

refers to all of the characters in the field starting with the second character from the left.

When you use reference modification, the first integer in the parentheses after a data name indicates the starting position within the field. As a result, the range of this value must be from one through the number of characters within the field. Then, the second integer represents the number of characters to be operated upon. This value must be coded so only characters within the field are referred to. If this second integer is omitted, all of the remaining characters in the field are referred to. If indexing or subscripting are used with a data name, the reference modification parentheses follow the indexing or subscripting parentheses.

Reference modification is useful because it gives you more control over the characters within a field. As a result, it can help you improve the coding of some character manipulation routines.

Omission of FILLER   As you know, FILLER can be used in place of a data name when a field isn't going to be referred to. Under the 1985 standards, though, you don't have to code the word FILLER if you are describing a record or field that isn't going to be referred to. For instance, figure 10-15 illustrates two record descriptions, one with FILLERs and one without.

Whether or not you omit the word FILLER, this provision of the 1985 standards shouldn't have much effect on your COBOL programs. However, Paul Noll recommends that you always code the word FILLER when you don't require a data name. That way there won't be any confusion about your intent. If you omit the FILLERs, it's harder to tell when you mistakenly omit a data name.

Expanded class tests   Do you remember what class tests are? Even though they aren't used much, we presented them in *Structured ANS COBOL, Part 1*. Briefly stated, under the 1974 standards, you can code a class test to determine whether an alphanumeric field is numeric or alphabetic.

Under the 1985 standards, you can also use the class test to find out whether a field contains lowercase (ALPHABETIC-LOWER) or uppercase (ALPHABETIC-UPPER) letters. Then, ALPHABETIC refers to a field that contains lowercase letters, uppercase letters, or both. In addition, you can use the class test to find out whether a field consists of only the characters you define for a *class name* in the SPECIAL-NAMES paragraph of the Environment Division.

Although you may find occasional use for these expanded class tests, you certainly won't use them much. In addition, we recommend

Record description with FILLERs

```
01   TOTAL-LINE-1.
*
     05   TL1-RECORD-COUNT        PIC Z(5).
     05   FILLER                  PIC X(15)  VALUE ' RECORDS IN THE'.
     05   FILLER                  PIC X(12)  VALUE ' MASTER FILE'.
     05   FILLER                  PIC X(19)  VALUE SPACE.
     05   TL1-SEL-LM-SALES-TOTAL     PIC $$$$,$$$,$$$.99.
     05   FILLER                  PIC X(2)   VALUE ' *'.
     05   FILLER                  PIC X(2)   VALUE SPACE.
     05   TL1-SEL-INVESTMENT-TOTAL   PIC $$$$,$$$,$$$.99.
     05   FILLER                  PIC X(2)   VALUE ' *'.
     05   FILLER                  PIC X(5)   VALUE SPACE.
     05   TL1-SEL-NO-OF-MONTHS-STOCK PIC ZZZ.9.
     05   FILLER                  PIC X(2)   VALUE ' *'.
     05   FILLER                  PIC X(33)  VALUE SPACE.
*
```

Record description without FILLERs

```
01   TOTAL-LINE-1.
*
     05   TL1-RECORD-COUNT        PIC Z(5).
     05                           PIC X(15)  VALUE ' RECORDS IN THE'.
     05                           PIC X(12)  VALUE ' MASTER FILE'.
     05                           PIC X(19)  VALUE SPACE.
     05   TL1-SEL-LM-SALES-TOTAL     PIC $$$$,$$$,$$$.99.
     05                           PIC X(2)   VALUE ' *'.
     05                           PIC X(2)   VALUE SPACE.
     05   TL1-SEL-INVESTMENT-TOTAL   PIC $$$$,$$$,$$$.99.
     05                           PIC X(2)   VALUE ' *'.
     05                           PIC X(5)   VALUE SPACE.
     05   TL1-SEL-NO-OF-MONTHS-STOCK PIC ZZZ.9.
     05                           PIC X(2)   VALUE ' *'.
     05                           PIC X(33)  VALUE SPACE.
*
```

Figure 10-15   A record description with and without the use of FILLERs

that you avoid the use of class names since it can reduce the readability of your Procedure Divisions by putting some of the logic in the Environment Division. That's why we won't take the time to show you how to code class names in the Environment Division. If class names are used in your shop, you can quickly learn how to use them on your own.

New ADD statement format   Under the 1974 standards, the word TO is illegal when the GIVING clause is used in an ADD statement, even though the word TO seems to be logical enough. If you refer to figure 10-14, though, you can see that the word TO can be used with GIVING when you use a 1985 compiler, although it's an optional word. This should eliminate an occasional coding error.

The ACCEPT DAY-OF-WEEK statement   We presented the ACCEPT DAY-OF-WEEK statement in *Structured ANS COBOL, Part 1*. In this statement, the identifier must be defined as a one-digit elementary item. After the statement has been executed, a value of 1 in the receiving field represents Monday; a value of 2, Tuesday; and so on.

The CONTINUE statement   The CONTINUE statement is a no operation statement. It can be used to satisfy the syntax of another statement while showing that no operation should be performed. For instance, figure 10-16 illustrates the use of the CONTINUE statement within an EVALUATE statement. You might code a statement like this when you want to provide for all transaction codes from 1 through 6 even though some of them aren't used at the time you code your program. Later on, you can replace the CONTINUE statements with the code your program requires. In this example, no operation is done for transaction codes 3 and 5.

Occasionally, the CONTINUE statement may help you improve the readability of a set of statements. However, you can usually code what you want in a readable style without using the CONTINUE statement.

The INITIALIZE statement   The INITIALIZE statement can give values to a field that is either an elementary or a group item. In its simplest form, it is coded without the REPLACING clause as in this example:

```
INITIALIZE INVENTORY-DATA.
```

Then, if INVENTORY-DATA is a group item, all numeric and numeric edited fields within it are set to zeros; all alphabetic, alphanumeric, and alphanumeric edited fields are set to spaces. If INVENTORY-DATA is an elementary item, it is set to spaces or zeros depending on what type of item it is.

If you don't want the fields to be initialized to spaces or zeros as described above, you can code the REPLACING clause. This implies a series of moves with identifier-1 as the receiving field and identifier-2 or literal-1 as the sending field. In this case, you can initialize each type of field within a group receiving item with whatever data you want.

If the REPLACING clause doesn't specify one or more types of fields, these fields are ignored during the execution of the statement.

```
EVALUATE ITR-TRAN-CODE
    WHEN 1      PERFORM 240-EDIT-CODE-1-FIELDS
    WHEN 2      PERFORM 250-EDIT-CODE-2-FIELDS
    WHEN 3      CONTINUE
    WHEN 4      PERFORM 260-EDIT-CODE-4-FIELDS
    WHEN 5      CONTINUE
    WHEN 6      PERFORM 270-EDIT-CODE-6-FIELDS
    WHEN OTHER MOVE MARK TO ITL-TYPE-CODE-ERROR
               MOVE 'N' TO VALID-TRAN-SWITCH
               ADD 1 TO INVALID-TRAN-CODE-COUNT.
```

Figure 10-16   The CONTINUE statement used within an EVALUATE statement

Also, fields defined as FILLER and fields that are redefined within a group item are ignored. For instance, this statement will only initialize the numeric and alphanumeric fields within a group item:

```
INITIALIZE INVENTORY-FIELDS
    REPLACING ALPHANUMERIC DATA BY SPACE
              NUMERIC       DATA BY ZERO.
```

When this statement is executed, it will ignore alphabetic fields, alphanumeric edited fields, numeric edited fields, fields defined as FILLER, and fields that are redefined within the area named INVENTORY-FIELDS.

Whenever logical, we recommend that you initialize fields in working storage with VALUE clauses. As a result, you shouldn't have much need for the INITIALIZE statement. In some programs, though, this statement makes it easy for you to define a table area or some other large area. It is also useful when you have to re-initialize the fields within a program.

Because the INITIALIZE statement makes it so easy for you to initialize fields within records, you should use it with some caution. If you use it carelessly, it can cause serious inefficiencies within a program. For instance, you can initialize a 50,000-byte table with a single INITIALIZE statement. But that doesn't mean you should initialize the table if it doesn't have to be initialized.

Some 1985 COBOL elements that you probably won't use

Although I'm not trying to present all of the 1985 COBOL elements in this book, I would like to present a couple of elements that you probably won't ever use. One of them relates to the de-editing of numeric items; the other relates to the new language for calling and writing subprograms.

De-editing numeric items   When you move a numeric field to a numeric edited field, it is *edited*. When you move a numeric edited field to a numeric field, you can theoretically *de-edit* it. Under the 1985 standards, the MOVE statement is supposed to de-edit a numeric edited item if it is moved to a numeric item. This means that the unedited numeric value should end up in the receiving field.

You probably won't ever use this facility of 1985 COBOL because you won't ever need to. But perhaps you'll run into an application some day that requires it.

New language for calling and writing subprograms   As I mentioned in chapter 7, the 1985 standards provide a considerable amount of new code for calling and writing subprograms. At this writing, we're not sure how it will be implemented or how it will be used. It appears, though, that the new language will be quite difficult to implement, so we don't expect to see it implemented by the compilers for microcomputers or minicomputers.

In general, we feel that the new language gives the programmer more control over the data that is operated upon by calling programs and subprograms than is required. As a result, we predict that the new language won't be used much, if at all, in most COBOL shops. That's why we aren't presenting the new language for calling and writing subprograms in this text or in this series.

In some COBOL shops, though, each module of a program is implemented as a subprogram. Based on a study we did a few years ago, less than ten percent of the COBOL shops develop programs in this way. Nevertheless, if you work in one of these shops, you'll probably have to master the new language for calling and writing subprograms. How you use it, though, will depend upon how it is implemented on your system and what your shop standards are for using it.

Discussion

Although we haven't presented all of the 1985 COBOL elements in this chapter or in this book, we think we've presented all the elements of significance. As we point out in chapter 12, though, professional programmers should occasionally review their reference manuals to make sure they're aware of all the code that may be useful to them. As a result, you should eventually find out what other 1985 COBOL code is available to you on your system.

Terminology

case structure
linear nest
reference modification
class name
de-editing

Objective

If you have a 1985 compiler available to you, apply the elements
presented in this topic to your application programs.

Topic 3   Compiler dependent code

At this writing, only a few 1985 compilers have been announced. One of these, the VS COBOL II compiler for IBM mainframes, was developed before the 1985 standards were officially adopted, so it doesn't conform completely to the standards. Although we believe it will be modified eventually to conform to the standards, we think you should be aware of its current incompatibilities. We think you should also realize that the EVALUATE statement may not be implemented on compilers for microcomputers and minicomputers.

The VS COBOL II compiler for IBM mainframes

We believe that the VS COBOL II compiler for IBM mainframes will be modified eventually so it qualifies as a "high subset" compiler under the provisions of the 1985 standards. To be a high subset compiler, a compiler must implement all of the elements in the first eight modules of the standards. These modules are summarized in chapter 12.

At this writing, though, the VS COBOL II compiler has not implemented all of the elements in the first eight modules. As a result, it must be considered a non-standard compiler. However, it does implement most of the 1985 code, so you only need to know what hasn't been implemented yet.

Right now, the VS COBOL II compiler supports all of the 1985 elements in topic 1 of this chapter. It also supports the EVALUATE statement, the omission of the word FILLER in data descriptions, the CONTINUE statement, the INITIALIZE statement, and most of the new language for calling and writing subprograms, as described in topic 2. However, this compiler doesn't currently support NOT clauses, BINARY and PACKED-DECIMAL usage, the new relational operators, reference modification, the expanded class tests, the new ADD statement format, the ACCEPT DAY-OF-WEEK statement, and de-editing, as described in topic 2.

You should also realize that some of the 1985 code presented in chapters 2 through 9 isn't supported by the VS COBOL II compiler right now. On this compiler, the LABEL RECORDS clause isn't optional, even though it is treated as documentation for VSAM files. For variable-length sequential files, you can't use the RECORD IS VARYING IN SIZE clause in the FD statement. You can't use the GREATER THAN OR EQUAL TO condition in the START statement for an indexed or relative file. The sort/merge feature for this compiler is based on the 1974 standards, not the 1985 standards, so you have to use sections for your input and output procedures along with EXIT paragraphs. You can't use relative subscripting for table handling. And this compiler only supports three levels of tables, not the seven that are supported by the 1985 standards.

The EVALUATE statement

The EVALUATE statement is complex. Also, it is defined as a high-level element in the nucleus module of the 1985 standards. Since most of these high-level elements aren't implemented by the compilers for small systems, we don't expect the EVALUATE statement to be implemented by the compilers for most microcomputers and minicomputers.

Terminology

None

Objective

Find out what features of the 1985 COBOL standards have been implemented on your compiler.

Related subjects

This section consists of two chapters. Chapter 11 introduces you to the structure and logic of edit, update, and file maintenance programs. By studying the examples in this chapter, you should begin to understand the basic structures of these programs. You can read this chapter any time after you read chapter 1, but we recommend that you read it before you start the case studies in appendix D.

In contrast, chapter 12 tells you what else you must know to become an effective COBOL programmer. It describes those subjects that aren't presented in either *Part 1* or *Part 2* of this course. You should read this chapter after you've completed the other eleven chapters in this book, or at least a major portion of them.

Chapter 11

The structure and logic of edit, update, and maintenance programs

In chapter 1, I introduced you to structured programming. I first presented the characteristics of a structured program. Then, I showed you how to design a program from the top down and how to plan the critical modules of a program using pseudocode. To illustrate these techniques, I used the report preparation program that is presented in appendix A.

Before you can use structured programming techniques effectively, you need to be familiar with the structure and logic of other types of business programs. As a result, I am now going to present the design and code for three more programs. These should show you how the techniques of chapter 1 can be applied to most business programs. Once you're familiar with these model programs, I will show you the basic structures that they contain. Last, I'll show you how you can use the model programs as a basis for designing new programs. By the time you complete this chapter, you should be able to create structure charts of your own, and you should be able to use pseudocode to plan the critical modules of your structure charts.

Three model programs

As we see it, there are four classes of programs common to all batch business systems. They are: (1) report preparation programs that prepare printed reports from one or more transaction or master files; (2) edit programs that check source data for validity; (3) sequential update or file-maintenance programs that update or maintain master files; and (4) random update or file-maintenance programs. Since *Structured ANS COBOL, Part 1* shows you how to design and develop report preparation programs, I'm going to concentrate on the other three types of batch programs in this chapter.

For each type of model program, I will present a set of program specifications, the structure chart for the entire program, and the COBOL code for some of the critical modules of the program. You should realize, however, that you don't have to know how you're going to code the modules when you design a program. I'm only presenting the code so you can see the relationships between the design and the code. Once you understand these relationships, you should be able to design most programs with little or no concern for the resulting code. You should also be able to use pseudocode to plan the critical modules of your programs before you actually code them.

If you have our *COBOL Programmer's Handbook*, you can refer to it for additional information about the model programs. If, for example, you want to see the complete COBOL code for a model program, you can find it in the *Handbook*. Similarly, you can find design alternatives in the *Handbook*. For now, I just want to show you one way of designing each type of program, but you should realize that other designs will work too.

For illustrative purposes, it was tempting to give specifications for the model programs that kept their designs and code simple. But we haven't done that because production programs are rarely without complication. As a result, you'll find some realistic complications in each of the model programs. Although this doesn't have much effect on any of the program designs, it does make the code for some of the modules quite complicated. This will give you a better idea of how production programs are designed and coded.

Because of the complications, you may be bothered by the complexity of the code for some of the modules in the model programs. So, let me make this point about the coding in a structured program. Often, a structured program will require a couple of complex modules. In other words, you can't avoid programming complexity just by using structured development techniques. But once you get the coding for the critical modules right, the development of the rest of the structured program is routine. In a 2000-line program, for example, you may struggle with 200 of the coding lines. But you'll be able to develop the other 1800 lines of the program at a high rate of speed with much of it picked up from old programs.

Model program 1: An edit program   An *edit program* checks the records in a transaction file to make sure they contain valid data. If the edit program detects an invalid field within a record, the record is not released for further processing. In addition, the error record is usually listed on an error listing so the errors can be corrected and the data can be resubmitted for processing. If the edit program doesn't detect any invalid fields for a record, it releases the record for further processing. It usually does this by writing the valid records on a sequential transaction file that will be used to update and maintain one or more master files.

Program: **INV2100 EDIT INVENTORY TRANSACTIONS**   Page: **1**

Designer: **Anne Prince**   Date: **08-17-84**

Input/output specifications

File	Description	Use
INVTRAN	Inventory transaction file	Input
PARTNUM	Part number file	Input
VINVTRAN	Valid inventory transaction file	Output
IINVTLST	Print file: Invalid inventory transaction listing	Output

Process specifications

This program edits a file of transaction records consisting of two record types: sales transactions and return transactions. Although the formats for these records are similar, they are not exactly alike.

For efficiency, since the company has less than 100 inventory items, load a part-number table at the start of the program that can be used to check for valid part numbers throughout the program. The part numbers can be read from the part-number file. The records in this file are in order of transaction frequency; the first part number has the most activity, the last part number has the least.

Print the output listing in the same order that the transactions are read. Print the editing totals on a separate page on the invalid transaction listing.

The records in the valid transaction file have the same format as the records in the input transaction file.

Figure 11-1   The program specifications for the edit program (part 1 of 4)

Program: **INV2100 EDIT INVENTORY TRANSACTIONS**   Page: 2

Designer: **Anne Prince**   Date: **08-17-84**

Process specifications

The basic processing requirements follow:

Load the part-number table.

Do until the end of the inventory transaction file:

1.   **Read an inventory transaction record.**

2.   **Edit the transaction fields.**

3.   **If the transaction is invalid, print a line on the invalid transaction listing.**

4.   **If the transaction is valid, write a record to the valid transaction file.**

After all transactions have been processed, print the total page.

Figure 11-1   The program specifications for the edit program (part 2 of 4)

Program: INV2100   EDIT INVENTORY TRANSACTIONS   Page: 3

Designer: Anne Prince   Date: 08-17-84

Process specifications

Editing rules for a sales transaction:

ITR-UPDATE-CODE	Must be "C"
ITR-TRAN-CODE	Must be 1
ITR-REF-NO	No restrictions
ITR-REF-DATE	Use DATEDIT subprogram; must be a valid date in the form MMDDYY
ITR-BRANCH-NO	Numeric, greater than zero, and less than 25
ITR-SALESMAN-NO	Numeric and greater than zero
ITR-CUSTOMER-NO	Numeric and greater than zero
ITR-QUANTITY	Numeric and greater than zero
ITR-PART-NO	Must match with a number in the part-number table that is loaded at the start of the program
ITR-RETURN-CODE	Not used

Editing rules for a return transaction:

ITR-UPDATE-CODE	Must be "C"
ITR-TRAN-CODE	Must be 2
ITR-REF-NO	No restrictions
ITR-REF-DATE	Use DATEDIT subprogram; must be a valid date in the form MMDDYY
ITR-BRANCH-NO	Not used
ITR-SALESMAN-NO	Not used
ITR-CUSTOMER-NO	Numeric and greater than zero
ITR-QUANTITY	Numeric and greater than zero
ITR-PART-NO	Must match with a number in the part-number table that is loaded at the start of the program
ITR-RETURN-CODE	Alphabetic

Figure 11-1   The program specifications for the edit program (part 3 of 4)

Document name Invalid Sales and Return Listing **Date** 8-17-84

Program name INV2100 **Designer** Anne Prince

Record Name		
Heading-Line-1	1	DATE: 99/99/99 MIKE MURACH & ASSOCIATES, INC. PAGE: ZZ9
Heading-Line-2	2	TIME: 99:99 XX INV2100
Heading-Line-3	3	INVALID SALES AND RETURN TRANSACTIONS
	4	
Heading-Line-4	5	TRAN REFERENCE DATE BRANCH SALESMAN CUSTOMER QUANTITY PART RETURN
Heading-Line-5	6	CODE UPDATE NUMBER NUMBER NUMBER NUMBER NUMBER CODE
	7	CODE
Invalid-Transaction-Line	8	*X *XXXXX *XX *XXXX *XXXX *XX *XX
	9	*XX *XX *XX *XXX *XXX *XX *XX *X
	10	XX XXXXXX XX XX XXX XXX XXX XXXX
	11	
	12	
	13	
	14	
	15	
Error-Code-Line	16	* INDICATES ERROR FIELDS
	17	
	18	
	19	
Total page:	20	
	21	
Heading-Line-1	22	DATE: 99/99/99 MIKE MURACH & ASSOCIATES, INC. PAGE: ZZ9
Heading-Line-2	23	TIME: 99:99 XX INV2100
	24	
Summary-Heading	25	SUMMARY FOR SALES AND RETURN EDITING RUN
	26	
Total-Line	27	VALID SALES ZZ,ZZ9-
	28	RETURNS ZZ,ZZ9-
	29	TOTAL ZZ,ZZ9-*
	30	
	31	INVALID SALES ZZ,ZZ9-
	32	RETURNS ZZ,ZZ9-
	33	TOTAL ZZ,ZZ9-*
	34	
	35	INVALID TRAN CODES ZZ,ZZ9-*
	36	
	37	TRANSACTIONS PROCESSED ZZ,ZZ9-* *
	38	
	39	
	40	
	41	
	42	
	43	
	44	
	45	
	46	
	47	
	48	
	49	
	50	

Figure 11-1   The program specifications for the edit program (part 4 of 4)

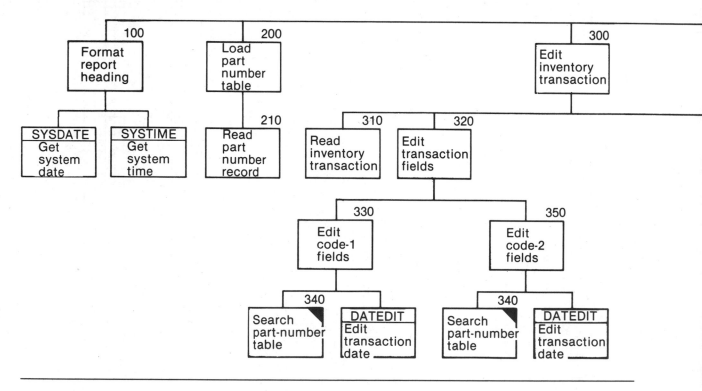

Figure 11-2   The structure chart for the edit program

In some shops, you will find an edit program referred to as a *validation*, or *verification*, *program*. However, these terms have taken on new meanings in interactive program environments. As a result, we prefer the term *edit* to either of these other terms.

Figure 11-1 presents the program specifications for the model edit program. As you can see, this program edits two types of records: sales and return records. However, the record formats are so similar that one output line format can be used to list both types of invalid transactions. The error fields are highlighted on the error listing by the printing of an asterisk (*) to the left of each error field.

If you check the editing rules in the program overview, you can see that all numeric fields are to be checked to make sure they contain valid numeric data that is greater than zero. Also, the date field must be edited using the DATEDIT subprogram, the branch-number field must contain a number under 25 for a sales transaction, and the part-number field must contain a number that can be found in the table of

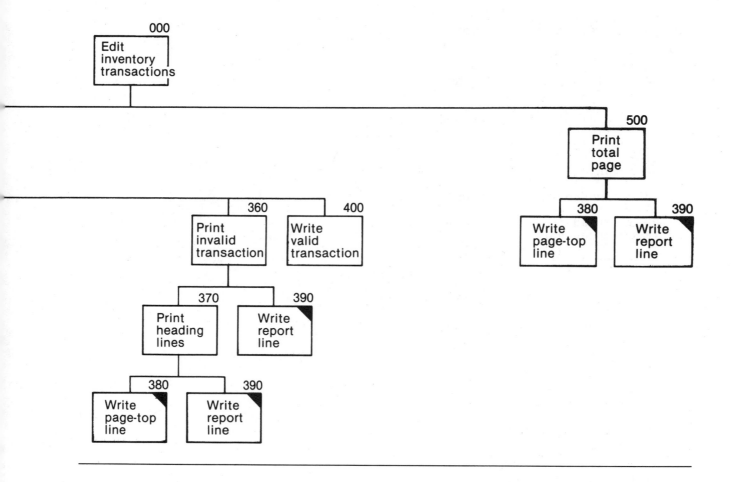

valid part numbers that is loaded into storage at the start of the program.

Figure 11-2 presents the structure chart for this program. Since this program is limited in complexity, there aren't too many different ways that this program can be designed. Obviously, the part-number table must be loaded into storage before starting to edit the transaction records. The report headings must be formatted before any printing can be done. And the total page must be printed after the records are edited.

To process each transaction, module 300 calls module 310 to read a record and module 320 to edit the record. Then, if the transaction is invalid, module 300 calls module 360 to print a line on the invalid transaction listing; if the transaction is valid, module 300 calls module 400 to write a record on the valid transaction file.

Figure 11-3 presents the pseudocode for the critical modules of this program. As you can see, module 000 uses DO UNTIL statements

```
000-edit-inventory-transactions.

    Open files.
    DO 100-format-report-heading.
    DO 200-load-part-number-table
        VARYING table-index from 1 by 1
        UNTIL part-number-eof.
    Do 300-edit-inventory-transaction
        UNTIL tran-eof.
    DO 500-print-total-page.
    Close files.
    Stop run.

300-edit-inventory-transaction.

    DO 310-read-inventory-transaction.
    IF NOT tran-eof
        DO 320-edit-transaction-fields
        IF NOT valid-tran
            DO 360-print-invalid-transaction
        ELSE
            DO 400-write-valid-transaction.

310-read-inventory-transaction.

    Read record
        AT END
            move 'Y' to tran-eof-switch.
    IF NOT tran-eof
        add 1 to trans-processed-count.

320-edit-transaction-fields.

    Move 'Y' to valid-tran-switch.
    Move space to invalid-transaction-line.
    IF transaction-code = 1
        DO 330-edit-code-1-fields
    ELSE IF transaction-code = 2
        DO 350-edit-code-2-fields
    ELSE
        move 'N' to valid-tran-switch
        move error-indicator to type-code-error
        add 1 to invalid-tran-code-count.
```

Figure 11-3   Pseudocode for the critical modules of the edit program

to perform modules 200 and 300 until there are no more records in the input files. And module 300 uses a nested IF statement to control the execution of modules 310, 320, 360, and 400. As for module 320, it checks the transaction code to decide which of the remaining two edit modules should be performed. If the code is invalid, it turns off the valid-transaction switch, moves an asterisk (error-indicator) into the proper position in the output line, and adds one to the invalid-transaction-code count. Modules 330 and 350 will contain similar code to handle any errors they find in the other transaction fields.

```
PROCEDURE DIVISION.
*
000-EDIT-INVENTORY-TRANS.
*
    OPEN INPUT   PARTNUM
                 INVTRAN
          OUTPUT VINVTRN
                 IINVTLST.
    PERFORM 100-FORMAT-REPORT-HEADING.
    PERFORM 200-LOAD-PART-NUMBER-TABLE
        VARYING PN-TABLE-INDEX FROM 1 BY 1
        UNTIL PART-NUMBER-EOF.
    PERFORM 300-EDIT-INVENTORY-TRAN
        UNTIL TRAN-EOF.
    PERFORM 500-PRINT-TOTAL-PAGE.
    CLOSE PARTNUM
          INVTRAN
          VINVTRN
          IINVTLST.
    STOP RUN.
*
100-FORMAT-REPORT-HEADING.
*
    CALL 'SYSDATE' USING TODAYS-DATE.
    MOVE TODAYS-DATE    TO HDG1-DATE.
    MOVE COMPANY-NAME   TO HDG1-COMPANY-NAME.
    CALL 'SYSTIME' USING  HDG2-TIME-DATA.
    MOVE 'INV2100'      TO HDG2-REPORT-NUMBER.
    MOVE REPORT-TITLE   TO HDG3-REPORT-TITLE.
*
200-LOAD-PART-NUMBER-TABLE.
*
    PERFORM 210-READ-PART-NUMBER-RECORD.
    IF NOT PART-NUMBER-EOF
        MOVE PNR-PART-NO TO PN-TABLE-ENTRY (PN-TABLE-INDEX)
    ELSE
        SET PN-TABLE-INDEX DOWN BY 1
        SET PN-ENTRY-COUNT TO PN-TABLE-INDEX.
*
210-READ-PART-NUMBER-RECORD.
*
    READ PARTNUM
        AT END
            MOVE 'Y' TO PART-NUMBER-EOF-SWITCH.
```

Figure 11-4   The COBOL code for the first seven modules of the edit program (part 1 of 2)

So you can see how the pseudocode relates to the actual code, figure 11-4 presents the Procedure Division code for the first seven modules of this program. In general, the COBOL code is an expanded and refined version of the pseudocode. As a result, if you can understand the pseudocode for a program, you should be able to understand the COBOL code for a program, and vice versa.

```
✿
 300-EDIT-INVENTORY-TRAN.
✿
     PERFORM 310-READ-INVENTORY-TRAN.
     IF NOT TRAN-EOF
         PERFORM 320-EDIT-TRANSACTION-FIELDS
         IF NOT VALID-TRAN
             PERFORM 360-PRINT-INVALID-TRANSACTION
         ELSE
             PERFORM 400-WRITE-VALID-TRANSACTION.
✿
 310-READ-INVENTORY-TRAN.
✿
     READ INVTRAN INTO INVENTORY-TRANSACTION-RECORD
         AT END
             MOVE 'Y' TO TRAN-EOF-SWITCH.
     IF NOT TRAN-EOF
         ADD 1 TO TRANS-PROCESSED-COUNT.
✿
 320-EDIT-TRANSACTION-FIELDS.
✿
     MOVE 'Y'   TO VALID-TRAN-SWITCH.
     MOVE SPACE TO INVALID-TRANSACTION-LINE.
     IF ITR-TRAN-CODE = 1
         PERFORM 330-EDIT-CODE-1-FIELDS
     ELSE IF ITR-TRAN-CODE = 2
         PERFORM 350-EDIT-CODE-2-FIELDS
     ELSE
         MOVE ERROR-INDICATOR TO ITL-TRAN-CODE-ERR
         MOVE 'N'                TO VALID-TRAN-SWITCH
         ADD 1                   TO INVALID-TRAN-CODE-COUNT.
```

Figure 11-4   The COBOL code for the first seven modules of the edit program (part 2 of 2)

For the next two programs, I will only present the COBOL code for the program; I won't present the pseudocode that corresponds to it. With the COBOL code as a guide, you should be able to develop the pseudocode for the critical modules of your own programs. The advantages of using COBOL code rather than pseudocode for illustrative purposes are (1) that the COBOL code is tested so you know it works, and (2) that the COBOL code shows the detailed requirements of a module.

Model program 2: A sequential file-maintenance program   In our shop, we distinguish between update and file-maintenance programs, although some shops don't make this distinction. We use the term *update* when a program changes the records in a file based on operational data such as sales, hours worked, or receipts to inventory. We use the term *file maintenance* when the transactions contain maintenance data such as address changes.

Figure 11-5 presents the program specifications for the next model program, which is a sequential file-maintenance program.

Program: **MNT1500   MAINTAIN INVENTORY FILE**   Page: 1

Designer: **Anne Prince**   Date: **08-30-84**

Input/output specifications

File	Description	Use
OLDMAST	Old inventory master file	Input
MNTTRAN	Maintenance transaction file	Input
NEWMAST	New inventory master file	Output
ERRTRAN	Maintenance transaction error file	Output
MNTLIST	Print file: Inventory maintenance listing	Output

Process specifications

Use the transaction records to maintain the master records. A
transaction record may change, add, or delete a master file
record. There may be none, one, or several transactions for each
master. Since the fields in the transaction record have already
been edited, this program does <u>not</u> have to do any field editing.

The master file is in sequence by item number. The transaction
file is in sequence by action code within item number. That means
that for any one item number, the types of transactions are in
this sequence: delete, add, changes. So it is possible to delete
an item number, add a new record with the same item number to the
file, and then update the new record one or more times.

The maintenance listing is to be printed with one line for each
valid transaction record as shown on the print chart. The totals
for the program are to be printed on a separate output page.

If an unmatched deletion or change transaction, or a matched
addition transaction is detected, write a record in the error
file. The error record should have the same format as the
transaction record.

Figure 11-5   The program specifications for the sequential file-maintenance program (part 1 of 3)

Program: **MNT1500   MAINTAIN INVENTORY FILE**   Page: 2

Designer: Anne Prince   Date: 08-30-84

Process specifications

The basic processing requirements follow:

Do until all records have been processed:

1. **Read an inventory transaction record.**

2. **Get inventory master records until a record with a matching or greater item number is found. This includes writing the previous master record to the new master file if there aren't any more transactions for the record and the record wasn't deleted.**

3. **Determine the processing to be performed--deletion, addition, change, or error.**

4. **For a delete transaction, mark the record as deleted and print a line on the maintenance listing.**

5. **For an addition transaction, format the addition record and print a line on the maintenance listing.**

6. **For a change transaction, make the changes and print a line on the maintenance listing.**

7. **For an error transaction, write a record to the error transaction file.**

After all records have been processed, print the transaction totals on the last page of the maintenance listing.

Figure 11-5   The program specifications for the sequential file-maintenance program (part 2 of 3)

Document name _Inventory Maintenance Listing_   Date _8-30-84_

Program name _MNT1500_   Designer _Anne Prince_

Record Name

Line	Record Name	Content
1	Heading-Line-1	DATE: 99/99/99
2	Heading-Line-2	TIME: 99:99 XX
3	Heading-Line-3	
4		
5	Heading-Line-4	ITEM NO ITEM DESCRIPTION
6		
7	Maintenance-Line	XXXXXX XXXXXXXXXXXXXXXXXXX
8		XXXXXX XXXXXXXXXXXXXXXXXXX
9		XXXXXX XXXXXXXXXXXXXXXXXXX
10		
11		
12		
13		
14	Total page data to be	
15	printed after the	
16	first two lines of	
17	the standard heading	
18		
19	Total-Line-1	SUMMARY FOR INVENTORY MAINTENANCE RUN
20		
21	Total-Line-2	DELETIONS ZZ,ZZ9
22	Total-Line-3	ADDITIONS ZZ,ZZ9
23	Total-Line-4	CHANGES ZZ,ZZ9
24	Total-Line-5	TOTAL ZZ,ZZ9 *
25		
26	Total-Line-6	ERRORS ZZ,ZZ9
27		
28	Total-Line-7	TRANSACTIONS PROCESSED ZZZ,ZZ9 **
29		
30		
...		
50		

Across print positions (heading area):

MIKE MURACH & ASSOCIATES, INC.   PAGE: ZZ9

INVENTORY MAINTENANCE LISTING   MNT1500

UNIT COST   UNIT PRICE   ON HAND   ACTION

ZZ9.99   ZZ9.99   ZZ9   CHANGED
ZZ9.99   ZZ9.99   ZZ9   ADDED
ZZ9.99   ZZ9.99   ZZ9   DELETED

Figure 11-5   The program specifications for the sequential file-maintenance program (part 3 of 3)

As you can see, this program requires two input files: an inventory master file and a maintenance transaction file. It produces three output files: a maintained, or new, master file; a listing of the records that were maintained; and an error file of transactions that couldn't be processed.

The logic in a program like this is based on a comparison of the *control fields* in the master and transaction records that are read. In this program, the control field is the inventory item number. In order for the program to work, both files must be in sequence by the control field because a sequential file-maintenance program reads all input files in sequence.

As the program reads the records in the input files, it compares the control fields in the transaction and master records. If a transaction record and a master record have the same control field value, the records are *matched*. If no master record has the same control field value as a transaction record, the transaction record is an *unmatched transaction*. If no transaction record has the same control field value as a master record, the master record is an *unmatched master*. In a sequential file-maintenance program, an unmatched transaction must be an addition record; otherwise, it can't be processed, so it represents an error transaction. On the other hand, an unmatched master doesn't indicate an error; it just means that no transaction applies to the master.

In contrast to a random update or maintenance program, a sequential program forces procedural thinking like this upon you. To a large extent, this thinking goes back to the days of computing when most files were kept on magnetic tapes rather than direct-access devices. That's why it's usually more difficult to develop a sequential update or maintenance program than it is to develop a random update or maintenance program. Instead of concentrating on the functions that the program requires, you have to be aware that the files are being read one record at a time and that you can't get a master record back once you've written it on the new master file. Also, unmatched master records have to be written on the new file, even though they haven't been changed.

With this as background, figure 11-6 presents a structure chart for this program. After module 310 reads a transaction record, module 320 gets the next master record. Here, the verb *get* means to both write a new master record and read an old master record, since you shouldn't do one without doing the other. After module 320 gets the appropriate master record, module 350 controls the processing of the inventory transaction.

If a transaction is matched and it is a deletion or a change, module 350 calls module 360 or 440 to apply the transaction to the master record. Here, the verb *apply* means to change the record in storage but not to actually delete or rewrite the record on the tape or disk. This is done by module 320 and its subordinates. If the transaction is unmatched and it is an addition, module 350 calls module 420 to apply the addition transaction to the master file. Otherwise, module 350 calls module 410 to write the transaction on the error file.

Figure 11-7 gives the COBOL code for the critical modules of this program. As you can see, the two most complicated modules are modules 320 and 350. Both are complicated by the requirement to process a deletion, an addition, and one or more changes for the same item number. As a result, the program can't just read the next master record when a record is deleted from the file. And it can't just write the new master record when a record is added to the file. This accounts for the use of the MASTER-DELETED and the MASTER-HELD-FOR-ADDITION switches that are used in these modules. Without this requirement, these modules would be quite straightforward.

Module 320 starts by using a FIRST-EXECUTION switch that is on at the start of the program. As a result, the first time this module is executed, it only performs module 330 to read a master record; then, it turns the FIRST-EXECUTION switch off. In subsequent executions, module 320 uses the MASTER-DELETED and MASTER-HELD-FOR-ADDITION switches to decide whether to write a new master record, read an old master record, or both. If a master hasn't been deleted and a master hasn't been held for addition, this module performs module 340 to write a new master record and performs module 330 to read an old master record. However, if a master record has been deleted, this module doesn't perform module 340 to write the record. Also, if a master has been held for addition to the file, this module doesn't perform module 330 to read a new master record; instead, it treats the record in the area named HELD-MASTER-RECORD as the new master record. To provide for all combinations of these conditions, module 320 requires an IF statement with three levels of nesting.

Module 350 controls the processing for the three types of transactions based on the condition names MT-DELETION, MT-ADDITION, and MT-CHANGE. In general, if a deletion or change transaction is matched, module 350 calls module 360 or module 440 to apply the transaction; if an addition transaction is unmatched, module 350 calls module 420 to apply the addition transaction. However, this module also provides for the possibility that a matching master record has already been deleted, even though it's still in storage. That's why this module requires five levels of nesting.

If you look at the apply modules for deletions and additions, you can see how they support the code in modules 320 and 350. In module 360, the MASTER-DELETED switch is turned on when a deletion transaction is applied. In module 420, unless the last master record has been deleted, the inventory master record in storage is moved to HELD-MASTER-RECORD and the MASTER-HELD-FOR-ADDITION switch is turned on. Then, the addition transaction is applied to the area named INVENTORY-MASTER-RECORD.

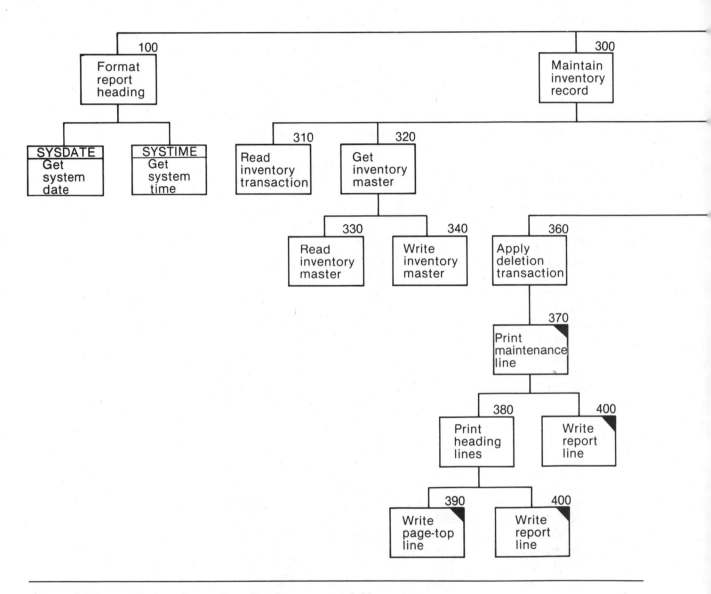

Figure 11-6   The structure chart for the sequential file-maintenance program

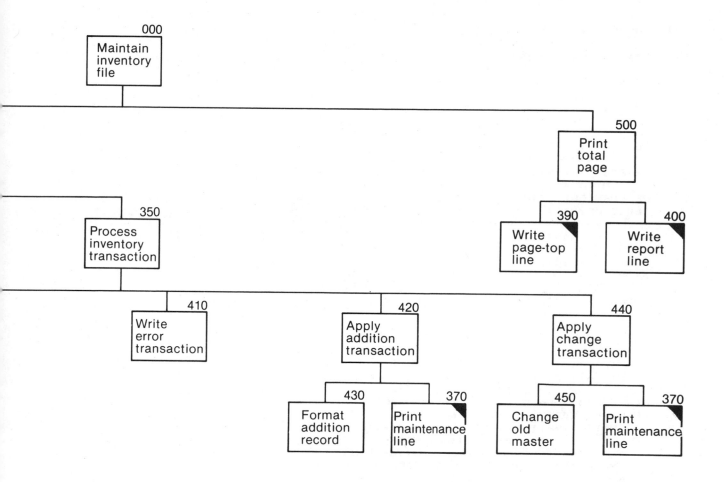

```
PROCEDURE DIVISION.
*
000-MAINTAIN-INVENTORY-FILE.
*
    OPEN INPUT   OLDMAST
                 MNTTRAN
         OUTPUT  NEWMAST
                 ERRTRAN
                 MNTLIST.
    PERFORM 100-FORMAT-REPORT-HEADING.
    MOVE LOW-VALUE TO IM-ITEM-NUMBER.
    PERFORM 300-MAINTAIN-INVENTORY-RECORD
        UNTIL ALL-RECORDS-PROCESSED.
    PERFORM 500-PRINT-TOTAL-PAGE.
    CLOSE OLDMAST
          MNTTRAN
          NEWMAST
          ERRTRAN
          MNTLIST.
    STOP RUN.
*
100-FORMAT-REPORT-HEADING.
*
        .
        .
        .
*
300-MAINTAIN-INVENTORY-RECORD.
*
    PERFORM 310-READ-INVENTORY-TRANSACTION.
    PERFORM 320-GET-INVENTORY-MASTER
        UNTIL IM-ITEM-NUMBER NOT < MT-ITEM-NUMBER.
    IF          MT-ITEM-NUMBER = HIGH-VALUE
            AND IM-ITEM-NUMBER = HIGH-VALUE
        MOVE 'Y' TO ALL-RECORDS-PROCESSED-SWITCH
    ELSE
        PERFORM 350-PROCESS-INVENTORY-TRAN.
*
310-READ-INVENTORY-TRANSACTION.
*
    READ MNTTRAN INTO MAINTENANCE-TRANSACTION
        AT END
            MOVE HIGH-VALUE TO MT-ITEM-NUMBER.
    IF MT-ITEM-NUMBER NOT = HIGH-VALUE
        ADD 1 TO TRAN-COUNT.
*
```

Figure 11-7   The COBOL code for the critical modules of the sequential file-maintenance program
              (part 1 of 4)

```
320-GET-INVENTORY-MASTER.
*
     IF FIRST-EXECUTION
         PERFORM 330-READ-INVENTORY-MASTER
         MOVE 'N' TO FIRST-EXECUTION-SWITCH
     ELSE
         IF NOT MASTER-DELETED
             PERFORM 340-WRITE-INVENTORY-MASTER
             IF MASTER-HELD-FOR-ADDITION
                 MOVE HELD-MASTER-RECORD
                     TO INVENTORY-MASTER-RECORD
                 MOVE 'N' TO MASTER-HELD-FOR-ADDITION-SWITCH
             ELSE
                 PERFORM 330-READ-INVENTORY-MASTER
         ELSE
             MOVE 'N' TO MASTER-DELETED-SWITCH
             IF MASTER-HELD-FOR-ADDITION
                 MOVE HELD-MASTER-RECORD
                     TO INVENTORY-MASTER-RECORD
                 MOVE 'N' TO MASTER-HELD-FOR-ADDITION-SWITCH
             ELSE
                 PERFORM 330-READ-INVENTORY-MASTER.
*
 330-READ-INVENTORY-MASTER.
*
     READ OLDMAST INTO INVENTORY-MASTER-RECORD
         AT END
             MOVE HIGH-VALUE TO IM-ITEM-NUMBER.
*
 340-WRITE-INVENTORY-MASTER.
*
     WRITE NEW-MASTER-RECORD FROM INVENTORY-MASTER-RECORD.
*
```

Figure 11-7   The COBOL code for the critical modules of the sequential file-maintenance program (part 2 of 4)

```
350-PROCESS-INVENTORY-TRAN.
*
    IF MT-DELETION
        IF IM-ITEM-NUMBER = MT-ITEM-NUMBER
            IF NOT MASTER-DELETED
                PERFORM 360-APPLY-DELETION-TRANSACTION
            ELSE
                PERFORM 410-WRITE-ERROR-TRANSACTION
        ELSE
            PERFORM 410-WRITE-ERROR-TRANSACTION
    ELSE
        IF MT-ADDITION
            IF IM-ITEM-NUMBER = MT-ITEM-NUMBER
                IF MASTER-DELETED
                    PERFORM 420-APPLY-ADDITION-TRANSACTION
                ELSE
                    PERFORM 410-WRITE-ERROR-TRANSACTION
            ELSE
                PERFORM 420-APPLY-ADDITION-TRANSACTION
        ELSE
            IF MT-CHANGE
                IF IM-ITEM-NUMBER = MT-ITEM-NUMBER
                    IF NOT MASTER-DELETED
                        PERFORM 440-APPLY-CHANGE-TRANSACTION
                    ELSE
                        PERFORM 410-WRITE-ERROR-TRANSACTION
                ELSE
                    PERFORM 410-WRITE-ERROR-TRANSACTION.
*
 360-APPLY-DELETION-TRANSACTION.
*
    MOVE 'Y'              TO MASTER-DELETED-SWITCH.
    MOVE DELETE-MESSAGE TO ML-ACTION.
    ADD 1                TO DELETION-COUNT.
    PERFORM 370-PRINT-MAINTENANCE-LINE.
*
    .
    .
    .
*
 420-APPLY-ADDITION-TRANSACTION.
*
    IF NOT MASTER-DELETED
        MOVE INVENTORY-MASTER-RECORD TO HELD-MASTER-RECORD
        MOVE 'Y' TO MASTER-HELD-FOR-ADDITION-SWITCH
    ELSE
        MOVE 'N' TO MASTER-DELETED-SWITCH.
    PERFORM 430-FORMAT-ADDITION-RECORD.
    MOVE ADD-MESSAGE      TO ML-ACTION.
    ADD 1                 TO ADDITION-COUNT.
    PERFORM 370-PRINT-MAINTENANCE-LINE.
*
```

Figure 11-7   The COBOL code for the critical modules of the sequential file-maintenance program (part 3 of 4)

```
430-FORMAT-ADDITION-RECORD.
*
      MOVE MT-ITEM-NUMBER            TO IM-ITEM-NUMBER.
      MOVE MT-ITEM-DESCRIPTION       TO IM-ITEM-DESCRIPTION.
      MOVE MT-UNIT-COST              TO IM-UNIT-COST.
      MOVE MT-UNIT-PRICE             TO IM-UNIT-PRICE.
      MOVE MT-ON-HAND-BALANCE        TO IM-ON-HAND-BALANCE.
      MOVE ZERO                      TO IM-SALES-THIS-MONTH
                                        IM-RECEIPTS-THIS-MONTH
                                        IM-SALES-THIS-YEAR
                                        IM-RECEIPTS-THIS-YEAR.
*
440-APPLY-CHANGE-TRANSACTION.
*
      PERFORM 450-CHANGE-OLD-MASTER.
      MOVE CHANGE-MESSAGE TO ML-ACTION.
      ADD 1                    TO CHANGE-COUNT.
      PERFORM 370-PRINT-MAINTENANCE-LINE.
*
      .
      .
      .
```

Figure 11-7   The COBOL code for the critical modules of the sequential file-maintenance program (part 4 of 4)

To better understand the nature of a sequential update or file-maintenance program, look back at the sequential update program in chapter 2 (figures 2-10 through 2-12). Since this program processes only one type of transaction, its structure and code are relatively simple. If you contrast this with the structure and code in figures 11-6 and 11-7, you can begin to appreciate the range of logical difficulties that you can encounter when you develop sequential update and maintenance programs.

Model program 3: A random update program with an internal sort
Another typical business program is a random update program. In this type of program, the *key field* in each transaction is used to directly access the related master record. If the master record is found, it is updated based on the transaction data, after which it is rewritten on the file. If the master record can't be found, it indicates an error condition. If the transactions haven't been edited in a previous run, they should be edited in the update program so invalid records won't be used to update master records.

On large systems, you often code a sort within an application program like an edit or a random update program. This is usually more efficient than sorting in one run and editing or updating in a separate run. To show you how the use of a COBOL sort affects a program's design, this next model program requires an internal sort in combination with a random update.

Figure 11-8 presents the program specifications for this model program. Here, an indexed master file is to be updated based on receipts to inventory. To improve the efficiency of this program, the transactions are to be sorted into the master-file sequence before they are processed. Then, this program is supposed to be written so each updated master record will only be read and written once no matter how many transactions apply to it.

Figure 11-9 is a structure chart for this program. If you haven't read chapter 5 yet, the top two levels of this chart may seem awkward to you. As I explained in chapter 5, though, the COBOL SORT statement forces this structure upon you. If the program didn't require a sort, it would have the structure represented by modules 300 through 800. Then, module 300 would be the top-level module of the program.

After the records have been sorted, module 300 performs module 600 until there are no more transactions. Each time module 600 is executed, it gets a transaction. In this case, the verb *get* means to read a transaction, edit it, and write a line on the invalid transaction listing if the transaction is invalid. If the transaction is valid, module 600 calls module 690 to apply the transaction to the master record, and it calls module 700 to write the transaction on the valid transaction file. When all the transaction records for a master record have been processed, module 600 calls module 710 to rewrite the master record on the master file.

Figure 11-10 gives the COBOL code for the critical modules of this program. As you can see, module 000 contains this SORT statement:

```
SORT SORTFILE
    ON ASCENDING KEY SF-ITEM-NUMBER
    USING RCPTTRAN
    OUTPUT PROCEDURE IS 300-PROCESS-SORTED-TRAN-FILE.
```

In other words, the SORT statement itself will read the transaction file (a dummy module), sort it (another dummy module), and then transfer control to the output procedure module. If an input procedure was used in the SORT statement, the get-transaction-file module wouldn't be a dummy module, but the sort module will always be a dummy module. This is explained in detail in chapter 5.

As you might expect, module 600 is the most complicated module in the program. The second most complicated module in this program is module 630, which edits the transaction records. Part of the complexity in both of these modules has to do with the requirement to read and write each updated master record only once so object program efficiency is improved. Without this requirement, the COBOL code would be much simpler.

Program: INV2300   UPDATE INVENTORY FILE   Page: 1

Designer: Anne Prince   Date: 08-23-84

Input/output specifications

File	Description	Use
RCPTTRAN	Receipt transaction file	Input
INVMAST	Inventory master file	Update
VRCPTRN	Valid receipt transaction file	Output
IRCPTLST	Print file: Invalid inventory receipt listing	Output
SORTFILE	Sorted inventory receipt transaction file	Output

Process specifications

The inventory master file has indexed file organization. It is a large
file with low receipt activity.

The input file of receipt transactions is in a random order. Before
the transactions are processed, they should be sorted into item-number
sequence.

For object program efficiency, the program should only read and write a
master record once for each group of transactions that affect the
master record.

The receipts must be edited and only valid receipts should be used to
update the master records. The error code on the invalid listing will
indicate only the first field that is invalid in each invalid record.

The totals for the update run should be printed on a separate page of
printer output.

Figure 11-8   The program specifications for the random update program (part 1 of 3)

Program: INV2300   UPDATE INVENTORY FILE   Page: 2

Designer: Anne Prince   Date: 08-23-84

Process specifications

The basic processing requirements follow:

   Sort the receipt transaction file in ascending item-number order.

   Do until the end of the sorted transaction file:

1.   Get the next transaction.

2.   Edit the transaction fields.

3.   If the transaction is not valid, print a line on the invalid inventory receipts listing.

4.   If the transaction is valid and has the same item number as the previous transaction, add the receipt quantity in the transaction record to the on hand balance in the master record, and write a valid transaction record.

5.   If the transaction is valid and has a different item number than the previous transaction, rewrite the current master record on the master file and then process the new transaction.

   Print the transaction totals on a separate page.

Editing rules for receipt transactions:

RT-ITEM-NUMBER   Must be a valid number in the inventory master file.

RT-VENDOR-NUMBER   Must be numeric and greater than zero.

RT-RECEIPT-DATE   Must be a valid date in the form MMDDYY and the year must be equal to the current year.

RT-RECEIPT-QUANTITY   Must be numeric and greater than zero.

Figure 11-8   The program specifications for the random update program (part 2 of 3)

Print Chart

Document name Invalid Inventory Receipts Listing **Date** 8-23-84

Program name INV2300   **Designer** Anne Prince

Print positions near the top right:

```
PAGE: ZZ9
INV2300
```

Record Name	Layout content
1 Heading-Line-1	DATE: 99/99/99 ... MIKE MURACH & ASSOCIATES, INC.
2 Heading-Line-2	TIME: 99:99 XX
3 Heading-Line-3	INVALID INVENTORY RECEIPTS LISTING
4	
5 Heading-Line-4	ITEM VENDOR DATE ERROR
6 Heading-Line-5	NUMBER NUMBER RECEIVED QUANTITY CODE
7	
8 Invalid-Transaction-Line	XXXXXX XXX XX/XX/XX ZZ9 FIELD 1
9	
10	XXXXXX XXX XX/XX/XX ZZ9 FIELD 2
11	
12	XXXXXX XXX XX/XX/XX ZZ9 FIELD 3
13	
14	XXXXXX XXX XX/XX/XX ZZ9 FIELD 4
15	
16	
17	
18	
19	
20	Total page date to be
21	printed after the
22	first two lines of
23	the standard headings.
24	
25 Total-Line-1	SUMMARY FOR INVENTORY RECEIPTS RUN
26	
27 Total-Line-2	ZZ,ZZ9 TRANSACTIONS READ
28 Total-Line-3	ZZ,ZZ9 VALID TRANSACTIONS
29 Total-Line-4	ZZ,ZZ9 INVALID TRANSACTIONS
30	
31–50	

Figure 11-8   The program specifications for the random update program (part 3 of 3)

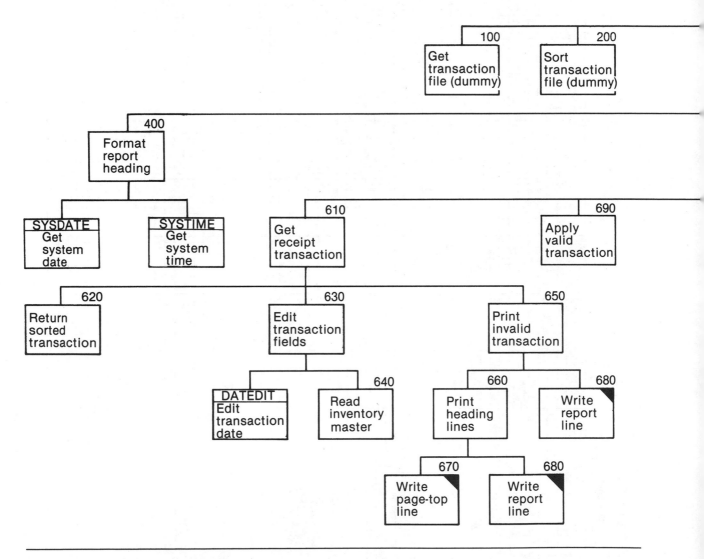

Figure 11-9   The structure chart for the random update program

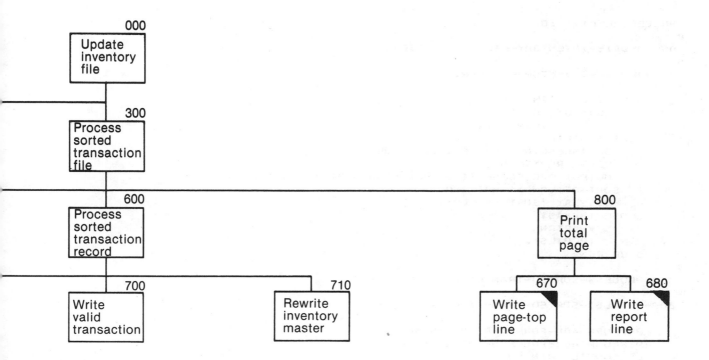

```
PROCEDURE DIVISION.
*
 000-UPDATE-INVENTORY-FILE     SECTION.
*
 000-UPDATE-INVENTORY-FILE-P.
*
     OPEN I-O    INVMAST
          OUTPUT VRCPTRN
                 IRCPTLST.
     SORT SORTFILE
         ON ASCENDING KEY SF-ITEM-NUMBER
         USING RCPTTRAN
         OUTPUT PROCEDURE IS 300-PROCESS-SORTED-TRAN-FILE.
     IF SORT-RETURN IS NOT ZERO
         DISPLAY 'SORT FAILED'.
     CLOSE INVMAST
           VRCPTRN
           IRCPTLST.
     STOP RUN.
*
 300-PROCESS-SORTED-TRAN-FILE     SECTION.
*
 300-PROCESS-SORTED-TRAN-FILE-P.
*
     PERFORM 400-FORMAT-REPORT-HEADING.
     PERFORM 600-PROCESS-SORTED-TRAN-RECORD
         UNTIL TRAN-EOF.
     PERFORM 800-PRINT-TOTAL-PAGE.
     GO TO 300-EXIT,
*
 400-FORMAT-REPORT-HEADING.
*
        .
        .
        .
*
 600-PROCESS-SORTED-TRAN-RECORD.
*
     MOVE 'N' TO VALID-TRAN-SWITCH.
     PERFORM 610-GET-RECEIPT-TRANSACTION
         UNTIL VALID-TRAN.
     IF NOT TRAN-EOF
        IF FIRST-RECORD
           MOVE RT-ITEM-NUMBER          TO OLD-ITEM-NUMBER
           MOVE NEXT-INVENTORY-RECORD TO INVENTORY-MASTER-RECORD
           MOVE 'N'                    TO FIRST-RECORD-SWITCH.
     IF NOT TRAN-EOF
        IF RT-ITEM-NUMBER = OLD-ITEM-NUMBER
            PERFORM 690-APPLY-VALID-TRANSACTION
            PERFORM 700-WRITE-VALID-TRANSACTION.
     IF RT-ITEM-NUMBER > OLD-ITEM-NUMBER
         PERFORM 710-REWRITE-INVENTORY-MASTER
         IF NOT TRAN-EOF
            MOVE NEXT-INVENTORY-RECORD TO INVENTORY-MASTER-RECORD
            MOVE RT-ITEM-NUMBER         TO OLD-ITEM-NUMBER
            PERFORM 690-APPLY-VALID-TRANSACTION
            PERFORM 700-WRITE-VALID-TRANSACTION.
```

Figure 11-10   The COBOL code for the critical modules of the random update program (part 1 of 2)

```
*
 610-GET-RECEIPT-TRANSACTION.
*
     MOVE 'Y' TO VALID-TRAN-SWITCH.
     PERFORM 620-RETURN-SORTED-TRANSACTION.
     IF NOT TRAN-EOF
         ADD 1 TO TRANSACTION-COUNT
         PERFORM 630-EDIT-TRANSACTION-FIELDS
         IF NOT VALID-TRAN
             PERFORM 650-PRINT-INVALID-TRANSACTION.
*
 620-RETURN-SORTED-TRANSACTION.
*
     RETURN SORTFILE INTO RECEIPT-TRANSACTION
         AT END
             MOVE HIGH-VALUE TO RT-ITEM-NUMBER
             MOVE 'Y' TO TRAN-EOF-SWITCH.
*
 630-EDIT-TRANSACTION-FIELDS.
*
     MOVE 'Y' TO MASTER-FOUND-SWITCH.
     IF RT-ITEM-NUMBER > OLD-ITEM-NUMBER
         MOVE RT-ITEM-NUMBER TO IR-ITEM-NUMBER
         PERFORM 640-READ-INVENTORY-MASTER.
     IF NOT MASTER-FOUND
         MOVE 'FIELD-1' TO ITL-ERROR-CODE
         MOVE 'N'       TO VALID-TRAN-SWITCH
     ELSE
         IF          RT-VENDOR-NUMBER NOT NUMERIC
                 OR RT-VENDOR-NUMBER NOT > ZERO
             MOVE 'FIELD-2' TO ITL-ERROR-CODE
             MOVE 'N'           TO VALID-TRAN-SWITCH
         ELSE
             CALL 'DATEDIT' USING RT-RECEIPT-DATE
                                  VALID-DATE-SWITCH
             IF NOT VALID-DATE
                 MOVE 'FIELD-3' TO ITL-ERROR-CODE
                 MOVE 'N'           TO VALID-TRAN-SWITCH
             ELSE IF RT-RECEIPT-YEAR NOT = TODAYS-YEAR
                 MOVE 'FIELD-3' TO ITL-ERROR-CODE
                 MOVE 'N'           TO VALID-TRAN-SWITCH
             ELSE
                 IF          RT-RECEIPT-QUANTITY NOT NUMERIC
                         OR RT-RECEIPT-QUANTITY NOT > ZERO
                     MOVE 'FIELD-4' TO ITL-ERROR-CODE
                     MOVE 'N'           TO VALID-TRAN-SWITCH.
*
 640-READ-INVENTORY-MASTER.
*
     READ INVMAST INTO NEXT-INVENTORY-RECORD
         INVALID KEY
             MOVE 'N' TO MASTER-FOUND-SWITCH.
     .
     .
     .
```

Figure 11-10   The COBOL code for the critical modules of the random update program (part 2 of 2)

Module 600 compares the item number in the transaction record (RT-ITEM-NUMBER) with the item number of the previous transaction record (OLD-ITEM-NUMBER) to determine when all the transactions for an item have been processed. If these item numbers are equal, it means that the transaction applies to the master record that has already been read. But if RT-ITEM-NUMBER is greater than OLD-ITEM-NUMBER, it means that all the records for the master record have been processed so the master record should be rewritten onto the master file. Note that this module doesn't call module 640 to read a master record because a master record is read as part of the editing routine for a transaction.

Module 630 also compares RT-ITEM-NUMBER with OLD-ITEM-NUMBER to determine when a transaction applies to a new master record. If the item number in the transaction is greater than the old item number, this module calls module 640 to read the new master record. If the master record is found, it continues by editing the other fields in the transaction record. If the master record isn't found, the transaction is treated as invalid.

To better understand the nature of a random update or file-maintenance program, look back at the random update program in chapter 3 (figures 3-13 through 3-15). Since this program doesn't edit the input transactions and since it doesn't include an internal sort, its structure and code are relatively simple. If you contrast this with the structure and code in figures 11-9 and 11-10, you can begin to appreciate the range of logical difficulties that you can encounter when you develop random update and maintenance programs.

Three basic program structures

Now that you're familiar with the model programs, I want you to see the basic structure that underlies the specific requirements in these programs. It is this basic structure that you can reuse from one program to the next.

Here, then, are the three basic structures of the model programs I've just presented. These structure charts don't show the lower-level modules that you'd have in a production program. And they use general module names. This should make it easier for you to see how one model program applies in a general way to all programs of its type.

The basic structure of an edit program   Figure 11-11 shows you the basic structure of an edit program that you can derive from the structure chart in figure 11-2. This design is for one type of record in a single transaction file. But with minor modifications it can be used for editing two or more different types of records in one or more files.

The basic structure of a sequential file-maintenance program
Figure 11-12 presents the basic structure of a sequential file-

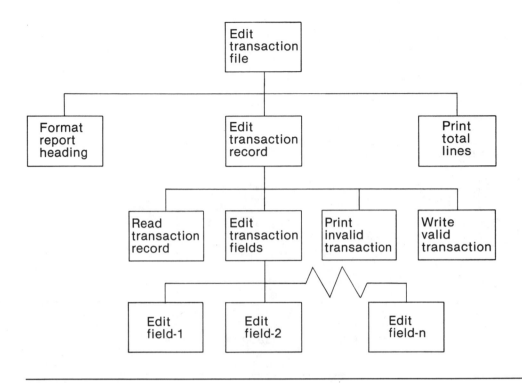

Figure 11-11 The basic structure of an edit program

maintenance program that you can derive from the structure chart in figure 11-6. It can easily be modified so it updates a master record based on one or more transactions. In fact, as you should realize by now, an update program usually has a simpler structure than a file-maintenance program does.

The basic structure of a random update program   Figure 11-13 gives the basic structure of a random update program that you can derive from the structure chart in figure 11-9. It can easily be modified so that it becomes a file-maintenance program that provides for changes, deletions, and additions.

How to reuse the model programs

Once you understand the basic structures that the model programs contain, you can use their designs as the basis for many different programs. Not only can you use one structure chart as the basis for designing a similar program, but you can combine elements taken from two or more structure charts to create the design for a new program. To give you a better idea about this, let me present two examples.

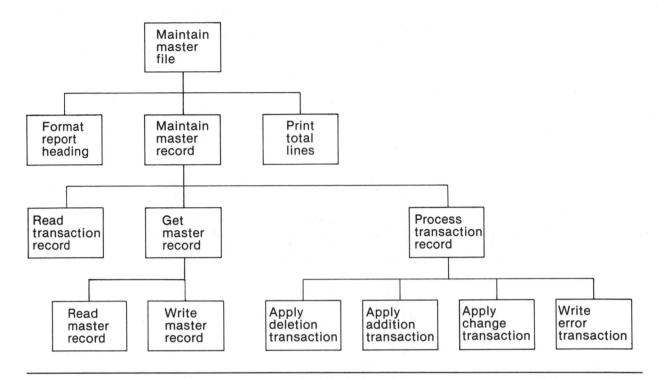

Figure 11-12   The basic structure of a sequential file-maintenance program

A sequential update program with editing   If you have to write a program that combines sequential updating with editing, you can combine portions of the structure chart in figure 11-2 with portions of the structure chart in figure 11-6. For instance, the structure chart in figure 11-14 is for a program that edits transaction records and then uses the valid transactions to update records in an inventory master file. Note that the print-invalid-transaction module is a common module in this program. That's because a transaction can be found to be invalid either during editing (if it contains invalid data) or during updating (if there's not a master record that matches it). Since this program doesn't provide for adding records to a file and deleting records from it, the update portion of the structure is simpler than the one in figure 11-6. Similarly, since the program edits only one type of transaction, the edit portion of the program is simpler than the one in figure 11-2.

A random update program that updates three master files   Figure 11-15 presents a structure chart for a random update program that updates three master files for each valid sales transaction. This structure assumes that the transaction file is in sequence by customer number, so for object program efficiency the program should only read and write one customer master record for each group of transac-

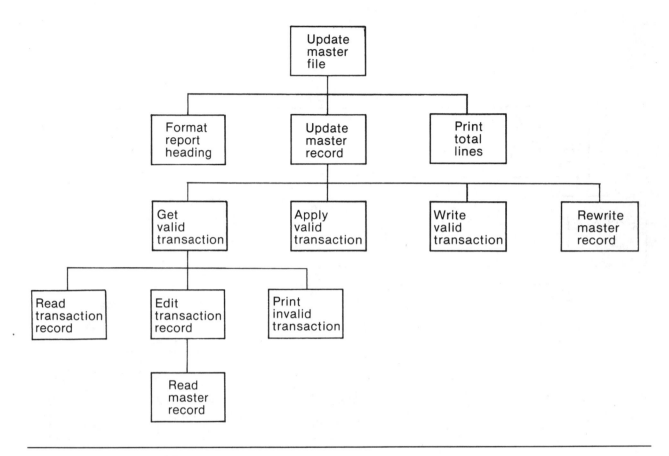

Figure 11-13 The basic structure of a random update program

tions with the same customer number. On the other hand, the transaction file isn't in sequence by salesman number or branch number, so these master records can be read and written once for each transaction. Can you see how you can derive this structure from the chart in figure 11-9?

Module 230 in this program calls modules 240, 250, and 260 to read three master records for each transaction. This helps determine whether the transaction is valid. If the edit leg finds the related record in each file, the transaction is considered valid and processing continues. Otherwise, the program prints a line on the invalid transaction listing.

Module 310 applies a valid transaction to the three master records read by modules 240, 250, and 260. For object program efficiency, the customer record is updated in storage, but it isn't rewritten on the master file until all of its transactions have been processed. That's why module 370 isn't subordinate to module 320. In contrast, the update modules for the salesman and branch records call rewrite modules so the master records are rewritten on the master files each time they are updated.

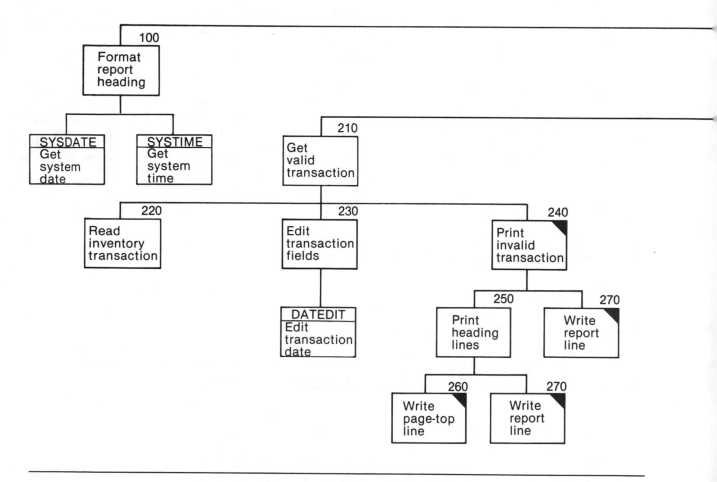

Figure 11-14   A structure chart for a sequential update program that edits the transaction records

The benefits of this design method

I hope by now you can see the benefits of this design method. Once you have your own library of model programs, you can often reuse entire structure charts, deleting modules that you don't need and adding modules that you do need. Otherwise, you can combine a portion of one structure chart with a portion of another to fit the requirements of the program you're developing.

Although this by itself can lead to a significant increase in programming productivity, this also means that you can reuse COBOL code from one program to another. The code in control modules, for

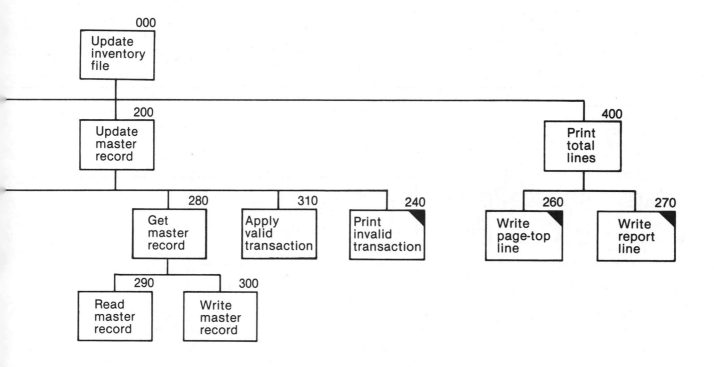

example, can often be reused by changing only a few of the data or procedure names. And the code in many edit, search, and I/O modules can also be reused with only minor modifications. In fact, we believe that you should code few modules from scratch. We believe that you should derive at least half the code in every new program you write from code that is available in old programs. If you do this, you can achieve impressive levels of programming productivity.

The presentation in this chapter should also show you how easy it is to modify a structured program if enhancements are requested. If, for example, the edit program is supposed to be changed so it edits a third type of record, you add a few modules to the structure chart,

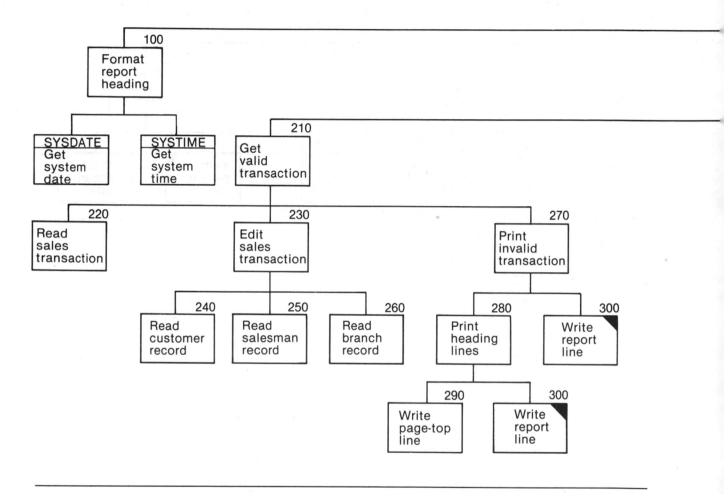

Figure 11-15   A structure chart for a random update program that updates three master records for each valid transaction

change one of the control modules, code the new modules, and the enhancement is done. Since you don't have to change any of the other modules in the program, you can make an enhancement like this with maximum efficiency. Similarly, it's easy to modify programs when editing rules change, print formats change, and so on.

When you plan the code for the modules of a program or when you actually code them, you will sometimes find that you will want to change the design. For instance, you may want to add another

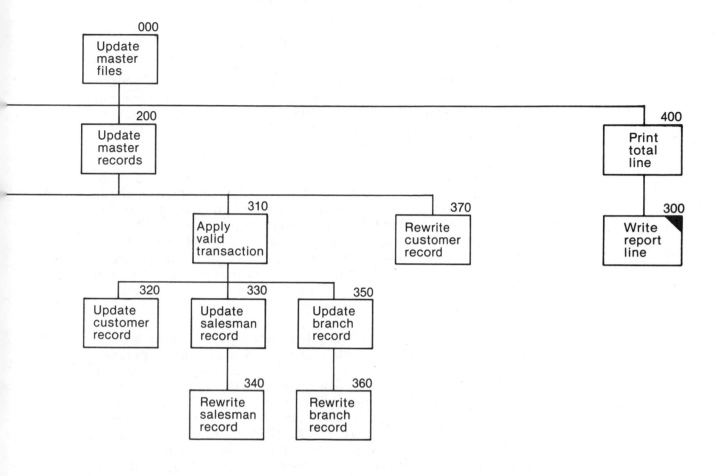

module to a chart. Or you may want to combine two or more modules into a single module. In some cases, if you find that a control module is extremely difficult to code, you may want to add some subordinate modules to the structure chart. When you decide to make one of these changes, you simply modify the structure chart and continue. That too is a benefit of this design method. You can make changes to the design of a program as you implement it without paying a price in terms of reduced productivity.

Discussion

At this point, you should be able to create structure charts of your own for edit, update, and maintenance programs. When you create new charts, you should base them on the model programs and basic program structures presented in this chapter. After you do this for a while, you can develop your own library of model programs, one for each type of program you write.

At first, you should expect to struggle a bit when you design a new program. Before you will be able to design a program with maximum efficiency, you need to study the model programs and the basic structures presented in this chapter. In particular, you need to understand the COBOL code for the critical modules of each program. Although I could describe the structure and code of the model programs in more detail, I think it's best that you figure out how the structures work and why the critical modules are coded the way they are. Once you do this, you'll be able to reuse the structures and code in your own programs.

You should realize, though, that this chapter is just an introduction to the structures of edit, update, and maintenance programs. That's why we offer two other books on structured programming for the COBOL programmer. The first, called *How to Design and Develop COBOL Programs*, presents all aspects of structured programming, including other techniques for design, module planning, and coding. The second, called *The COBOL Programmer's Handbook*, presents complete guidelines for developing structured programs as well as seven model programs that you can use as the basis for developing your own programs.

We recommend that you use the *Handbook* in conjunction with this course because our students have found that it helps them learn more quickly. Later on, we recommend that you read *How to Design and Develop COBOL Programs* because it deals with the questions of design and development that can't be covered in a COBOL course.

Terminology

edit program	control field
validation program	matched records
verification program	unmatched transaction
update program	unmatched master
file-maintenance program	key field

Objective

Given the specifications for an edit, update, or file-maintenance program, design an acceptable structure chart for it and write the pseudocode for its critical modules.

Chapter 12

What else an effective
COBOL programmer must know

You should read this chapter after you've read the other eleven chapters in this book. Its purpose is to show you what else a COBOL programmer must know in order to be effective. When you complete this book, you should be able to develop batch COBOL programs that prepare reports, edit data, and update sequential, indexed, or relative files. You should also be able to use the sort/merge feature of COBOL within these programs. Even so, there's more to COBOL programming than that.

In brief, effective COBOL programmers must know how to use all of the standard COBOL language that is available to them on their systems. They must know how to use the non-standard COBOL features that make it possible for them to write interactive programs. If their system uses data base software, they must know how to access data bases in their COBOL programs. They must know how to make use of the features that their operating system provides. And they must know the programming techniques that let them develop reliable programs that are easy to code, test, debug, and maintain.

Standard COBOL and its features

Figure 12-1 summarizes the COBOL modules that are defined in the 1974 and 1985 ANS standards. In general, both sets of standards consist of the same modules. However, the table handling module of 1974 COBOL is part of the nucleus module in 1985 COBOL. Similarly, the "library" module of 1974 COBOL is called the "source text manipulation" module in 1985 COBOL.

Each set of standards provides for several levels of language in each module, as shown by the "levels" columns in figure 12-1. For

Module name	1974 levels	1985 levels	Remarks
Nucleus	3	3	The 1985 nucleus includes table handling code.
Table handling	2	0	Included in the nucleus in 1985 COBOL.
Sequential I-O	2	3	
Relative I-O	2	2	
Indexed I-O	2	2	
Library	2	2	Called "source text manipulation" in 1985 COBOL. Provides for the use of the COPY library.
Inter-program communication	2	3	Provides for the use of subprograms.
Sort-merge	2	2	
Report Writer	1	1	Not required in a 1985 compiler.
Communication	2	2	Not required in a 1985 compiler.
Segmentation	2	2	Not required in a 1985 compiler, and it will be deleted from the next set of standards.
Debug	2	2	Not required in a 1985 compiler, and it will be deleted from the next set of standards.

Note: All of the modules listed are required in a "full standard" 1974 compiler. However, only the modules above the line are required in a "high subset" 1985 compiler; the modules below the line are optional.

Figure 12-1   The modules of 1974 and 1985 ANS COBOL

instance, there are three levels to the nucleus in both the 1974 and 1985 standards. In contrast, there are two levels for the inter-program communication module in the 1974 standards, but three levels in the 1985 standards.

Each level consists of more COBOL elements than the level below it. For example, the simple DIVIDE statement is part of level 1 of the nucleus module, while the DIVIDE statement with the RE-MAINDER clause is part of level 2. To be classified as "standard," a minimum 1974 compiler only has to provide for the lowest level in each of the first three modules listed in figure 12-1, and a 1985 compiler only has to provide for the lowest level in the nucleus, sequential I-O, and inter-program communication modules.

To be classified as a "full standard" compiler, a 1974 compiler has to provide for the highest level in all of the modules. Similarly, to be classified as a "high subset" compiler, a 1985 compiler has to provide for the highest level in all the modules above the line in figure 12-1; the modules below the line are optional.

Many compilers, though, are neither minimum nor full standard or high subset compilers. Instead, they provide for a subset of COBOL elements that are above the minimum standard but below the full, or high, standard. That's why you must study the COBOL manuals for your system to find out exactly what language it provides.

Structured ANS COBOL, Part 1 and *Part 2* present the essential elements in the first eight modules in figure 12-1. In general, *Part 1* presents a subset of the elements in the nucleus, table handling, sequential I-O, indexed I-O, library, and inter-program communication modules. Then, *Part 2* presents the rest of the essential elements in these modules, plus the essential elements in the relative I-O and sort-merge modules.

I think it's obvious which modules of COBOL are taught by chapters 2 through 8 in this book since each of these chapters corresponds to one COBOL module. Then, chapter 9 presents the character manipulation elements that are defined in the nucleus module of COBOL, and chapter 10 presents the 1985 COBOL elements, which are also defined in the nucleus module.

If you look at the four modules below the line in figure 12-1, you can see that two will not be included in subsequent sets of standards: the segmentation module and the debug module. Neither of these modules is used much today, and we expect them to be used even less frequently in the future. As a result, we don't present them in our COBOL series. For the same reasons, we don't present the communication module in our series. On the other hand, we believe that effective COBOL programmers should know how to use the Report Writer module if it is available on their systems.

The Report Writer module   The Report Writer module of COBOL lets you define a report in detail in the Data Division. Then, you can prepare the report by using just a few statements in the Procedure Division.

For instance, figure 12-2 presents the structure chart for a multilevel report preparation program using Report Writer. This chart is for one of the programs that we presented without Report Writer in *Structured ANS COBOL, Part 1* (figure 12-16). In this case, the program with Report Writer requires only four modules, while the program without Report Writer requires eleven different modules. Similarly, the Procedure Division of the program with

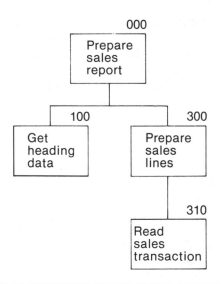

Figure 12-2   The structure chart for a multilevel report preparation program when using the Report Writer feature of COBOL

Report Writer is less than one-third as many lines of code as the Procedure Division without Report Writer. Finally, the number of lines of code in the Data Division of the Report Writer program is actually less than the number of lines in the program without Report Writer. As a result, the complete program with Report Writer is only 65 percent as long as the complete program without Report Writer.

Because it lets you reduce the number of modules in your structure charts and the number of lines of code in your programs, we believe the Report Writer module will help you increase your productivity. Nevertheless, many compilers don't provide this module and many COBOL shops don't use it even when the compiler does provide it. That's why Report Writer isn't one of the required modules in the 1985 standards. If you do need to learn this module, our *Report Writer* text will help you learn it quickly and use it effectively.

COBOL for interactive programs

If you refer again to figure 12-1, you can see that neither the 1974 nor the 1985 COBOL standards provide for interactive programs. Today, however, most systems are interactive, so almost all COBOL compilers provide non-standard language that lets a program send data to a terminal screen and receive data from a terminal keyboard.

To illustrate one way that this is done, figure 12-3 shows some interactive COBOL code for a Wang VS compiler. This code sends a customer entry screen to a user's terminal. Then, after the user enters data on the terminal using the keyboard, the program receives this

```
01   CUSTOMER-ENTRY-SCREEN  DISPLAY-WS.
*
     05   FILLER             LINE 1
                             COLUMN 1
                             PIC X(80)
                             SOURCE DSP-HEADING-LINE.
     05   FILLER             LINE 6
                             COLUMN 2
                             PIC X(14)
                             VALUE "CUSTOMER CODE:".
     05   CES-CUST-CODE      LINE 6
                             COLUMN 19
                             PIC X(5)
                             SOURCE CM-CUSTOMER-CODE.
     05   FILLER             LINE 8
                             COLUMN 2
                             PIC X(5)
                             VALUE "NAME:".
     05   CES-NAME           LINE 8
                             COLUMN 19
                             PIC X(30)
                             SOURCE CM-NAME
                             OBJECT CM-NAME.
     05   FILLER             LINE 9
                             COLUMN 2
                             PIC X(8)
                             VALUE "ADDRESS:".
     05   CES-ADDRESS        LINE 9
                             COLUMN 19
                             PIC X(30)
                             SOURCE CM-ADDRESS
                             OBJECT CM-ADDRESS.
          .
          .
     05   FILLER             LINE 24
                             COLUMN 1
                             PIC X(80)
                             SOURCE DSP-MESSAGE-LINE.
*
          .
          .
420-ACCEPT-CUSTOMER-DATA.
*
     MOVE "PF16 = CANCEL ENTRY" TO DSP-MESSAGE-AREA.
     MOVE SCREEN-ORDER-AREA
         TO ORDER-AREA OF CUSTOMER-ENTRY-SCREEN.
     DISPLAY AND READ CUSTOMER-ENTRY-SCREEN ON SCREEN
         PFKEY 16
         ON PFKEY 16
             MOVE "Y" TO CANCEL-ENTRY-SW.
     SET WCC-BEEP IN SOA-WCC OFF.
*
```

Figure 12-3   Getting data from a terminal using Wang VS COBOL

```
1300-SEND-CUSTOMER-SCREEN SECTION.
*
      PERFORM 1310-SET-ENTRY-FACS.
      MOVE CWA-DATE TO CDM-D-DATE.
      EXEC CICS
          SEND MAP('MT21MP2')
               MAPSET('MT21SET')
               FROM(CUSTOMER-DATA-MAP)
               CURSOR
          END-EXEC.
*
         .
         .
         .
*
  2100-RECEIVE-CUSTOMER-SCREEN SECTION.
*
      EXEC CICS
          HANDLE AID CLEAR(2100-CLEAR-KEY)
                     ANYKEY(2100-ANYKEY)
      END-EXEC.
      EXEC CICS
          RECEIVE MAP('MT21MP2')
                  MAPSET('MT21SET')
                  INTO(CUSTOMER-DATA-MAP)
      END-EXEC.
      GO TO 2100-EXIT.
*
```

Figure 12-4   Getting data from a terminal using CICS on an IBM mainframe

data. In module 420, the shaded statement is the one that sends and receives the screen data. It is the DISPLAY AND READ statement. Otherwise, the Procedure Division code is standard COBOL. Similarly, the Data Division uses only a few non-standard clauses to define the fields in the terminal screen that is being sent and received. Otherwise, it looks a lot like standard Data Division code.

Figure 12-4 shows another way that data can be sent to and received from terminals. It shows some Procedure Division code when using CICS for handling terminal screens on an IBM mainframe. Here, one COBOL module is used to send the screen to the terminal; another module is used to receive the data from the terminal. The statements that send and receive the data are shaded in this figure. They are EXEC statements that call subprograms to send and receive the data.

In general, each type of system supports interactive processing in COBOL in a different way. Most microcomputers and minicomputers provide language for interactive processing that is similar to standard

COBOL, but most mainframes provide for it by using language that is similar to CALL statements. If you're going to develop interactive programs, you have to learn how to use the interactive provisions of your system.

COBOL for processing data bases

Data base software lets you organize the data that your system requires in a way that is both logical and efficient. The resulting collection of data is called a *data base*. I'm not going to describe data bases at all here. Just be aware that they're organized differently than the records and files you've learned to handle in this book.

Data base software is used on most large systems today. In the future, we expect data base software to be used on medium and even small systems. Nevertheless, neither the 1974 nor the 1985 COBOL standards provide language for processing data bases. As a result, the COBOL compiler for a system that uses data base software must have some other way to access its data bases.

Figure 12-5 illustrates one way that a COBOL program can access the data in a data base. This is part of a COBOL program for an IBM mainframe that accesses a data base using DL/I (Data Language I). If you study this code, you can see that it is all standard COBOL since the access to the data base is made by calling a subprogram with a standard CALL statement (shaded). To access the data base using DL/I, you must learn what subprograms to call, what fields must be passed to each subprogram, and so on.

Although many systems use CALLs to access data bases, some provide a special language for it. If you're going to develop programs that access your system's data bases, you must learn how to use whatever facility your system provides.

The operating system and its features

To be an effective COBOL programmer, it's not enough to master the COBOL for your system. You must also learn how to use the operating system and its features. This includes its interactive editor, its job control language, its debugging aids, and its utilities.

Although this book doesn't show you how to use interactive editors and job control language, you probably have used them to develop the case studies for this course. An interactive editor lets you enter your COBOL programs into the system and modify them later on. It may also let you compile and test your COBOL programs. In addition, you usually need to know the job control language for your system so you can test and run your programs.

The debug module of COBOL isn't presented in this series because most operating systems provide debugging aids that are more

```
LINKAGE SECTION.
*
 01  INVENTORY-PCB-MASK.
*
     05   IPCB-DBD-NAME              PIC X(8).
     05   IPCB-SEGMENT-LEVEL         PIC XX.
     05   IPCB-STATUS-CODE           PIC XX.
     05   IPCB-PROC-OPTIONS          PIC X(4).
     05   FILLER                     PIC S9(5)          COMP.
     05   IPCP-SEGMENT-NAME          PIC X(8).
     05   IPCB-KEY-LENGTH            PIC S9(5)          COMP.
     05   IPCB-NUMB-SENS-SEGS        PIC S9(5)          COMP.
     05   IPCB-KEY                   PIC X(11).
*
     .
     .
     .
*
 110-GET-INVENTORY-SEGMENT.
*
     CALL 'CBLTDLI' USING DLI-GN
                          INVENTORY-PCB-MASK
                          SEGMENT-I-O-AREA.
     IF IPCB-STATUS-CODE = 'GB'
         MOVE 'Y' TO END-OF-DATA-BASE-SW
     ELSE
         IF          IPCB-STATUS-CODE NOT = 'GA'
             AND IPCB-STATUS-CODE NOT = SPACE
           MOVE 'Y' TO END-OF-DATA-BASE-SW
           DISPLAY 'INV2100  I  1  DATA BASE ERROR - STATUS CODE '
                   IPCB-STATUS-CODE.
*
```

Figure 12-5   Accessing a data base using DL/I on an IBM mainframe

efficient than it is. The debugging aids may be part of the interactive editor, or they may be separate programs within the operating system. In any event, you should find out what debugging aids are available on your system and master them. If you do, they can save you many hours of debugging time each month.

Utilities are general-purpose programs that are provided as part of an operating system. They let you list the data in files, generate test data, and so on. Because they can help you during testing, you should learn how to use the utilities that are available on your system.

Programming techniques

Some programmers do a poor job even though they master the COBOL language and the features of their operating systems. In other words, mastering COBOL and an operating system isn't enough to make you an effective COBOL programmer. In addition, you must learn how to get complete program specifications, how to design programs, how to plan the modules of a program, how to test a program, and so on. I introduced you to some of these techniques in chapter 1, but there's much more to them than that.

By the mid-1970's, many people realized that most programmers were working at a dismally low level of performance. As a result, many techniques were developed that were designed to improve program quality and programmer productivity. Unfortunately, most COBOL shops didn't make dramatic improvements in programmer performance by changing to these techniques, and there's little doubt that most programmers today still use techniques that are inefficient and ineffective. But programming doesn't have to be that way.

If you're interested in learning techniques that have proven to be effective in thousands of COBOL shops throughout the country, let me recommend two books. The first is a text called *How to Design and Develop COBOL Programs*. This 528-page book is a complete presentation of the techniques that apply to all phases of program development. It assumes that you are an experienced COBOL programmer, but you can read it any time after you complete this book. It will teach you the programming techniques that aren't usually presented in a course that teaches the COBOL language.

The second book is a reference book called *The COBOL Programmer's Handbook*. It presents complete standards for the development of COBOL programs. It also presents seven model programs—four batch and three interactive—that will show you how to apply the COBOL language to the most common types of business programs. If you use this handbook for reference as you continue your study in COBOL, we're confident that you'll learn COBOL more quickly and more completely.

Standard COBOL elements that haven't been covered in this series

In *Structured ANS COBOL, Part 1* and *Part 2*, we have tried to present all of the standard COBOL elements that you are likely to use in your shop. However, we didn't include all of the 1974 and 1985 COBOL elements. First, we excluded an element whenever we felt that the element shouldn't be used in a modern COBOL shop due to its negative effect on program quality or programmer productivity. Second, we excluded an element if we didn't think it is used in enough COBOL shops to justify its inclusion in this series.

Now, I would like to introduce you to some of the elements we haven't covered in this series. Then, if some of them are used in your shop or you discover that you have a need for some of them, you can learn how to use them on your own. In general, the excluded elements don't let you code anything that you couldn't code in some other way. Also, most of the excluded elements are easy to learn on your own.

Environment Division elements   The code in the Environment Division is used to describe the conditions in a specific operating environment. As a result, this division varies the most from one shop to another. Whenever you begin to work in a new shop, one of the first things you should find out is what you are expected to code in this division.

To give you some idea of what you can code in the Environment Division, let's start by considering the SPECIAL-NAMES paragraph of the Configuration Section. Here, you can assign names to switches that are set outside of the COBOL program, and you can assign condition names to the off and on statuses of these conditions. You can also assign names to the collating sequences that are used within a program, and you can establish a special collating sequence if a standard sequence isn't adequate for your program. If you're working outside the United States, you can establish a currency sign to be used instead of the dollar sign, and you can specify that the comma rather than the decimal point be used to separate dollars and cents. Under the 1985 standards, you can also establish symbolic characters and class names.

In the OBJECT-COMPUTER paragraph in the Configuration Section, you can identify the collating sequence to be used by the program. In the I-O-CONTROL paragraph in the Input-Output Section, you can specify three options related to rerunning programs, reusing I/O areas, and positioning tape reels. Beyond this, many compilers offer extensions to the standards that allow you to specify or establish other factors in the operating environment.

In our shop, we use COBOL extensions in the Environment Divisions of all our interactive programs. These extensions let us control the operation of interactive terminals. In our batch programs, though, we don't use any special code in the Environment Division.

Data Division elements   In *Structured ANS COBOL, Part 1*, I mentioned that you can assign a level number of 77 to items in the Working-Storage Sections of your programs. However, we recommend that you avoid using 77 levels because they imply that a data item is unrelated to any other data items. Instead, we try to show the relationships between items by defining all data items in working storage as elementary items within group items. Similarly, we avoid using 77 levels in the Linkage Sections of subprograms.

You can also use 66 levels in the Data Division to rename data items that have already been defined. However, we don't recommend the use of 66 levels because they are unnecessary. Using REDEFINES, you can rename a data item at the same time you redefine it. And if the item doesn't need to be redefined, why should it have two names?

Finally, the SIGN, SYNCHRONIZED, and JUSTIFIED clauses can be used to describe an item in the Data Division. On most systems, though, you don't need to code these clauses. The SIGN clause tells the compiler whether the sign for a field is leading or trailing, and whether it is embedded in the field or separate. If this clause isn't specified, the default for the system is assumed. The SYNC clause tells the compiler to synchronize a field with any system requirements, which we feel should be done automatically. And the JUSTIFIED clause right-justifies an alphabetic or alphanumeric field, instead of left-justifying it. Occasionally, these clauses can be useful, but we never use them in our shop.

Section names in the Procedure Division   In chapter 5, I showed you how to use *section names* in the Procedure Division of a program as required by the sort/merge feature of 1974 COBOL. You should realize, though, that section names can be used in the Procedure Division of any COBOL program. Then, the Procedure Division is divided into one or more sections, and each section is divided into one or more paragraphs. To create a section name, you code a paragraph name followed by a space and the word SECTION.

In *How to Design and Develop COBOL Programs*, we recommend that each module of a program be implemented as a single COBOL paragraph whenever that is practical. Then, you don't need to use sections at all. Sometimes, though, this isn't practical. For instance, when you develop an interactive program for an IBM mainframe using CICS, we recommend that you implement each module of the program as a section. (I won't try to explain why sections are more logical than paragraphs for a CICS program, but they are.) In any case, when sections are required, they're easy to use as illustrated by chapter 5 in this book.

Declarative Sections in the Procedure Division   You can start a Procedure Division with one or more *declarative sections*. These sections are used to handle special conditions that occur during the execution of a program. For instance, declarative sections have often been used in the past for handling various types of I/O errors. Today, however, declarative sections are used infrequently, so you probably won't use them in your shop.

The PERFORM THRU statement   In this book, the PERFORM statements are coded so they perform one paragraph. In some shops, though, PERFORM statements are coded so they perform more than one paragraph or section. For instance, this statement

```
PERFORM 210-LOAD-TABLE THRU 210-EXIT
```

performs all of the paragraphs or sections from 210-LOAD-TABLE through 210-EXIT. Since we believe each module of a program should be coded as a single paragraph or section, we don't recommend this form of coding, but some shops insist that all PERFORM statements be coded in this way.

The PERFORM TIMES statement   Occasionally, the PERFORM TIMES statement can be useful. It is coded like this:

```
PERFORM 210-CALCULATE-INTEREST
    LOAN-TERM TIMES.
```

In this example, module 210 will be executed as many times as are indicated by the integer value in LOAN-TERM. Since you can code a function like this using a PERFORM UNTIL statement, we rarely use the PERFORM TIMES statement in our shop. The limitation of the PERFORM TIMES statement is that you can't vary one or more indexes with it.

NEXT SENTENCE in an IF statement   Instead of an imperative statement, you can code the words NEXT SENTENCE in an IF statement as in this example:

```
IF INVMAST-EOF
    NEXT SENTENCE
ELSE
    PERFORM 320-CALCULATE-INVENTORY-FIELDS
    PERFORM 330-PREPARE-INVESTMENT-LINE.
```

In this case, if the INVMAST-EOF condition is on, the program skips to the next sentence, which is the first sentence after the period that ends the IF statement. Since this is roughly equivalent to a GO TO statement, we don't recommend the use of NEXT SENTENCE. In our shop, we always find satisfactory ways to code our IF statements without using NEXT SENTENCE.

Qualification   Up to this point, I haven't told you that you can define the same name twice within a program. If you do, though, you have to refer to it using *qualification*. If, for example, you have defined a field named ITEM-NUMBER once within an input record named OLD-INVENTORY-MASTER and again within an output record named NEW-INVENTORY-MASTER, you have to qualify ITEM-NUMBER whenever you refer to it. If you want the field in the old record, you can refer to it like this:

```
ITEM-NUMBER IN OLD-INVENTORY-MASTER
```

If you want the field in the new record, you can refer to it like this:

```
ITEM-NUMBER IN NEW-INVENTORY-MASTER
```

When you use qualification, you can use either IN or OF to show the relationship. And you can use qualification within qualification so you can refer to a field within a record within a file as

```
ITEM-NUMBER OF INVENTORY-MASTER OF OLDMAST
```

where ITEM-NUMBER is a field name, INVENTORY-MASTER is a record name, and OLDMAST is a file name.

You can also use qualification to qualify paragraph names within sections. In other words, you can give the same paragraph name to two or more paragraphs as long as they're coded in different sections.

We don't recommend the use of qualification because it can easily get so cumbersome that it reduces the readability of a program. As a result, a program without qualification is likely to be more readable than a program that uses it. In addition, qualification increases the amount of coding that you have to do, which reduces your productivity. Nevertheless, qualification is used in some COBOL shops.

The MOVE, ADD, and SUBTRACT CORRESPONDING statements
When you use qualification, you can use the CORRESPONDING options of the MOVE, ADD, and SUBTRACT statements. Here, for example, is a MOVE CORRESPONDING statement:

```
MOVE CORRESPONDING OLD-INVENTORY-MASTER
     TO NEW-INVENTORY-MASTER.
```

When it is executed, all of the fields in OLD-INVENTORY-MASTER that have the same names as fields in NEW-INVENTORY-MASTER are moved to the corresponding fields in NEW-INVENTORY-MASTER. Similarly, an ADD CORRESPONDING statement adds the fields in one record to the fields with the same name in another record, and a SUBTRACT CORRESPONDING statement subtracts the fields in one record from the corresponding fields in another record. In all of these statements, if a field in the sending record doesn't have a corresponding field in the receiving record, it is ignored.

We don't recommend the use of the CORRESPONDING options for two primary reasons. First, when you use CORRESPONDING, you have to use qualification, and I've already explained why we don't recommend qualification. Second, when a CORRESPONDING statement operates on large records, you lose control of what's happening. As a result, a field can get operated upon that you didn't want to be operated upon, or a field that you want to be operated upon can get ignored. In either case, you end up with debugging problems. Nevertheless, the CORRESPONDING statements are used in some shops.

Discussion

I hope you can see by now that there's a lot to learn if you want to become an effective COBOL programmer. After you've taken courses like this one for your basic training in COBOL, you should go through the technical manuals for your system to find out specific details that may be of use to you. You should also go through your shop standards to make sure you use COBOL and all development software in a way that is consistent with the goals of your company.

For instance, our COBOL books present standard COBOL that should work on any full or high subset compiler. However, your compiler may not be a full standard compiler. In addition, it may offer extensions to the standards that are useful on your system. That's why you should study the COBOL manuals for your system to learn all of the language that is available to you that wasn't presented in the COBOL courses you've taken. You should also find out whether all of the language that was presented in your COBOL courses is available on your compiler. After you study the manuals, you should study your shop standards to find out what restrictions your shop places on the use of the COBOL language.

I hope this chapter hasn't sounded too much like an advertisement for our books. In case you enjoyed this book, I just wanted you to know that we offer a complete selection of books for COBOL training. In addition, we offer books on operating system features, JCL, interactive editors, DL/I, and CICS. Please check our catalog for books that may apply to your system.

Terminology

data base
section name
declarative section
qualification

Objective

This chapter is only intended to show you what you must know if you want to become an effective COBOL programmer. As a result, there are no behavioral objectives for it.

Appendixes

A structured
report preparation program

This appendix presents the program specifications, structure chart, and COBOL listing for a structured report preparation program. This is the program that was used as an example in chapter 5 of *Structured ANS COBOL, Part 1*. If you haven't read *Part 1*, you should study this program until you become familiar with it. It illustrates the style of program that is used in this book, and it will be referred to throughout this book.

This program also can help you decide whether you've met the prerequisites for this course. If you can read and understand all of the code in this program, you're ready for this course. If you can't, you should learn how to use the code that is giving you problems before you start this course. However, if the only code that you're unfamiliar with is that in the COPY and CALL statements, you're ready for this course because these statements are taught in chapters 6 and 7.

Program: INV3520   PREPARE INVESTMENT LISTING   Page: 1

Designer: Anne Prince   Date: 04-03-86

Input/output specifications

File	Description	Use
INVMAST	Inventory master file	Input
INVLIST	Print file: Investment listing	Output

Process specifications

This program prepares an investment listing from a sequential file of inventory master records. The records are in sequence by item number, and the report should be printed in the same sequence. For each master record, a line should be printed on the investment listing only if the investment amount is greater than $10,000.

The basic processing requirements for each inventory master record follow:

1. Read the master record.

2. Calculate the investment amount.
    (Investment amount = on-hand balance x unit price)

3. If the investment amount is greater than $10,000, add the investment amount to the investment total and format and print an investment line. To figure the number of months inventory on hand, divide the investment amount by last month's sales.

After all records have been processed, prepare and print the total lines.

The COPY member for the inventory master record (INVMAST)

```
01   INVENTORY-MASTER-RECORD.
*
     05   IM-DESCRIPTIVE-DATA.
          10   IM-ITEM-NO             PIC 9(5).
          10   IM-ITEM-DESC           PIC X(20).
          10   IM-UNIT-COST           PIC 999V99.
          10   IM-UNIT-PRICE          PIC 999V99.
     05   IM-INVENTORY-DATA.
          10   IM-REORDER-POINT       PIC S9(5).
          10   IM-ON-HAND             PIC S9(5).
          10   IM-ON-ORDER            PIC S9(5).
     05   IM-SALES-DATA.
          10   IM-LAST-ORDER-DATE       PIC 9(6).
          10   IM-LAST-ORDER-DATE-R REDEFINES IM-LAST-ORDER-DATE.
             15   IM-LAST-ORDER-MONTH PIC 99.
             15   IM-LAST-ORDER-DAY   PIC 99.
             15   IM-LAST-ORDER-YEAR  PIC 99.
          10   IM-LAST-MONTH-SALES    PIC S9(5)V99.
          10   IM-LAST-YEAR-SALES     PIC S9(7)V99.
     05   FILLER                      PIC X(8).
```

The print chart for the investment listing (INVLIST)

```
DATE: 99/99/99                    MIKE MURACH & ASSOCIATES, INC.                              PAGE: ZZ9
TIME: 99:99 XX                                                                               INV3520
              INVENTORY INVESTMENT LISTING -- ITEMS WITH RETAIL VALUE OVER $10,000

ITEM                      UNIT    QUANTITY   LAST        LAST MONTH     INVESTMENT     NO. OF MONTHS
NO.   ITEM DESCRIPTION    PRICE   ON HAND    ORDER DATE  SALES IN $     IN RETAIL $    INVENTORY ON HAND

ZZZZZ XXXXXXXXXXXXXXXXXXXX ZZZ.99 ZZ,ZZ9    99/99/99    ZZ,ZZZ.99      ZZ,ZZZ.99      ZZ9.9

ZZZZZ RECORDS IN THE MASTER FILE          $$$,$$$,$$$.99* $$$,$$$,$$$.99*  ZZZ.9*
ZZZZZ RECORDS IN THIS SELECTED LISTING
```

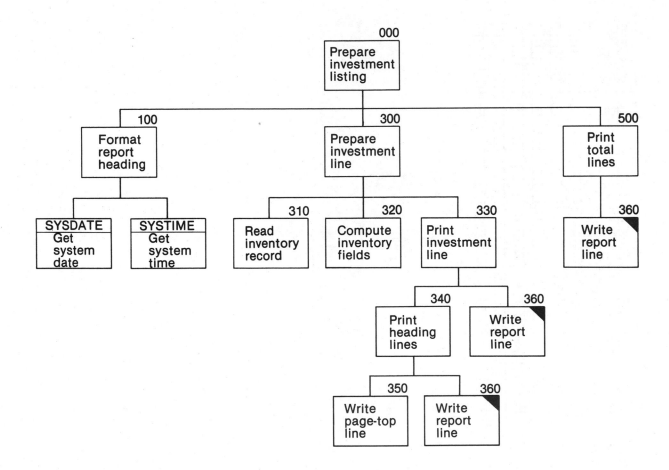

```
  1   IBM DOS/VS COBOL                              REL 3.0


 CBL LIB,APOST
00001    000100 IDENTIFICATION DIVISION.
00002    000200*
00003    000300 PROGRAM-ID.          INV3520.
00004    000400*AUTHOR.           MIKE MURACH.
00005    000500*
00006    000600 ENVIRONMENT DIVISION.
00007    000700*
00008    000800 INPUT-OUTPUT SECTION.
00009    000900*
00010    001000 FILE-CONTROL.
00011    001100     SELECT INVMAST ASSIGN TO SYS020-AS-INVMAST.
00012    001200     SELECT INVLIST ASSIGN TO SYS006-UR-1403-S.
00013    001300*
00014    001400 DATA DIVISION.
00015    001500*
00016    001600 FILE SECTION.
00017    001700*
00018    001800 FD   INVMAST
00019    001900     LABEL RECORDS ARE STANDARD
00020    002000     RECORD CONTAINS 80 CHARACTERS.
00021    002100*
00022    002200 01   INVENTORY-MASTER         PIC X(80).
00023    002300*
00024    002400 FD   INVLIST
00025    002500     LABEL RECORDS ARE OMITTED
00026    002600     RECORD CONTAINS 132 CHARACTERS.
00027    002700*
00028    002800 01   PRINT-AREA               PIC X(132).
00029    002900*
00030    003000 WORKING-STORAGE SECTION.
00031    003100*
00032    003200 01   SWITCHES.
00033    003300*
00034    003400     05   INVMAST-EOF-SWITCH          PIC X      VALUE 'N'.
00035    003500         88   INVMAST-EOF                        VALUE 'Y'.
00036    003600     05   INVESTMENT-SIZE-ERROR-SWITCH  PIC X    VALUE 'N'.
00037    003700         88   INVESTMENT-SIZE-ERROR              VALUE 'Y'.
00038    003800*
00039    003900 01   PRINT-FIELDS             COMP-3.
00040    004000*
00041    004100     05   SPACE-CONTROL        PIC S9.
00042    004200     05   LINES-ON-PAGE        PIC S999 VALUE +55.
00043    004300     05   LINE-COUNT           PIC S999 VALUE +99.
00044    004400     05   PAGE-COUNT           PIC S999 VALUE ZERO.
00045    004500*
00046    004600 01   DATE-FIELDS.
00047    004700*
00048    004800     05   TODAYS-DATE          PIC 9(6).
00049    004900     05   TODAYS-DATE-R REDEFINES TODAYS-DATE.
00050    005000         10   TODAYS-MONTH     PIC 99.
00051    005100         10   TODAYS-DAY       PIC 99.
00052    005200         10   TODAYS-YEAR      PIC 99.
00053    005300*
00054    005400 01   COUNT-FIELDS             COMP-3.
00055    005500*
```

```
00056   005600      05   RECORD-COUNT              PIC S9(5)          VALUE ZERO.
00057   005700      05   SELECTED-RECORD-COUNT     PIC S9(5)          VALUE ZERO.
00058   005800*
00059   005900 01   CALCULATED-FIELDS             COMP-3.
00060   006000*
00061   006100      05   INVESTMENT-AMOUNT         PIC S9(7)V99.
00062   006200      05   NO-OF-MONTHS-STOCK        PIC S9(3)V9.
00063   006300*
00064   006400 01   TOTAL-FIELDS                  COMP-3.
00065   006500*
00066   006600      05   SELECTED-LM-SALES-TOTAL   PIC S9(9)V99       VALUE ZERO.
00067   006700      05   SELECTED-INVESTMENT-TOTAL PIC S9(9)V99       VALUE ZERO.
00068   006800*
00069   006900 COPY INVMAST.
00070 C       *
00071 C          01   INVENTORY-MASTER-RECORD.
00072 C       *
00073 C          05   IM-DESCRIPTIVE-DATA.
00074 C             10   IM-ITEM-NO             PIC 9(5).
00075 C             10   IM-ITEM-DESC           PIC X(20).
00076 C             10   IM-UNIT-COST           PIC 999V99.
00077 C             10   IM-UNIT-PRICE          PIC 999V99.
00078 C          05   IM-INVENTORY-DATA.
00079 C             10   IM-REORDER-POINT       PIC S9(5).
00080 C             10   IM-ON-HAND             PIC S9(5).
00081 C             10   IM-ON-ORDER            PIC S9(5).
00082 C          05   IM-SALES-DATA.
00083 C             10   IM-LAST-ORDER-DATE     PIC 9(6).
00084 C             10   IM-LAST-ORDER-DATE-R REDEFINES IM-LAST-ORDER-DATE.
00085 C                15   IM-LAST-ORDER-MONTH PIC 99.
00086 C                15   IM-LAST-ORDER-DAY   PIC 99.
00087 C                15   IM-LAST-ORDER-YEAR  PIC 99.
00088 C             10   IM-LAST-MONTH-SALES    PIC S9(5)V99.
00089 C             10   IM-LAST-YEAR-SALES     PIC S9(7)V99.
00090 C          05   FILLER                    PIC X(8).
00091   007000*
00092   007100 COPY RPTHDG14.
00093 C          01   HEADING-LINE-1.
00094 C       *
00095 C          05   FILLER         PIC X(7)    VALUE 'DATE:'.
00096 C          05   HDG1-DATE      PIC 99/99/99.
00097 C          05   FILLER         PIC X(36)   VALUE SPACE.
00098 C          05   FILLER         PIC X(20)   VALUE 'MIKE MURACH & ASSOCI'.
00099 C          05   FILLER         PIC X(20)   VALUE 'ATES, INC.          '.
00100 C          05   FILLER         PIC X(31)   VALUE SPACE.
00101 C          05   FILLER         PIC X(6)    VALUE 'PAGE:'.
00102 C          05   HDG1-PAGE-NO   PIC ZZ9.
00103 C          05   FILLER         PIC X       VALUE SPACE.
00104 C       *
00105 C          01   HEADING-LINE-2.
00106 C       *
00107 C          05   HDG2-TIME-DATA.
00108 C             10   FILLER        PIC X(7)   VALUE 'TIME:'.
00109 C             10   HDG2-HOURS    PIC 99.
00110 C             10   FILLER        PIC X      VALUE ':'.
00111 C             10   HDG2-MINUTES  PIC 99.
```

3   14.05.29   11/20/86

```
00112 C                   10  FILLER                PIC X          VALUE SPACE.
00113 C                   10  HDG2-TIME-SUFFIX      PIC X(8).
00114 C               05  FILLER                    PIC X(101)  VALUE SPACE.
00115 C               05  HDG2-REPORT-NUMBER        PIC X(10)   VALUE 'XXXX9999'.
00116     007200*
00117     007300 01  HEADING-LINE-3.
00118     007400*
00119     007500     05  FILLER  PIC X(20)   VALUE '                    '.
00120     007600     05  FILLER  PIC X(20)   VALUE '            INVENTOR'.
00121     007700     05  FILLER  PIC X(20)   VALUE 'Y INVESTMENT LISTING'.
00122     007800     05  FILLER  PIC X(20)   VALUE ' -- ITEMS WITH RETAI'.
00123     007900     05  FILLER  PIC X(20)   VALUE 'L VALUE OVER $10,000'.
00124     008000     05  FILLER  PIC X(20)   VALUE '                    '.
00125     008100     05  FILLER  PIC X(12)   VALUE '            '.
00126     008200*
00127     008300 01  HEADING-LINE-4.
00128     008400*
00129     008500     05  FILLER  PIC X(20)   VALUE 'ITEM                '.
00130     008600     05  FILLER  PIC X(20)   VALUE '          UNIT   QUAN'.
00131     008700     05  FILLER  PIC X(20)   VALUE 'TITY    LAST     LAST'.
00132     008800     05  FILLER  PIC X(20)   VALUE ' MONTH        INVEST'.
00133     008900     05  FILLER  PIC X(20)   VALUE 'MENT    NO. OF MONTH'.
00134     009000     05  FILLER  PIC X(20)   VALUE 'S                   '.
00135     009100     05  FILLER  PIC X(12)   VALUE '            '.
00136     009200*
00137     009300 01  HEADING-LINE-5.
00138     009400*
00139     009500     05  FILLER  PIC X(20)   VALUE ' NO.    ITEM DESCRIPT'.
00140     009600     05  FILLER  PIC X(20)   VALUE 'ION      PRICE   ON H'.
00141     009700     05  FILLER  PIC X(20)   VALUE 'AND ORDER DATE   SALE'.
00142     009800     05  FILLER  PIC X(20)   VALUE 'S IN $        IN RET'.
00143     009900     05  FILLER  PIC X(20)   VALUE 'AIL $  INVENTORY ON '.
00144     010000     05  FILLER  PIC X(20)   VALUE 'HAND                '.
00145     010100     05  FILLER  PIC X(12)   VALUE '            '.
00146     010200*
00147     010300 01  INVESTMENT-LINE.
00148     010400*
00149     010500     05  IL-ITEM-NO                PIC Z(5).
00150     010600     05  FILLER                    PIC X(2)   VALUE SPACE.
00151     010700     05  IL-ITEM-DESC              PIC X(20).
00152     010800     05  FILLER                    PIC X(2)   VALUE SPACE.
00153     010900     05  IL-UNIT-PRICE             PIC ZZZ.99.
00154     011000     05  FILLER                    PIC X(2)   VALUE SPACE.
00155     011100     05  IL-ON-HAND                PIC -----9.
00156     011200     05  FILLER                    PIC X(2)   VALUE SPACE.
00157     011300     05  IL-LAST-ORDER-DATE        PIC 99/99/99.
00158     011400     05  FILLER                    PIC X(3)   VALUE SPACE.
00159     011500     05  IL-LAST-MONTH-SALES       PIC ---,---.99
00160     011600                                   BLANK WHEN ZERO.
00161     011700     05  FILLER                    PIC X(6)   VALUE SPACE.
00162     011800     05  IL-INVESTMENT-AMOUNT  PIC --,---,---.99.
00163     011900     05  IL-INVESTMENT-AMT-MESSAGE REDEFINES IL-INVESTMENT-AMOUNT
00164     012000                                   PIC X(13).
00165     012100     05  FILLER                    PIC X(6)   VALUE SPACE.
00166     012200     05  IL-NO-OF-MONTHS-STOCK PIC ----.9.
00167     012300     05  IL-NO-OF-MONTHS-STOCK-MESSAGE
```

```
00168   012400                    REDEFINES IL-NO-OF-MONTHS-STOCK
00169   012500                                    PIC X(6).
00170   012600        05   FILLER                  PIC X(35)  VALUE SPACE.
00171   012700*
00172   012800 01   TOTAL-LINE-1.
00173   012900*
00174   013000        05   TL1-RECORD-COUNT        PIC Z(5).
00175   013100        05   FILLER                  PIC X(15)  VALUE ' RECORDS IN THE'.
00176   013200        05   FILLER                  PIC X(12)  VALUE ' MASTER FILE'.
00177   013300        05   FILLER                  PIC X(19)  VALUE SPACE.
00178   013400        05   TL1-SEL-LM-SALES-TOTAL    PIC $$$$,$$$,$$$.99.
00179   013500        05   FILLER                  PIC X(2)   VALUE ' *'.
00180   013600        05   FILLER                  PIC X(2)   VALUE SPACE.
00181   013700        05   TL1-SEL-INVESTMENT-TOTAL   PIC $$$$,$$$,$$$.99.
00182   013800        05   FILLER                  PIC X(2)   VALUE ' *'.
00183   013900        05   FILLER                  PIC X(5)   VALUE SPACE.
00184   014000        05   TL1-SEL-NO-OF-MONTHS-STOCK PIC ZZZ.9.
00185   014100        05   FILLER                  PIC X(2)   VALUE ' *'.
00186   014200        05   FILLER                  PIC X(33)  VALUE SPACE.
00187   014300*
00188   014400 01   TOTAL-LINE-2.
00189   014500*
00190   014600        05   TL2-SEL-RECORD-COUNT  PIC Z(5).
00191   014700        05   FILLER                  PIC X(15)  VALUE ' RECORDS IN THI'.
00192   014800        05   FILLER                  PIC X(18)  VALUE 'S SELECTED LISTING'.
00193   014900        05   FILLER                  PIC X(94)  VALUE SPACE.
00194   015000*
00195   015100 PROCEDURE DIVISION.
00196   015200*
00197   015300 000-PREPARE-INVENTORY-LISTING.
00198   015400*
00199   015500        OPEN INPUT   INVMAST
00200   015600             OUTPUT INVLIST.
00201   015700        PERFORM 100-FORMAT-REPORT-HEADING.
00202   015800        PERFORM 300-PREPARE-INVESTMENT-LINE
00203   015900            UNTIL INVMAST-EOF.
00204   016000        PERFORM 500-PRINT-TOTAL-LINES.
00205   016100        CLOSE INVMAST
00206   016200             INVLIST.
00207   016300        DISPLAY 'INV3520  I  1  NORMAL EOJ'.
00208   016400        STOP RUN.
00209   016500*
00210   016600 100-FORMAT-REPORT-HEADING.
00211   016700*
00212   016800        CALL 'SYSDATE' USING TODAYS-DATE.
00213   016900        MOVE TODAYS-DATE TO HDG1-DATE.
00214   017000        CALL 'SYSTIME' USING HDG2-TIME-DATA.
00215   017100        MOVE 'INV3520' TO HDG2-REPORT-NUMBER.
00216   017200*
00217   017300 300-PREPARE-INVESTMENT-LINE.
00218   017400*
00219   017500        PERFORM 310-READ-INVENTORY-RECORD.
00220   017600        IF NOT INVMAST-EOF
00221   017700            PERFORM 320-COMPUTE-INVENTORY-FIELDS
00222   017800            IF INVESTMENT-AMOUNT > 10000
00223   017900                PERFORM 330-PRINT-INVESTMENT-LINE.
```

```
00224   018000*
00225   018100 310-READ-INVENTORY-RECORD.
00226   018200*
00227   018300      READ INVMAST RECORD INTO INVENTORY-MASTER-RECORD
00228   018400          AT END
00229   018500              MOVE 'Y' TO INVMAST-EOF-SWITCH.
00230   018600      IF NOT INVMAST-EOF
00231   018700          ADD 1 TO RECORD-COUNT.
00232   018800*
00233   018900 320-COMPUTE-INVENTORY-FIELDS.
00234   019000*
00235   019100      COMPUTE INVESTMENT-AMOUNT = IM-ON-HAND * IM-UNIT-PRICE
00236   019200          ON SIZE ERROR
00237   019300              MOVE 9999999.99 TO INVESTMENT-AMOUNT
00238   019400              MOVE 'Y' TO INVESTMENT-SIZE-ERROR-SWITCH.
00239   019500      IF        NOT INVESTMENT-SIZE-ERROR
00240   019600          AND IM-LAST-MONTH-SALES POSITIVE
00241   019700          COMPUTE NO-OF-MONTHS-STOCK ROUNDED =
00242   019800              INVESTMENT-AMOUNT / IM-LAST-MONTH-SALES
00243   019900              ON SIZE ERROR
00244   020000                  MOVE 999.9 TO NO-OF-MONTHS-STOCK
00245   020100      ELSE
00246   020200          MOVE 999.9 TO NO-OF-MONTHS-STOCK.
00247   020300*
00248   020400 330-PRINT-INVESTMENT-LINE.
00249   020500*
00250   020600      IF LINE-COUNT > LINES-ON-PAGE
00251   020700          PERFORM 340-PRINT-HEADING-LINES.
00252   020800      MOVE IM-ITEM-NO             TO IL-ITEM-NO.
00253   020900      MOVE IM-ITEM-DESC           TO IL-ITEM-DESC.
00254   021000      MOVE IM-UNIT-PRICE          TO IL-UNIT-PRICE.
00255   021100      MOVE IM-ON-HAND             TO IL-ON-HAND.
00256   021200      MOVE IM-LAST-ORDER-DATE     TO IL-LAST-ORDER-DATE.
00257   021300      MOVE IM-LAST-MONTH-SALES    TO IL-LAST-MONTH-SALES.
00258   021400      ADD IM-LAST-MONTH-SALES     TO SELECTED-LM-SALES-TOTAL.
00259   021500      IF NOT INVESTMENT-SIZE-ERROR
00260   021600          MOVE INVESTMENT-AMOUNT    TO IL-INVESTMENT-AMOUNT
00261   021700          ADD INVESTMENT-AMOUNT     TO SELECTED-INVESTMENT-TOTAL
00262   021800          MOVE NO-OF-MONTHS-STOCK TO IL-NO-OF-MONTHS-STOCK
00263   021900      ELSE
00264   022000          MOVE '   SIZE ERROR'     TO IL-INVESTMENT-AMT-MESSAGE
00265   022100          MOVE '   N/A'            TO IL-NO-OF-MONTHS-STOCK-MESSAGE
00266   022200          MOVE 'N'                 TO INVESTMENT-SIZE-ERROR-SWITCH.
00267   022300      MOVE INVESTMENT-LINE         TO PRINT-AREA.
00268   022400      PERFORM 360-WRITE-REPORT-LINE.
00269   022500      MOVE 1 TO SPACE-CONTROL.
00270   022600      ADD 1 TO SELECTED-RECORD-COUNT.
00271   022700*
00272   022800 340-PRINT-HEADING-LINES.
00273   022900*
00274   023000      ADD 1 TO PAGE-COUNT.
00275   023100      MOVE PAGE-COUNT TO HDG1-PAGE-NO.
00276   023200      PERFORM 350-WRITE-PAGE-TOP-LINE.
00277   023300      MOVE HEADING-LINE-2 TO PRINT-AREA.
00278   023400      MOVE 1 TO SPACE-CONTROL.
00279   023500      PERFORM 360-WRITE-REPORT-LINE.
```

```
00280    023600      MOVE HEADING-LINE-3 TO PRINT-AREA.
00281    023700      PERFORM 360-WRITE-REPORT-LINE.
00282    023800      MOVE HEADING-LINE-4 TO PRINT-AREA.
00283    023900      MOVE 2 TO SPACE-CONTROL.
00284    024000      PERFORM 360-WRITE-REPORT-LINE.
00285    024100      MOVE HEADING-LINE-5 TO PRINT-AREA.
00286    024200      MOVE 1 TO SPACE-CONTROL.
00287    024300      PERFORM 360-WRITE-REPORT-LINE.
00288    024400      MOVE 2 TO SPACE-CONTROL.
00289    024500*
00290    024600 350-WRITE-PAGE-TOP-LINE.
00291    024700*
00292    024800      WRITE PRINT-AREA FROM HEADING-LINE-1
00293    024900          AFTER ADVANCING PAGE.
00294    025000      MOVE 1 TO LINE-COUNT.
00295    025100*
00296    025200 360-WRITE-REPORT-LINE.
00297    025300*
00298    025400      WRITE PRINT-AREA
00299    025500          AFTER ADVANCING SPACE-CONTROL LINES.
00300    025600      ADD SPACE-CONTROL TO LINE-COUNT.
00301    025700*
00302    025800 500-PRINT-TOTAL-LINES.
00303    025900*
00304    026000      MOVE RECORD-COUNT TO TL1-RECORD-COUNT.
00305    026100      MOVE SELECTED-LM-SALES-TOTAL TO TL1-SEL-LM-SALES-TOTAL.
00306    026200      MOVE SELECTED-INVESTMENT-TOTAL
00307    026300          TO TL1-SEL-INVESTMENT-TOTAL.
00308    026400      COMPUTE TL1-SEL-NO-OF-MONTHS-STOCK ROUNDED =
00309    026500          SELECTED-INVESTMENT-TOTAL / SELECTED-LM-SALES-TOTAL
00310    026600          ON SIZE ERROR
00311    026700              MOVE 999.9 TO TL1-SEL-NO-OF-MONTHS-STOCK.
00312    026800      MOVE TOTAL-LINE-1 TO PRINT-AREA.
00313    026900      MOVE 3 TO SPACE-CONTROL.
00314    027000      PERFORM 360-WRITE-REPORT-LINE.
00315    027100      MOVE SELECTED-RECORD-COUNT TO TL2-SEL-RECORD-COUNT.
00316    027200      MOVE TOTAL-LINE-2 TO PRINT-AREA.
00317    027300      MOVE 1 TO SPACE-CONTROL.
00318    027400      PERFORM 360-WRITE-REPORT-LINE.
```

COBOL reference summary

This appendix presents a summary of the COBOL language presented in *Structured ANS COBOL, Part 1* and *Part 2*. In sequence, you will find the following:

General Information
Identification Division
Environment Division
Data Division
Procedure Division

The notation used in this appendix conforms to the notation used in the ANS COBOL standards. This notation is also used in COBOL reference manuals. The rules for this notation follow:

1. Words printed entirely in capital letters are COBOL reserved words.

2. Words printed in lowercase letters represent names, literals, or statements that must be supplied by the programmer.

3. Braces { } enclosing a group of items indicate that the programmer must choose one of them.

4. When a single item is enclosed in braces, it means the ellipsis that follows applies only to that item—not to the entire statement or clause (see rule 6 below).

5.   Brackets [ ] indicate that the enclosed item may be used or omitted, depending on the requirements of the program.

6.   The ellipsis ... indicates that an element may be repeated as many times as necessary.

7.   Underlined reserved words are required unless the element itself is optional. Words that aren't underlined are optional.

8.   In general, the clauses and phrases in a statement should be coded in the sequence shown. This is particularly true for statements in the Procedure Division.

The formats in this summary use the word *identifier* to indicate that the programmer must identify a data item. Most of the time an identifier is coded as a data name, but it can also be a data name followed by an index or a subscript enclosed in parentheses as described in chapter 8.

This summary presents elements from both the 1974 and the 1985 COBOL standards. If an element is included in the 1985 standards but not in the 1974 standards, it's shaded. That means that you shouldn't use it unless you are using a 1985 compiler. In contrast, all of the unshaded elements are acceptable to both 1974 and 1985 compilers.

GENERAL INFORMATION

Character set

Characters used for words and names

A-Z	Letters
0-9	Digits
-	Hyphen

Characters used for punctuation

"	Quotation mark
'	Single quote (apostrophe)
(	Left parenthesis
)	Right parenthesis
.	Period
	Space
,	Comma

Characters used in arithmetic expressions

+	Addition
-	Subtraction
*	Multiplication
/	Division
**	Exponentiation

Characters used to show relationships

=	Equals
<	Less than
>	Greater than

Characters used in editing

Z   Zero suppression

,   Comma

.   Period

–   Minus

+   Plus

C R   Credit

D B   Debit

*   Asterisk

$ Dollar sign

/   Stroke

B   Blank

0   Zero

Logical operators

NOT

OR

AND

Name formation

Program name

1. Maximum of 30 characters.
2. Letters, numbers, and hyphens only.
3. Cannot start or end with a hyphen.
4. Should conform to the requirements of your system.

Data name

1. Maximum of 30 characters.
2. Letters, numbers, and hyphens only.
3. Cannot start or end with a hyphen.
4. Must contain at least one letter.

Paragraph or section name (procedure name)

1. Maximum of 30 characters.
2. Letters, numbers, and hyphens only.
3. Cannot start or end with a hyphen.
4. A section name is followed by the word SECTION.

File name, record name, or condition name

Same as for data name.

Figurative constants

```
ZERO, ZEROS, ZEROES
SPACE, SPACES
HIGH-VALUE, HIGH-VALUES
LOW-VALUE, LOW-VALUES
QUOTE, QUOTES
ALL literal
```

Rules for forming literals

Numeric literals

1. Maximum of 18 digits.
2. Consisting of 0-9, + or − , and the decimal point.
3. Only one sign character (if unsigned, assumed positive).
4. Only one decimal point.

Non-numeric literals

1. Maximum of 120 characters in the 1974 standards, 160 characters in the 1985 standards.
2. Enclosed in quotation marks.

Comment lines

1. An asterisk (*) in position 7.
2. Any other characters in positions 8-72.

Debugging lines

1. The letter D in position 7.
2. Any valid COBOL code in positions 8-72.
3. When the WITH DEBUGGING MODE clause is coded in the SOURCE-COMPUTER paragraph in the Environment Division, the debugging lines are compiled and executed. When the WITH DEBUGGING MODE clause isn't coded, the debugging lines are treated as comments.

Indexing format

```
data-name ({integer-1                       } ... )
           {index-name-1 [{±} integer-2]}
```

Subscripting format

```
data-name ({integer-1                     } ... )
           {data-name-2 [{±} integer-2]}
```

Condition formats

Relation conditions

```
{identifier-1             }  (IS [NOT] GREATER THAN        )  {identifier-2             }
{literal-1                }  {IS [NOT] LESS THAN           }  {literal-2                }
{arithmetic-expression-1  }  {IS [NOT] EQUAL TO            }  {arithmetic-expression-2  }
{index-name-1             }  {IS GREATER THAN OR EQUAL TO  }  {index-name-2             }
                            (IS LESS THAN OR EQUAL TO     )
```

```
{identifier-1             }  (IS [NOT] >  )  {identifier-2             }
{literal-1                }  {IS [NOT] <  }  {literal-2                }
{arithmetic-expression-1  }  {IS [NOT] =  }  {arithmetic-expression-2  }
{index-name-1             }  {IS >=       }  {index-name-2             }
                            (IS <=       )
```

Class condition

```
identifier IS [NOT] {NUMERIC          }
                    {ALPHABETIC       }
                    {ALPHABETIC-LOWER }
                    {ALPHABETIC-UPPER }
                    (class-name-1     )
```

Sign condition

```
arithmetic-expression IS [NOT]  {POSITIVE}
                                {NEGATIVE}
                                {ZERO    }
```

Condition-name condition

```
condition-name
```

Reference modification format

```
data-name (leftmost-character-position: [length])
```

Identifier format

```
data-name [({index    } ... )] [(leftmost-character-position: [length])]
           {subscript }
```

IDENTIFICATION DIVISION

```
IDENTIFICATION DIVISION.
PROGRAM-ID.   program-name.
```

Notes:

1. Your program name should conform to the requirements of your system.
2. To provide other identifying information in this division, you should use comment lines.

ENVIRONMENT DIVISION

General format

```
ENVIRONMENT DIVISION.
[CONFIGURATION SECTION.
SOURCE-COMPUTER.  computer-name [WITH DEBUGGING MODE].
OBJECT-COMPUTER.  computer-name.]
INPUT-OUTPUT SECTION.
FILE-CONTROL.
     SELECT-statement ...
```

Notes:

1. Computer names are defined by the computer manufacturer.
2. The entire Configuration System is optional on some 1974 compilers, and it is optional under the 1985 standards.

SELECT statement formats

Format 1: Sequential file

```
SELECT file-name

     ASSIGN TO system-name

     [[ORGANIZATION IS] SEQUENTIAL]

     [ACCESS MODE IS SEQUENTIAL]

     [FILE STATUS IS data-name].
```

Format 2: Indexed file

```
SELECT file-name

    ASSIGN TO system-name

    [ORGANIZATION IS] INDEXED

    ⎡                ⎧SEQUENTIAL⎫⎤
    ⎢ACCESS MODE IS  ⎨RANDOM    ⎬⎥
    ⎣                ⎩DYNAMIC   ⎭⎦

    RECORD KEY IS data-name-1

    [ALTERNATE RECORD KEY IS data-name-2 [WITH DUPLICATES]] ...

    [FILE STATUS IS data-name-3].
```

Format 3: Relative file

```
SELECT file-name

    ASSIGN TO system-name

    [ORGANIZATION IS] RELATIVE

    ⎡                ⎧SEQUENTIAL [RELATIVE KEY IS data-name-1]⎫⎤
    ⎢ACCESS MODE IS  ⎨⎧RANDOM ⎫                              ⎬⎥
    ⎢                ⎩⎩DYNAMIC⎭ RELATIVE KEY IS data-name-1  ⎭⎥
    ⎣                                                        ⎦

    [FILE STATUS IS data-name-2].
```

Format 4: Sort or merge file

```
SELECT file-name

    ASSIGN TO system-name.
```

DATA DIVISION

General format

```
DATA DIVISION.

[FILE SECTION.

 ⌈file-description-entry {record-description-entry} ...            ⌉ ...]
 ⌊sort-merge-file-description-entry {record-description-entry} ...⌋

[WORKING-STORAGE SECTION.

 [record-description-entry]...]

[LINKAGE SECTION.

 [record-description-entry]...]
```

File description entry format

```
FD file-name

    [LABEL  ⎰RECORD IS  ⎱ ⎰STANDARD⎱   ]
           ⎱RECORDS ARE⎰ ⎱OMITTED ⎰

    ⎡BLOCK CONTAINS [integer-1 TO] integer-2 ⎰RECORDS   ⎱⎤
    ⎣                                        ⎱CHARACTERS⎰⎦

    ⎡      ⎰CONTAINS integer-3 CHARACTERS                      ⎱⎤
    ⎢      ⎪IS VARYING IN SIZE                                 ⎪⎥
    ⎢RECORD⎨    [[FROM integer-4] [TO integer-5] CHARACTERS]   ⎬⎥ .
    ⎢      ⎪    [DEPENDING ON data-name]                       ⎪⎥
    ⎣      ⎩CONTAINS integer-6 TO integer-7 CHARACTERS         ⎭⎦
```

Sort-merge file description format

```
SD file-name

    ⎡      ⎰CONTAINS integer-1 CHARACTERS                      ⎱⎤
    ⎢      ⎪IS VARYING IN SIZE                                 ⎪⎥
    ⎢RECORD⎨    [[FROM integer-2] [TO integer-3] CHARACTERS]   ⎬⎥ .
    ⎢      ⎪    [DEPENDING ON data-name]                       ⎪⎥
    ⎣      ⎩CONTAINS integer-4 TO integer-5 CHARACTERS         ⎭⎦
```

Data description entry format

Format 1: 01 through 49 levels

```
level-number    ⎡data-name-1⎤
                ⎣FILLER     ⎦

        [REDEFINES data-name-2]

        ⎡⎧PICTURE⎫  IS character-string⎤
        ⎣⎩PIC    ⎭                     ⎦

                        ⎧BINARY        ⎫
                        ⎪COMPUTATIONAL ⎪
        ⎡[USAGE IS]     ⎨COMP          ⎬⎤
        ⎣               ⎪DISPLAY       ⎪⎦
                        ⎪INDEX         ⎪
                        ⎩PACKED-DECIMAL⎭

⎡ ⎛ OCCURS integer-2 TIMES                                        ⎞ ⎤
⎢ ⎜                                                               ⎟ ⎥
⎢ ⎜     ⎡⎧ASCENDING ⎫ KEY IS {data-name-3}  ...⎤ ...              ⎟ ⎥
⎢ ⎜     ⎣⎩DESCENDING⎭                          ⎦                  ⎟ ⎥
⎢ ⎜                                                               ⎟ ⎥
⎢ ⎨         INDEXED BY {index-name-1} ...                         ⎬ ⎥
⎢ ⎜ OCCURS integer-1 TO integer-2 TIMES DEPENDING ON data-name-4  ⎟ ⎥
⎢ ⎜                                                               ⎟ ⎥
⎢ ⎜     ⎡⎧ASCENDING ⎫ KEY IS {data-name-3}  ...⎤ ...              ⎟ ⎥
⎢ ⎜     ⎣⎩DESCENDING⎭                          ⎦                  ⎟ ⎥
⎣ ⎝         INDEXED BY {index-name-1} ...                         ⎠ ⎦

        [BLANK WHEN ZERO]

        [VALUE IS literal].
```

Note: Although COMP-3 usage is non-standard, it is accepted by many compilers and it is the preferred usage on some systems.

Format 2: 88 levels

```
88  condition-name  ⎧VALUE IS ⎫  ⎧literal-1 ⎡⎧THROUGH⎫ literal-2⎤⎫... .
                    ⎩VALUES ARE⎭  ⎩         ⎣⎩THRU   ⎭          ⎦⎭
```

PROCEDURE DIVISION

General format

```
[PROCEDURE DIVISION  [USING  {data-name-1} ...].

{section-name SECTION.

[paragraph-name.

      [sentence]  ... ] ... } ... ]
```

Statement formats

```
ACCEPT identifier FROM  { DATE        }
                        { DAY         }
                        { DAY-OF-WEEK }
                        { TIME        }

ADD  {identifier-1}  ... TO {identifier-2 [ROUNDED]} ...
     {literal     }

     [ON SIZE ERROR imperative-statement-1]

     [NOT ON SIZE ERROR imperative-statement-2]

     [END-ADD]


ADD  {identifier-1}  ... TO {identifier-2}
     {literal     }         {literal-2  }

     GIVING {identifier-3 [ROUNDED]} ...

     [ON SIZE ERROR imperative-statement-1]

     [NOT ON SIZE ERROR imperative-statement-2]

     [END-ADD]


CALL subprogram-name  [USING identifier-1 ...]

     [END-CALL]

CLOSE  {file-name-1} ...


CLOSE  {file-name-1  [WITH NO REWIND]} ...
```

```
COMPUTE  {identifier-1  [ROUNDED]} ... = arithmetic-expression

    [ON SIZE ERROR imperative-statement-1]

    [NOT ON SIZE ERROR imperative-statement-2]

    [END-COMPUTE]


CONTINUE


COPY text-name   [{OF}  library-name]
                  [{IN}             ]

    [          ({==pseudo-text-1==}     ({==pseudo-text-2==}    ]
    [          {identifier-1     }      {identifier-2    }      ]
    [REPLACING {literal-1        }  BY  {literal-2       }} ... ]
    [          {word-1           }      {word-2          }      ]


DELETE file-name RECORD

    [INVALID KEY imperative-statement-1]

    [NOT INVALID KEY imperative-statement-1]

    [END-DELETE]

DISPLAY  {identifier-1}  ...
         {literal-1   }

DIVIDE  {identifier-1}  INTO  {identifier-2  [ROUNDED]} ...
        {literal     }

    [ON SIZE ERROR imperative-statement-1]

    [NOT ON SIZE ERROR imperative-statement-2]

    [END-DIVIDE]
```

DIVIDE {identifier-1} INTO {identifier-2}
        {literal-1   }   {literal-2   }

    GIVING {identifier-3 [ROUNDED]} ...

    [ON SIZE ERROR imperative-statement-1]

    [NOT ON SIZE ERROR imperative-statement-2]

    [END-DIVIDE]

DIVIDE {identifier-1} BY {identifier-2}
        {literal-1   }   {literal-2   }

    GIVING {identifier-3 [ROUNDED]} ...

    [ON SIZE ERROR imperative-statement-1]

    [NOT ON SIZE ERROR imperative-statement-2]

    [END-DIVIDE]

DIVIDE {identifier-1} INTO {identifier-2}
        {literal-1   }   {literal-2   }

    GIVING identifier-3 [ROUNDED]

    REMAINDER identifier-4

    [ON SIZE ERROR imperative-statement-1]

    [NOT ON SIZE ERROR imperative-statement-2]

    [END-DIVIDE]

DIVIDE {identifier-1} BY {identifier-2}
        {literal-1   }   {literal-2   }

    GIVING identifier-3 [ROUNDED]

    REMAINDER identifier-4

    [ON SIZE ERROR imperative-statement-1]

    [NOT ON SIZE ERROR imperative-statement-2]

    [END-DIVIDE]

```
         ⎧identifier-1 ⎫   ⎡      ⎧identifier-2 ⎫ ⎤
         ⎪literal-1    ⎪   ⎪      ⎪literal-2    ⎪ ⎪
EVALUATE ⎨expression-1 ⎬   ⎢ ALSO ⎨expression-2 ⎬ ⎥ ...
         ⎪TRUE         ⎪   ⎪      ⎪TRUE         ⎪ ⎪
         ⎩FALSE        ⎭   ⎣      ⎩FALSE        ⎭ ⎦
```

```
{{WHEN

   ⎧ANY                                                                      ⎫
   ⎪condition-1                                                              ⎪
   ⎪TRUE                                                                     ⎪
   ⎨FALSE                                                                    ⎬
   ⎪       ⎧identifier-3           ⎫ ⎡⎧THROUGH⎫ ⎧identifier-4           ⎫⎤   ⎪
   ⎪[NOT] ⎨literal-3              ⎬ ⎢⎨THRU   ⎬ ⎨literal-4              ⎬⎥   ⎪
   ⎩       ⎩arithmetic-expression-1⎭ ⎣⎩       ⎭ ⎩arithmetic-expression-2⎭⎦   ⎭

[ALSO

   ⎧ANY                                                                         ⎫
   ⎪condition-2                                                                 ⎪
   ⎪TRUE                                                                        ⎪
   ⎨FALSE                                                                       ⎬ ... } ...
   ⎪       ⎧identifier-5           ⎫ ⎡⎧THROUGH⎫ ⎧identifier-6           ⎫⎤      ⎪
   ⎪[NOT] ⎨literal-5              ⎬ ⎢⎨THRU   ⎬ ⎨literal-6              ⎬⎥      ⎪
   ⎩       ⎩arithmetic-expression-3⎭ ⎣⎩       ⎭ ⎩arithmetic-expression-4⎭⎦      ⎭

imperative-statement-1} ...

[WHEN OTHER imperative-statement-2]

[END-EVALUATE]
```

```
EXIT

EXIT PROGRAM

IF condition-1 ⎧{statement-1}   ⎫   ⎡⎧ELSE {statement-2} ... [END-IF]⎫⎤
               ⎨               ⎬...⎢⎨ELSE NEXT SENTENCE              ⎬⎥
               ⎩NEXT SENTENCE  ⎭   ⎣⎩END-IF                         ⎭⎦

INITIALIZE {identifier-1} ...
```

```
⎡           ⎧ALPHABETIC        ⎫            ⎧identifier-2⎫    ⎤
⎢ REPLACING ⎪ALPHANUMERIC      ⎪ DATA BY   ⎨            ⎬ ...⎥
⎢           ⎨NUMERIC           ⎬            ⎩literal     ⎭    ⎥
⎢           ⎪ALPHANUMERIC-EDITED⎪                            ⎥
⎣           ⎩NUMERIC-EDITED    ⎭                             ⎦
```

```
INSPECT identifier-1 TALLYING
⎧                 ⎧CHARACTERS ⎡⎧BEFORE⎫ INITIAL ⎧identifier-4⎫⎤ ...              ⎫
⎪                 ⎪          ⎣⎨AFTER ⎬         ⎨literal-2   ⎬⎦                   ⎪
⎪identifier-2 FOR ⎨           ⎩      ⎭                                           ⎬ ... } ...
⎪                 ⎪⎧ALL   ⎫ ⎧identifier-3⎫ ⎡⎧BEFORE⎫ INITIAL ⎧identifier-4⎫⎤ ... ⎪
⎩                 ⎩⎨LEADING⎬ ⎨literal-1   ⎬ ⎣⎨AFTER ⎬         ⎨literal-2   ⎬⎦ ... ⎭
                   ⎩      ⎭ ⎩            ⎭   ⎩      ⎭         ⎩            ⎭
```

```
INSPECT identifier-1 REPLACING

  ⎧  CHARACTERS BY  {identifier-5}  [{BEFORE}  INITIAL  {identifier-4}]  ...  ⎫
  ⎪                 {literal-3  }   [{AFTER }           {literal-2  }]        ⎪
  ⎨                                                                          ⎬ ...
  ⎪  ⎧ALL    ⎫  ⎧{identifier-3}     {identifier-5}  [{BEFORE}  INITIAL  {identifier-4}]  ⎫     ⎪
  ⎪  ⎨LEADING⎬  ⎨{literal-1  }  BY  {literal-3  }   [{AFTER }           {literal-2  }]  ⎬ ... ⎪
  ⎩  ⎩FIRST  ⎭  ⎩                                                                       ⎭     ⎭


INSPECT identifier-1 TALLYING

  ⎧                 ⎧ CHARACTERS  [{BEFORE}  INITIAL  {identifier-4}]  ...                                        ⎫      ⎫
  ⎪                 ⎪             [{AFTER }           {literal-2  }]                                               ⎪      ⎪
  ⎨ identifier-2 FOR⎨                                                                                             ⎬ ... ⎬ ...
  ⎪                 ⎪ ⎧ALL    ⎫  ⎧{identifier-3}  [{BEFORE}  INITIAL  {identifier-4}]  ...⎫  ...                   ⎪      ⎪
  ⎩                 ⎩ ⎨LEADING⎬  ⎨{literal-1  }   [{AFTER }           {literal-2  }]       ⎬                       ⎭      ⎭
                      ⎩       ⎭  ⎩                                                       ⎭

REPLACING

  ⎧  CHARACTERS BY  {identifier-5}  [{BEFORE}  INITIAL  {identifier-4}]  ...  ⎫
  ⎪                 {literal-3  }   [{AFTER }           {literal-2  }]        ⎪
  ⎨                                                                          ⎬ ...
  ⎪  ⎧ALL    ⎫  ⎧{identifier-3}     {identifier-5}  [{BEFORE}  INITIAL  {identifier-4}]  ...⎫  ...  ⎪
  ⎪  ⎨LEADING⎬  ⎨{literal-1  }  BY  {literal-3  }   [{AFTER }           {literal-2  }]       ⎬       ⎪
  ⎩  ⎩FIRST  ⎭  ⎩                                                                           ⎭       ⎭


INSPECT identifier-1 CONVERTING  {identifier-2}  TO  {identifier-3}
                                 {literal-1  }       {literal-2  }

    [{BEFORE}  INITIAL  {identifier-4}]  ...
    [{AFTER }           {literal-3  }]


MERGE file-name-1  ⎧ON  {ASCENDING }  KEY  {data-name-1}  ...⎫  ...
                   ⎩    {DESCENDING}                         ⎭

    [COLLATING SEQUENCE IS alphabet-name]

    USING file-name-2  {file-name-3}  ...

    ⎧OUTPUT PROCEDURE IS procedure-name⎫
    ⎨GIVING  {file-name-4}  ...        ⎬
    ⎩                                  ⎭


MOVE  {identifier-1}  TO  {identifier-2}  ...
      {literal     }


MULTIPLY  {identifier-1}  BY  {identifier-2  [ROUNDED]}  ...
          {literal     }

    [ON SIZE ERROR imperative-statement-1]

    [NOT ON SIZE ERROR imperative-statement-2]

    [END-MULTIPLY]
```

```
MULTIPLY  {identifier-1}  BY  {identifier-2}
          {literal-1   }      {literal-2   }

    GIVING {identifier-3  [ROUNDED]} ...

    [ON SIZE ERROR imperative-statement-1]

    [NOT ON SIZE ERROR imperative-statement-2]

    [END-MULTIPLY]


OPEN  { INPUT   {file-name-1  [WITH NO REWIND]}  ... }
      { OUTPUT  {file-name-2  [WITH NO REWIND]}  ... } ...
      { I-O     {file-name-3}  ...                    }
      { EXTEND  {file-name 4}  ...                    }


PERFORM  [procedure-name]

    [WITH TEST {BEFORE}]  [UNTIL condition]
               {AFTER }

    [imperative-statement

    END-PERFORM]


PERFORM  [procedure-name]

    [WITH TEST {BEFORE}]
               {AFTER }

    VARYING {identifier-1 }  FROM {identifier-2 }
            {index-name-1 }       {index-name-2 }
                                  {literal-1    }

        BY {identifier-3}  UNTIL condition-1
           {literal-2   }

        [AFTER {identifer-4  }  FROM {identifier-5 }
               {index-name-3 }       {index-name-4 }
                                     {literal-3    }

            BY {identifier-6}  UNTIL condition-2] ...
               {literal-4   }

    [imperative-statement

    END-PERFORM]
```

READ file-name [NEXT] RECORD [INTO identifier]

   [AT END imperative-statement-1]

   [NOT AT END imperative-statement-2]

   [END-READ]

READ file-name RECORD [INTO identifier]

   [KEY IS data-name]

   [INVALID KEY imperative-statement-1]

   [NOT INVALID KEY imperative-statement-2]

   [END-READ]

RELEASE record-name [FROM identifier]

RETURN file-name RECORD [INTO identifier]

   [AT END imperative-statement-1]

   [NOT AT END imperative-statement-2]

   [END-RETURN]

REWRITE record-name [FROM identifier]

   [INVALID KEY imperative-statement-1]

   [NOT INVALID KEY imperative-statement-2]

   [END-REWRITE]

SEARCH identifier-1 $\left[\text{VARYING} \begin{Bmatrix} \text{identifier-2} \\ \text{index-name} \end{Bmatrix} \right]$

   [AT END imperative-statement-1]

   $\begin{Bmatrix} \text{WHEN condition-1} \begin{Bmatrix} \text{imperative-statement-2} \\ \text{NEXT SENTENCE} \end{Bmatrix} \end{Bmatrix}$ ...

   [END-SEARCH]

```
SEARCH ALL identifier-1  [AT END imperative-statement-1]


    WHEN   ⎰data-name-1  ⎰IS EQUAL TO⎱  ⎰identifier-2                  ⎱⎱
           ⎱           ⎩IS =      ⎭  ⎱literal-1                      ⎱⎱
                                         ⎩arithmetic-expression-1⎭⎭
           ⎩condition-name-1


       ⎡        ⎰data-name-2  ⎰IS EQUAL TO⎱  ⎰identifier-3               ⎱⎱⎤
       ⎢  AND   ⎱           ⎩IS =      ⎭  ⎱literal-2                   ⎱⎱⎥ ...
       ⎢                                     ⎩arithmetic-expr ession-2⎭⎭⎥
       ⎣        ⎩condition-name-2                                       ⎦


           ⎰imperative-statement-2⎱
           ⎱NEXT SENTENCE          ⎭

       [END-SEARCH]


    SET   ⎰index-name-1⎱  ...  TO  ⎰index-name-2⎱
          ⎱identifier-1⎭           ⎱identifier-2⎱
                                    ⎩integer     ⎭

    SET   {index-name-1}  ...  ⎰UP BY   ⎱  ⎰identifier⎱
                               ⎱DOWN BY⎭  ⎱integer   ⎭

    SET   {condition-name}  ...   TO TRUE

    SORT file-name-1  ⎰ON ⎰ASCENDING ⎱  KEY {data-name-1}  ...⎱ ...
                      ⎱   ⎩DESCENDING⎭                        ⎭

       [WITH DUPLICATES IN ORDER]

       [COLLATING SEQUENCE IS alphabet-name]

       ⎰INPUT PROCEDURE IS procedure-name-1⎱
       ⎱USING  {file-name-2}  ...           ⎭

       ⎰OUTPUT PROCEDURE IS procedure-name-2⎱
       ⎱GIVING  {file-name-3}  ...           ⎭
```

```
                                 ┌ IS EQUAL TO      ┐
                                 │ IS =             │
                                 │ IS GREATER THAN  │
START file-name  [  KEY          │ IS >             │          data-name  ]
                                 │ IS NOT LESS THAN │
                                 │ IS NOT <         │
                                 │ IS GREATER THAN OR EQUAL TO │
                                 └ IS >=            ┘
```

[INVALID KEY imperative-statement-1]

[NOT INVALID KEY imperative-statement-2]

[END-START]

STOP RUN

STRING { {identifier-1} ... DELIMITED BY { identifier-2 } } ...
        { {literal-1   }   { literal-2   } }
                                            { SIZE   }

    INTO identifier-3

    [WITH POINTER identifier-4]

    [ON OVERFLOW imperative-statement-1]

    [NOT ON OVERFLOW imperative-statement-2]

    [END-STRING]

SUBTRACT {identifier-1} ... FROM {identifier-2 [ROUNDED]} ...
          {literal-1   }

    [ON SIZE ERROR imperative-statement-1]

    [NOT ON SIZE ERROR imperative-statement-2]

    [END-SUBTRACT]

SUBTRACT {identifier-1} ... FROM {identifier-2}
          {literal-1   }   {literal-2   }

    GIVING {identifier-3 [ROUNDED]} ...

    [ON SIZE ERROR imperative-statement-1]

    [NOT ON SIZE ERROR imperative-statement-2]

    [END-SUBTRACT]
```
```

UNSTRING identifier-1

    [DELIMITED BY [ALL] {identifier-2 / literal-1} [OR [ALL] {identifier-3 / literal-2}] ...]

    INTO {identifier-4 [DELIMITER IN identifier-5] [COUNT IN identifier-6]} ...

    [WITH POINTER identifier-7]

    [TALLYING IN identifier-8]

    [ON OVERFLOW imperative-statement-1]

    [NOT ON OVERFLOW imperative-statement-2]

    [END-UNSTRING]

WRITE record-name [FROM identifier-1]

    [{BEFORE / AFTER} ADVANCING {identifier-2 / integer-1 / PAGE} {LINE / LINES}]

    [END-WRITE]

WRITE record-name [FROM identifier]

    [INVALID KEY imperative-statement-1]

    [NOT INVALID KEY imperative-statement-2]

    [END-WRITE]

Appendix C

Case study problems by chapter

The case study problems that follow involve three programs that we call LISTMAST, MAINTMST, and CREATMST. LISTMAST is a report preparation program that lists the records in an inventory master file. MAINTMST is a file maintenance program that maintains the records in the inventory master file based upon transactions that are read from a sequential transaction file. And CREATMST is a program that creates a new inventory master file from the old one.

In the pages that follow, you will find complete documentation, including the source listings, for initial versions of LISTMAST, MAINTMST, and CREATMST. After this documentation, you will find problems for chapters 2 through 10 in the text. Each problem asks you to modify one of the three programs.

Right before these problems, though, you'll find the overview for a fourth program that we call LISTTRAN. This program is like LISTMAST, except that it lists the records in the maintenance transaction file, rather than the records in the inventory master file. You can use this program to list the records in the transaction file so you know what data the file contains.

When you do the problems in this appendix, the source code for these four programs should be available to you on your system. Then, you won't have to take the time to enter it. As a result, you can concentrate on the COBOL elements that the problems ask you to apply, rather than on the COBOL elements you already know. This means that you'll be able to apply most of the COBOL code presented in *Structured ANS COBOL, Part 2* without taking the time to create any programs from scratch.

You should be able to do all the problems in this appendix, because the required programs closely parallel the programs and examples given in chapters 2 through 10 in the text. If you complete all of the problems, you will have used all of the significant COBOL elements described in this book. In addition, though, your instructor may assign one or more of the case studies in appendix D. Although those case studies don't require the use of any additional COBOL elements, they are more demanding in terms of structure and logic than the problems in this appendix.

When you do one of the problems in this appendix, you should start by modifying the structure chart for the program you're going to work on. Sometimes, no modifications are required, but more often they are. Then, you can modify the COBOL code and test the resulting program. When you complete each problem, you should have a revised structure chart, a revised source listing, and the test run output.

If you're using a 1985 compiler, feel free to use 1985 code for any of the problems in this appendix. In addition, the problems for chapter 10 ask you to use 1985 code within a specific program, but only if the code helps improve the structure or clarity of the program.

Program: LISTMAST   List inventory master file   Page: 1

Designer: MM   Date: 10-20-86

Input/output specifications

File	Description	Use
INVMAST	Inventory master file	Input
INVLIST	Print file: Inventory master listing	Output

Process specifications

This program reads the inventory master file (INVMAST) and prepares an
inventory master listing from it (INVLIST). The program listing that
follows is for an initial version of this program that reads a sequential
inventory master file with fixed-length records.

For chapter 2, you will be asked to modify this program so it reads a
sequential file with variable-length records. For chapters 3 and 4, you
will be asked to modify this program so it reads indexed and relative
master files. For chapter 5, you will be asked to modify this program so
it includes an internal sort. And for chapters 6 through 10, you will be
asked to modify this program so it uses other features of COBOL or so it
performs additional functions.

When you test MAINTMST or CREATMST, you can use LISTMAST to make sure the
master file was maintained or created correctly. When you test MAINTMST,
for example, you can use LISTMAST to list the contents of the master file
before it is maintained and after it has been maintained. By comparing
the two listings, you can figure out whether or not MAINTMST ran
correctly.

Program: LISTMAST   List inventory master file   Page: 2

Designer: MM   Date: 10-20-86

Process specifications

Compiler dependent code

Before you can run this program on your system, you may need to modify
the following items so they conform to your system requirements or shop
standards:

The program name in the Identification Division
The Configuration Section
The system name in the SELECT statement for the disk file
The system name in the SELECT statement for the printer file
The FD statement for the disk file
The FD statement for the printer file
Quotation marks (from single to double quotes)
Computational usage (from COMP-3 to COMP)

File identification

Unless you're told otherwise, you can assume that the external name for
the inventory master file is INVMAST. However, you may also have to get
other identifying information, such as what volume the file is on, what
library it's in, or what catalog is used to locate it.

Record layout for the inventory master record (INVMAST)

```
01    INVENTORY-MASTER-RECORD.
*
      05   IM-STATUS                              PIC X.
           88   IM-IN-PRINT                       VALUE 'I'.
           88   IM-OUT-OF-PRINT                   VALUE 'O'.
      05   IM-DESCRIPTIVE-DATA.
           10   IM-BOOK-CODE                      PIC X(4).
           10   IM-AUTHOR-LAST-NAME               PIC X(10).
           10   IM-BOOK-TITLE                     PIC X(40).
      05   IM-RETAIL-PRICES.
           10   IM-RETAIL-1-THRU-9-PRICE          PIC S999V99.
           10   IM-RETAIL-10-THRU-24-PRICE        PIC S999V99.
           10   IM-RETAIL-25-OR-MORE-PRICE        PIC S999V99.
      05   IM-INVENTORY-DATA.
           10   IM-DATE-OFF-PRESS.
                15   IM-MONTH-OFF-PRESS           PIC XX.
                15   IM-DAY-OFF-PRESS             PIC XX.
                15   IM-YEAR-OFF-PRESS            PIC XX.
           10   IM-QUANTITY-ON-HAND               PIC S9(5).
           10   IM-QUANTITY-BACK-ORDERED          PIC S9(5).
      05   IM-SALES-DATA-IN-UNITS.
           10   IM-UNIT-SALES-YTD                 PIC S9(5).
           10   IM-NUMBER-OF-PAST-YEARS-DATA      PIC S9.
           10   IM-PAST-YEARS-DATA.
                15   IM-UNIT-SALES-LAST-YEAR      PIC S9(5).
                15   IM-UNIT-SALES-2-YEARS-AGO    PIC S9(5).
                15   IM-UNIT-SALES-3-YEARS-AGO    PIC S9(5).
                15   IM-UNIT-SALES-4-YEARS-AGO    PIC S9(5).
                15   IM-UNIT-SALES-5-YEARS-AGO    PIC S9(5).
      05   FILLER                                 PIC X(11).
```

Document name Inventory master listing Date 10-20-86

Program name LISTMAST Designer MM

Record Name

```
      1         DATE: 99/99/99                    LISTING OF INVENTORY MASTER RECORDS              PAGE: ZZ9
      2         TIME: 99:99                                                                        LISTMAST
      3
      4         CODE  AUTHOR       TITLE                          RETAIL PRICES
      5
      6         XXXX  XXXXXXXXXX   XXXXXXXXXXXXXXXXXXXXXXXXXXXXXX  ZZZ.99 ZZZ.99 ZZZ.99
      7
      8
      9         ZZ9 RECORDS IN THE MASTER FILE
     10
     11
     12
```

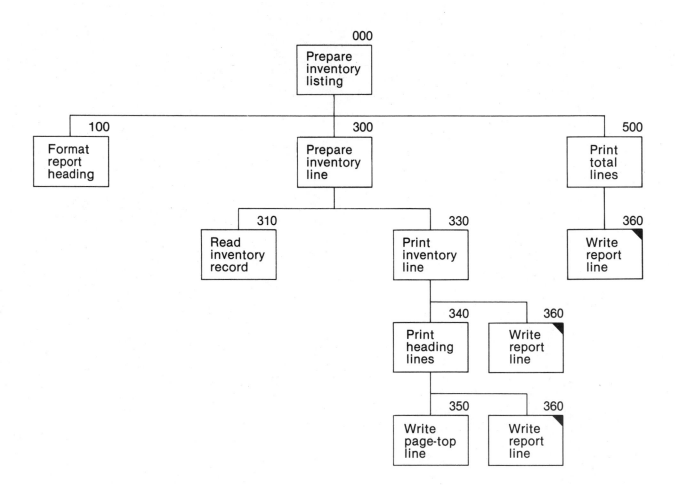

```
 IDENTIFICATION DIVISION.
*
 PROGRAM-ID.     LISTMAST.
*
 ENVIRONMENT DIVISION.
*
 INPUT-OUTPUT SECTION.
*
 FILE-CONTROL.
     SELECT INVMAST ASSIGN TO SYS020-AS-INVMAST.
     SELECT INVLIST ASSIGN TO SYS006-UR-1403-S.
*
 DATA DIVISION.
*
 FILE SECTION.
*
 FD  INVMAST
     LABEL RECORDS ARE STANDARD
     RECORD CONTAINS 128 CHARACTERS.
*
 01  INVENTORY-MASTER        PIC X(128).
*
 FD  INVLIST
     LABEL RECORDS ARE OMITTED
     RECORD CONTAINS 132 CHARACTERS.
*
 01  PRINT-AREA              PIC X(132).
*
 WORKING-STORAGE SECTION.
*
 01  SWITCHES.
*
     05  INVMAST-EOF-SWITCH          PIC X        VALUE 'N'.
         88  INVMAST-EOF                          VALUE 'Y'.
*
 01  PRINT-FIELDS            COMP-3.
*
     05  SPACE-CONTROL      PIC S9.
     05  LINES-ON-PAGE      PIC S999 VALUE +55.
     05  LINE-COUNT         PIC S999 VALUE +99.
     05  PAGE-COUNT         PIC S999 VALUE ZERO.
*
 01  DATE-AND-TIME-FIELDS.
*
     05  TODAYS-DATE        PIC X(6).
     05  TODAYS-DATE-R REDEFINES TODAYS-DATE.
         10  TODAYS-YEAR    PIC XX.
         10  TODAYS-MONTH   PIC XX.
         10  TODAYS-DAY     PIC XX.
     05  TODAYS-TIME        PIC X(8).
     05  TODAYS-TIME-R REDEFINES TODAYS-TIME.
         10  TODAYS-HOURS   PIC S99.
         10  TODAYS-MINUTES PIC XX.
         10  FILLER         PIC X(4).
*
```

```
   01   COUNT-FIELDS                  COMP-3.
*
      05   RECORD-COUNT              PIC S9(3)        VALUE ZERO.
*
   01   INVENTORY-MASTER-RECORD.
*
      05   IM-STATUS                              PIC X.
         88   IM-IN-PRINT                         VALUE 'I'.
         88   IM-OUT-OF-PRINT                     VALUE 'O'.
      05   IM-DESCRIPTIVE-DATA.
         10   IM-BOOK-CODE                        PIC X(4).
         10   IM-AUTHOR-LAST-NAME                 PIC X(10).
         10   IM-BOOK-TITLE                       PIC X(40).
      05   IM-RETAIL-PRICES.
         10   IM-RETAIL-1-THRU-9-PRICE            PIC S999V99.
         10   IM-RETAIL-10-THRU-24-PRICE          PIC S999V99.
         10   IM-RETAIL-25-OR-MORE-PRICE          PIC S999V99.
      05   IM-INVENTORY-DATA.
         10   IM-DATE-OFF-PRESS.
            15   IM-MONTH-OFF-PRESS               PIC XX.
            15   IM-DAY-OFF-PRESS                 PIC XX.
            15   IM-YEAR-OFF-PRESS                PIC XX.
         10   IM-QUANTITY-ON-HAND                 PIC S9(5).
         10   IM-QUANTITY-BACK-ORDERED            PIC S9(5).
      05   IM-SALES-DATA-IN-UNITS.
         10   IM-UNIT-SALES-YTD                   PIC S9(5).
         10   IM-NUMBER-OF-PAST-YEARS-DATA        PIC S9.
         10   IM-PAST-YEARS-DATA.
            15   IM-UNIT-SALES-LAST-YEAR          PIC S9(5).
            15   IM-UNIT-SALES-2-YEARS-AGO        PIC S9(5).
            15   IM-UNIT-SALES-3-YEARS-AGO        PIC S9(5).
            15   IM-UNIT-SALES-4-YEARS-AGO        PIC S9(5).
            15   IM-UNIT-SALES-5-YEARS-AGO        PIC S9(5).
      05   FILLER                                 PIC X(11).
*
   01   HEADING-LINE-1.
*
      05   FILLER           PIC X(7)  VALUE 'DATE:'.
      05   HDG1-DATE.
         10   HDG1-MONTH    PIC X(2).
         10   FILLER        PIC X     VALUE '/'.
         10   HDG1-DAY      PIC X(2).
         10   FILLER        PIC X     VALUE '/'.
         10   HDG1-YEAR     PIC X(2).
      05   FILLER           PIC X(25) VALUE SPACE.
      05   FILLER           PIC X(20) VALUE 'LISTING OF INVENTORY'.
      05   FILLER           PIC X(20) VALUE ' MASTER RECORDS       '.
      05   FILLER           PIC X(42) VALUE SPACE.
      05   FILLER           PIC X(6)  VALUE 'PAGE:'.
      05   HDG1-PAGE-NO     PIC ZZ9.
      05   FILLER           PIC X     VALUE SPACE.
*
   01   HEADING-LINE-2.
*
      05   HDG2-TIME-DATA.
         10   FILLER        PIC X(7)  VALUE 'TIME:'.
```

```
           10   HDG2-HOURS       PIC XX.
           10   FILLER           PIC X         VALUE ':'.
           10   HDG2-MINUTES     PIC XX.
           10   FILLER           PIC X(9)      VALUE SPACE.
       05  FILLER               PIC X(101) VALUE SPACE.
       05  HDG2-PROGRAM-NAME PIC X(10)  VALUE 'LISTMAST  '.
*
 01    HEADING-LINE-3.
*
       05  FILLER  PIC X(20)  VALUE 'CODE   AUTHOR        TI'.
       05  FILLER  PIC X(20)  VALUE 'TLE                  '.
       05  FILLER  PIC X(20)  VALUE '                     '.
       05  FILLER  PIC X(20)  VALUE '        RETAIL PRICES '.
       05  FILLER  PIC X(20)  VALUE '                     '.
       05  FILLER  PIC X(20)  VALUE '                     '.
       05  FILLER  PIC X(12)  VALUE '             '.
*
 01    INVENTORY-LINE.
*
       05  IL-BOOK-CODE               PIC X(4).
       05  FILLER                     PIC X(2)   VALUE SPACE.
       05  IL-AUTHOR-LAST-NAME        PIC X(10).
       05  FILLER                     PIC X(2)   VALUE SPACE.
       05  IL-BOOK-TITLE              PIC X(40).
       05  FILLER                     PIC X(2)   VALUE SPACE.
       05  IL-RETAIL-1-THRU-9-PRICE   PIC ZZZ.99.
       05  FILLER                     PIC X(2)   VALUE SPACE.
       05  IL-RETAIL-10-THRU-24-PRICE PIC ZZZ.99.
       05  FILLER                     PIC X(2)   VALUE SPACE.
       05  IL-RETAIL-25-OR-MORE-PRICE PIC ZZZ.99.
       05  FILLER                     PIC X(50)  VALUE SPACE.
*
 01    TOTAL-LINE-1.
*
       05  TL1-RECORD-COUNT PIC ZZ9.
       05  FILLER             PIC X(7)   VALUE ' RECORD'.
       05  FILLER             PIC X(20)  VALUE 'S IN THE MASTER FILE'.
       05  FILLER             PIC X(102) VALUE SPACE.
*
 PROCEDURE DIVISION.
*
 000-PREPARE-INVENTORY-LISTING.
*
     OPEN INPUT   INVMAST
          OUTPUT  INVLIST.
     PERFORM 100-FORMAT-REPORT-HEADING.
     PERFORM 300-PREPARE-INVENTORY-LINE
          UNTIL INVMAST-EOF.
     PERFORM 500-PRINT-TOTAL-LINES.
     CLOSE INVMAST
           INVLIST.
     DISPLAY 'LISTMAST  I  1  NORMAL EOJ'.
     STOP RUN.
*
 100-FORMAT-REPORT-HEADING.
*
```

```
        ACCEPT TODAYS-DATE FROM DATE.
        MOVE TODAYS-MONTH TO HDG1-MONTH.
        MOVE TODAYS-DAY TO HDG1-DAY.
        MOVE TODAYS-YEAR TO HDG1-YEAR.
        ACCEPT TODAYS-TIME FROM TIME.
        MOVE TODAYS-HOURS TO HDG2-HOURS.
        MOVE TODAYS-MINUTES TO HDG2-MINUTES.
*
  300-PREPARE-INVENTORY-LINE.
*
        PERFORM 310-READ-INVENTORY-RECORD.
        IF NOT INVMAST-EOF
            PERFORM 330-PRINT-INVENTORY-LINE.
*
  310-READ-INVENTORY-RECORD.
*
        READ INVMAST RECORD INTO INVENTORY-MASTER-RECORD
            AT END
                MOVE 'Y' TO INVMAST-EOF-SWITCH.
        IF NOT INVMAST-EOF
            ADD 1 TO RECORD-COUNT.
*
  330-PRINT-INVENTORY-LINE.
*
        IF LINE-COUNT > LINES-ON-PAGE
            PERFORM 340-PRINT-HEADING-LINES.
        MOVE IM-BOOK-CODE          TO IL-BOOK-CODE.
        MOVE IM-AUTHOR-LAST-NAME   TO IL-AUTHOR-LAST-NAME.
        MOVE IM-BOOK-TITLE         TO IL-BOOK-TITLE.
        MOVE IM-RETAIL-1-THRU-9-PRICE
            TO IL-RETAIL-1-THRU-9-PRICE.
        MOVE IM-RETAIL-10-THRU-24-PRICE
            TO IL-RETAIL-10-THRU-24-PRICE.
        MOVE IM-RETAIL-25-OR-MORE-PRICE
            TO IL-RETAIL-25-OR-MORE-PRICE.
        MOVE INVENTORY-LINE        TO PRINT-AREA.
        PERFORM 360-WRITE-REPORT-LINE.
        MOVE 1 TO SPACE-CONTROL.
*
  340-PRINT-HEADING-LINES.
*
        ADD 1 TO PAGE-COUNT.
        MOVE PAGE-COUNT TO HDG1-PAGE-NO.
        PERFORM 350-WRITE-PAGE-TOP-LINE.
        MOVE HEADING-LINE-2 TO PRINT-AREA.
        MOVE 1 TO SPACE-CONTROL.
        PERFORM 360-WRITE-REPORT-LINE.
        MOVE HEADING-LINE-3 TO PRINT-AREA.
        MOVE 2 TO SPACE-CONTROL.
        PERFORM 360-WRITE-REPORT-LINE.
*
  350-WRITE-PAGE-TOP-LINE.
*
        WRITE PRINT-AREA FROM HEADING-LINE-1
            AFTER ADVANCING PAGE.
        MOVE 1 TO LINE-COUNT.
```

```
*
 360-WRITE-REPORT-LINE.
*
      WRITE PRINT-AREA
          AFTER ADVANCING SPACE-CONTROL LINES.
      ADD SPACE-CONTROL TO LINE-COUNT.
*
 500-PRINT-TOTAL-LINES.
*
      MOVE RECORD-COUNT TO TLI-RECORD-COUNT.
      MOVE TOTAL-LINE-1 TO PRINT-AREA.
      MOVE 3 TO SPACE-CONTROL.
      PERFORM 360-WRITE-REPORT-LINE.
```

Program: **MAINTMST**   Maintain inventory master file   Page: 1

Designer: **MM**   Date: 10-20-86

Input/output specifications

File	Description	Use
MNTTRAN	Maintenance transaction file	Input
INVMAST	Inventory master file	Input
NEWMAST	New inventory master file (chapter 2 only)	Output

Process specifications

This program maintains an inventory master file (INVMAST) based on
transactions in a maintenance transaction file (MNTTRAN). The program
listing that follows is for an initial version of this program that
maintains the master file based on change transactions only and creates a
new inventory master file (NEWMAST).

For chapter 2, you will be asked to modify this program so it maintains
the sequential master file based on deletion and addition transactions as
well as change transactions. For chapters 3 and 4, you will be asked to
modify this program so it processes change, deletion, and addition
transactions as it maintains indexed and relative master files.

When all transactions have been processed, the program displays a count
of the invalid transactions. In the initial version of the program, a
transaction is invalid if it isn't a change transaction or if a change
transaction isn't matched by a master record. In subsequent versions of
the program, a deletion transaction is invalid if it isn't matched by a
master record, and an addition transaction is invalid if it is matched by
a master record.

Program: **MAINTMST**   Maintain inventory master file   Page: 2

Designer: **MM**   Date: 10-20-86

Process specifications

Compiler dependent code

Before you can run this program on your system, you may need to modify the following items so they conform to your system requirements or shop standards:

The program name in the Identification Division
The Configuration Section
The system names in the SELECT statements for the disk files
The FD statements for the disk files
Quotation marks (from single to double quotes)
Computational usage (from COMP-3 to COMP)

File identification

Unless you're told otherwise, you can assume that the external names for the transaction and the master files are **MNTTRAN, INVMAST,** and **NEWMAST.** However, you may also have to get other identifying information, such as what volume the files are on, what library they're in, or what catalog is used to locate the files.

Record layout for the maintenance transaction record (MNTTRAN)

```
01    MAINTENANCE-TRANSACTION-RECORD.
*
      05   MT-MAINTENANCE-CODE                    PIC X.
           88   MT-DELETION                       VALUE 'D'.
           88   MT-CHANGE                         VALUE 'C'.
           88   MT-ADDITION                       VALUE 'A'.
      05   MT-DESCRIPTIVE-DATA.
           10   MT-BOOK-CODE                      PIC X(4).
           10   MT-AUTHOR-LAST-NAME               PIC X(10).
           10   MT-BOOK-TITLE                     PIC X(40).
      05   MT-RETAIL-PRICES.
           10   MT-RETAIL-1-THRU-9-PRICE          PIC S999V99.
           10   MT-RETAIL-1-THRU-9-PRICE-X     REDEFINES
                MT-RETAIL-1-THRU-9-PRICE          PIC X(5).
           10   MT-RETAIL-10-THRU-24-PRICE        PIC S999V99.
           10   MT-RETAIL-10-THRU-24-PRICE-X   REDEFINES
                MT-RETAIL-10-THRU-24-PRICE        PIC X(5).
           10   MT-RETAIL-25-OR-MORE-PRICE        PIC S999V99.
           10   MT-RETAIL-25-OR-MORE-PRICE-X   REDEFINES
                MT-RETAIL-25-OR-MORE-PRICE        PIC X(5).
      05   FILLER                                 PIC X(10).
```

Record layout for the inventory master record (INVMAST)

```
01    INVENTORY-MASTER-RECORD.
*
      05   IM-STATUS                              PIC X.
           88   IM-IN-PRINT                       VALUE 'I'.
           88   IM-OUT-OF-PRINT                   VALUE 'O'.
      05   IM-DESCRIPTIVE-DATA.
           10   IM-BOOK-CODE                      PIC X(4).
           10   IM-AUTHOR-LAST-NAME               PIC X(10).
           10   IM-BOOK-TITLE                     PIC X(40).
      05   IM-RETAIL-PRICES.
           10   IM-RETAIL-1-THRU-9-PRICE          PIC S999V99.
           10   IM-RETAIL-10-THRU-24-PRICE        PIC S999V99.
           10   IM-RETAIL-25-OR-MORE-PRICE        PIC S999V99.
      05   IM-INVENTORY-DATA.
           10   IM-DATE-OFF-PRESS.
                15   IM-MONTH-OFF-PRESS           PIC XX.
                15   IM-DAY-OFF-PRESS             PIC XX.
                15   IM-YEAR-OFF-PRESS            PIC XX.
           10   IM-QUANTITY-ON-HAND               PIC S9(5).
           10   IM-QUANTITY-BACK-ORDERED          PIC S9(5).
      05   IM-SALES-DATA-IN-UNITS.
           10   IM-UNIT-SALES-YTD                 PIC S9(5).
           10   IM-NUMBER-OF-PAST-YEARS-DATA      PIC S9.
           10   IM-PAST-YEARS-DATA.
                15   IM-UNIT-SALES-LAST-YEAR      PIC S9(5).
                15   IM-UNIT-SALES-2-YEARS-AGO    PIC S9(5).
                15   IM-UNIT-SALES-3-YEARS-AGO    PIC S9(5).
                15   IM-UNIT-SALES-4-YEARS-AGO    PIC S9(5).
                15   IM-UNIT-SALES-5-YEARS-AGO    PIC S9(5).
      05   FILLER                                 PIC X(11).
```

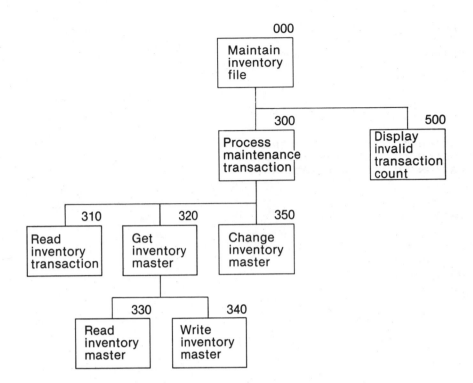

```
 IDENTIFICATION DIVISION.
*
 PROGRAM-ID.      MAINTMST.
*
 ENVIRONMENT DIVISION.
*
 INPUT-OUTPUT SECTION.
*
 FILE-CONTROL.
     SELECT MNTTRAN   ASSIGN TO SYS020-AS-MNTTRAN.
     SELECT INVMAST   ASSIGN TO SYS021-AS-INVMAST.
     SELECT NEWMAST   ASSIGN TO SYS022-AS-NEWMAST.
*
 DATA DIVISION.
*
 FILE SECTION.
*
 FD  MNTTRAN
     LABEL RECORDS ARE STANDARD
     RECORD CONTAINS 80 CHARACTERS.
*
 01  MAINTENANCE-TRANSACTION-AREA     PIC X(80).
*
 FD  INVMAST
     LABEL RECORDS ARE STANDARD
     RECORD CONTAINS 128 CHARACTERS.
*
 01  MASTER-RECORD-AREA              PIC X(128).
*
 FD  NEWMAST
     LABEL RECORDS ARE STANDARD
     RECORD CONTAINS 128 CHARACTERS.
*
 01  NEW-MASTER-AREA                 PIC X(128).
*
 WORKING-STORAGE SECTION.
*
 01  SWITCHES.
*
     05   ALL-RECORDS-PROCESSED-SWITCH  PIC X     VALUE 'N'.
          88   ALL-RECORDS-PROCESSED              VALUE 'Y'.
     05   FIRST-EXECUTION-SWITCH       PIC X     VALUE 'Y'.
          88   FIRST-EXECUTION                    VALUE 'Y'.
*
 01  COUNT-FIELDS.
*
     05   INVALID-TRANSACTION-COUNT    PIC 9(5) VALUE ZERO.
*
 01  MAINTENANCE-TRANSACTION-RECORD.
*
     05   MT-MAINTENANCE-CODE               PIC X.
          88   MT-DELETION                  VALUE 'D'.
          88   MT-CHANGE                    VALUE 'C'.
          88   MT-ADDITION                  VALUE 'A'.
     05   MT-DESCRIPTIVE-DATA.
```

```
          10   MT-BOOK-CODE                   PIC X(4).
          10   MT-AUTHOR-LAST-NAME            PIC X(10).
          10   MT-BOOK-TITLE                  PIC X(40).
      05   MT-RETAIL-PRICES.
          10   MT-RETAIL-1-THRU-9-PRICE       PIC S999V99.
          10   MT-RETAIL-1-THRU-9-PRICE-X     REDEFINES
               MT-RETAIL-1-THRU-9-PRICE       PIC X(5).
          10   MT-RETAIL-10-THRU-24-PRICE     PIC S999V99.
          10   MT-RETAIL-10-THRU-24-PRICE-X   REDEFINES
               MT-RETAIL-10-THRU-24-PRICE     PIC X(5).
          10   MT-RETAIL-25-OR-MORE-PRICE     PIC S999V99.
          10   MT-RETAIL-25-OR-MORE-PRICE-X   REDEFINES
               MT-RETAIL-25-OR-MORE-PRICE     PIC X(5).
      05   FILLER                             PIC X(10).
 *
  01   INVENTORY-MASTER-RECORD.
 *
      05   IM-STATUS                          PIC X.
          88   IM-IN-PRINT                    VALUE 'I'.
          88   IM-OUT-OF-PRINT                VALUE 'O'.
      05   IM-DESCRIPTIVE-DATA.
          10   IM-BOOK-CODE                   PIC X(4).
          10   IM-AUTHOR-LAST-NAME            PIC X(10).
          10   IM-BOOK-TITLE                  PIC X(40).
      05   IM-RETAIL-PRICES.
          10   IM-RETAIL-1-THRU-9-PRICE       PIC S999V99.
          10   IM-RETAIL-10-THRU-24-PRICE     PIC S999V99.
          10   IM-RETAIL-25-OR-MORE-PRICE     PIC S999V99.
      05   IM-INVENTORY-DATA.
          10   IM-DATE-OFF-PRESS.
              15   IM-MONTH-OFF-PRESS         PIC XX.
              15   IM-DAY-OFF-PRESS           PIC XX.
              15   IM-YEAR-OFF-PRESS          PIC XX.
          10   IM-QUANTITY-ON-HAND            PIC S9(5).
          10   IM-QUANTITY-BACK-ORDERED       PIC S9(5).
      05   IM-SALES-DATA-IN-UNITS.
          10   IM-UNIT-SALES-YTD              PIC S9(5).
          10   IM-NUMBER-OF-PAST-YEARS-DATA   PIC S9.
          10   IM-PAST-YEARS-DATA.
              15   IM-UNIT-SALES-LAST-YEAR    PIC S9(5).
              15   IM-UNIT-SALES-2-YEARS-AGO  PIC S9(5).
              15   IM-UNIT-SALES-3-YEARS-AGO  PIC S9(5).
              15   IM-UNIT-SALES-4-YEARS-AGO  PIC S9(5).
              15   IM-UNIT-SALES-5-YEARS-AGO  PIC S9(5).
      05   FILLER                             PIC X(11).
 *
  PROCEDURE DIVISION.
 *
  000-MAINTAIN-INVENTORY-FILE.
 *
      OPEN INPUT   MNTTRAN
                   INVMAST
           OUTPUT NEWMAST.
      MOVE LOW-VALUE TO IM-BOOK-CODE.
      PERFORM 300-PROCESS-MAINTENANCE-TRAN
          UNTIL ALL-RECORDS-PROCESSED.
```

```
      CLOSE MNTTRAN
            INVMAST
            NEWMAST.
      IF INVALID-TRANSACTION-COUNT > ZERO
          PERFORM 500-DISPLAY-INVALID-TRAN-COUNT.
      DISPLAY 'MAINTMST  I  1  NORMAL EOJ'.
      STOP RUN.
*
 300-PROCESS-MAINTENANCE-TRAN.
*
      PERFORM 310-READ-INVENTORY-TRAN.
      PERFORM 320-GET-INVENTORY-MASTER
          UNTIL IM-BOOK-CODE NOT < MT-BOOK-CODE.
      IF         IM-BOOK-CODE = HIGH-VALUE
          AND MT-BOOK-CODE = HIGH-VALUE
          MOVE 'Y' TO ALL-RECORDS-PROCESSED-SWITCH
      ELSE
          IF         IM-BOOK-CODE = MT-BOOK-CODE
              AND  MT-CHANGE
              PERFORM 350-CHANGE-INVENTORY-MASTER
          ELSE
              ADD 1 TO INVALID-TRANSACTION-COUNT.
*
 310-READ-INVENTORY-TRAN.
*
      READ MNTTRAN INTO MAINTENANCE-TRANSACTION-RECORD
          AT END
              MOVE HIGH-VALUE TO MT-BOOK-CODE.
*
 320-GET-INVENTORY-MASTER.
*
      IF FIRST-EXECUTION
          PERFORM 330-READ-INVENTORY-MASTER
          MOVE 'N' TO FIRST-EXECUTION-SWITCH
      ELSE
          PERFORM 340-WRITE-INVENTORY-MASTER
          PERFORM 330-READ-INVENTORY-MASTER.
*
 330-READ-INVENTORY-MASTER.
*
      READ INVMAST INTO INVENTORY-MASTER-RECORD
          AT END
              MOVE HIGH-VALUE TO IM-BOOK-CODE.
*
 340-WRITE-INVENTORY-MASTER.
*
      WRITE NEW-MASTER-AREA FROM INVENTORY-MASTER-RECORD.
*
 350-CHANGE-INVENTORY-MASTER.
*
      IF MT-AUTHOR-LAST-NAME NOT = SPACE
          MOVE MT-AUTHOR-LAST-NAME TO IM-AUTHOR-LAST-NAME.
      IF MT-BOOK-TITLE NOT = SPACE
          MOVE MT-BOOK-TITLE TO IM-BOOK-TITLE.
      IF MT-RETAIL-1-THRU-9-PRICE-X NOT = SPACE
          MOVE MT-RETAIL-1-THRU-9-PRICE
```

```
                TO IM-RETAIL-1-THRU-9-PRICE.
        IF MT-RETAIL-10-THRU-24-PRICE-X NOT = SPACE
            MOVE MT-RETAIL-10-THRU-24-PRICE
                TO IM-RETAIL-10-THRU-24-PRICE.
        IF MT-RETAIL-25-OR-MORE-PRICE-X NOT = SPACE
            MOVE MT-RETAIL-25-OR-MORE-PRICE
                TO IM-RETAIL-25-OR-MORE-PRICE.
 *
  500-DISPLAY-INVALID-TRAN-COUNT.
 *
       DISPLAY 'MAINTMST  A  2  '
                 INVALID-TRANSACTION-COUNT
                 ' INVALID TRANSACTIONS'.
```

Program: **CREATMST** Create inventory master file	Page: 1
Designer: **MM**	Date: 10-20-86

Input/output specifications

File	Description	Use
INVMAST	Inventory master file	Input
NEWMAST	New inventory master file	Output

Process specifications

This program reads an inventory master file (INVMAST) and creates a new inventory master file (NEWMAST). The record layout for both files is the same as for the inventory master file in the two preceding programs. The program listing that follows is for an initial version of this program that reads a sequential input file with fixed-length records and creates a sequential output file in the same format.

For chapter 2, you will be asked to modify this program so it creates a new master file with variable-length records. For chapter 3, you will be asked to modify this program so it creates an indexed master file. For chapter 4, you will be asked to modify this program so it creates a relative master file.

Compiler dependent code

Before you can run this program on your system, you may need to modify the following items so they conform to your system requirements or shop standards:

The program name in the Identification Division
The Configuration Section
The system names in the SELECT statements for the disk files
The FD statements for the disk files
Quotation marks (from single to double quotes)
Computational usage (from COMP-3 to COMP)

File identification

Unless you're told otherwise, you can assume that the external names for the transaction and the master file are INVMAST and NEWMAST. However, you may also have to get other identifying information, such as what volume the files are on, what library they're in, or what catalog is used to locate the files.

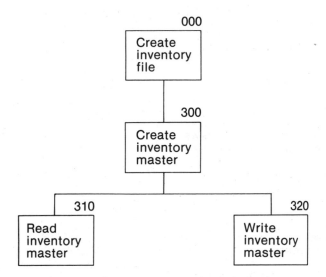

```
 IDENTIFICATION DIVISION.
*
 PROGRAM-ID.     CREATMST.
*
 ENVIRONMENT DIVISION.
*
 INPUT-OUTPUT SECTION.
*
 FILE-CONTROL.
     SELECT INVMAST   ASSIGN TO SYS020-AS-INVMAST.
     SELECT NEWMAST   ASSIGN TO SYS021-AS-NEWMAST.
*
 DATA DIVISION.
*
 FILE SECTION.
*
 FD  INVMAST
     LABEL RECORDS ARE STANDARD
     RECORD CONTAINS 128 CHARACTERS.
*
 01   INVENTORY-MASTER-AREA         PIC X(128).
*
 FD  NEWMAST
     LABEL RECORDS ARE STANDARD
     RECORD CONTAINS 128 CHARACTERS.
*
 01   NEW-MASTER-AREA          PIC X(128).
*
 WORKING-STORAGE SECTION.
*
 01   SWITCHES.
*
     05   INVMAST-EOF-SWITCH      PIC X      VALUE 'N'.
          88   INVMAST-EOF                   VALUE 'Y'.
*
 01   INVENTORY-MASTER-RECORD.
*
     05   IM-STATUS                          PIC X.
          88   IM-IN-PRINT                   VALUE 'I'.
          88   IM-OUT-OF-PRINT               VALUE 'O'.
     05   IM-DESCRIPTIVE-DATA.
          10   IM-BOOK-CODE                  PIC X(4).
          10   IM-AUTHOR-LAST-NAME           PIC X(10).
          10   IM-BOOK-TITLE                 PIC X(40).
     05   IM-RETAIL-PRICES.
          10   IM-RETAIL-1-THRU-9-PRICE      PIC S999V99.
          10   IM-RETAIL-10-THRU-24-PRICE    PIC S999V99.
          10   IM-RETAIL-25-OR-MORE-PRICE    PIC S999V99.
     05   IM-INVENTORY-DATA.
          10   IM-DATE-OFF-PRESS.
               15   IM-MONTH-OFF-PRESS       PIC XX.
               15   IM-DAY-OFF-PRESS         PIC XX.
               15   IM-YEAR-OFF-PRESS        PIC XX.
          10   IM-QUANTITY-ON-HAND           PIC S9(5).
          10   IM-QUANTITY-BACK-ORDERED      PIC S9(5).
```

```
        05   IM-SALES-DATA-IN-UNITS.
             10   IM-UNIT-SALES-YTD                    PIC S9(5).
             10   IM-NUMBER-OF-PAST-YEARS-DATA         PIC S9.
             10   IM-PAST-YEARS-DATA.
                  15   IM-UNIT-SALES-LAST-YEAR         PIC S9(5).
                  15   IM-UNIT-SALES-2-YEARS-AGO       PIC S9(5).
                  15   IM-UNIT-SALES-3-YEARS-AGO       PIC S9(5).
                  15   IM-UNIT-SALES-4-YEARS-AGO       PIC S9(5).
                  15   IM-UNIT-SALES-5-YEARS-AGO       PIC S9(5).
        05   FILLER                                    PIC X(11).
*
 PROCEDURE DIVISION.
*
 000-CREATE-INVENTORY-FILE.
*
     OPEN INPUT   INVMAST
          OUTPUT  NEWMAST.
     PERFORM 300-CREATE-INVENTORY-MASTER
         UNTIL INVMAST-EOF.
     CLOSE INVMAST
           NEWMAST.
     DISPLAY 'CREATMST  I  1   NORMAL EOJ'.
     STOP RUN.
*
 300-CREATE-INVENTORY-MASTER.
*
     PERFORM 310-READ-INVENTORY-MASTER.
     IF NOT INVMAST-EOF
         PERFORM 320-WRITE-INVENTORY-MASTER.
*
 310-READ-INVENTORY-MASTER.
*
     READ INVMAST INTO INVENTORY-MASTER-RECORD
         AT END
             MOVE 'Y' TO INVMAST-EOF-SWITCH.
*
 320-WRITE-INVENTORY-MASTER.
*
     WRITE NEW-MASTER-AREA FROM INVENTORY-MASTER-RECORD.
```

Program: LISTTRAN List transaction file	Page: 1
Designer: MM	Date: 10-20-86

Input/output specifications

File	Description	Use
MNTTRAN	Maintenance transaction file	Input
TRANLIST	Print file: Transaction listing	Output

Process specifications

This program reads the maintenance transaction file (MNTTRAN) and prepares a transaction listing from it (TRANLIST). This program can be used to list the contents of the transaction file so you know what transactions it contains. Then, you can figure out what output you should get when you test MAINTMST.

Compiler dependent code

Before you can run this program on your system, you may need to modify the following items so they conform to your system requirements or shop standards:

The program name in the Identification Division
The Configuration Section
The system name in the SELECT statement for the disk file
The system name in the SELECT statement for the printer file
The FD statement for the disk file
The FD statement for the printer file
Quotation marks (from single to double quotes)
Computational usage (from COMP-3 to COMP)

File identification

Unless you're told otherwise, you can assume that the external name for the transaction file is MNTTRAN. However, you may also have to get other identifying information, such as what volume the file is on, what library it's in, or what catalog is used to locate it.

PROBLEMS BY CHAPTER

Chapter 2   Sequential file handling

Topic 2   COBOL for sequential files of fixed-length records

1. Modify MAINTMST so it maintains the inventory master file based on deletion and addition transactions as well as change transactions. To simplify the logic within the COBOL program, you can assume that there can only be one type of transaction for any one master record. If, for example, there is a deletion transaction for book code DDBS, there can't be an addition or change transaction for that code. However, there can be more than one change transaction for the same master record.

Topic 3   COBOL for sequential files of variable-length records

If you review the documentation for LISTMAST, you can see that the last five unit sales fields in the inventory master record may contain zeros. As a result, the records in the master file could be variable in length. If, for example, a book has come off press in the current year, the unit sales for the last five years could be dropped from the master record. If a book came off press in the previous year, the last four unit sales fields could be dropped from the master record. For each record, the value in IM-NUMBER-OF-PAST-YEARS-DATA tells how many of the unit sales fields for past years are in use.

2. Modify CREATMST so it creates a variable-length inventory master file from the fixed-length master file. The variable-length records should have the same basic format as the fixed-length records, but unit sales fields that aren't being used should be dropped from each record. Although you could use OCCURS DEPENDING ON for the output file in this program, use multiple record definitions instead. In other words, you should define six different record sizes for the output file.

3. Modify LISTMAST so it will read the records in the variable-length inventory master file.

Chapter 3   Indexed file handling

Topic 2   COBOL for indexed files with one index

1. Modify CREATMST so it creates an indexed inventory master file from the sequential master file. The indexed file should have the same record format as the sequential file. The primary key for the indexed file should be the book code. If your program detects a duplicate record, it should display an error message and continue processing. If it detects an out-of-sequence record, it should display a message and end processing. And if it detects some other type of write error for the output file, it should display an error message and end processing. All three error messages should be in the form required by your installation and all three should give the book code of the record being processed. If the error isn't for a duplicate record or an out-of-sequence record, the message should also give the file status code for the error condition.

2. Modify MAINTMST so it maintains the indexed inventory master file based on change, deletion, and addition transactions. This maintenance should be done on a random basis. To simplify the logic within the COBOL program, you don't have to worry about its efficiency. In other words, it's okay to rewrite a changed master record after each transaction is processed, even though there may be more than one change transaction for a master record. If any I/O errors occur when a WRITE, REWRITE, or DELETE statement is executed, your program should display an error message in the form required by your installation and end processing. Each error message should give the book code of the transaction being processed and the file status code for the error condition.

3. Modify LISTMAST so it will list the records in the indexed inventory master file. Then, you can use LISTMAST to get before and after versions of the master file so you can figure out whether or not the maintenance has been done correctly.

Topic 3   COBOL for indexed files with alternate indexes

4. Modify the CREATMST program you developed for problem 1 in this chapter so it reads the sequential inventory master file and creates an indexed master file with one alternate key. The indexed file should have the same record format as the sequential file. The primary key for the indexed file should be the book code. And the alternate key should be the author's last name.

If you're using an IBM mainframe, you can't create a file with alternate indexes using COBOL alone. Instead, you have to use the 3-step procedure described on page 156. In this case, the COBOL program you developed for problem 1 will create the file with its primary index (step 2). As a result, you don't need to modify your program for problem 1. However, unless you know how to use AMS, your instructor will probably have to help you with steps 1 and 3.

5. Modify the MAINTMST program you developed for problem 2 in this chapter so it updates the alternate index as well as the primary index during the maintenance function. Otherwise, the program is the same as for problem 2.

   If you're using an IBM mainframe, the alternate index is automatically updated if the file is defined by AMS with the UPGRADE option on. In this case, the COBOL program you developed for problem 2 will update the alternate index during file maintenance. As a result, you don't need to modify your program for problem 2.

6. Modify LISTMAST so it will list the records in the indexed inventory master file in sequence by author's last name. You should do this by reading the records sequentially by alternate key.

Chapter 4   Relative file handling

Topic 2   COBOL for relative files

The problems for this topic ask you to treat the inventory master file as a relative file. To convert a book code to a relative record number, you should convert each of the first three characters in the code to a number from 1 through 9 as shown in this table:

A-C	1
D-F	2
G-I	3
J-L	4
M-O	5
P-R	6
S-U	7
V-X	8
Y-Z	9
Space	9

You can assume for this program that letters, numbers, and spaces are the only characters your program will find in a book code field. If you know how to use the INSPECT statement as presented in chapter 9, you should use it for this conversion. Otherwise, you can use whatever code you're familiar with to get this conversion done.

Once you have converted the first three characters of a book code to numbers, you have a number from 111 through 999. Then, to derive the relative record number, you should divide this number by 4 and subtract 26 from the quotient. This means the relative record numbers for the master file will range from 1 through 223, so at least 223 record areas must be allocated to this file.

Since it's possible that two or more book codes will randomize to the same relative record number, the programs that process this file must provide for duplicates. If a duplicate is detected during file creation or file maintenance, the duplicate record should be written in the first available record area after the relative record number derived from the book code. Then, to read records from the file on a random basis, a program must include logic that provides for duplicates.

1. Modify CREATMST so it creates a relative inventory master file from the sequential master file. The relative file should have the same record format as the sequential file. Records should be written on the relative output file on a random basis. If, for some reason, a record can't be written on the file, the program should display an error message in the form required by your installation and the program should end. The message should give the book code of the record that couldn't be written as well as the file status code for the error condition.

2. Modify MAINTMST so it maintains the relative inventory master file based on change, deletion, and addition transactions. This maintenance should be done on a random basis. If you've already done the program for problem 2 in chapter 3, you should modify that program because it will be easier to modify than MAINT-MST. To simplify the logic of this program, you don't have to worry about its efficiency. In other words, it's okay to rewrite a changed master record after each transaction is processed, even though there may be more than one change transaction for a master record.

When you code this program, remember that duplicates are stored in the first available record area after the relative record number derived by the randomizing routine. As a result, you can't actually delete a record from the file. If you did, the logic for finding duplicate records that originally randomized to the deleted record area wouldn't work. Instead, you should just change the status code for a deleted record from in-print to out-of-print.

If an I/O error occurs when a WRITE or REWRITE statement is executed, your program should display an error message in the form required by your installation and end processing.

Each error message should give the book code of the transaction being processed as well as the file status code for the error condition.

3. Modify LISTMAST so it will list the records in the relative inventory master file in sequence by relative record number. After the prices for each record, starting in print position 85, this program should list the relative record number derived by the randomizing routine and the relative record number that the record is actually stored in, as in this example:

```
DERIVED RR NO. = 123; ACTUAL RR NO. = 124
```

Chapter 5   The sort/merge feature

Topic 2   COBOL for sorting or merging

1. Modify the original version of LISTMAST so it will list the records in the sequential inventory master file in sequence by book code within author's last name. The format of the listing should be the same as it was in the original version of LISTMAST, but only books that came off press in 1985 and 1986 should be listed. To do this, the program requires an internal sort with both an input and an output procedure. For efficiency, the sort work record should be as short as possible.

Chapter 6   How to use the COPY library

Topic 1   Basic use of the COPY library

1. Modify the original version of LISTMAST so it uses two COPY members. The first one, named INVMAST, contains the record description for the inventory master file. The second one, named RPTHDG14, contains the record descriptions for the first two lines of a standard report heading. It uses the same names for the date and time data that LISTMAST uses, and it uses HDG1-TITLE for the report title field and HDG2-PROGRAM-NAME for the program name field.

Topic 2   Advanced use of the COPY library

2. Modify the version of LISTMAST that you created for problem 1 in this chapter so it uses a COPY member for the read module

that reads a sequential master file. The name of this COPY member is READSEQ, and its code is as follows:

```
READ SEQREC RECORD INTO SEQUENTIAL-MASTER-RECORD
    AT END
        MOVE 'Y' TO SEQREC-EOF-SWITCH.
IF NOT SEQREC-EOF
    ADD 1 TO RECORD-COUNT.
```

To make this COPY member consistent with the rest of the LISTMAST program, you must use the REPLACING clause of the COPY statement to change SEQUENTIAL and SEQREC to appropriate values.

Chapter 7   How to use subprograms

Topic 1   How to call subprograms

1.   Modify the original version of LISTMAST so it uses two subprograms. The first one, named SYSDATE, gets the system date and puts it in an eight-character field in this form: XX/XX/XX. The second one, named SYSTIME, gets the system time and puts it in a 21-character field in this form:

```
TIME:   HH:MM XXXXXXX
```

Here, HH stands for hours, MM for minutes, and the X's can contain AM, PM, NOON, or MIDNIGHT. You should use these subprograms to put the date and time in the heading of the report.

2.   Modify the version of LISTMAST that you created for problem 1 in this chapter so it uses a subprogram named DATEDITC. This subprogram edits a six-character, alphanumeric date field (MMDDYY) to determine whether or not it is valid. If it is valid, the subprogram puts Y in a one-character, alphanumeric switch field; otherwise, it puts N into this field. The date and switch fields must be passed to the subprogram in that order.

 LISTMAST should use the subprogram to edit the off-press dates in the master records. If a date is invalid, the program should print the date and an error message starting in print position 85 of the master record line, as in this example:

```
033285   INVALID DATE
```

Topic 2   How to write subprograms

3.   Write the DATEDITC subprogram described in problem 2. A valid date should be numeric. Also, the month should be a value

from 1 through 12, the day should be a value from 1 through 31, and the year should be less than or equal to the current year. If any of these rules are violated, the date is invalid.

Chapter 8   How to handle tables

Topic 1   How to handle single-level tables using indexes

1. Modify the original version of LISTMAST so it edits the off-press date (MMDDYY) to determine whether or not it is valid. If a date is invalid, the program should print the date starting in print position 85 followed by an error message, as in this example:

```
023086   INVALID DATE
```

To determine the validity of a date, the program should use a table that contains the month numbers (from 01 through 12) and the maximum number of days in each month (from 29 in February through 31). For instance, the entries in the table might look like this:

```
0131
0229
0331
  .
  .
  .
```

Then, if a month number can't be found in the table, it is invalid; and if a day number doesn't range from one through the maximum value for the month in the table, it is invalid. Since the problem is designed to get you to use a one-level table, you don't have to check the year for validity.

Topic 2   How to handle multilevel tables using indexes

2. Modify the original version of LISTMAST so it edits the retail prices stored in each master record. To do this, the program should start by loading a price table into storage. The table in storage should be described like this:

```
01  PRICE-TABLE.
*
    05  PT-PRICE-GROUP    OCCURS 50 TIMES
                          INDEXED BY PT-PRICE-GROUP-INDEX.
        10  PT-PRICE      OCCURS 3 TIMES
                          INDEXED BY PT-PRICE-INDEX
                          PIC S999V99      COMP.
```

The file that holds the price table records is a sequential file named PRICES with this record format:

```
01   PRICE-TABLE-RECORD.
*
     05   PTR-PRICE-GROUP                   OCCURS 5 TIMES.
          10   PTR-RETAIL-1-THRU-9-PRICE    PIC S999V99.
          10   PTR-RETAIL-10-THRU-24-PRICE  PIC S999V99.
          10   PTR-RETAIL-24-OR-MORE-PRICE  PIC S999V99.
     05   FILLER                            PIC X(5).
```

After the table has been loaded, LISTMAST should read each inventory master record and edit its prices. To do this, the program should first search the table to find a retail-1-through-9 price that matches the price in the master record. If no match is found, the retail-1-through-9 price is invalid, and the editing routine should stop. If the retail-1-through-9 price is found in the table, though, the program should check the other two prices in the master record. These prices should match the corresponding prices in the table that have the same occurrence number as the matching retail-1-through-9 price. If either of these prices in the master record doesn't match the corresponding price in the table, it is considered to be invalid.

If one or more of the prices in the master record are invalid, this error message should be printed starting in print position 85 of the inventory line:

```
PRICE X IS INVALID
```

Here, X is either a 1, 2, or 3 that indicates whether the first, second, or third price for a record is invalid. If more than one price is invalid, X indicates the first price that was found to be invalid.

Topic 3   How to use subscripts

3.   Modify the original version of LISTMAST so it prints the sales total for the last five years for each inventory master record. To do this, the last five unit sales fields in each master record should be redefined with an OCCURS clause so subscripts can be used to process them. The unit sales total should be printed starting in print position 85 of an inventory line, as in this example:

```
SALES LAST 5 YEARS = 39721
```

Chapter 9 How to manipulate characters

Topic 1 INSPECT, STRING, and UNSTRING

1. Modify the original version of LISTMAST so it creates new book codes from the book titles. To do this, the program should unstring the first four words in each book title, ignoring any punctuation marks within these titles. Then, the program should string together the first character from each of the four words to create a four-character code. The program should print this code starting in print position 85, as in this example:

```
NEW BOOK CODE = CFTC
```

Chapter 10 The 1985 COBOL elements

Topic 1 The 1985 COBOL elements for structured programming

1. If you're using a 1985 COBOL compiler and you haven't used 1985 code in the program for problem 2 in chapter 8, you should revise that program so it uses the 1985 elements for structured programming whenever they are appropriate. Start by modifying the structure chart, because the code can have an effect on the structure. Then, modify the code, but only use the 1985 elements when you think they improve the clarity of your code. If you haven't done problem 2 in chapter 8, your instructor will specify another program that you should modify.

Topic 2 Other 1985 COBOL elements

2. Modify the program that you did for problem 1 in this chapter so it uses the 1985 COBOL elements presented in topic 2 of chapter 10. Here again, only use the 1985 elements when you think they improve the clarity of your code.

Appendix D

Four more case studies

Appendix C presents case study problems that ask you to modify one or more programs after you complete chapters 2 through 10 of the text. By the time you complete these problems, you will have used most of the COBOL elements described in this book. However, those problems do *not* test your ability to design and develop programs from scratch. Also, they aren't demanding in terms of structure and logic.

This appendix presents four more case studies. Case study 1 asks you to develop an edit program from scratch. Then, case study 2 asks you to enhance that program. Similarly, case study 3 asks you to develop a sequential update program from scratch. Then, case study 4 asks you to modify that program so it becomes a random update program using an indexed master file.

In contrast to the case study problems in appendix C, the case studies in this appendix are more realistic and more demanding. If you can complete them with a minimum of outside help, we believe that you exceed the requirements for an entry-level programmer in industry. In fact, we feel you are qualified to develop batch programs on any system.

You can start case study 1 in this appendix as soon as you read chapter 1 in this text because it doesn't require any COBOL elements that you shouldn't already know. And if you've taken the course for *Structured ANS COBOL, Part 1*, you can skip chapter 1. Whether or not you took the *Part 1* course, though, before you start case study 1, you may want to read (1) topic 1 in chapter 8 so you know how to handle one-level tables, and (2) chapter 11 so you become more familiar with the design and logic of edit programs. Then, as you complete chapters 5 through 10, you can do the enhancements required by case study 2.

As for case study 3, you can start work on it as soon as you complete chapter 2. In addition, you may want to read (1) topic 1 in chapter 8 so you know how to handle one-level tables, and (2) chapter 11 so you become more familiar with the design and code for sequential update programs. After you read chapter 3 and complete case study 3, you can start case study 4. Before you start this case study, you may want to review chapter 11 so you become more familiar with the design and code for random update programs.

Test files should be available for each of the case studies, but you will have to get the identifying information for each of the files from your instructor. Similarly, COPY members should be available for the record descriptions provided with the program specifications for each case study, but you will have to get the identifying information for each of the COPY members from your instructor. If you already know how to use COPY members, you should use the available COPY members in your programs. Otherwise, you should start using them as soon as you complete chapter 6.

If you already know how to use subprograms, you should use the available subprograms in your programs. Otherwise, you should start using them as soon as you complete chapter 7. SYSDATE and SYSTIME subprograms should be available to you for all four of these case studies, but you should check to see whether your installation provides any other subprograms that may be of use to you as you develop these programs.

If you are using a 1985 compiler, feel free to use 1985 code as you develop the programs for these case studies. Also, because these case studies are relatively complicated, we suggest that you use top-down coding and testing as you develop these programs. If you do use it, be sure to create a test plan for each program as described in chapter 1 before you begin coding and testing.

Case study D-1

Program: AR1100 Edit accounts receivable transactions	Page: 1
Designer: MM	Date: 10-21-86

Input/output specifications

File	Description	Use
ARTRANX	Accounts receivable transactions	Input
VALTRAN	Valid accounts receivable transactions	Output
TRANLST	Print file: Invalid transaction listing	Output

Process specifications

This program edits an input file of accounts receivable transactions
(ARTRANX). It produces a new file of valid transactions (VALTRAN) and a
listing of invalid transactions (TRANLST). The format of the
transaction record is the same for the output file as it is for the
input file.

If one or more of the first seven fields in a transaction are invalid,
they should be preceded by an asterisk on the invalid transaction
listing as indicated by the print chart. If one of the billing fields
(code, charge, or cost) is invalid, this message should be printed in
print positions 71-101:

    INVALID ENTRY IN BILLING FIELDS

The editing rules for the fields in the transaction record are given on
page 2 of this overview.

You can start this program as soon as you start this course, because it
doesn't require any COBOL elements that you don't already know.
However, you should design the program using a structure chart as
described in chapter 1 of the text, and you should code the program so
each module on the structure chart is a single paragraph in the
Procedure Division of the source program. If you haven't designed and
coded programs this way before, you should read chapter 11 before you do
this program so you can become more familiar with the design and code
for edit programs.

If you took the Structured ANS COBOL, Part 1 course, your instructor may
decide that you don't need to do this case study. Then, you will be
given the structure chart and code for this program so you can enhance
it as described in case study 2.

Program: AR1100 Edit accounts receivable transactions	Page: 2
Designer: **MM**	Date: 10-21-86

Process specifications

Editing rules

Field	Rule
TR-TRANSACTION-CODE	Must be B, C, or P.
TR-CUSTOMER-NUMBER	Must be numeric and greater than zero.
TR-INVOICE-NUMBER	Must be numeric and greater than zero.
TR-PAYMENT-CREDIT-AMOUNT	If the transaction code is B, this field must be blank. If the code is P or C, this field must be numeric and greater than zero.
TR-TRANSACTION-DATE	Must be numeric in the form MMDDYY with MM ranging from 1 through 12 and DD ranging from 1 through 31.
TR-BRANCH-NUMBER	Must be numeric and greater than zero.
TR-SALES-REP-NUMBER	Must be numeric and greater than zero.
TR-SERVICE-CODE-n	If the transaction code is B, at least the first service code must be alphabetic. If the transaction code is C or P, the service code fields must be blank.
TR-SERVICE-CHARGE-n and TR-SERVICE-COST-n	If the transaction code is C or P, these fields must be blank. If the transaction code is B, each set of charge and cost fields should be numeric with a value greater than zero if the related service code isn't blank; if the service code field is blank, the related charge and cost fields should be blank.

The record description for ARTRANX

```
01    AR-TRANSACTION-RECORD-X.
*
      05   TR-TRANSACTION-CODE          PIC X.
           88   TR-PAYMENT              VALUE 'P'.
           88   TR-BILLING              VALUE 'B'.
           88   TR-CREDIT               VALUE 'C'.
      05   TR-CUSTOMER-NUMBER           PIC X(5).
      05   TR-INVOICE-NUMBER            PIC X(5).
      05   TR-PAYMENT-CREDIT-AMOUNT     PIC X(7).
      05   TR-TRANSACTION-DATE.
           10   TR-TRANSACTION-MONTH    PIC XX.
           10   TR-TRANSACTION-DAY      PIC XX.
           10   TR-TRANSACTION-YEAR     PIC XX.
      05   TR-BRANCH-NUMBER             PIC X.
      05   TR-SALES-REP-NUMBER          PIC XX.
      05   TR-BILLING-FIELDS.
           10   TR-SERVICE-CODE-1       PIC X(3).
           10   TR-SERVICE-CHARGE-1     PIC X(7).
           10   TR-SERVICE-COST-1       PIC X(7).
           10   TR-SERVICE-CODE-2       PIC X(3).
           10   TR-SERVICE-CHARGE-2     PIC X(7).
           10   TR-SERVICE-COST-2       PIC X(7).
           10   TR-SERVICE-CODE-3       PIC X(3).
           10   TR-SERVICE-CHARGE-3     PIC X(7).
           10   TR-SERVICE-COST-3       PIC X(7).
      05   FILLER                       PIC XX.
```

Document name Invalid transaction listing   Date 10/21/86

Program name AR1100   Designer MM

Record Name

INVALID ACCOUNTS RECEIVABLE TRANSACTIONS

Detail page

1	DATE: 99/99/99	PAGE: ZZ9
2	TIME: 99:99 XX	AR1100
3		
4	TRAN CUSTOMER INVOICE TRAN BRANCH SALES PAYMENT OR	
5	CODE NUMBER NUMBER DATE NUMBER REP CREDIT AMOUNT BILLING FIELDS	
6		
7	* X *XXXXX *XX XX *X *XX *XXXXXXX XXXXXXXXXXXXXXXXXXXXXXXXXXXXXX	
8	X XXXXX XX XX X XX XXXXXXX XXXXXXXXXXXXXXXXXXXXXXXXXXXX	
9		
10		
11		
12		
13		
14		

Total page

15	DATE: 99/99/99	PAGE: ZZ9
16	TIME: 99:99 XX	AR1100
17	INVALID ACCOUNTS RECEIVABLE TRANSACTIONS	
18	VALID TRANSACTIONS ZZ,ZZ9	
19	INVALID TRANSACTIONS ZZ,ZZ9	
20		
21	TOTAL TRANSACTIONS ZZ,ZZ9 **	
22		
23		
24		

Case study D-2

Program: AR1100X Edit accounts receivable transactions	Page: 1
Designer: **MM**	Date: 10-21-86

Input/output specifications

File	Description	Use
ARTRANX	Accounts receivable transactions	Input
SLSREP	Sales rep master (for chapter 8 enhancement)	Input
VALTRAN	Valid accounts receivable transactions	Output
TRANLST	Print file: Invalid transaction listing	Output

Process specifications

Case study 1 gives the specifications for an edit program (AR1100).
If you didn't do case study 1, you will be given the structure chart
and code for the program it requires. Then, this case study asks you
to enhance that program. The enhancements are given on a
chapter-by-chapter basis so you can do portions of this case study as
they are assigned by your instructor.

One thing you should learn from this case study is how easy it is to
modify a structured program. For each part of this case study, you
will modify the code within one or more of the original modules. In
addition, you may have to add new modules to the program. In either
case, you should be able to code and test the modifications with
relative ease.

Enhancements by chapter

Chapter 5 (Sort/merge)   Because the transaction records are in the
same sequence in which they were entered into the system, the file of
valid transactions must be sorted before it can be used to update the
customer master file. Modify this program, then, so the valid
transactions are sorted into sequence by customer number before they
are written on the valid transaction file.

Chapter 6 (COPY members)   Use the COPY member for the transaction
record format (ARTRANX). Also, check your shop's standards to see
whether there are any other COPY members you can use in this program.

Program: AR1100X Edit accounts receivable transactions	Page: 2
Designer: MM	Date: 10-21-86

Process specifications

Enhancements by chapter (continued)

Chapter 7 (Subprograms)   Three general-purpose subprograms are available that can be useful in this program: SYSDATE, SYSTIME, and DATEDITD. Use the SYSDATE subprogram to get the date for your program. It returns the date in the form MM/DD/YY in the eight-character field that you pass to it. Use SYSTIME to get the time for your program. It returns the time in the form

      TIME: 99:99 XXXXXXXX

in the 21-character field that you pass to it. Use DATEDITD to edit the transaction date in each record. It edits the six-character date that you pass to it in the form MMDDYY. If the date is valid, it returns the code Y in the one-character switch field that you pass to it; otherwise, it returns the code N in the switch field. The two fields must be passed as one record to the subprogram; within this record, the transaction date field must be followed by the switch field.

If your installation has its own versions of these subprograms, your instructor may tell you to use them. If so, you must find out the sequence and format of the fields that are to be passed to these subprograms.

Chapter 8 (Table handling)   For the initial version of this program, branch and sales rep number are valid if they are numeric and greater than zero. This, of course, means that the edit program will accept fields as valid, even if there is no such branch or sales rep number.

To improve the editing of these fields, make use of the sales rep master file (SLSREP). This file is a sequential file in sequence by sales rep number within branch number, and there is one master record for each sales rep. The company has 9 branches with as many as 20 sales representatives in a single branch, and the same sales rep number can be used in more than one branch. (The SLSREP record description follows this program overview.)

Use this file to load a table at the start of the edit program that can be used for editing branch and sales rep numbers. If a branch or sales rep number isn't in the table, the field is considered to be invalid, so the transaction should be shown on the transaction listing. As you code the routines for loading and searching the table, try to code them so they will execute as efficiently as possible.

Program: **AR1100X** Edit accounts receivable	Page: 3
transactions	
Designer: **MM**	Date: 10-21-86

Process specifications

Enhancements by chapter (continued)

Chapter 9 (Character manipulation)   During a data entry review, two
kinds of entry errors were found to be common in the service code
fields. First, U's were often entered as V's. Second, the code MRS
often appeared on the source documents, even though it had been
replaced by the code MIS several months before. This meant invalid
service codes were entered into the system.

To eliminate these errors, two program changes were recommended.
First, since none of the valid service codes contain the letter V, the
edit program should change all V's in the service code fields to U's.
Second, since MRS is an invalid code, the edit program should replace
it with the new code, MIS.

Use INSPECT to make these code conversions. Since this is the type of
routine that may have to be dropped from the program some day (if MRS
or V's become valid), put this routine in a separate module that is
called by the main editing routine.

Chapter 10 (1985 COBOL)   If you are using a 1985 compiler, you
should be using 1985 code as you develop all of the programs in this
appendix. In particular, you should use 1985 code when it helps you
improve the structure of a program or the clarity of its code. If you
haven't been using 1985 code, you should revise the structure and code
for this program now using 1985 code, but you should only make
revisions if you think they improve the program.

The record description for SLSREP

```
01    SALES-REP-RECORD.
*
      05    SR-SALES-REP-NUMBER              PIC XX.
      05    SR-SALES-REP-BRANCH-NUMBER       PIC X.
      05    SR-SALES-REP-DATA.
            10    SR-SALES-REP-NAME          PIC X(20).
            10    SR-SALES-REP-ADDRESS       PIC X(20).
            10    SR-SALES-REP-CITY          PIC X(11).
            10    SR-SALES-REP-STATE         PIC XX.
            10    SR-SALES-REP-ZIP-CODE.
                  15    SR-SALES-REP-ZIP-CODE-5 PIC X(5).
                  15    FILLER               PIC X(4).
      05    FILLER                           PIC X(15).
```

Case study D-3

Program: AR1200S Update A/R master file (sequential)	Page: 1
Designer: MM	Date: 10-21-86

Input/output specifications

File	Description	Use
ARTRAN	Accounts receivable transactions	Input
ARMAST	Accounts receivable master file	Input
NEWMAST	New accounts receivable master file	Output
POSTRAN	Posted accounts receivable transactions	Output
UPDLIST	Print file: Update listing	Output

Process specifications

This program updates the accounts receivable master file. The old
master file (ARMAST) is a sequential file in sequence by customer
number. The transaction file (ARTRAN) is also a sequential file in
sequence by customer number. This file contains the valid transactions
that were edited by AR1100 or AR1100X.

This program produces three output files. The first file is a new
(updated) master file (NEWMAST). The second file is a file of posted
transactions (POSTRAN); these are the transactions that were used for
updating the master records. The third file is an update listing
(UPDLIST). This listing includes transactions that couldn't be
processed because they contained one or more invalid fields as well as
those transactions that led to other exceptional conditions.

Program details

1. Each transaction in the valid transaction file may represent a
    payment, a credit, or a new billing. Also, there may be one,
    several, or no transactions for each master.

2. This program should compare the customer number, invoice number,
    branch number, and sales rep number fields in the transaction record
    with the data in the matching master record. If one or more fields
    is invalid, a line should be printed on the update listing and the
    invalid transaction should <u>not</u> be used to update the master record.
    For all transactions, the customer, branch, and sales rep numbers in
    the transaction must match those in the master. If the transaction
    is a payment or a credit, the invoice number in the transaction must
    match one of the invoice numbers in the master record. If the
    transaction is a new billing, the invoice number in the transaction
    must <u>not</u> match an invoice number in the master record. In the

Program: AR1200S Update A/R master file (sequential)	Page: 2
Designer: MM	Date: 10-21-86

Process specifications

invoice locations of a master record, data is stored randomly; in other words, location 2 may contain data even though location 1 does not.

3. On the update listing, the invalid fields should be indicated by an asterisk as shown on the print chart. In the message area, this message should be printed:

NOT POSTED - INVALID TRANSACTION DATA

4. When posting a new billing to a master record, the new billing should be stored in the first invoice location that has an invoice balance of zero. If the master record has no room for a new billing (no invoice with a balance of zero), the transaction should be listed on the update listing followed by this message:

NOT POSTED - MASTER RECORD IS FULL

As a new billing is posted, the customer's balance due may become greater than the credit limit. In this case, the master record should be updated, but the record should be listed on the update listing with this message in the message area:

POSTED - BUT CUSTOMER OVER CREDIT LIMIT

5. The invoice amount and invoice balance for a new billing are equal to the sum of the service charges in the transaction record.

6. If the transaction is a payment or a credit, the payment-credit amount must be applied to the balance of the corresponding invoice in the master record. In some cases, the payment-credit amount may be greater than the invoice balance. If so, the payment-credit amount should be applied as follows:

   a. If the transaction is a payment, a portion of the payment amount equal to the invoice balance should be applied to the matching invoice. Any leftover money should be applied to any of the customer's other unpaid invoices. If a payment amount remains after all the unpaid invoices have been zero balanced, the remaining amount should be applied to the invoice indicated in the transaction, thus leaving a credit (negative) balance for this invoice. In this case, the transaction should be listed on the update listing with this message in the message area:

   POSTED - BUT CUSTOMER HAS CREDIT BALANCE

Program: Update A/R master file (sequential)	Page: 3
Designer: MM	Date: 10-21-86

Process specifications

b. If the transaction is a credit, do <u>not</u> apply the remaining credit amount to other invoices. Instead, apply the entire credit amount to the corresponding invoice, leaving a credit balance. List the transaction on the update listing with this message in the message area:

POSTED - BUT INVOICE HAS CREDIT BALANCE

7. If the master record is updated by at least one valid transaction, calculate the new balance due for that master. Also, calculate the number of open items; that is, the number of invoices per master whose balance is not equal to zero.

8. After a valid transaction has been used to update the master file, it should be written on the sequential file of posted transactions. The format of the records for the output file is the same as the format for the input transaction file.

9. All master records, whether updated or not, must be written on the new master file. But a master record shouldn't be written until it has been updated by all applicable, valid transactions.

The record description for ARTRAN

```
01    AR-TRANSACTION-RECORD.
*
      05   TR-TRANSACTION-CODE           PIC X.
           88   TR-PAYMENT               VALUE 'P'.
           88   TR-CREDIT                VALUE 'C'.
           88   TR-BILLING               VALUE 'B'.
      05   TR-CUSTOMER-NUMBER            PIC X(5).
      05   TR-INVOICE-NUMBER             PIC X(5).
      05   TR-PAYMENT-CREDIT-AMOUNT      PIC S9(5)V99.
      05   TR-TRANSACTION-DATE.
           10   TR-TRANSACTION-MONTH     PIC XX.
           10   TR-TRANSACTION-DAY       PIC XX.
           1Q   TR-TRANSACTION-YEAR      PIC XX.
      05   TR-BRANCH-NUMBER              PIC X.
      05   TR-SALES-REP-NUMBER           PIC XX.
      05   TR-BILLING-DATA               OCCURS 3 TIMES
                                         INDEXED BY TR-BILLING-INDEX.
           10   TR-SERVICE-CODE          PIC X(3).
           10   TR-SERVICE-CHARGE        PIC S9(5)V99.
           10   TR-SERVICE-COST          PIC S9(5)V99.
      05   FILLER                        PIC XX.
```

The record description for ARMAST

```
01    CUSTOMER-MASTER-RECORD.
*
      05   CM-STATUS-CODE                PIC X.
      05   CM-CUSTOMER-DATA.
           10   CM-CUSTOMER-NUMBER       PIC X(5).
           10   CM-CUSTOMER-NAME         PIC X(20).
           10   CM-CUSTOMER-ADDRESS      PIC X(20).
           10   CM-CUSTOMER-CITY         PIC X(11).
           10   CM-CUSTOMER-STATE        PIC XX.
           10   CM-CUSTOMER-ZIP-CODE.
                15   CM-CUSTOMER-ZIP-CODE-5  PIC X(5).
                15   FILLER              PIC X(4).
           10   CM-BRANCH-NUMBER         PIC X.
           10   CM-SALES-REP-NUMBER      PIC XX.
      05   CM-CREDIT-DATA.
           10   CM-CREDIT-LIMIT          PIC S9(5)V99.
           10   CM-BALANCE-DUE           PIC S9(6)V99.
           10   CM-OPEN-ITEMS            PIC S9.
      05   CM-INVOICE-DATA               OCCURS 5 TIMES
                                         INDEXED BY CM-INVOICE-INDEX.
           10   CM-INVOICE-NUMBER        PIC X(5).
           10   CM-INVOICE-DATE.
                15   CM-INVOICE-MONTH     PIC XX.
                15   CM-INVOICE-DAY       PIC XX.
                15   CM-INVOICE-YEAR      PIC XX.
           10   CM-INVOICE-AMOUNT        PIC S9(5)V99.
           10   CM-INVOICE-BALANCE       PIC S9(5)V99.
      05   FILLER                        PIC X(44).
```

Document name __Update listing__   Date __10/21/86__

Program name __AR1200__   Designer __M.M.__

Record Name

Detail Page

1	DATE: 99/99/99 ACCOUNTS RECEIVABLE UPDATE LISTING
2	TIME: 99:99 XX PAGE: ZZ9
3	AR1200
4	TRAN CUSTOMER INVOICE BRANCH SALES
5	CODE NUMBER NUMBER NUMBER REP MESSAGE AREA
6	
7	X * XXXXX * X *XX XXXXXXXXXXXXXXXXXXXXXXXXXX
8	X XXXXX X XX XXXXXXXXXXXXXXXXXXXXXXXXXX
9	
10	
11	
12	
13	
14	

Total Page

15	DATE: 99/99/99 ACCOUNTS RECEIVABLE UPDATE LISTING
16	TIME: 99:99 XX PAGE: ZZ9
17	AR1200
18	VALID TRANSACTIONS ZZ,ZZ9
19	INVALID TRANSACTIONS ZZ,ZZ9
20	
21	TOTAL TRANSACTIONS ZZ,ZZ9 *
22	
23	
24	

Case study D-4

Program: AR1200R Update A/R master file (random)	Page: 1
Designer: MM	Date: 10-21-86

Input/output specifications

File	Description	Use
ARTRAN	Accounts receivable transactions	Input
ARMAST	Accounts receivable master file	Update
POSTRAN	Posted accounts receivable transactions	Output
UPDLIST	Print file: Update listing	Output

Process specifications

Modify the program for case study 3 (AR1200S) so it does a random rather than a sequential update. In this case, the accounts receivable master file (ARMAST) is an indexed file with customer number as the primary key. As a result, instead of creating a new master file, this program should update the master records in place. Otherwise, the processing details for this case study are the same as those for case study 3.

To simplify this program, you can assume that there will usually be only one transaction for each master record. As a result, you don't have to worry about the efficiency of your program. In other words, it's okay to read and rewrite one master record for each transaction record. You don't have to code the program so it reads and rewrites each master record only once no matter how many transaction records apply to it.

To save time, you should develop this program from the structure chart and code that you have for case study 3. This will have a dramatic effect on your productivity. In some cases, your instructor will give you the structure chart and code for the solution to case study 3 so you will be modifying someone else's program, not your own. Either way, this case study will once again show you how easy it is to modify a program when it has been developed in an effective structured style.

Index

Comment Form

Your opinions count

Your opinions today will affect our future products and policies. So if you have questions, criticisms, or suggestions, I'm eager to get them. You can expect a response within a week of the time we receive your comments.

Also, if you discover any errors in this book, typographical or otherwise, please point them out. We'll correct them when the book is reprinted.

Thanks for your help!

Mike Murach, President
Mike Murach and Associates, Inc.

Book title: Structured ANS COBOL: Part 2 (Second Edition)

Dear Mike: _____

_____

_____

_____

_____

_____

_____

_____

_____

_____

_____

_____

_____

_____

_____

_____

Name & Title _____
Company (if company address) _____
Address _____
City, State, Zip_____

Fold where indicated and staple.
No postage necessary if mailed in the U.S.

fold

fold

BUSINESS REPLY MAIL
FIRST CLASS   PERMIT NO. 3063   FRESNO, CA

POSTAGE WILL BE PAID BY ADDRESSEE

Mike Murach & Associates, Inc.

4697 West Jacquelyn Avenue
Fresno, California 93722-9986

Order Form

Our Unlimited Guarantee

To our customers who order directly from us: You must be satisfied. Our books must work for you, or you can send them back for a full refund . . . no matter how many you buy, no matter how long you've had them.

Name & Title _____

Company (if company address) _____

Address_____

City, State, Zip _____

Phone number (including area code) _____

Qty	Product code and title	Price*

COBOL Language Elements

Qty	Code	Title	Price*
_____	SC1R	Structured ANS COBOL: Part 1	$27.50
_____	C1IG	COBOL, Part 1, Instructor's Guide	75.00
_____	C1ME	COBOL, Part 1, Training Minireel—EBCDIC	75.00
_____	C1MA	COBOL, Part 1, Training Minireel—ASCII	75.00
_____	SC2R	Structured ANS COBOL: Part 2	27.50
_____	C2IG	COBOL, Part 2, Instructor's Guide	75.00
_____	C2ME	COBOL, Part 2, Training Minireel—EBCDIC	75.00
_____	C2MA	COBOL, Part 2, Training Minireel—ASCII	75.00
_____	RW	Report Writer	15.00
_____	VC2R	VS COBOL II (Second Edition)	25.00

COBOL Program Development

Qty	Code	Title	Price*
_____	DDCP	How to Design and Develop COBOL Programs	$30.00
_____	CPHB	The COBOL Programmer's Handbook	20.00

☐ Bill me the appropriate price plus UPS shipping and handling (and sales tax in California) for each book ordered.

☐ Bill the appropriate book prices plus UPS shipping and handling (and sales tax in California) to my _____VISA _____MasterCard:

Card number_____

Valid thru (month/year)_____

Cardowner's signature_____
(not valid without signature)

☐ I want to **save** UPS shipping and handling charges. Here's my check or money order for $_____. California residents, please add 6¼% sales tax to your total. (Offer valid in the U.S. only.)

Operating System Subjects

Qty	Code	Title	Price*
_____	VJLR	DOS/VSE JCL (Second Edition)	$32.50
_____	ICCF	DOS/VSE ICCF	27.50
_____	MJCL	MVS JCL	32.50
_____	TSO	MVS TSO	27.50
_____	VMCC	VM/CMS: Commands and Concepts	25.00
_____	VMXE	VM/CMS: XEDIT	25.00

CICS

Qty	Code	Title	Price*
_____	CIC1	CICS for the COBOL Programmer: Part 1	$27.50
_____	CIC2	CICS for the COBOL Programmer: Part 2	27.50
_____	CREF	The CICS Programmer's Desk Reference	35.00

Data Base Processing

Qty	Code	Title	Price*
_____	IMS1	IMS for the COBOL Programmer Part 1: DL/I Data Base Processing	$30.00
_____	IMS2	IMS for the COBOL Programmer Part 2: Data Communications and MFS	32.50

VSAM

Qty	Code	Title	Price*
_____	VSMR	VSAM for the COBOL Programmer (Second Edition)	$17.50
_____	VSMX	VSAM: AMS and Application Programming	25.00

To order more quickly,

Call **toll-free** 1-800-221-5528

(Weekdays, 8:30 a.m. to 5 p.m. Pacific Std. Time)

Mike Murach & Associates, Inc

4697 West Jacquelyn Avenue
Fresno, California 93722
(209) 275-3335
Fax: (209) 275-9035

*Prices are subject to change.
Please call for current prices.

fold

fold

fold

fold